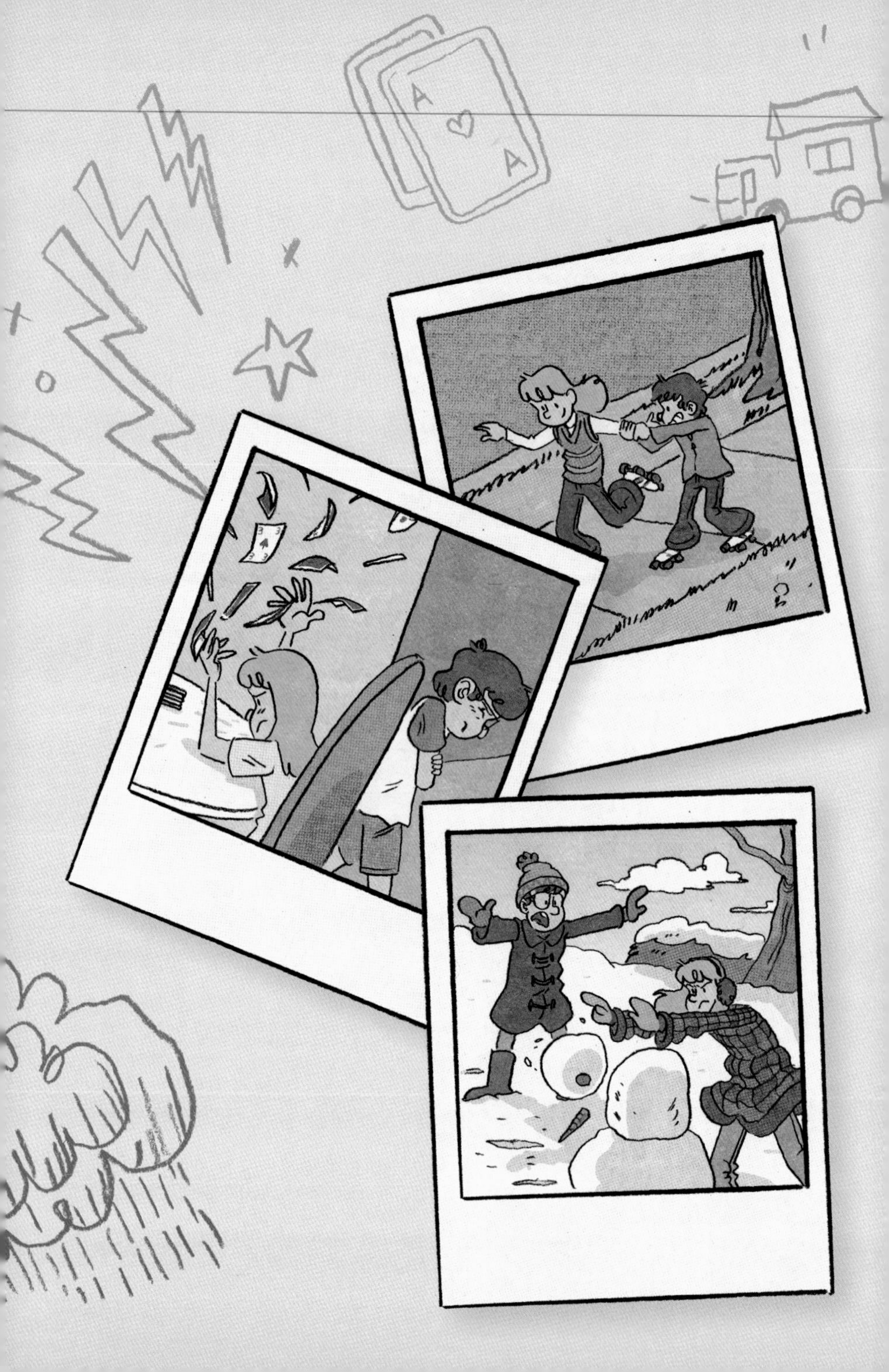

BAD SISTER

Written by
Charise Mericle Harper

Art by
Rory Lucey

:01
First Second
New York

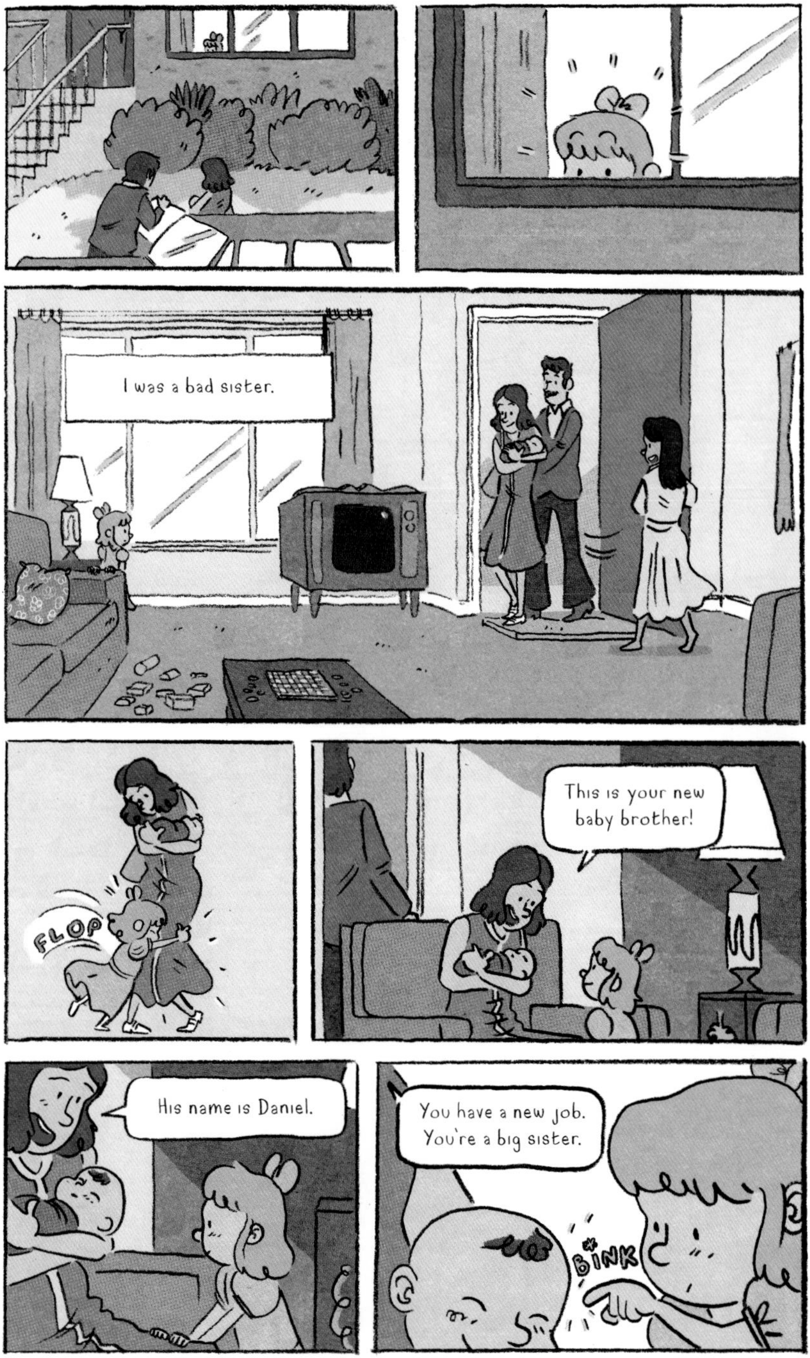
I was a bad sister.
FLOP
This is your new baby brother!
His name is Daniel.
You have a new job. You're a big sister.
BINK

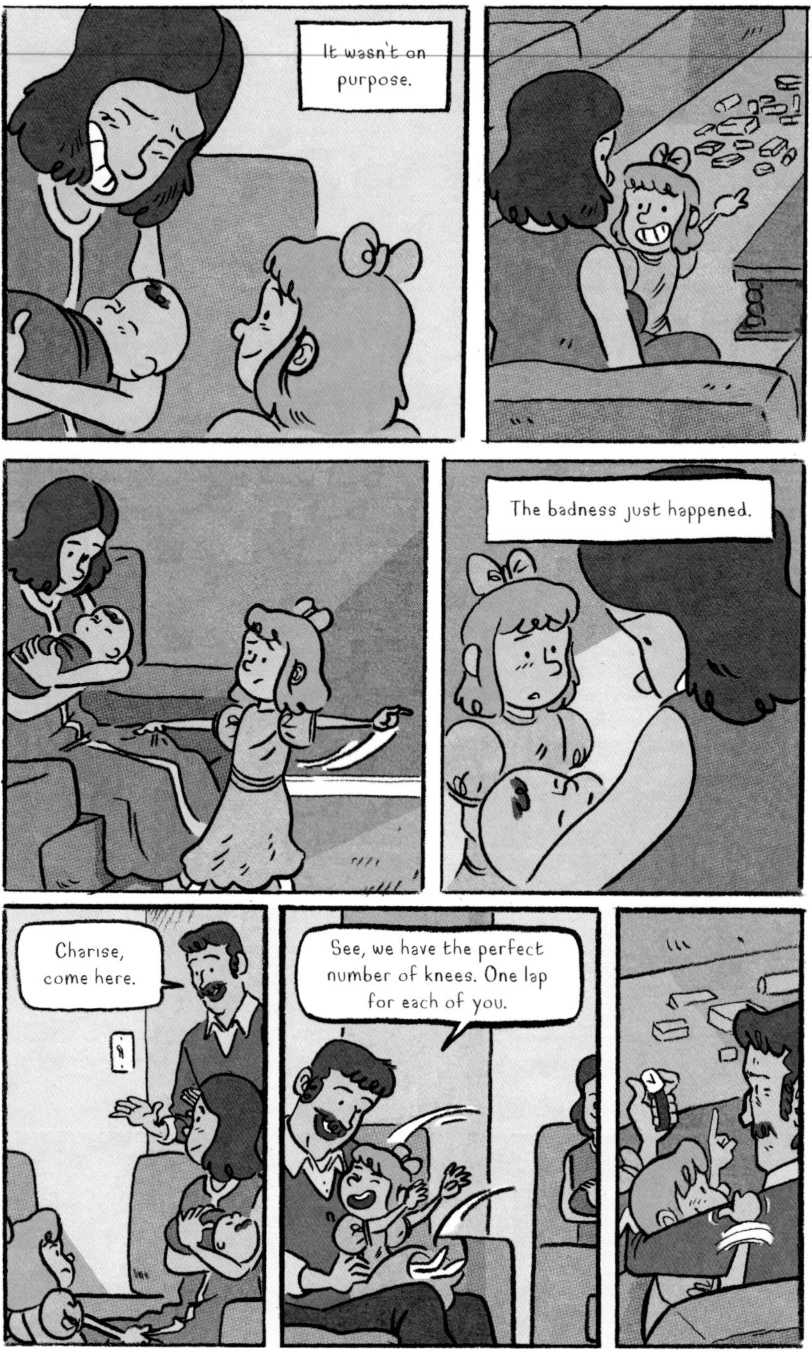
It wasn't on purpose.
The badness just happened.
Charise, come here.
See, we have the perfect number of knees. One lap for each of you.

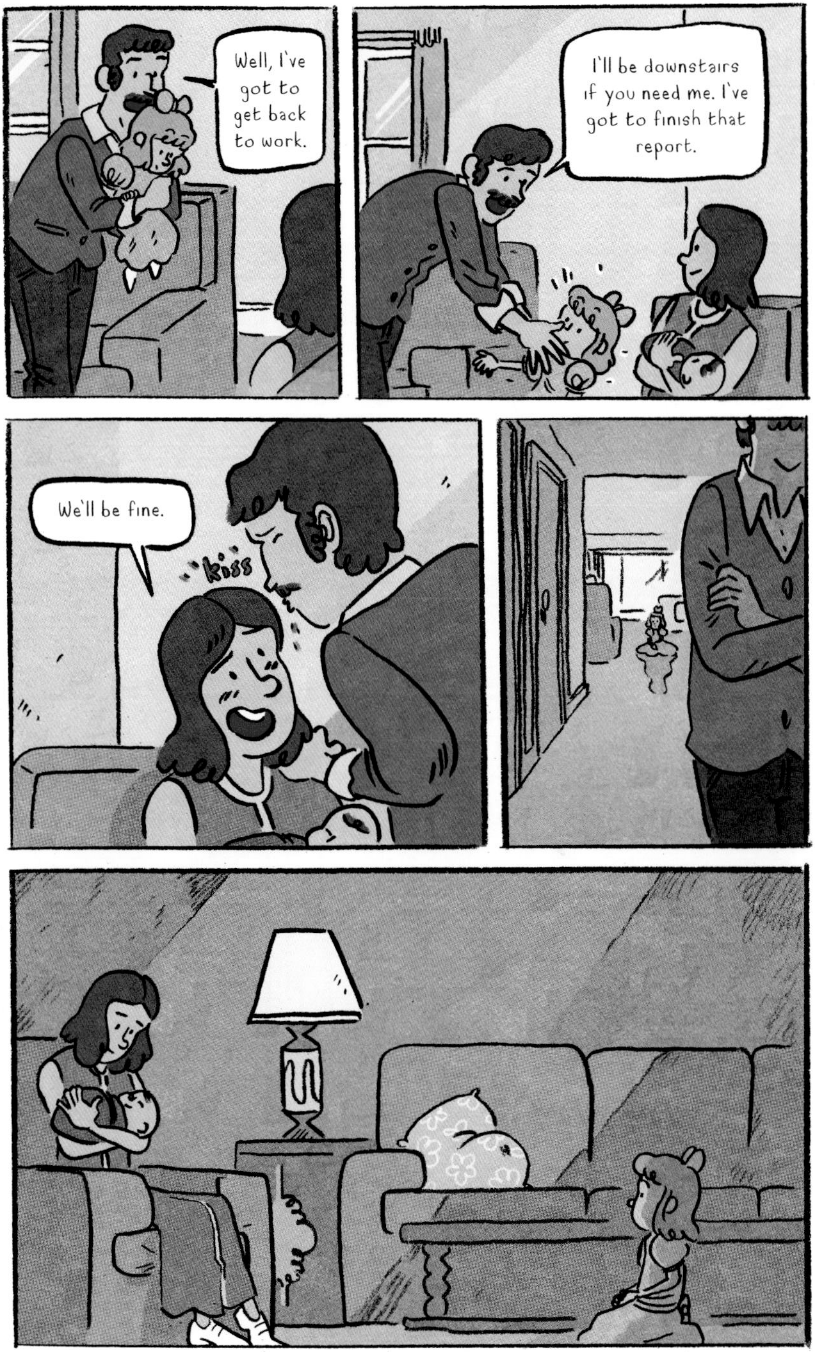
Well, I've got to get back to work.
I'll be downstairs if you need me. I've got to finish that report.
We'll be fine.
KISS

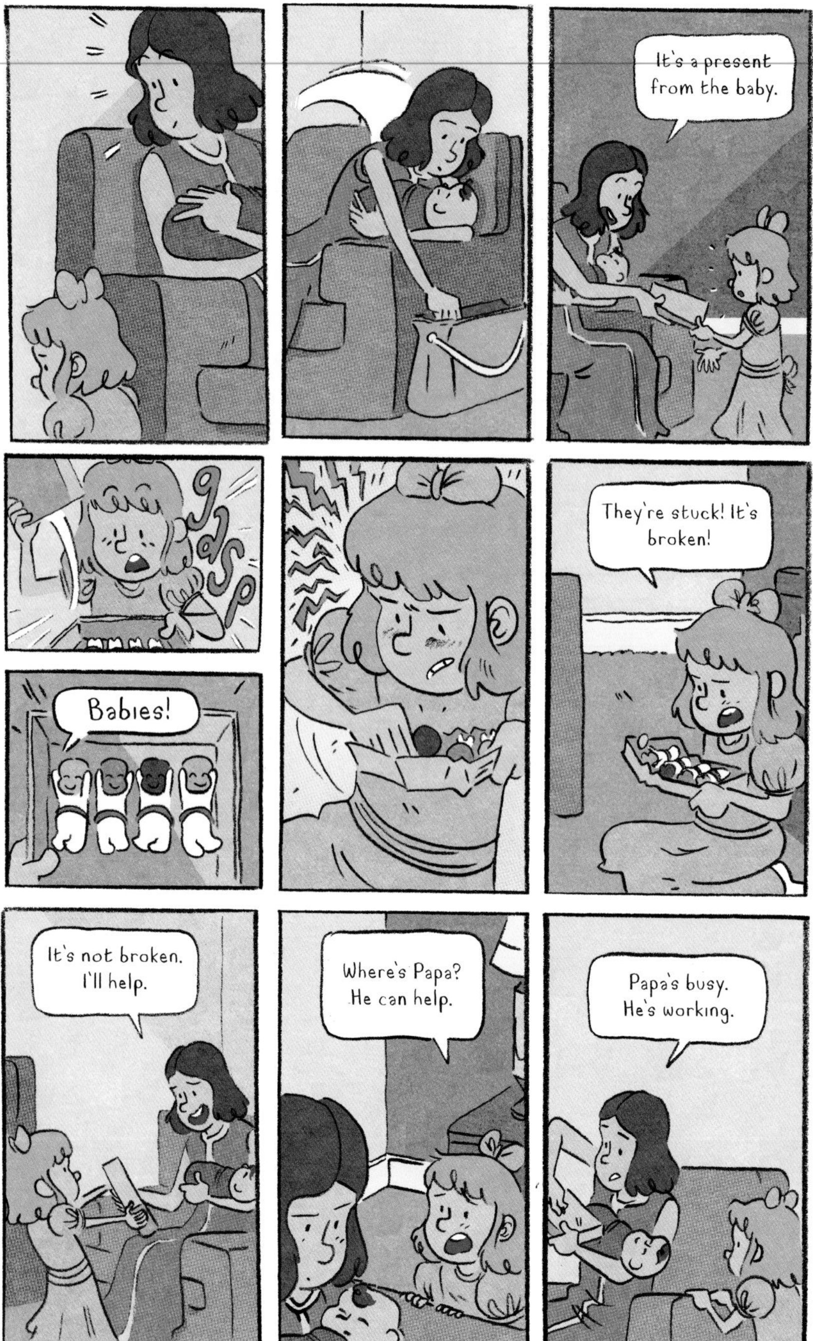

It's a present from the baby.
gasp
Babies!
They're stuck! It's broken!
It's not broken. I'll help.
Where's Papa? He can help.
Papa's busy. He's working.

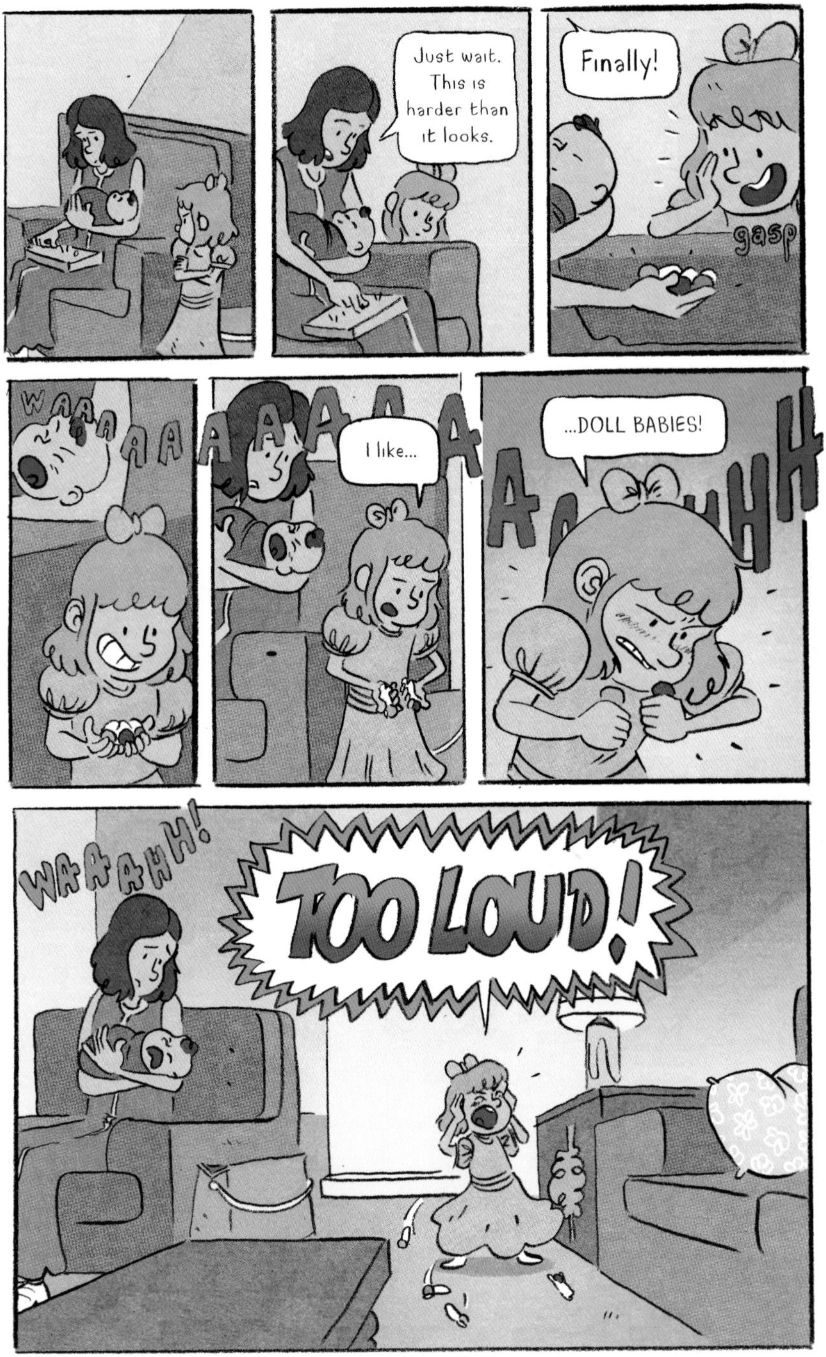

Just wait. This is harder than it looks.
Finally!
gasp
WAAAAAAAAAA
I like...
AAHHH
...DOLL BABIES!
WAAAHH!
TOO LOUD!

The Power of the Trick!

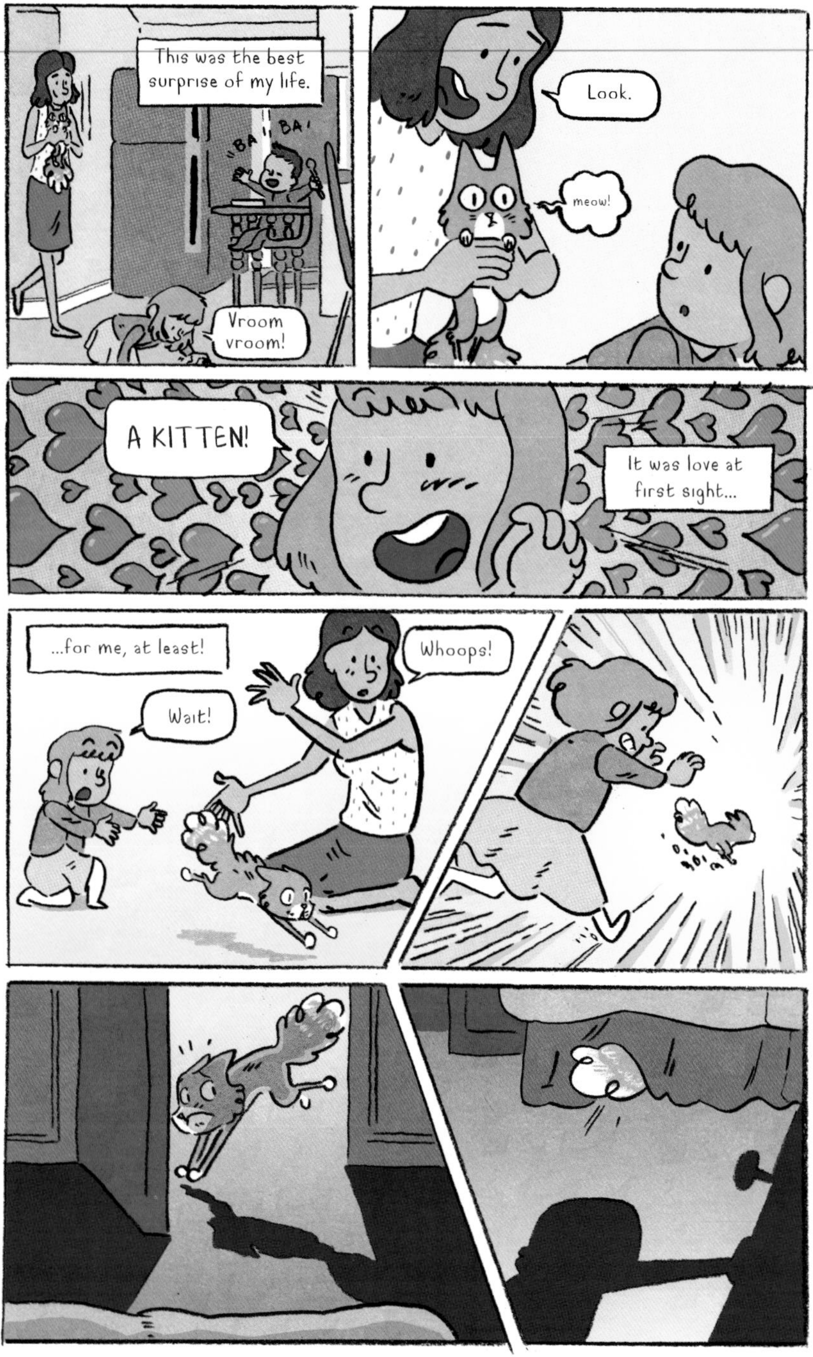
This was the best surprise of my life.
BA BA
Vroom vroom!
Look.
meow!
A KITTEN!
It was love at first sight...
...for me, at least!
Whoops!
Wait!

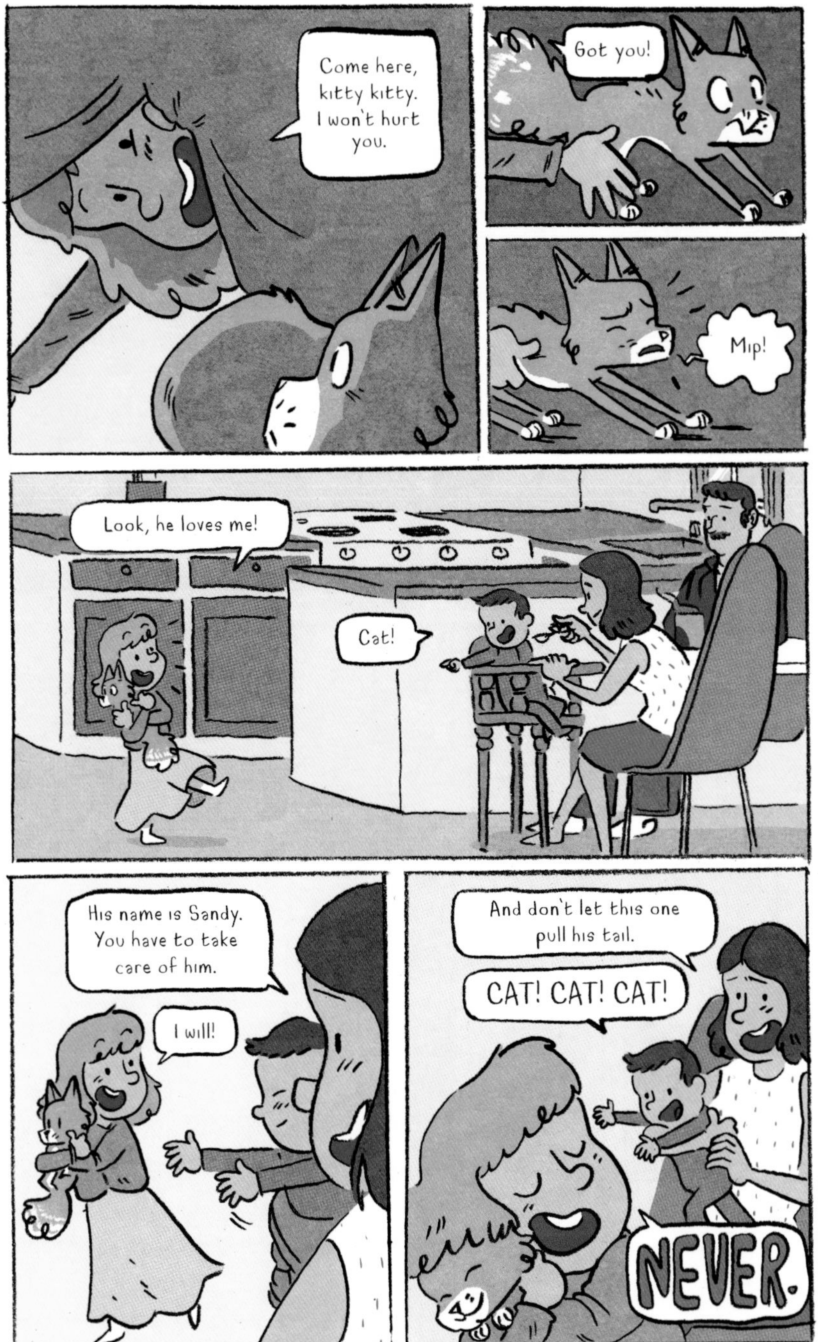
Come here, kitty kitty. I won't hurt you.
Got you!
Mip!
Look, he loves me!
Cat!
His name is Sandy. You have to take care of him.
I will!
And don't let this one pull his tail.
CAT! CAT! CAT!
NEVER.

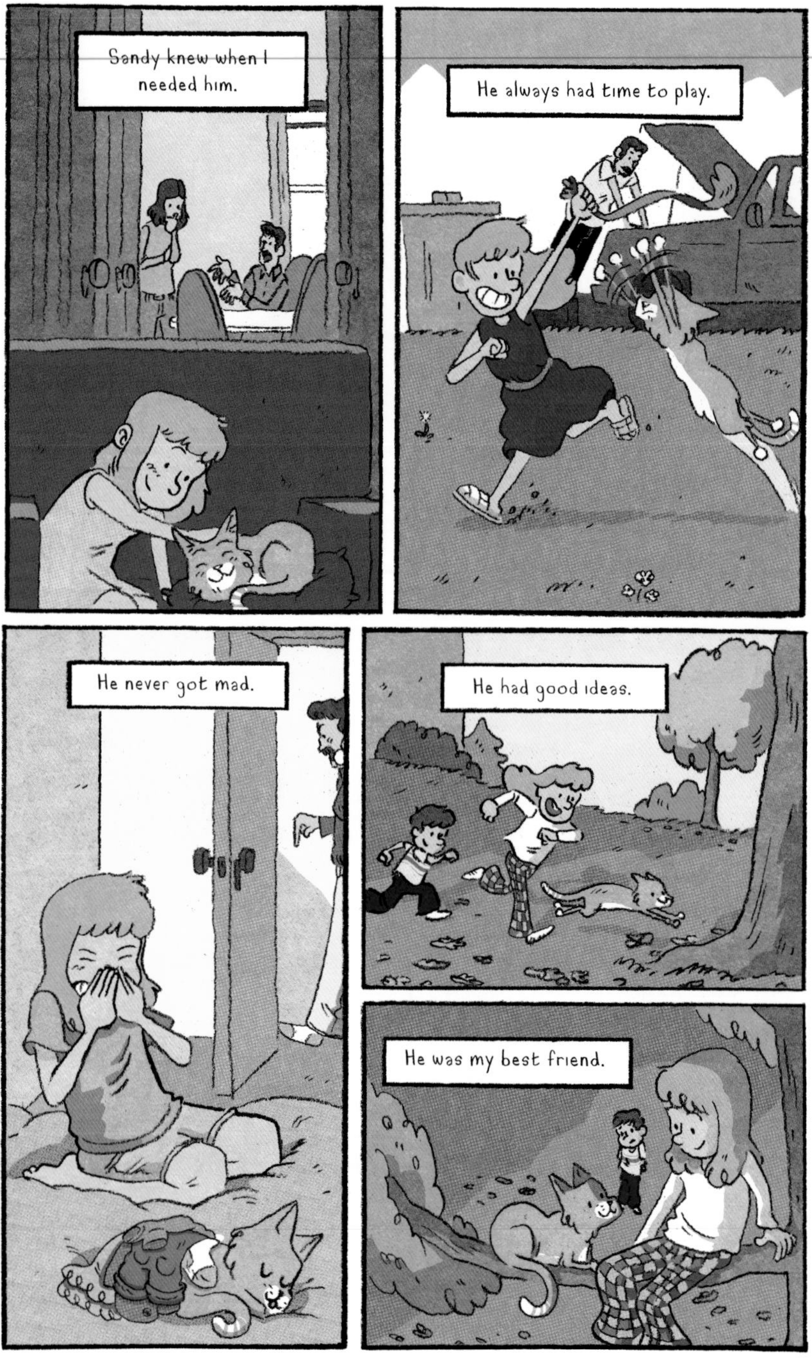
Sandy knew when I needed him.
He always had time to play.
He never got mad.
He had good ideas.
He was my best friend.

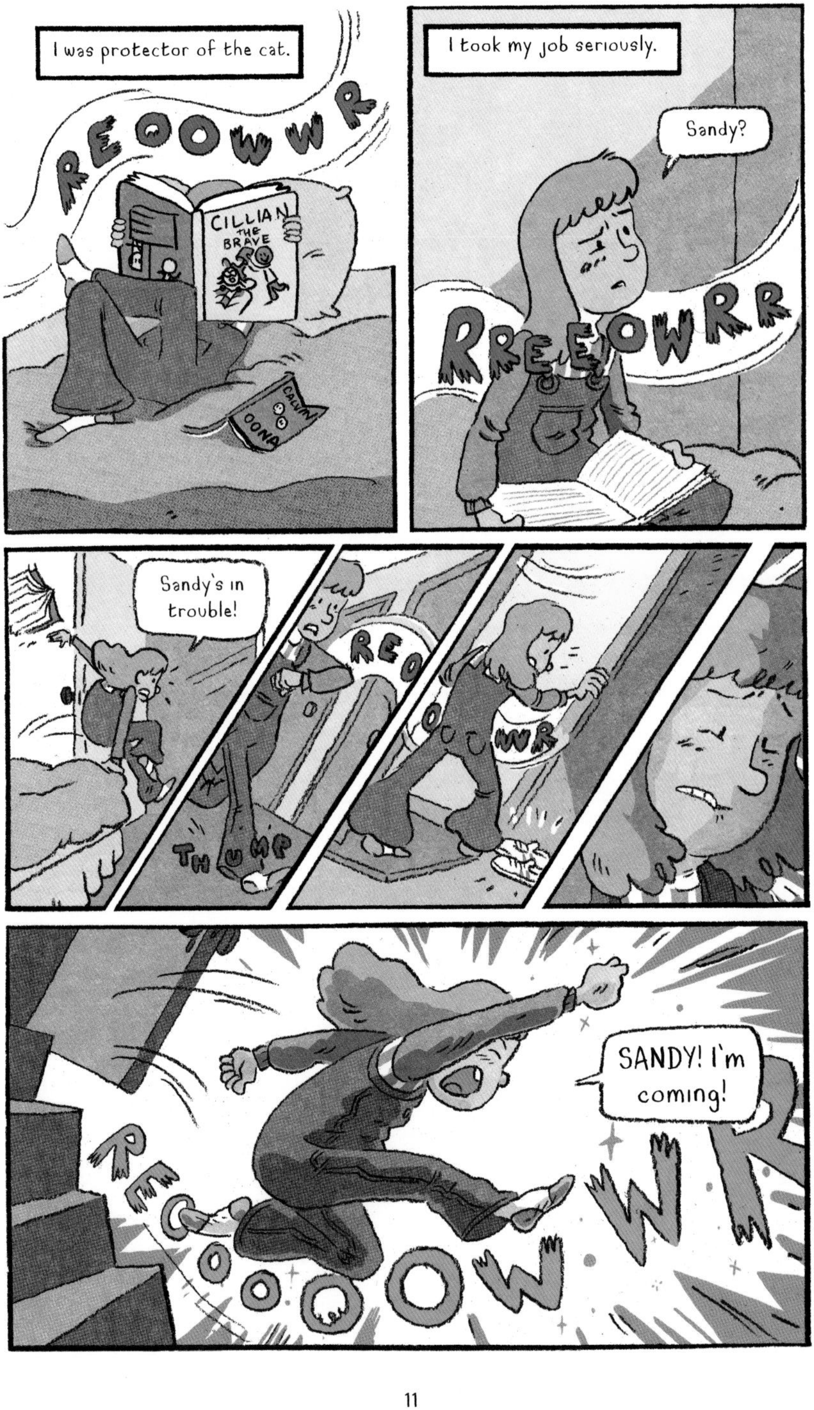
I was protector of the cat.
REOOWWR
CILLIAN THE BRAVE
CALVIN
OONA
I took my job seriously.
Sandy?
RREEOWRR
Sandy's in trouble!
REO
THUMP
OWR
SANDY! I'm coming!
REOOOOOWWR

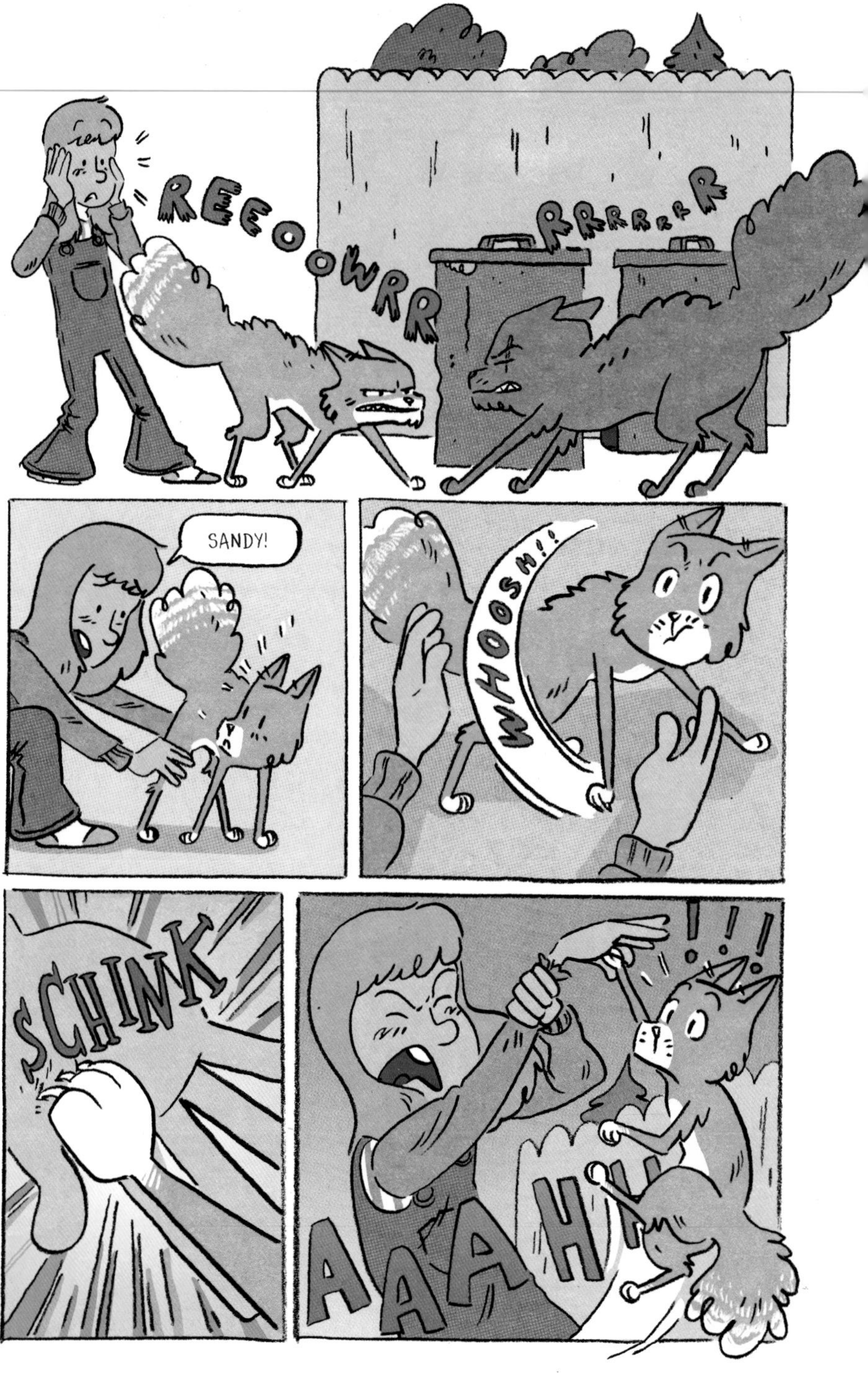
REEOOOWRR
RRRRRRRR
SANDY!
WHOOSH!!
SCHINK
!!!
AAAHH

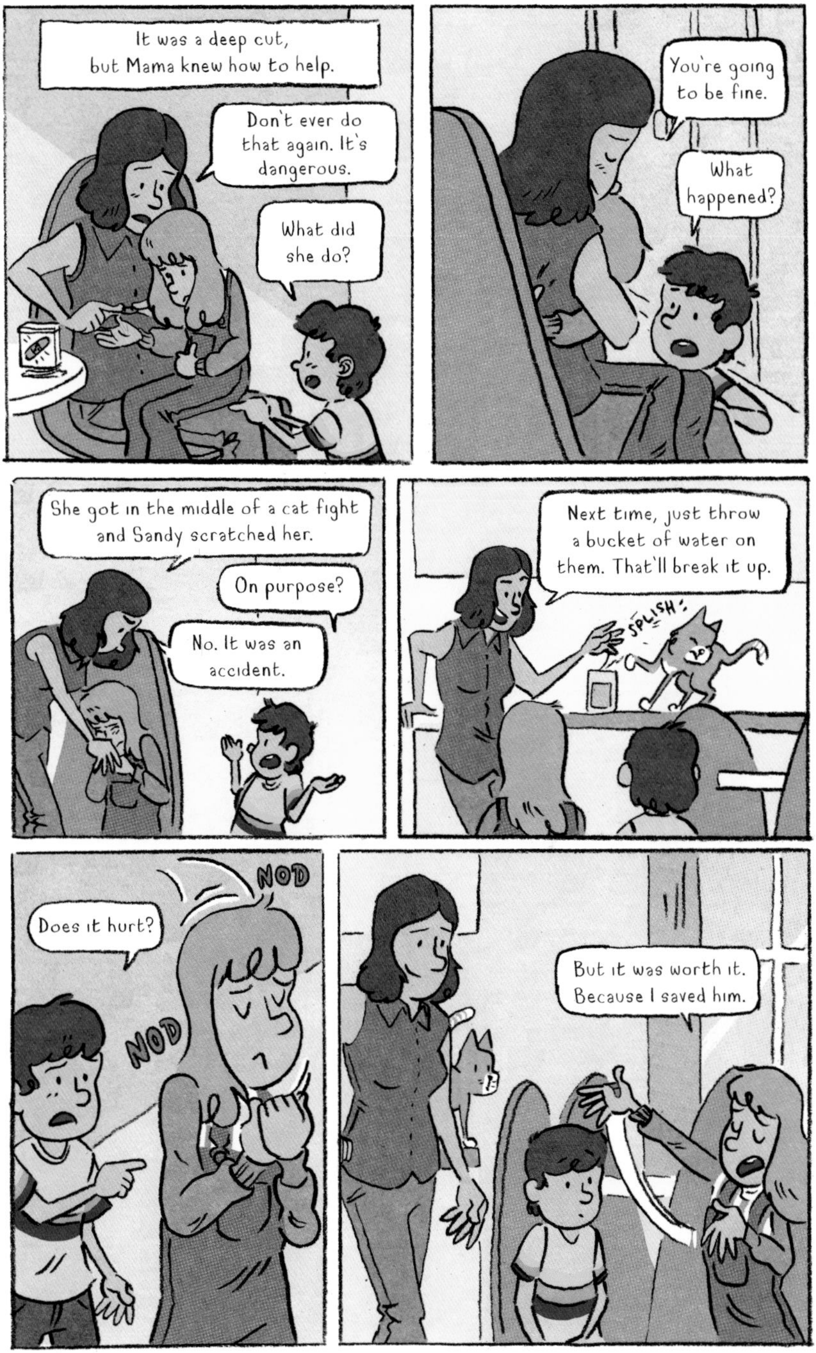
It was a deep cut, but Mama knew how to help.
Don't ever do that again. It's dangerous.
What did she do?
You're going to be fine.
What happened?
She got in the middle of a cat fight and Sandy scratched her.
On purpose?
No. It was an accident.
Next time, just throw a bucket of water on them. That'll break it up.
SPLISH
Does it hurt?
NOD
NOD
But it was worth it. Because I saved him.

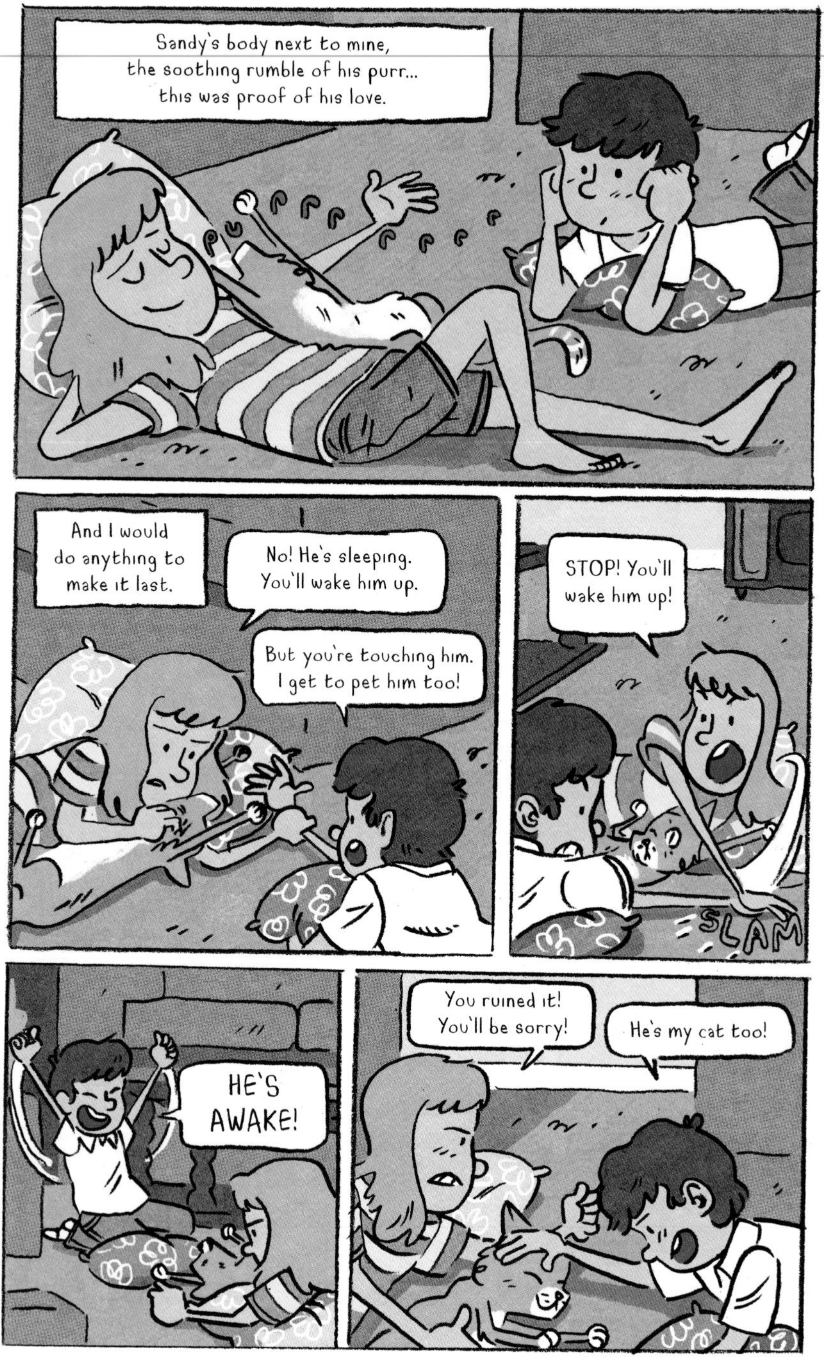
Sandy's body next to mine, the soothing rumble of his purr... this was proof of his love.
PURRRRRRR
And I would do anything to make it last.
No! He's sleeping. You'll wake him up.
But you're touching him. I get to pet him too!
STOP! You'll wake him up!
SLAM
HE'S AWAKE!
You ruined it! You'll be sorry!
He's my cat too!

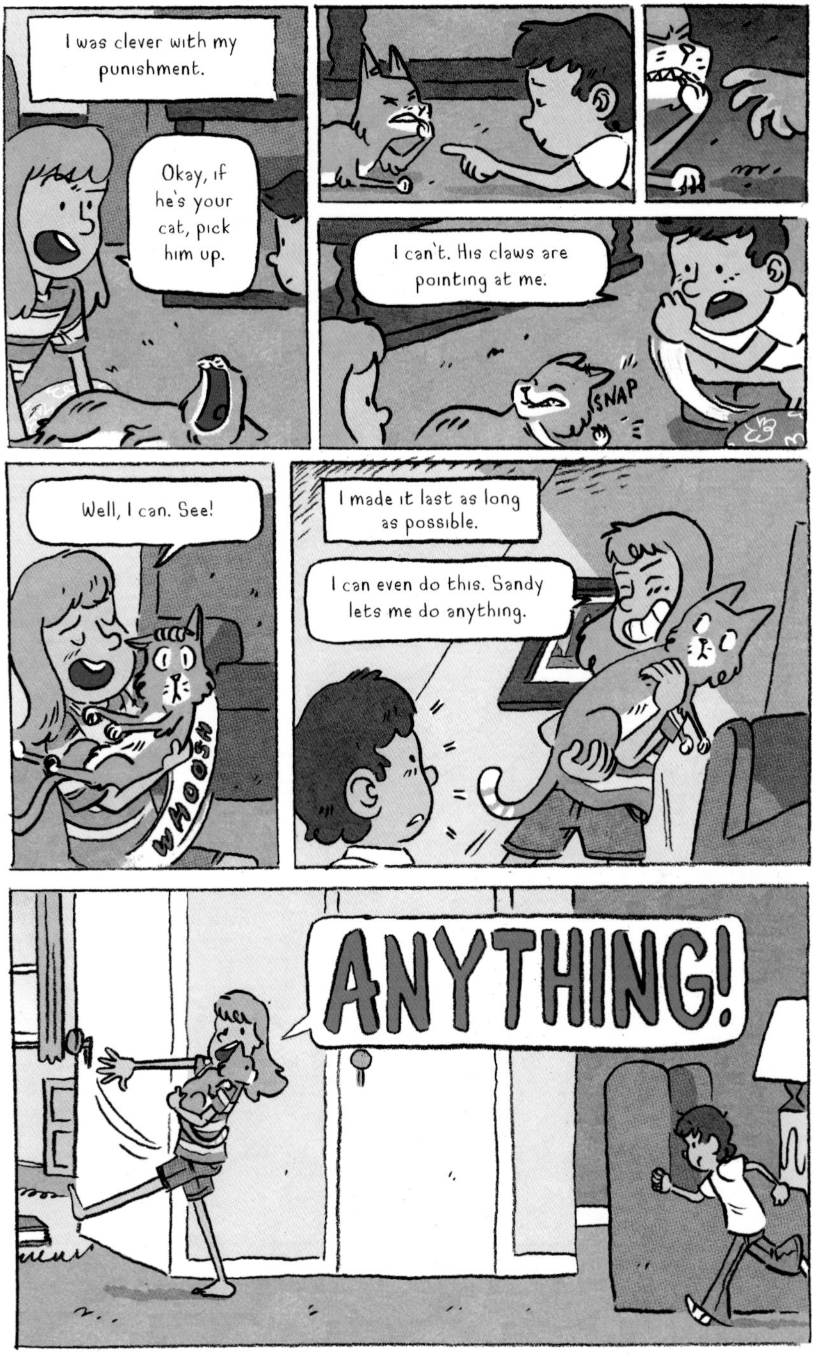
I was clever with my punishment.
Okay, if he's your cat, pick him up.
I can't. His claws are pointing at me.
SNAP
Well, I can. See!
WHOOSH
I made it last as long as possible.
I can even do this. Sandy lets me do anything.
ANYTHING!

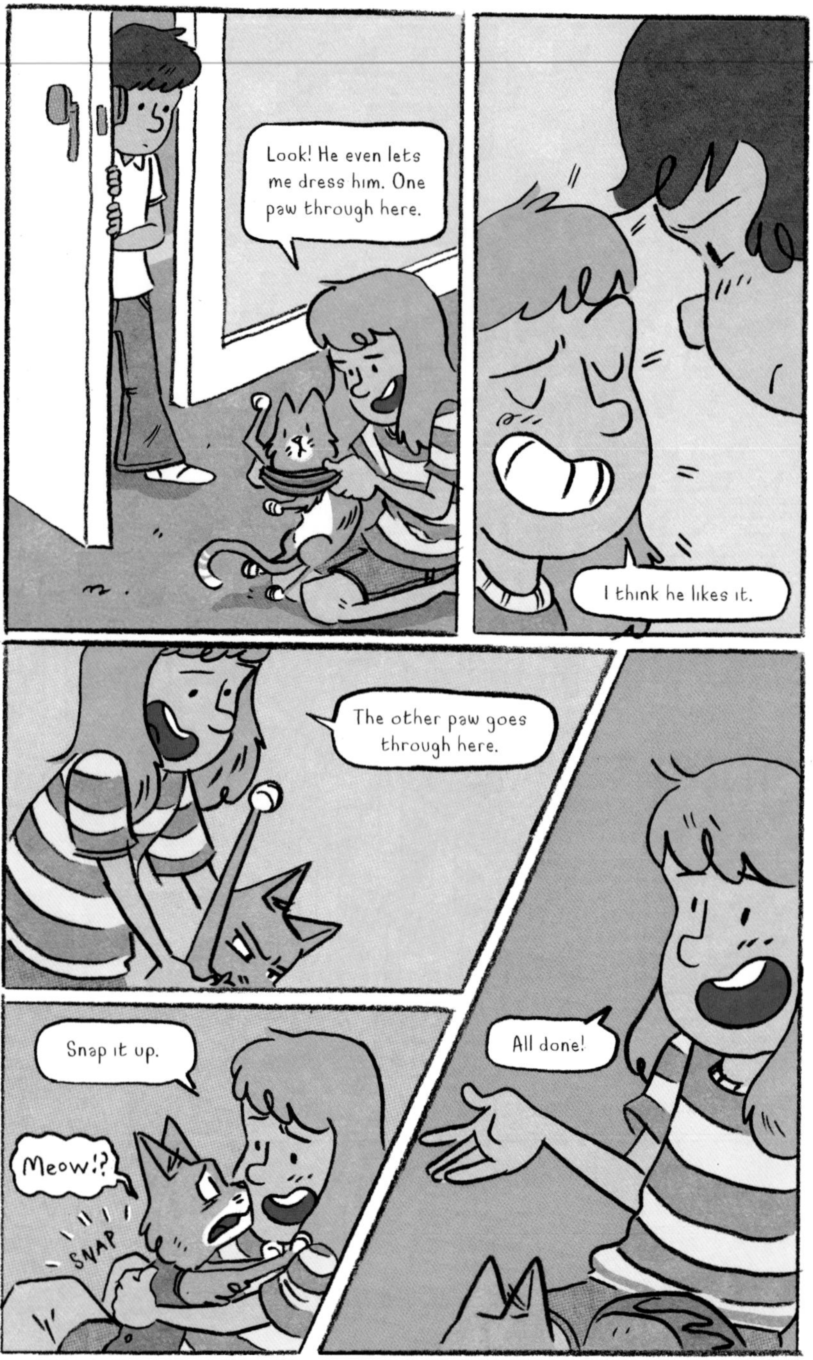
Look! He even lets me dress him. One paw through here.
I think he likes it.
The other paw goes through here.
Snap it up.
Meow!?
SNAP
All done!

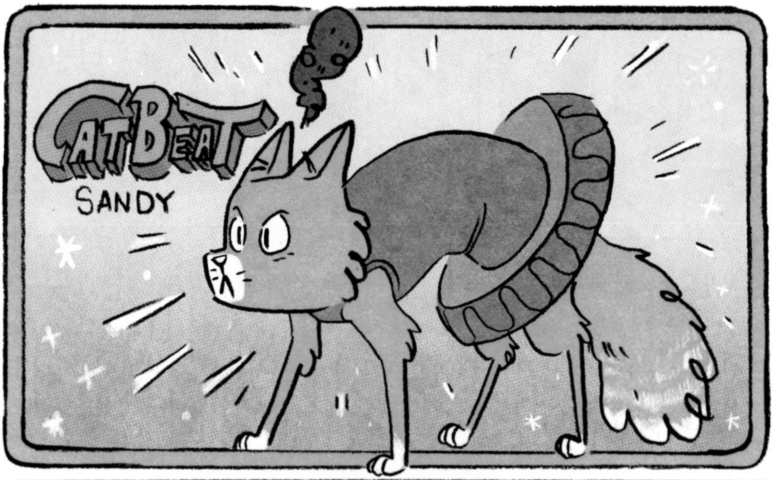
CATBEAT
SANDY

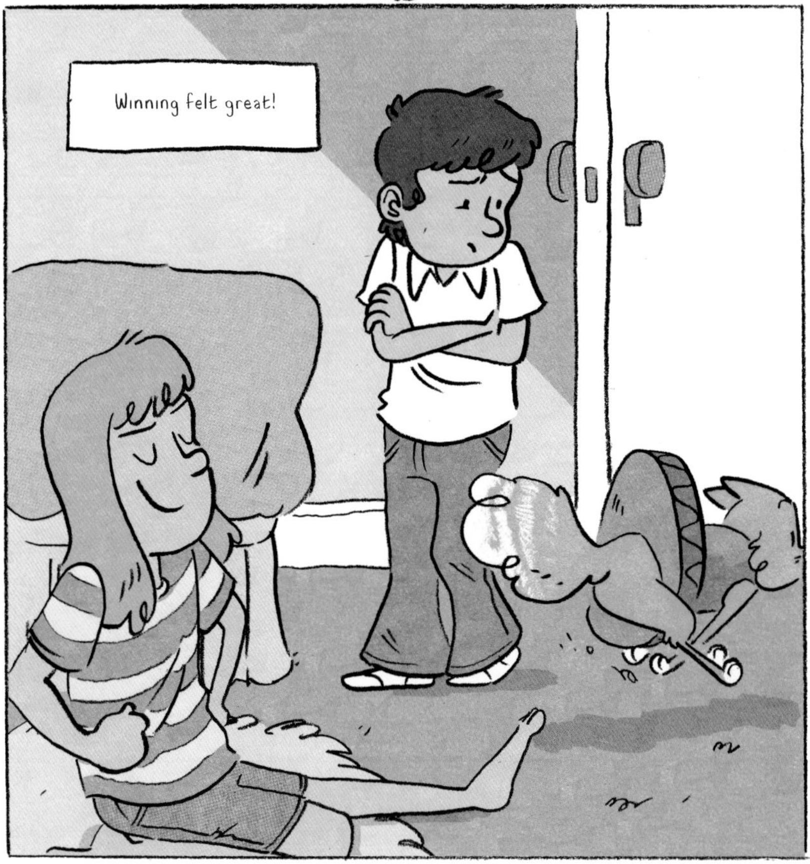
Winning felt great!

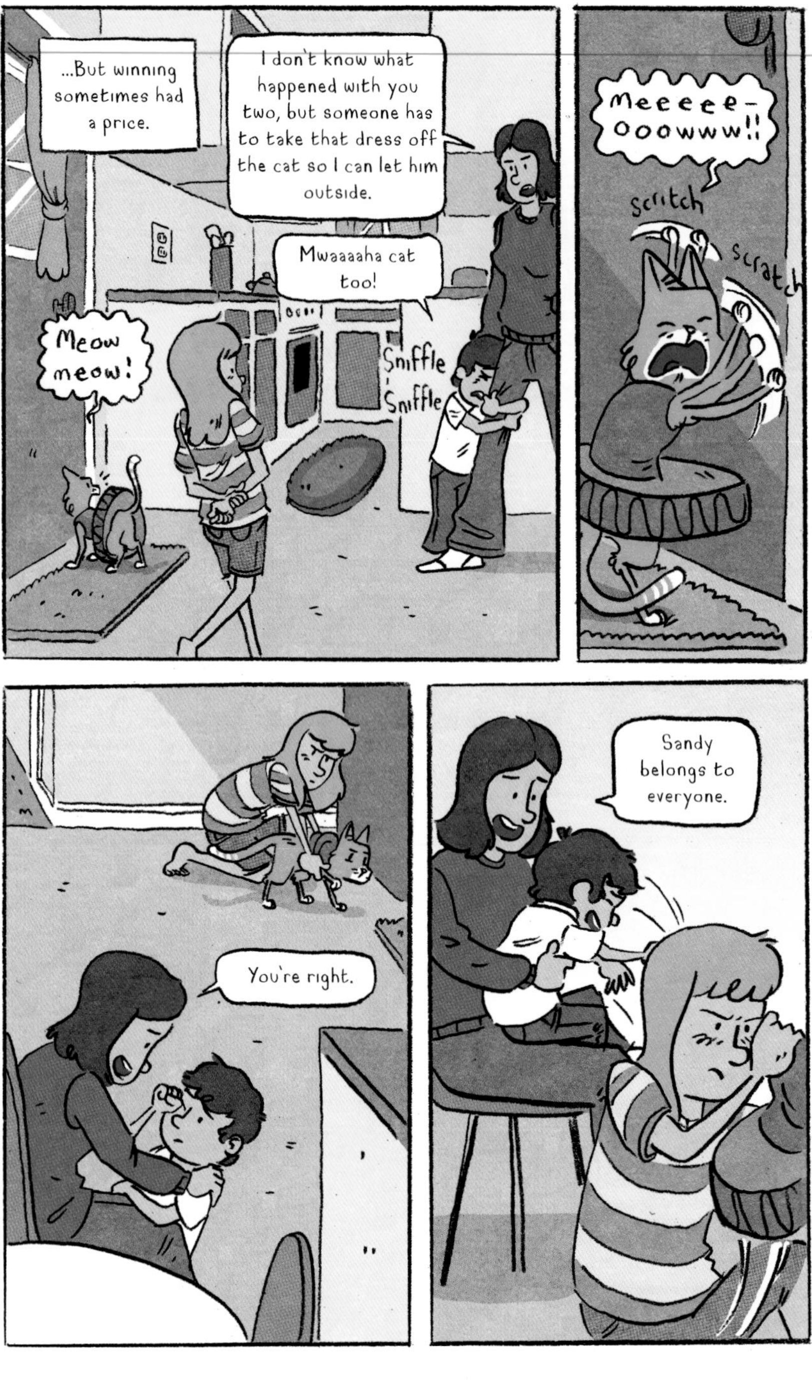
...But winning sometimes had a price.
I don't know what happened with you two, but someone has to take that dress off the cat so I can let him outside.
Mwaaaaha cat too!
Meow meow!
Sniffle Sniffle
Meeeee-ooowww!!
Scritch
Scratch
You're right.
Sandy belongs to everyone.

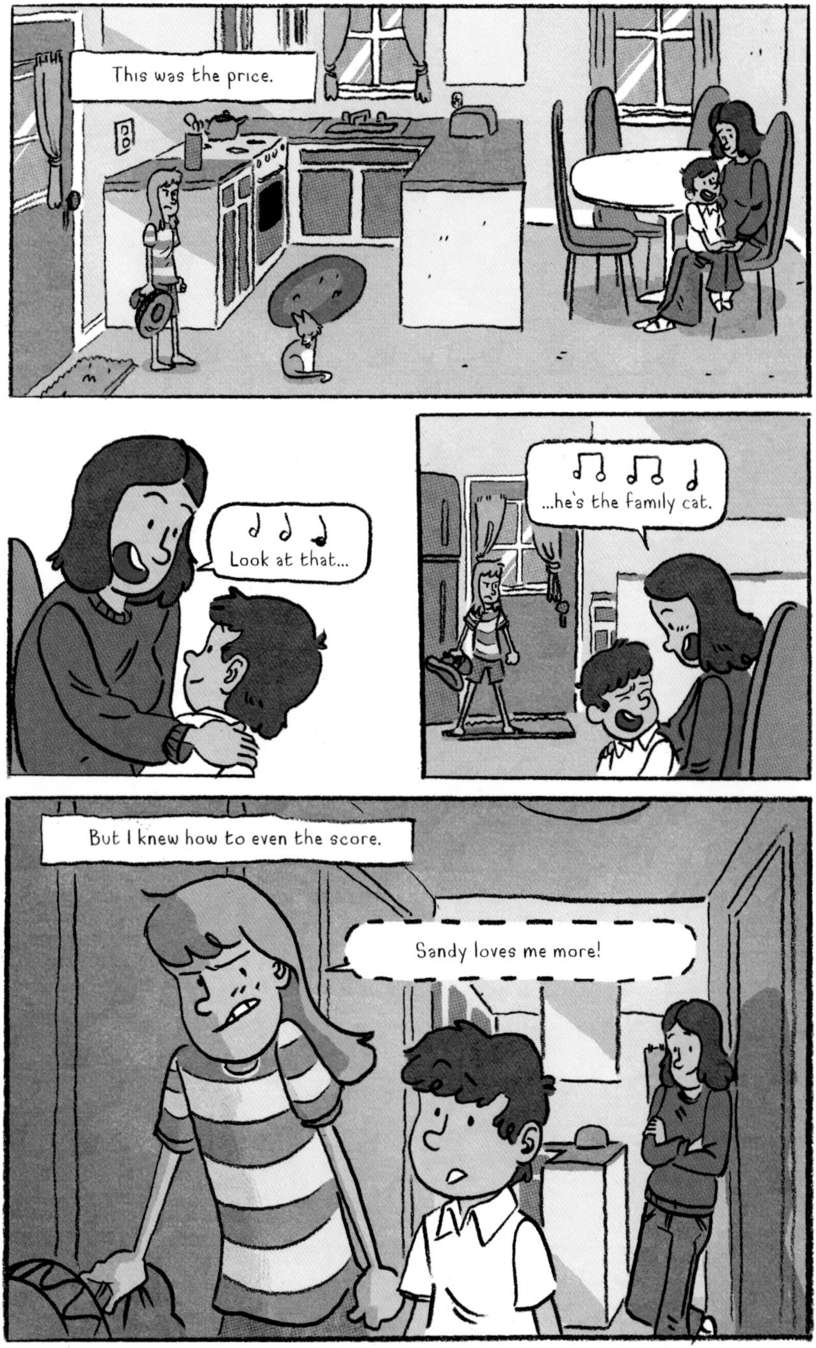
This was the price.
Look at that...
...he's the family cat.
But I knew how to even the score.
Sandy loves me more!

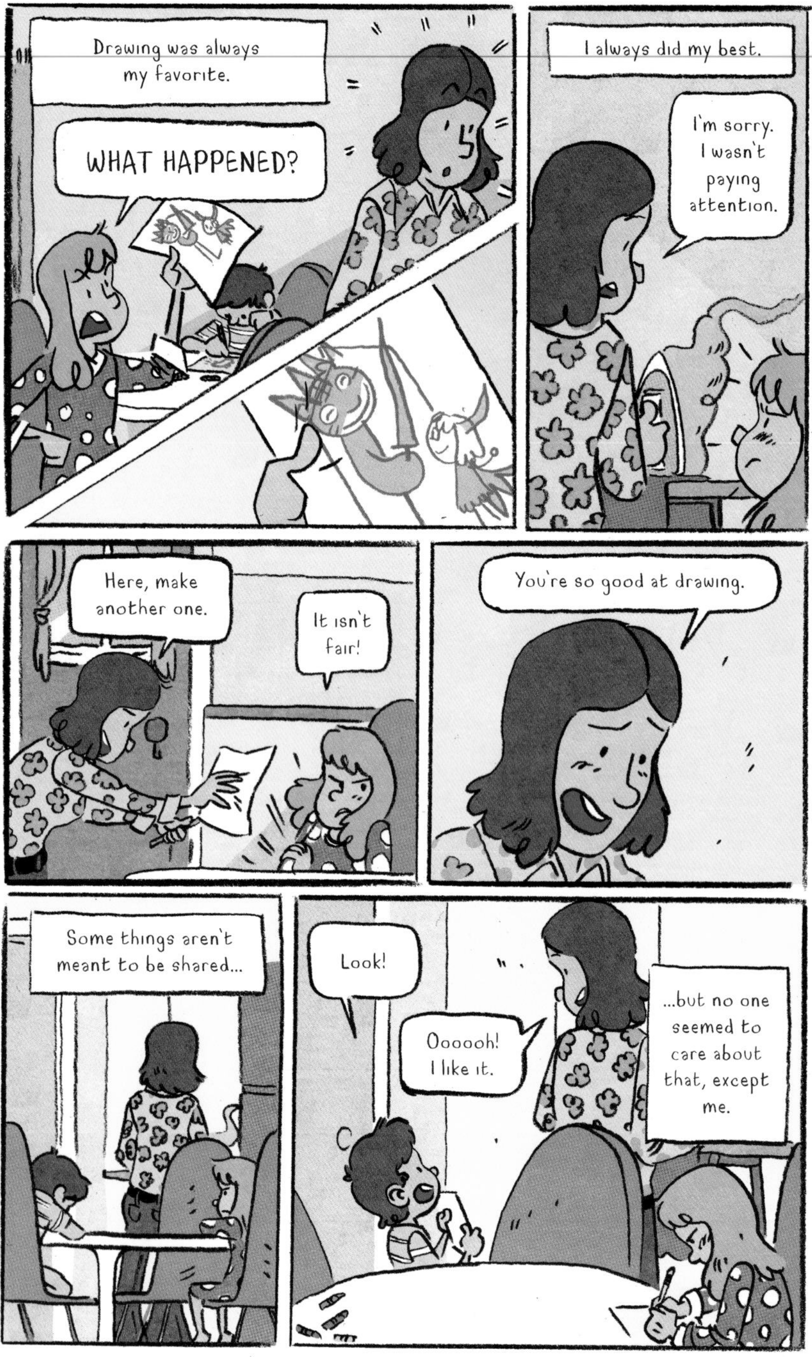
Drawing was always my favorite.
WHAT HAPPENED?
I always did my best.
I'm sorry. I wasn't paying attention.
Here, make another one.
It isn't fair!
You're so good at drawing.
Some things aren't meant to be shared...
Look!
Oooooh! I like it.
...but no one seemed to care about that, except me.

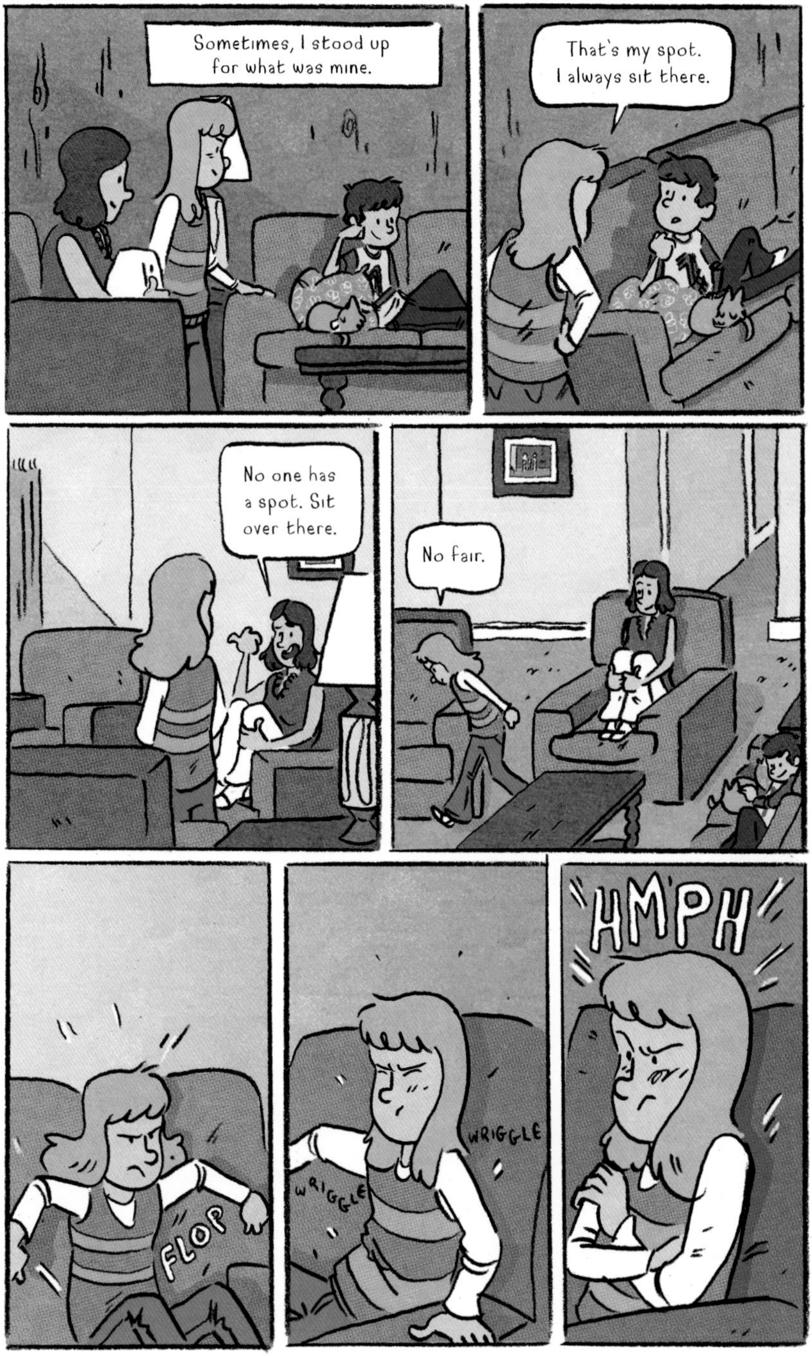
Sometimes, I stood up for what was mine.
That's my spot. I always sit there.
No one has a spot. Sit over there.
No fair.
FLOP
WRIGGLE
WRIGGLE
HMPH

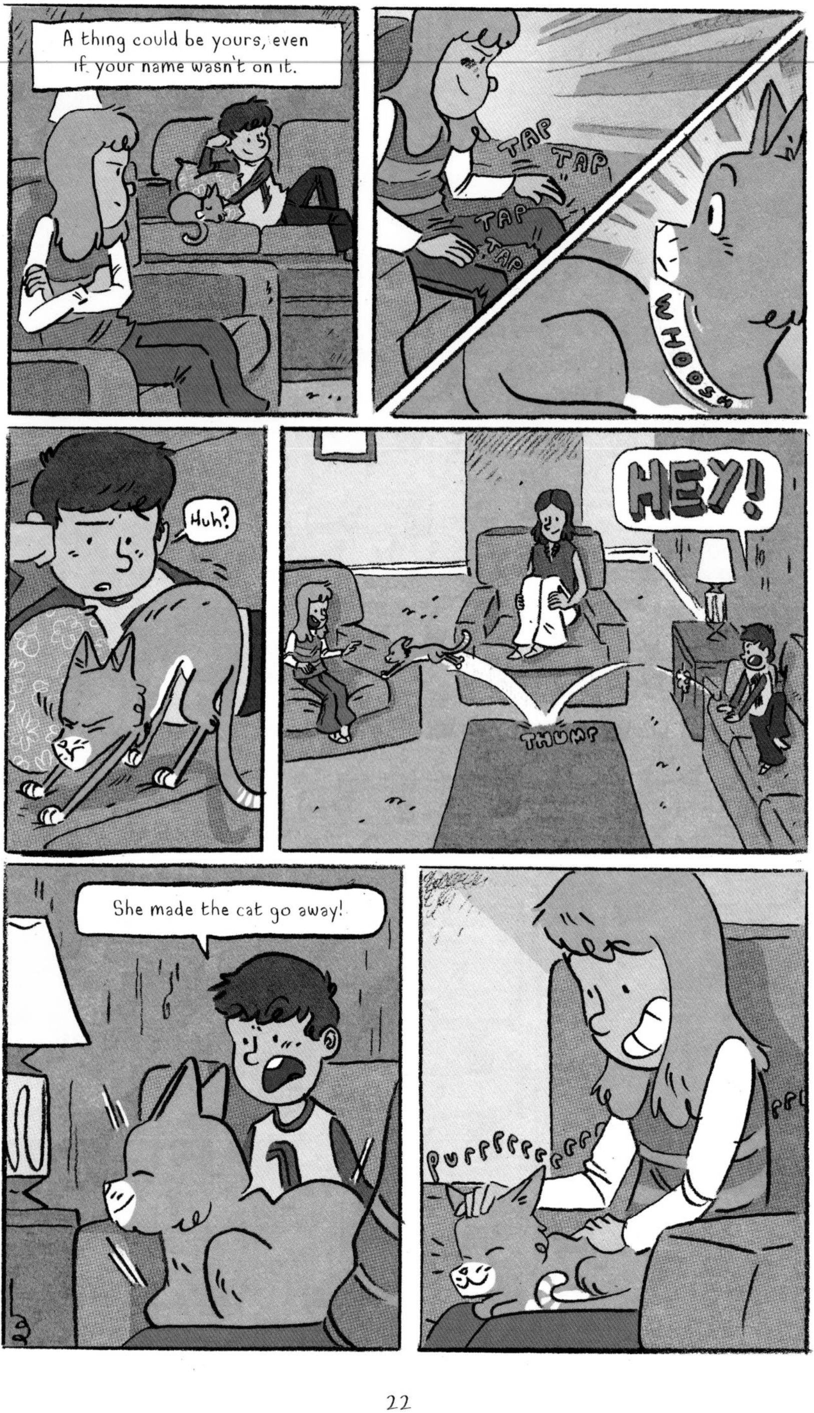
A thing could be yours, even if your name wasn't on it.
TAP
TAP
TAP
TAP
WHOOSH
Huh?
HEY!
THUMP
She made the cat go away!
purrrrrrrrr

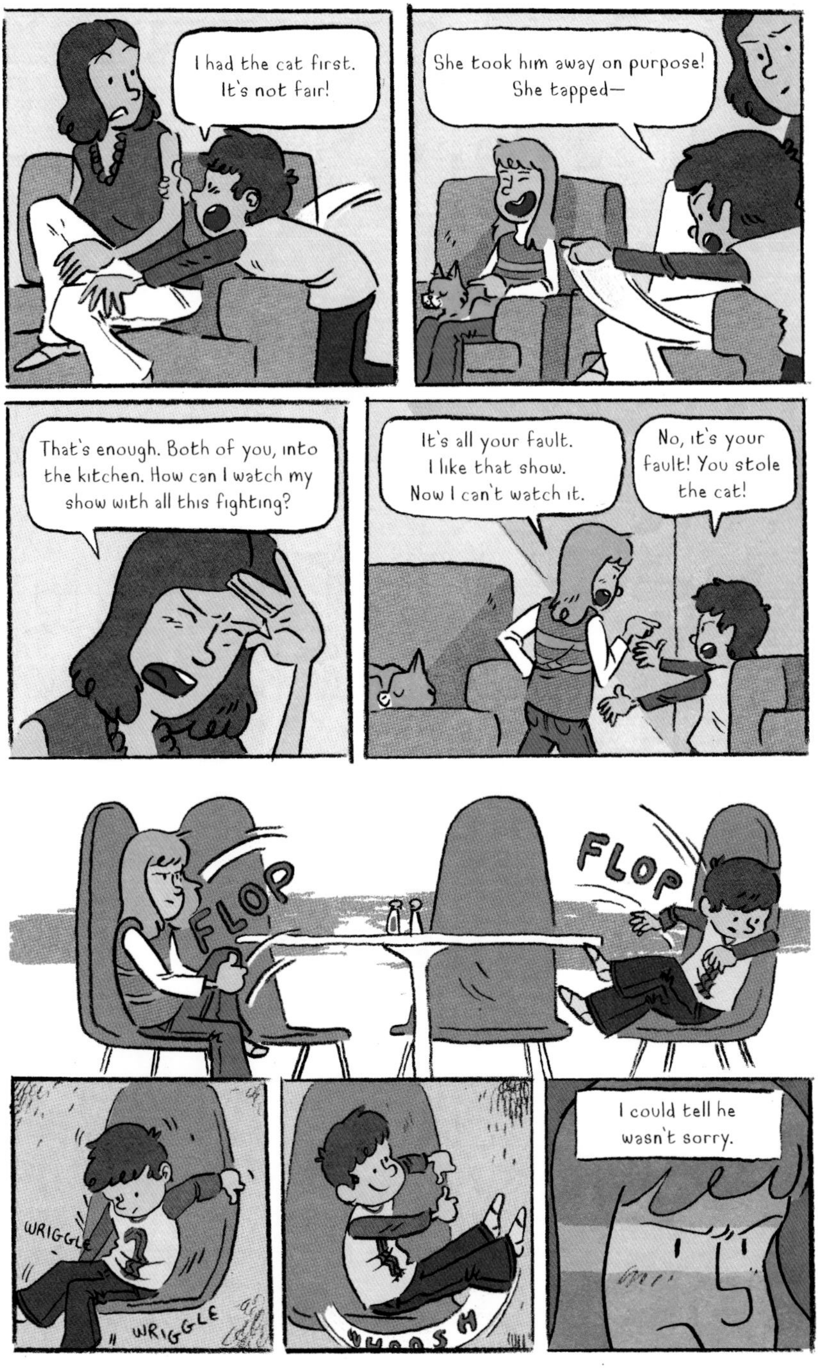
I had the cat first. It's not fair!
She took him away on purpose! She tapped—
That's enough. Both of you, into the kitchen. How can I watch my show with all this fighting?
It's all your fault. I like that show. Now I can't watch it.
No, it's your fault! You stole the cat!
FLOP
FLOP
WRIGGLE
WRIGGLE
I could tell he wasn't sorry.

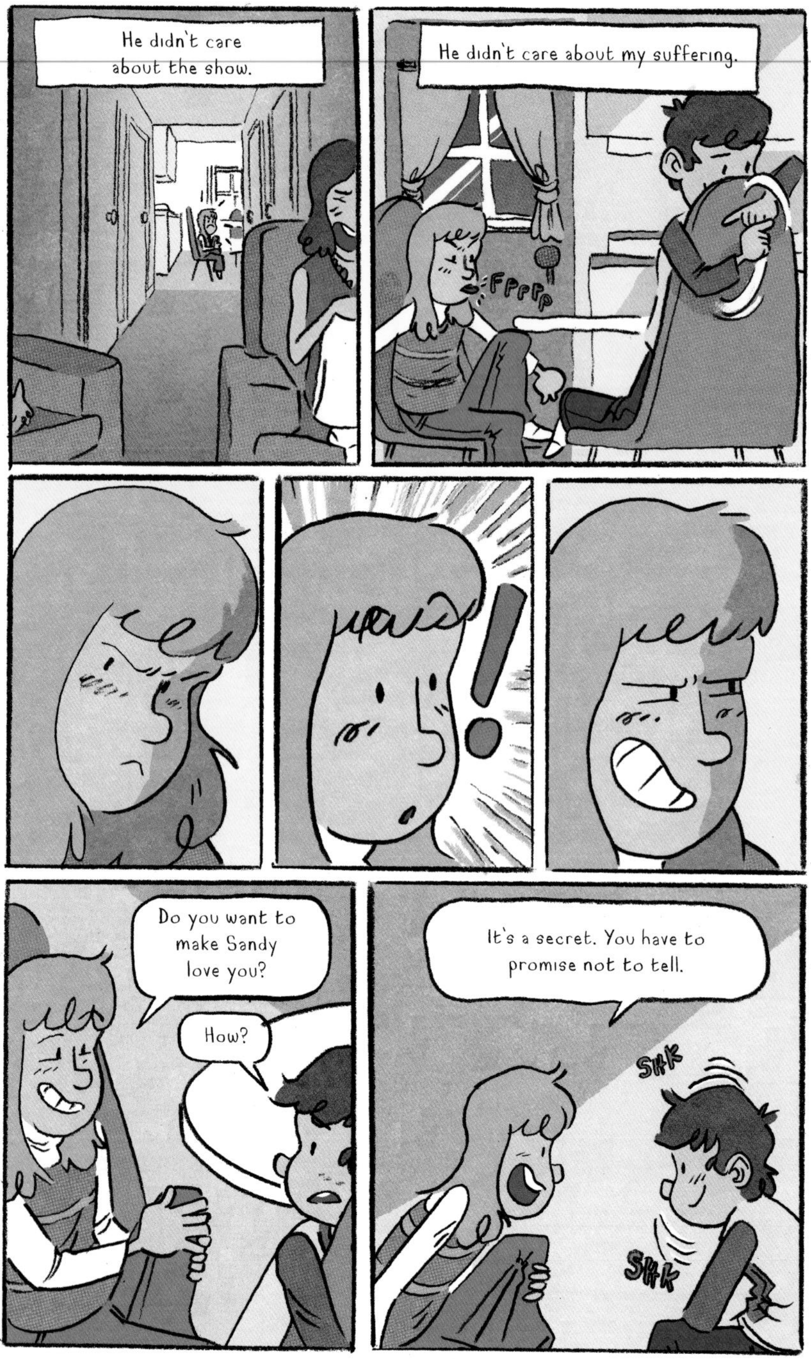
He didn't care about the show.
He didn't care about my suffering.
FPPPp
Do you want to make Sandy love you?
How?
It's a secret. You have to promise not to tell.
SHK
SHK

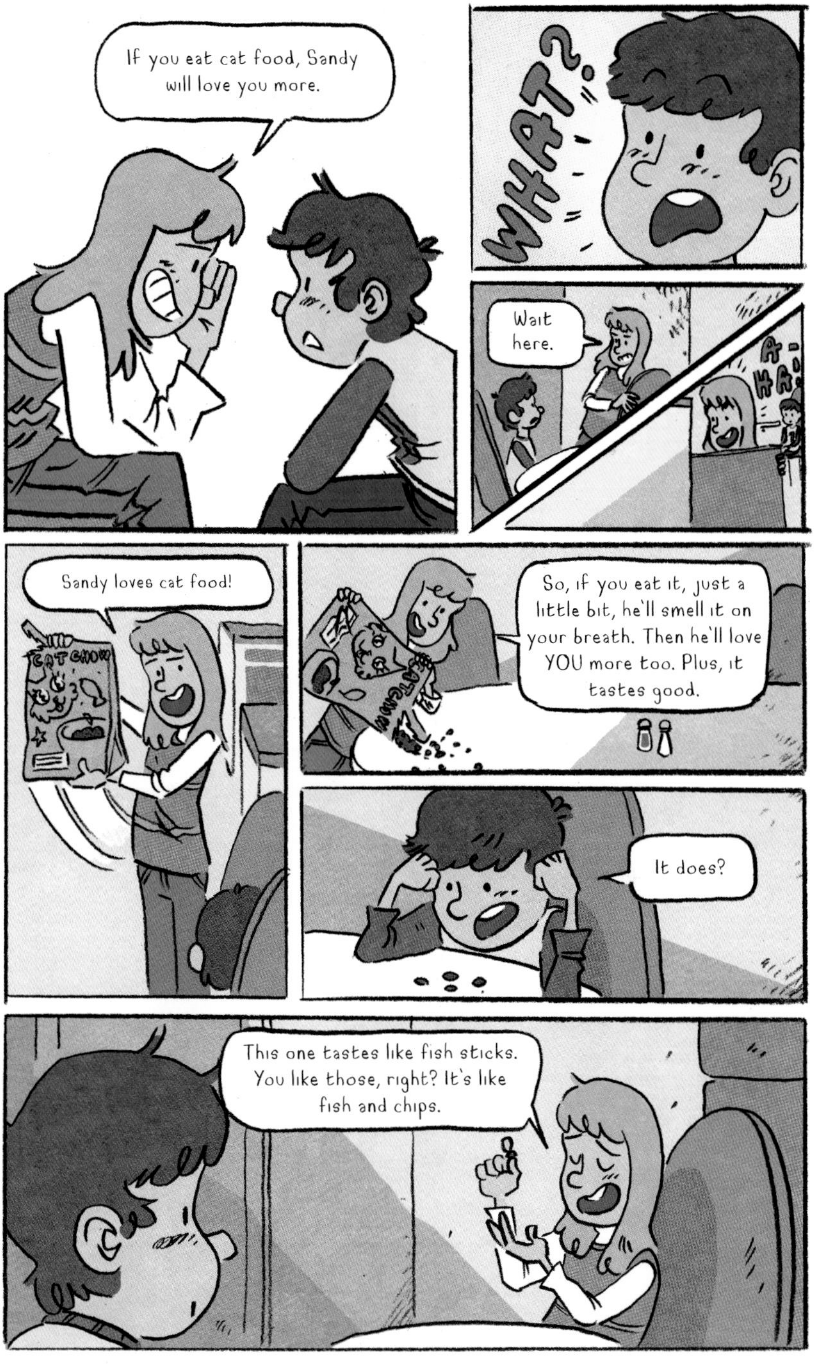
If you eat cat food, Sandy will love you more.
WHAT?
Wait here.
A-HA!
Sandy loves cat food!
CAT CHOW
So, if you eat it, just a little bit, he'll smell it on your breath. Then he'll love YOU more too. Plus, it tastes good.
It does?
This one tastes like fish sticks. You like those, right? It's like fish and chips.

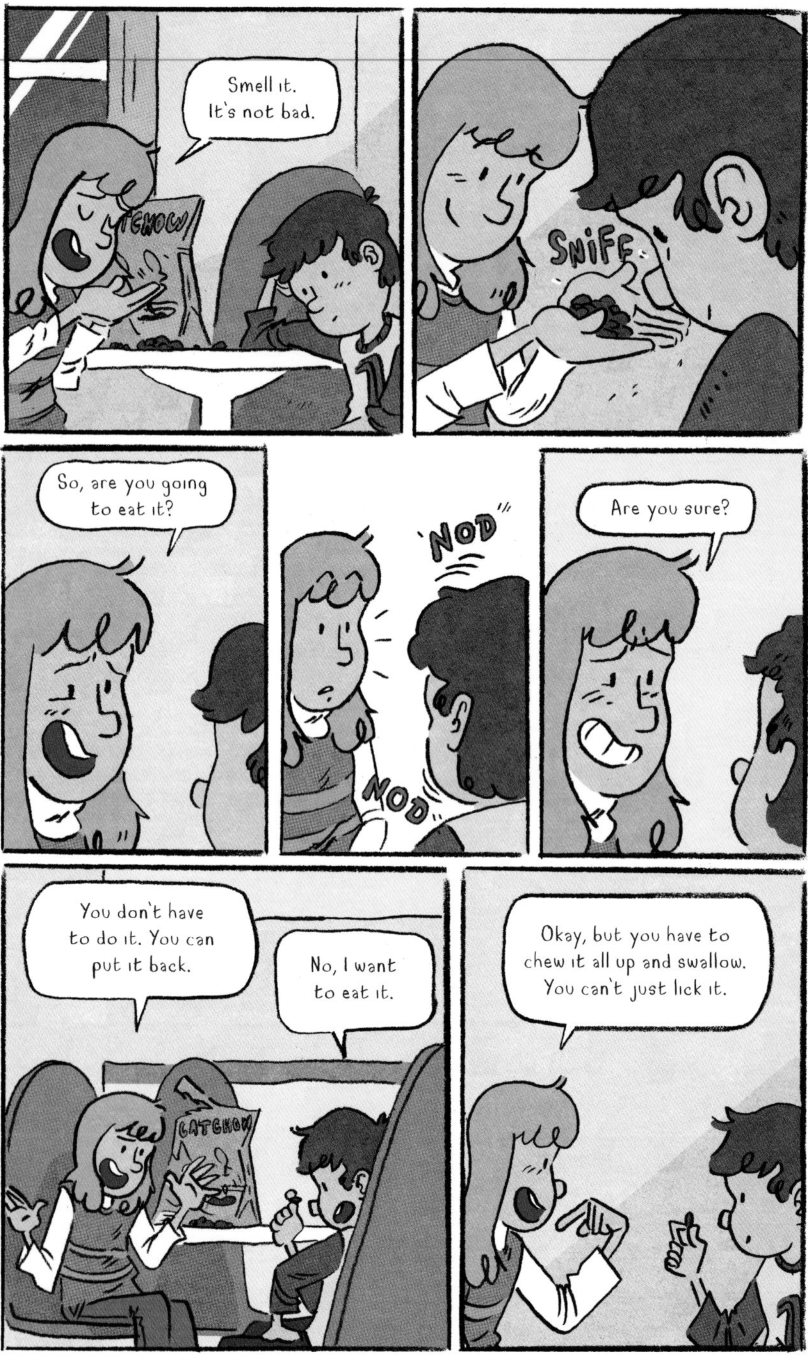
Smell it. It's not bad.
SNIFF
So, are you going to eat it?
NOD
NOD
Are you sure?
You don't have to do it. You can put it back.
No, I want to eat it.
Okay, but you have to chew it all up and swallow. You can't just lick it.

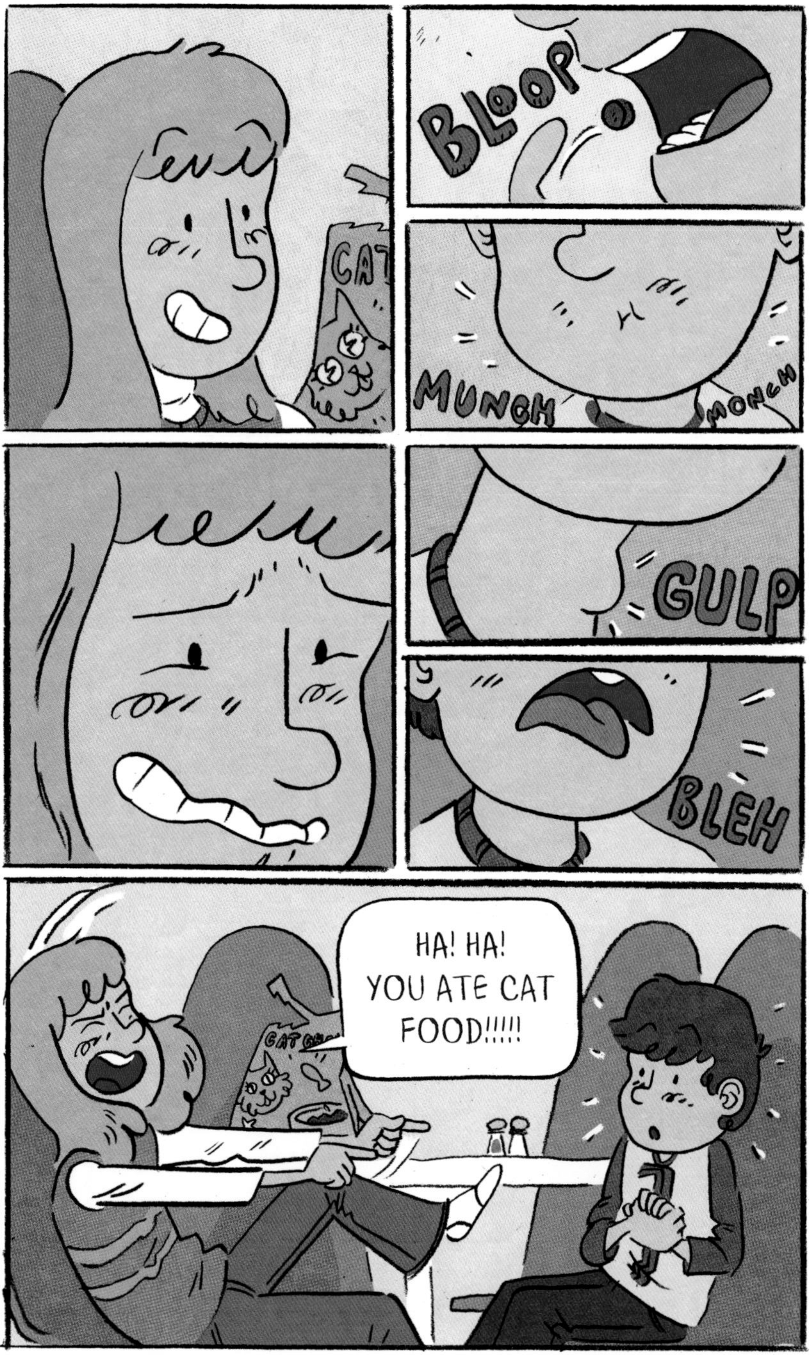
CAT
BLOOP
MUNCH
MONCH
GULP
BLEH
CAT
HA! HA!
YOU ATE CAT
FOOD!!!!!

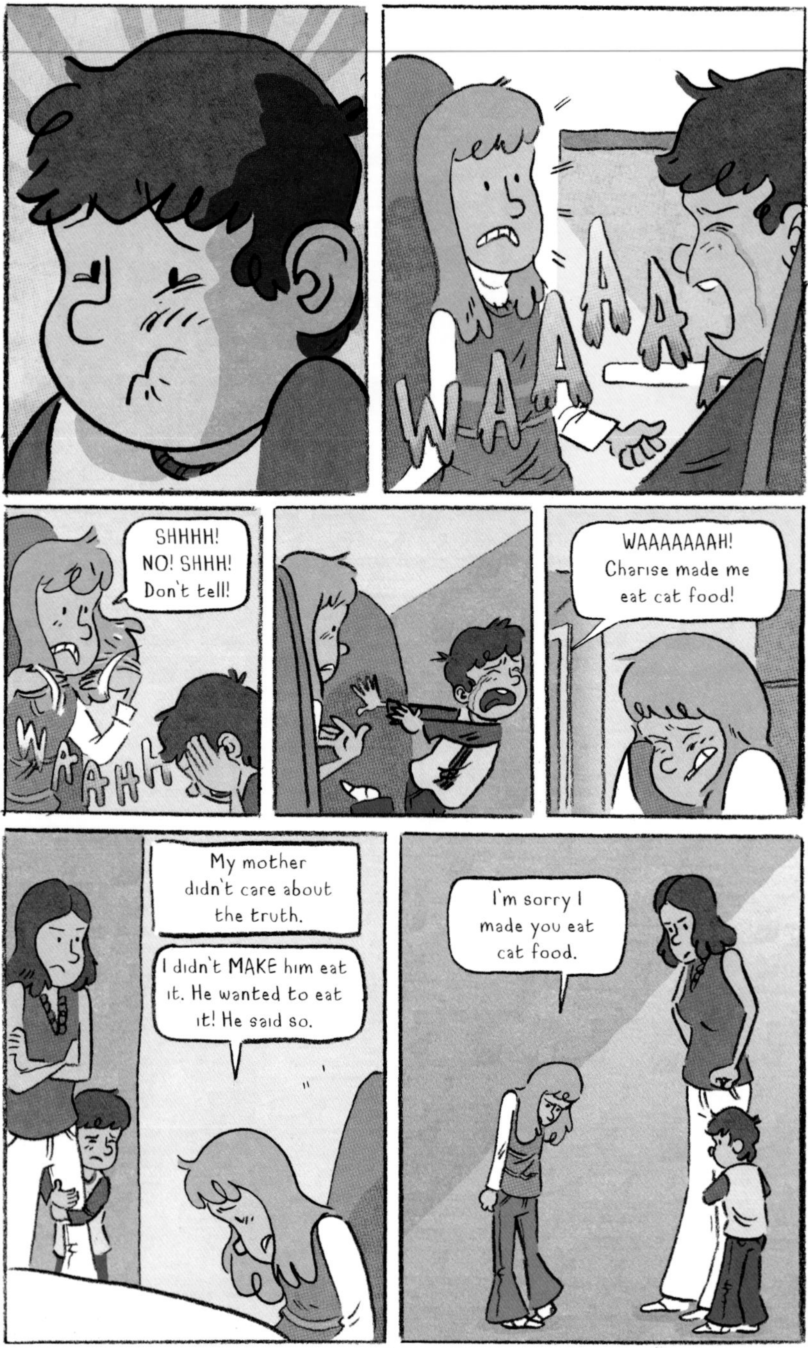
WAAAAA
SHHHH! NO! SHHH! Don't tell!
WAAHH
WAAAAAAAH! Charise made me eat cat food!
My mother didn't care about the truth.
I didn't MAKE him eat it. He wanted to eat it! He said so.
I'm sorry I made you eat cat food.

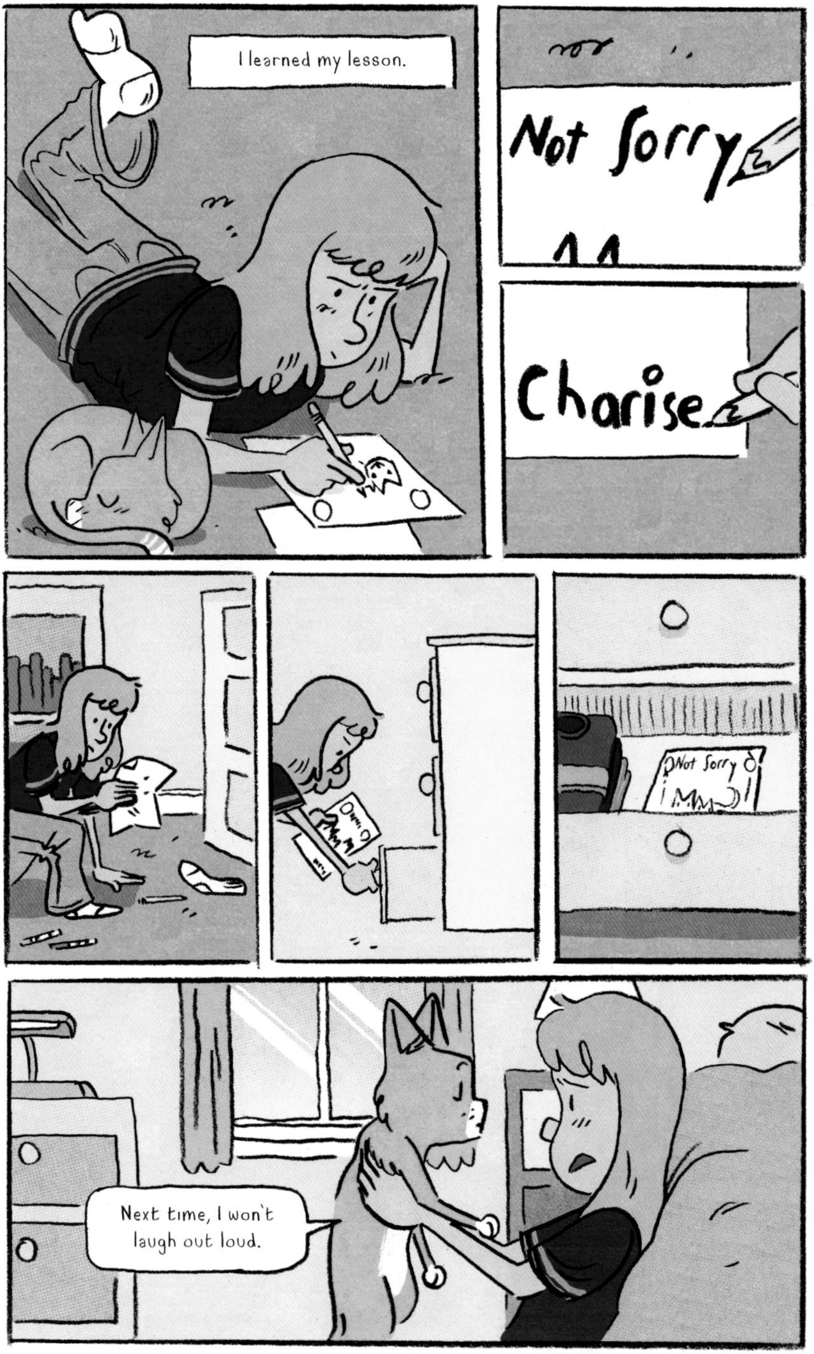
I learned my lesson.
Not Sorry
Charise
Not Sorry
Next time, I won't laugh out loud.

The Power of Seeing and Knowing

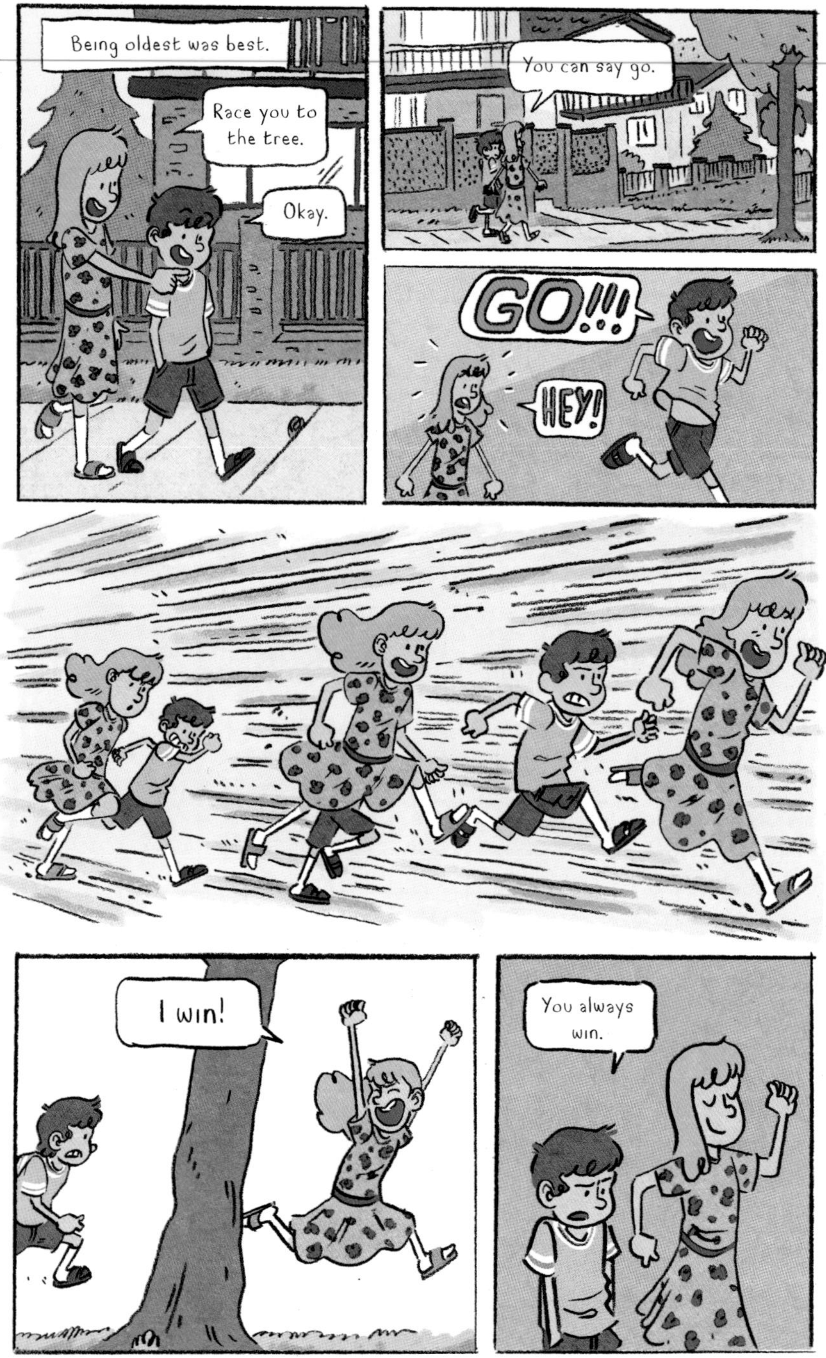

Being oldest was best.
Race you to the tree.
Okay.
You can say go.
GO!!!
HEY!
I win!
You always win.

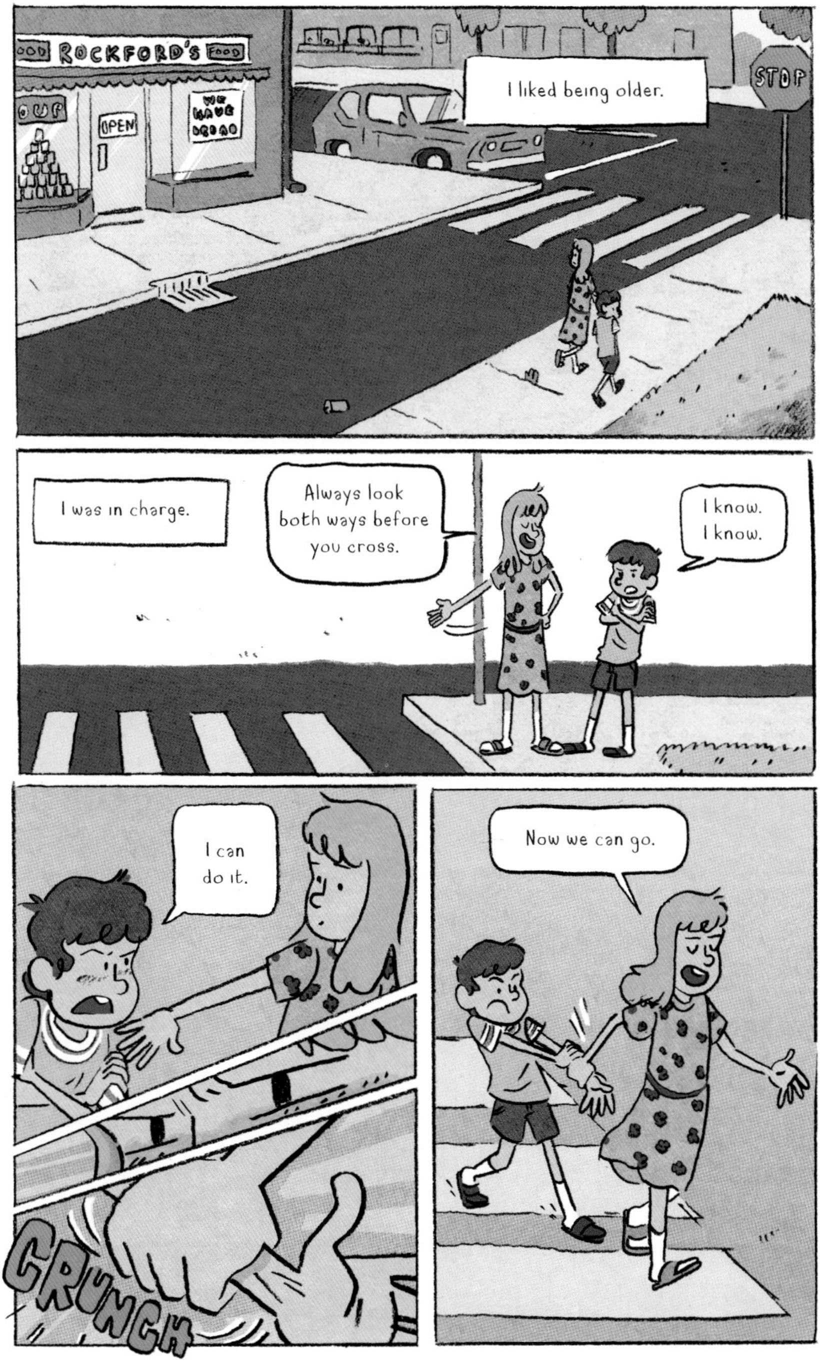
ROCKFORD'S
FOOD
OPEN
WE HAVE BREAD
STOP
I liked being older.
I was in charge.
Always look both ways before you cross.
I know. I know.
I can do it.
CRUNCH
Now we can go.

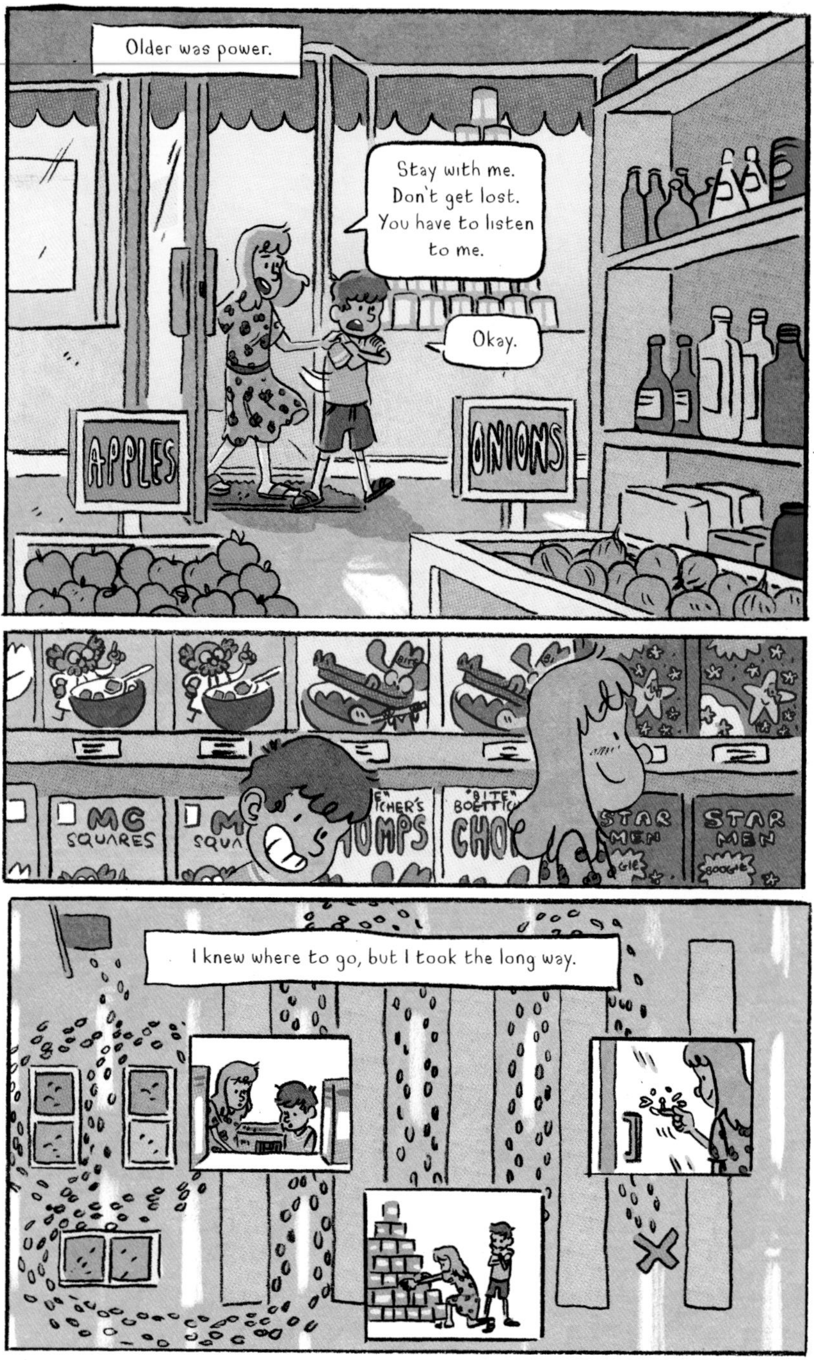
Older was power.
Stay with me. Don't get lost. You have to listen to me.
Okay.
APPLES
ONIONS
MC SQUARES
STAR MEN
I knew where to go, but I took the long way.

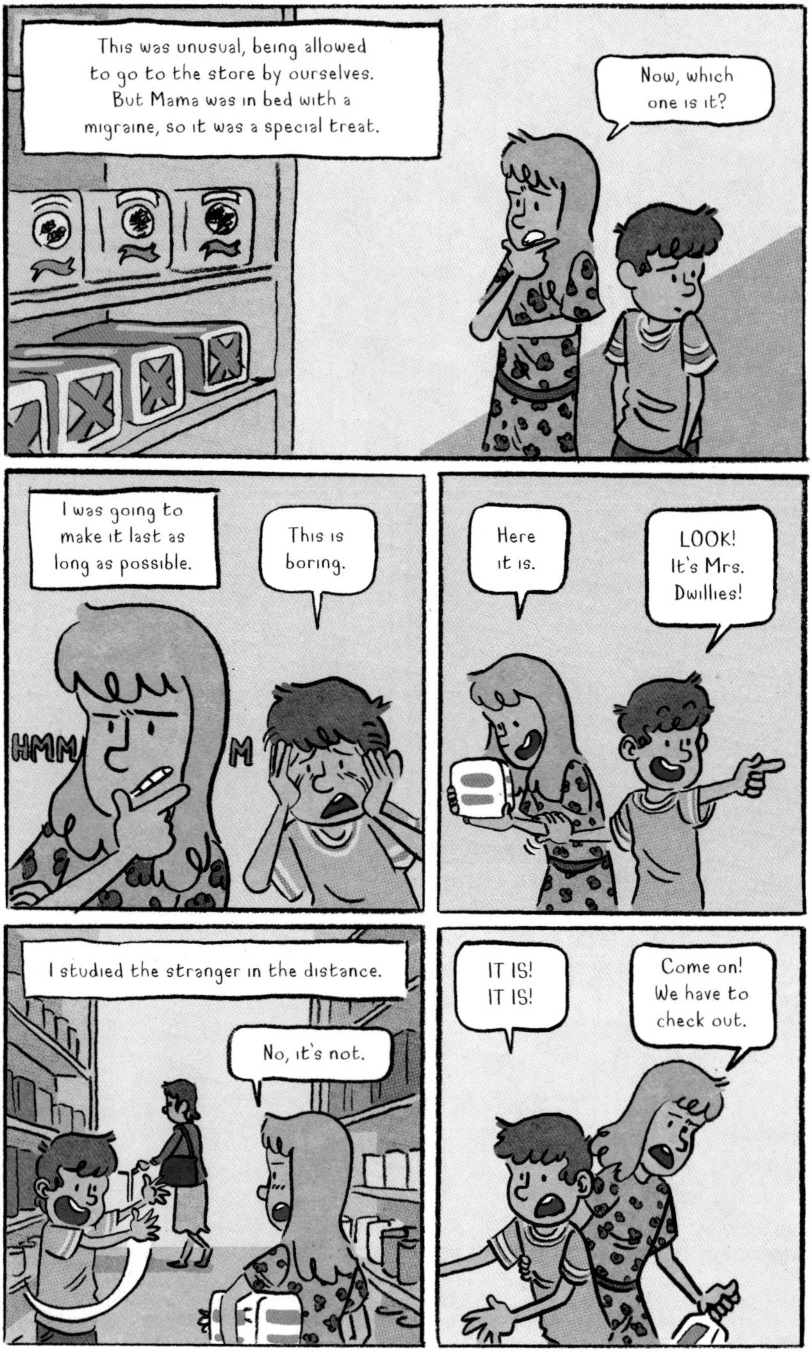
This was unusual, being allowed to go to the store by ourselves. But Mama was in bed with a migraine, so it was a special treat.
Now, which one is it?
I was going to make it last as long as possible.
This is boring.
HMMM
Here it is.
LOOK! It's Mrs. Dwillies!
I studied the stranger in the distance.
No, it's not.
IT IS! IT IS!
Come on! We have to check out.

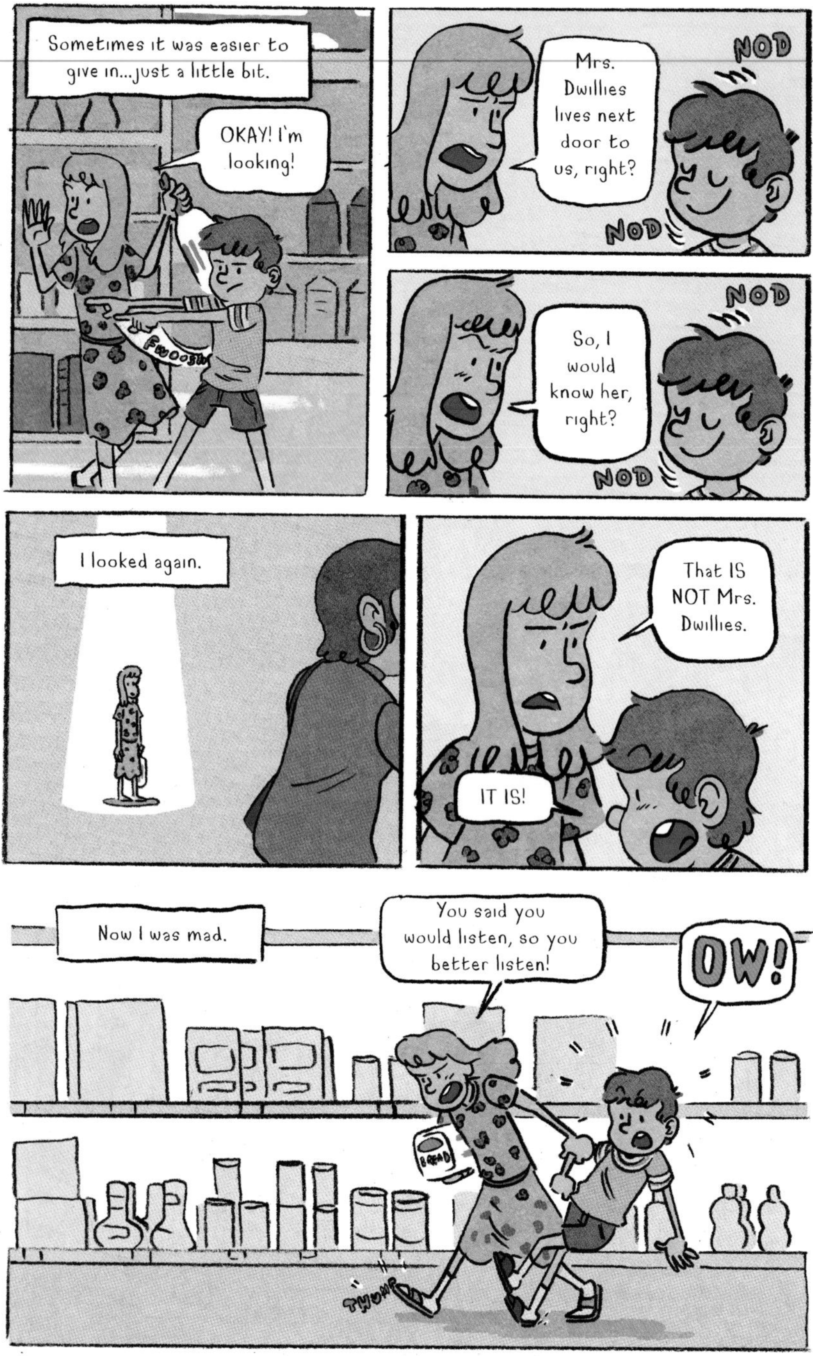
Sometimes it was easier to give in...just a little bit.
OKAY! I'm looking!
FWOOSH
Mrs. Dwillies lives next door to us, right?
NOD
NOD
So, I would know her, right?
NOD
NOD
I looked again.
That IS NOT Mrs. Dwillies.
IT IS!
Now I was mad.
You said you would listen, so you better listen!
OW!
BREAD
THUMP

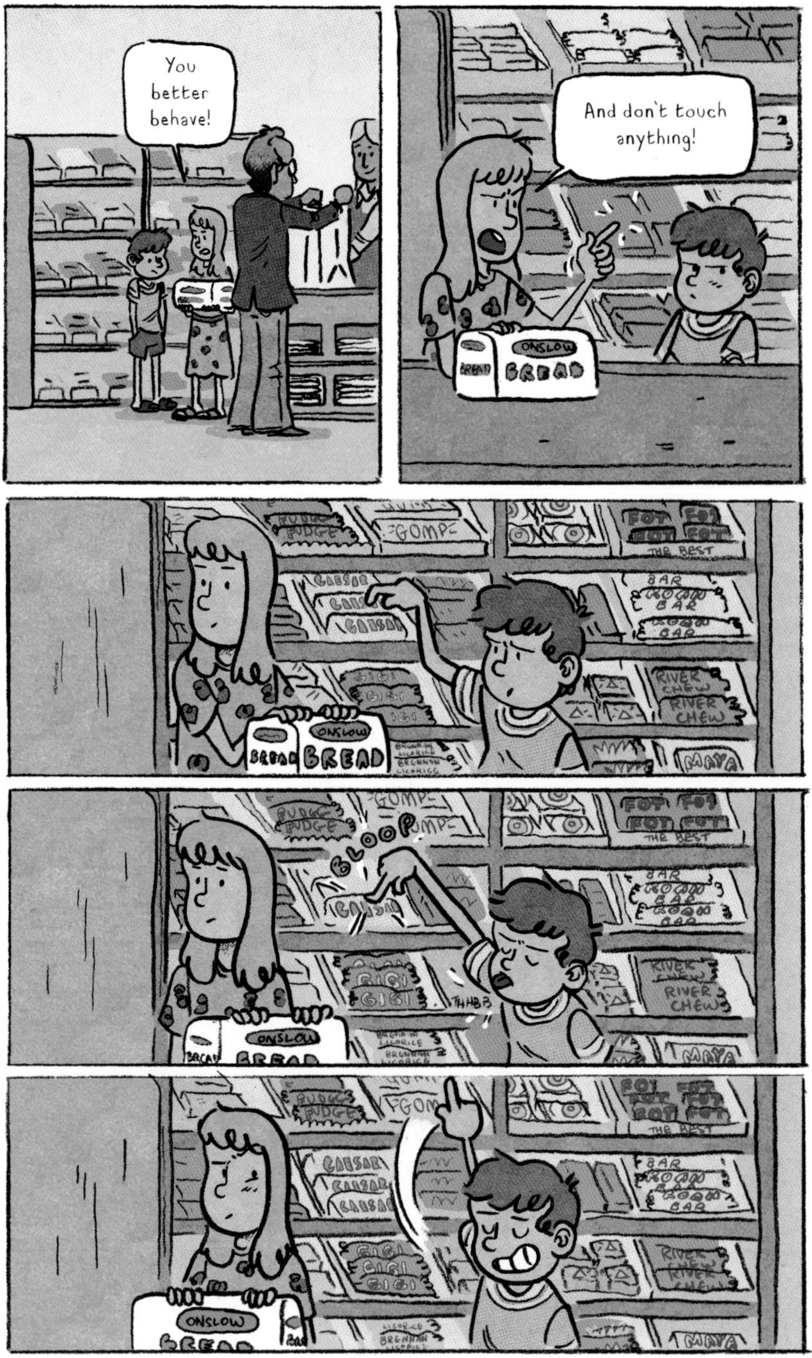
You better behave!
And don't touch anything!
ONSLOW
BREAD
BLOOP
THBB

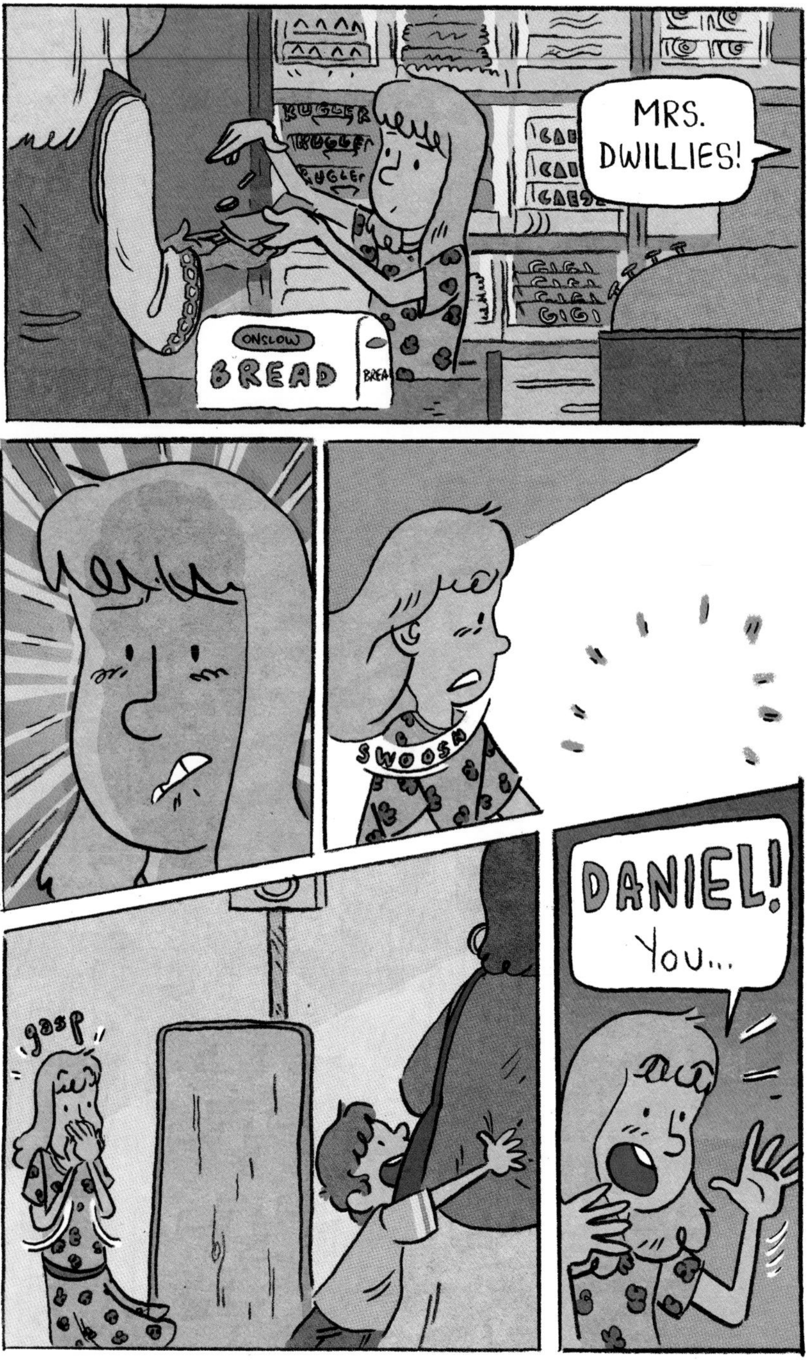
MRS. DWILLIES!
ONSLOW
BREAD
SWOOSH
DANIEL! You...
gasp

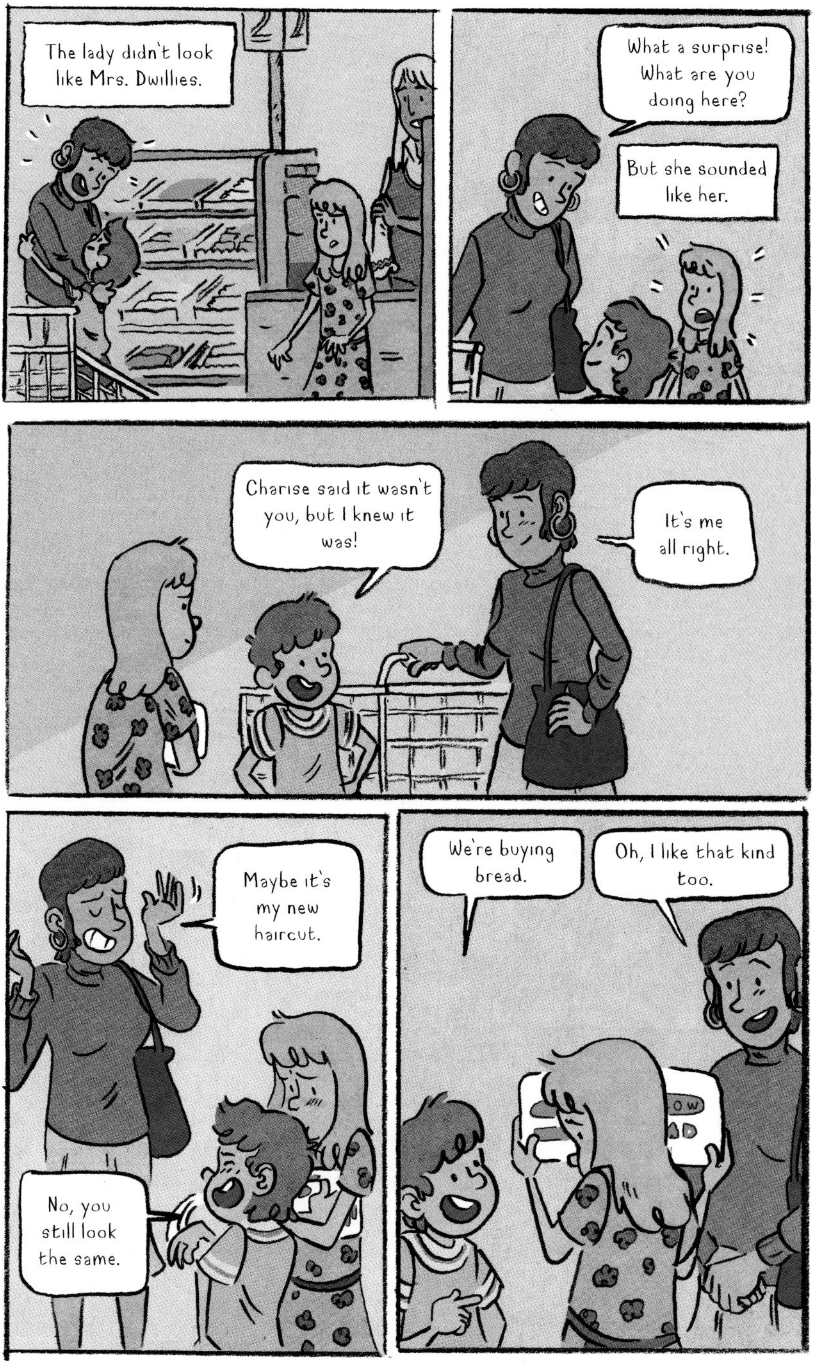
The lady didn't look like Mrs. Dwillies.
What a surprise! What are you doing here?
But she sounded like her.
Charise said it wasn't you, but I knew it was!
It's me all right.
Maybe it's my new haircut.
No, you still look the same.
We're buying bread.
Oh, I like that kind too.

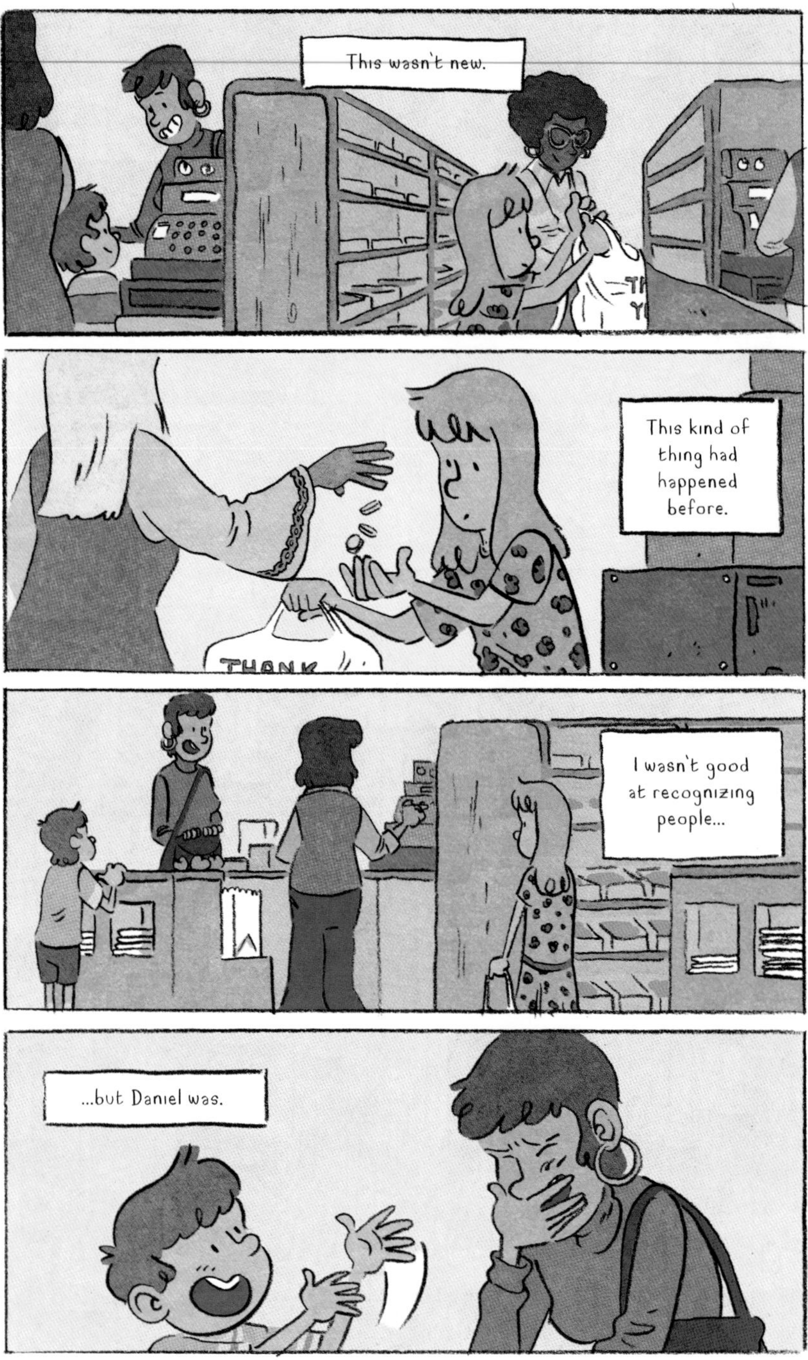
This wasn't new.
THANK
This kind of thing had happened before.
I wasn't good at recognizing people...
...but Daniel was.

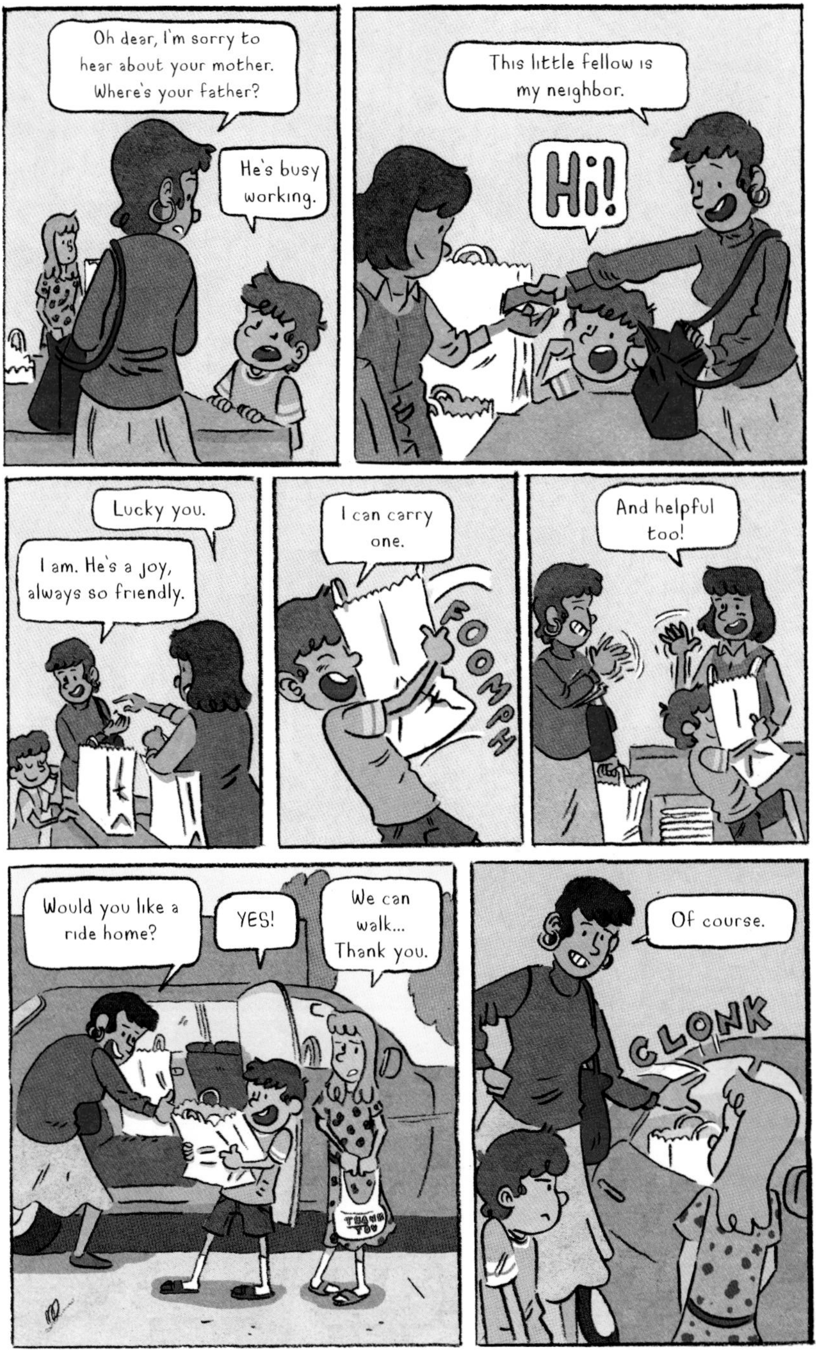

Oh dear, I'm sorry to hear about your mother. Where's your father?
He's busy working.
This little fellow is my neighbor.
Hi!
Lucky you.
I am. He's a joy, always so friendly.
I can carry one.
FOOMPH
And helpful too!
Would you like a ride home?
YES!
We can walk... Thank you.
Of course.
CLONK

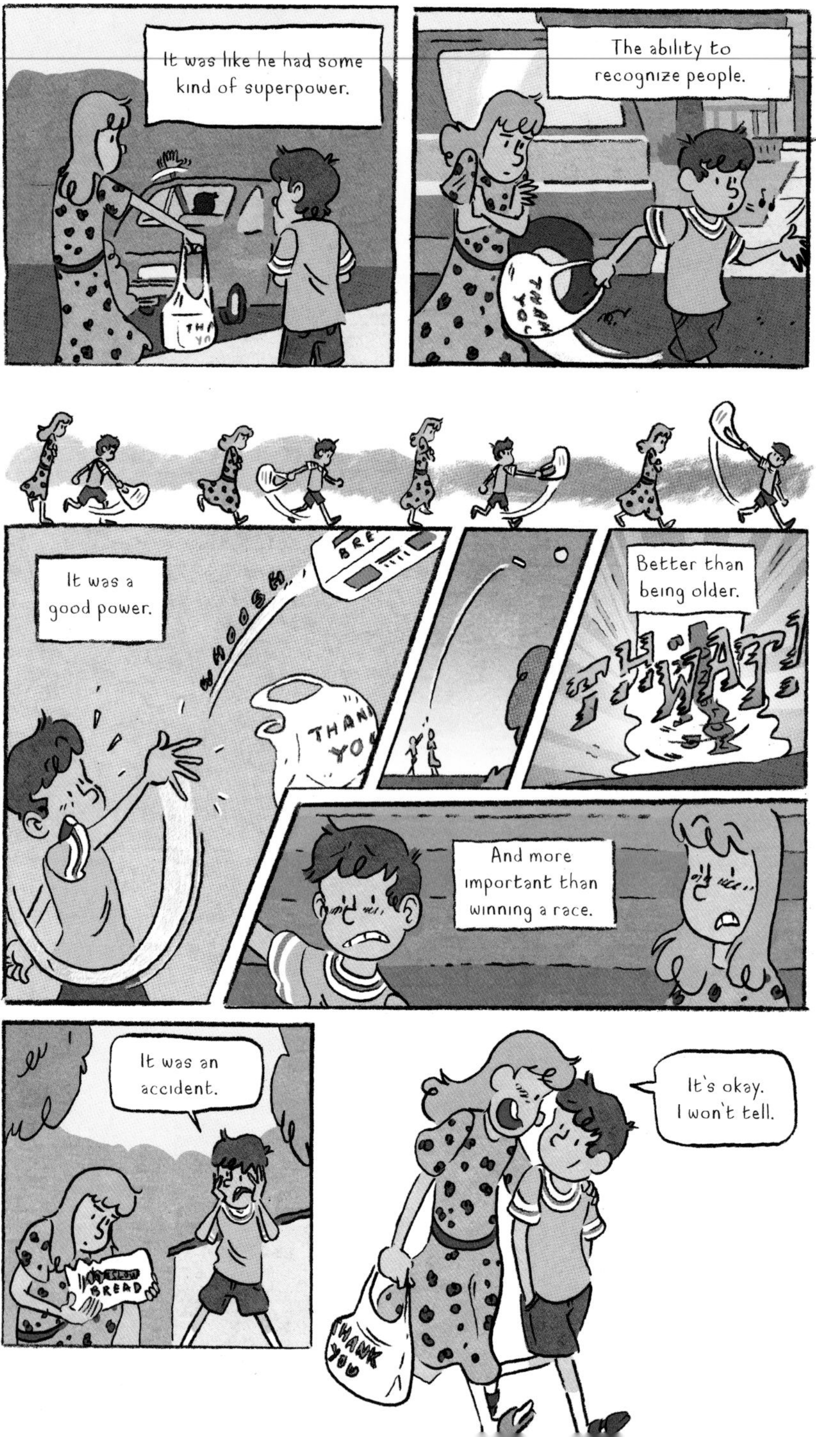
It was like he had some kind of superpower.
THANK YOU
The ability to recognize people.
THANK YOU
It was a good power.
WHOOSH...
BRE
THANK YOU
Better than being older.
THWAT!
And more important than winning a race.
It was an accident.
BREAD
It's okay. I won't tell.
THANK YOU

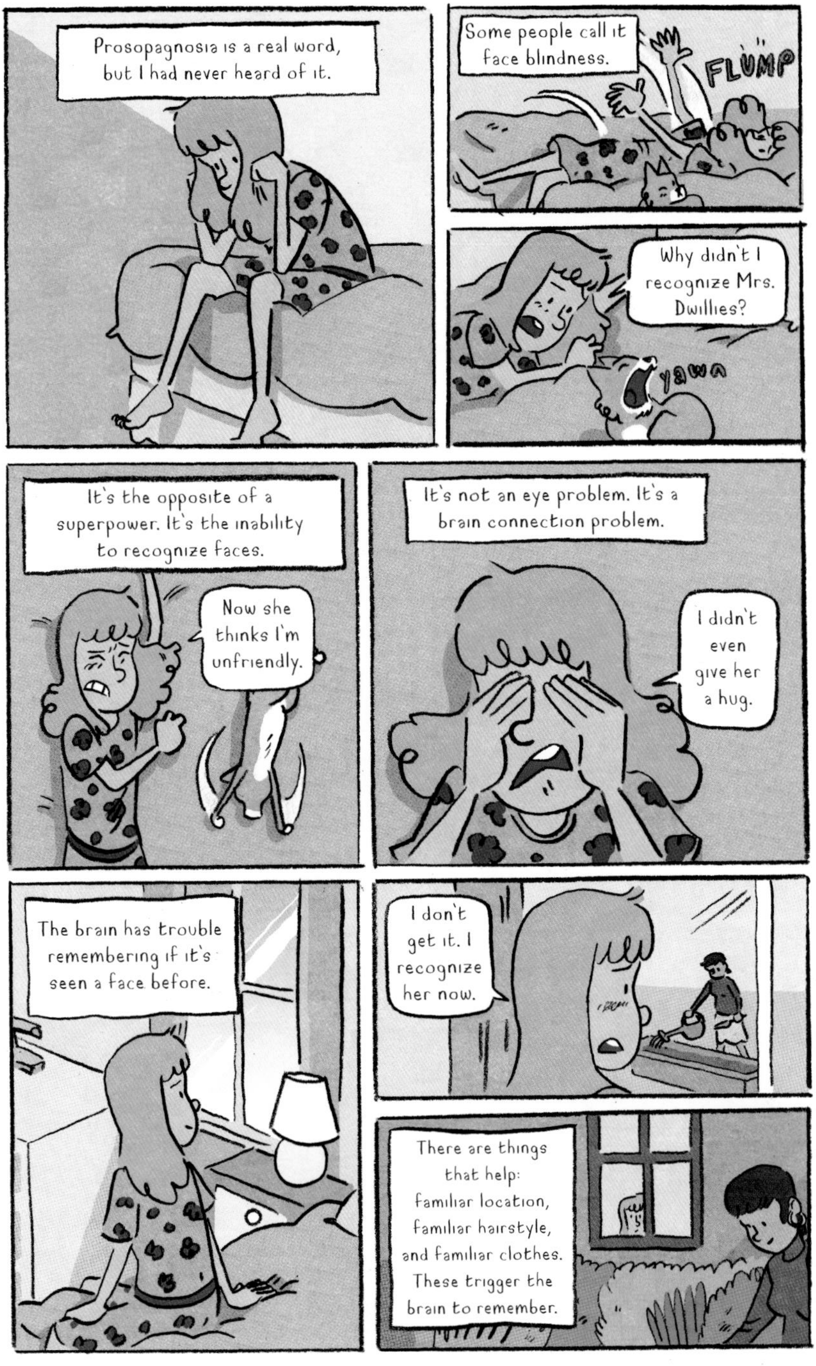
Prosopagnosia is a real word, but I had never heard of it.
Some people call it face blindness.
FLUMP
Why didn't I recognize Mrs. Dwillies?
yawn
It's the opposite of a superpower. It's the inability to recognize faces.
Now she thinks I'm unfriendly.
It's not an eye problem. It's a brain connection problem.
I didn't even give her a hug.
The brain has trouble remembering if it's seen a face before.
I don't get it. I recognize her now.
There are things that help: familiar location, familiar hairstyle, and familiar clothes. These trigger the brain to remember.

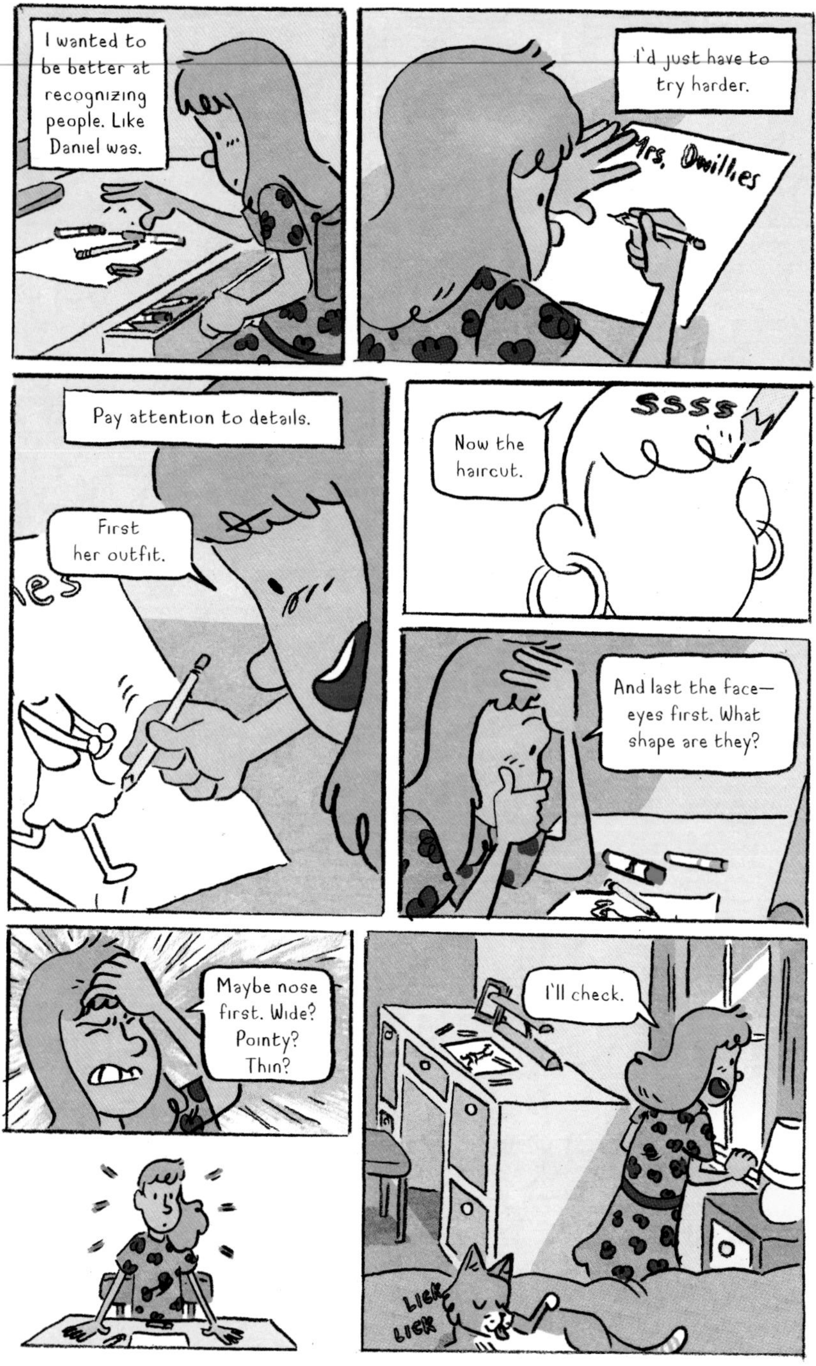
I wanted to be better at recognizing people. Like Daniel was.
I'd just have to try harder.
Mrs. Dwillies
Pay attention to details.
First her outfit.
Now the haircut.
SSSS
And last the face—eyes first. What shape are they?
Maybe nose first. Wide? Pointy? Thin?
I'll check.
LICK
LICK

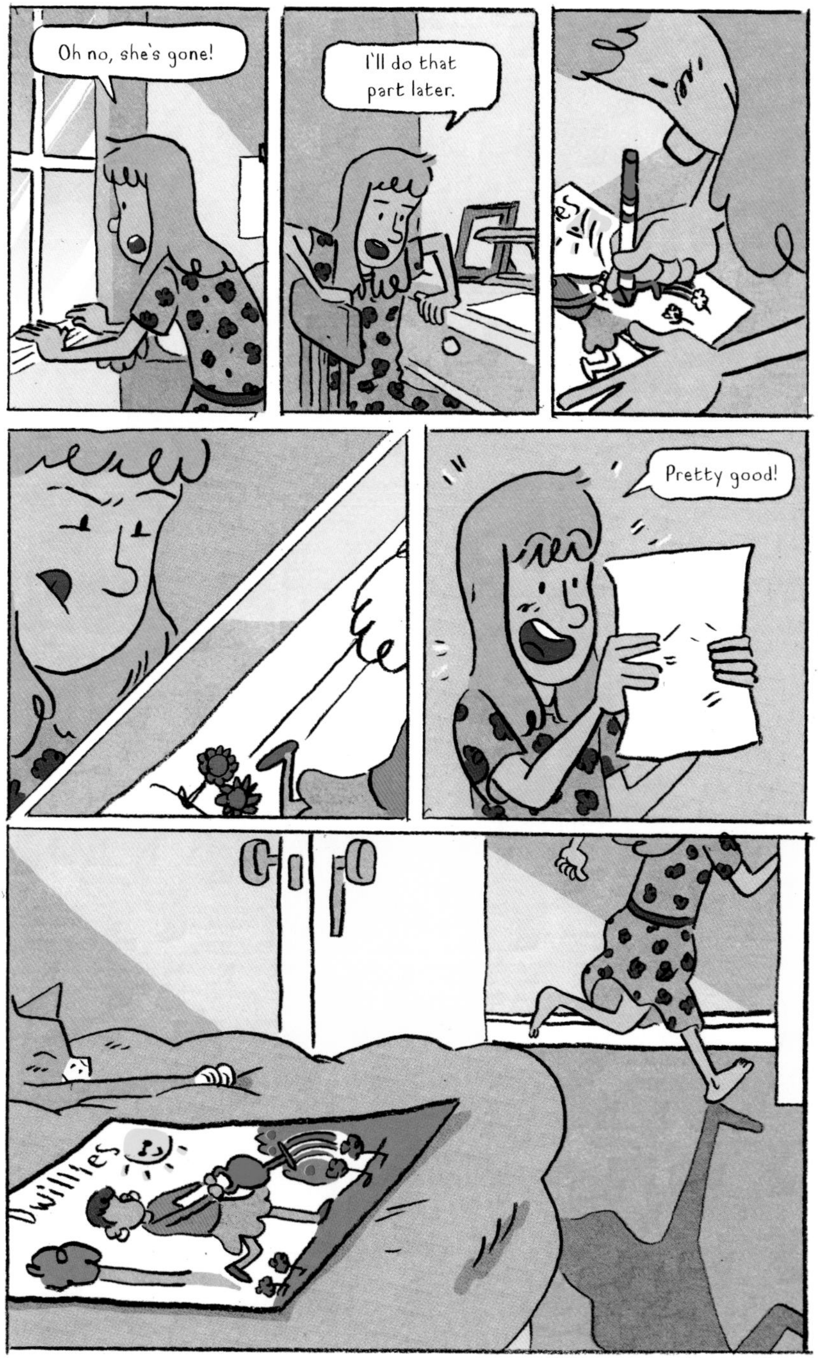
Oh no, she's gone!
I'll do that part later.
Pretty good!
Willies

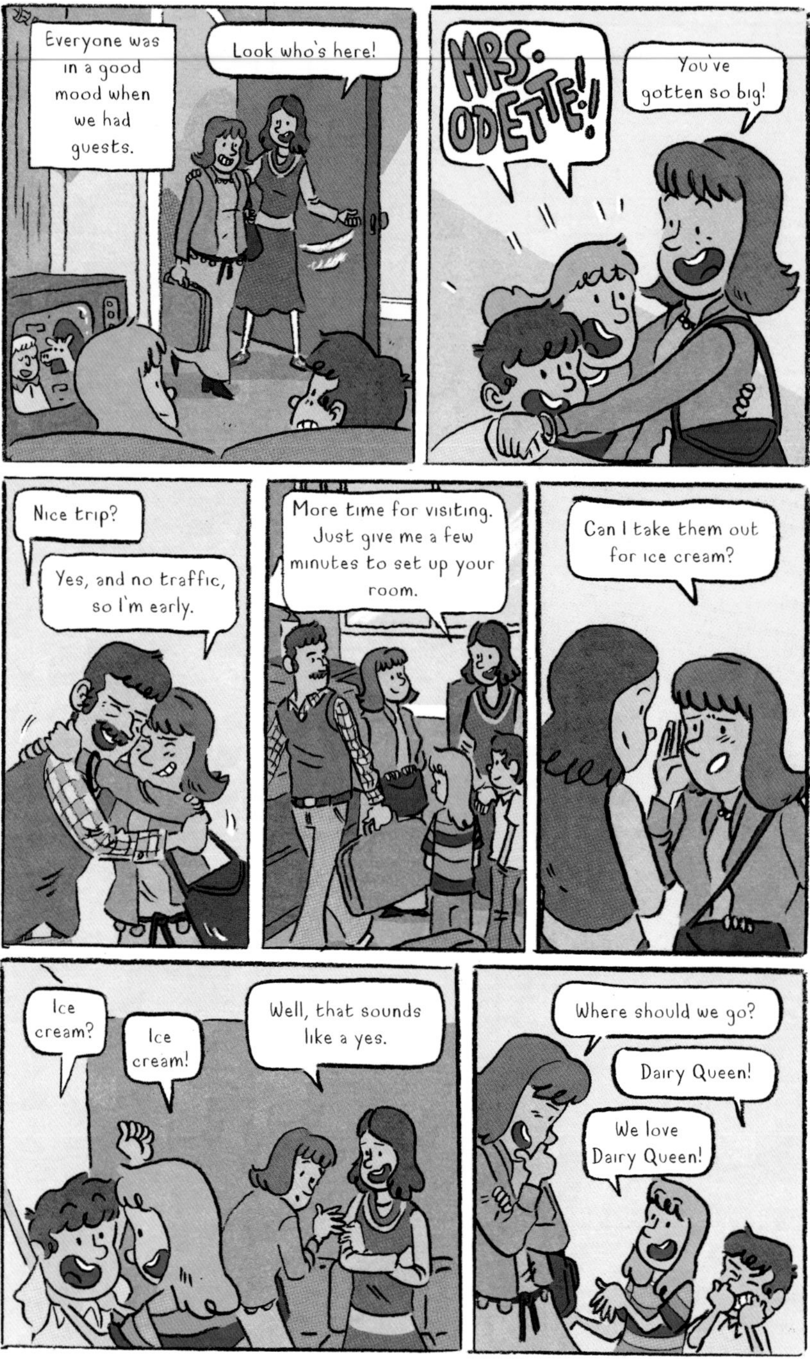
Everyone was in a good mood when we had guests.
Look who's here!
MRS. ODETTE!
You've gotten so big!
Nice trip?
Yes, and no traffic, so I'm early.
More time for visiting. Just give me a few minutes to set up your room.
Can I take them out for ice cream?
Ice cream?
Ice cream!
Well, that sounds like a yes.
Where should we go?
Dairy Queen!
We love Dairy Queen!

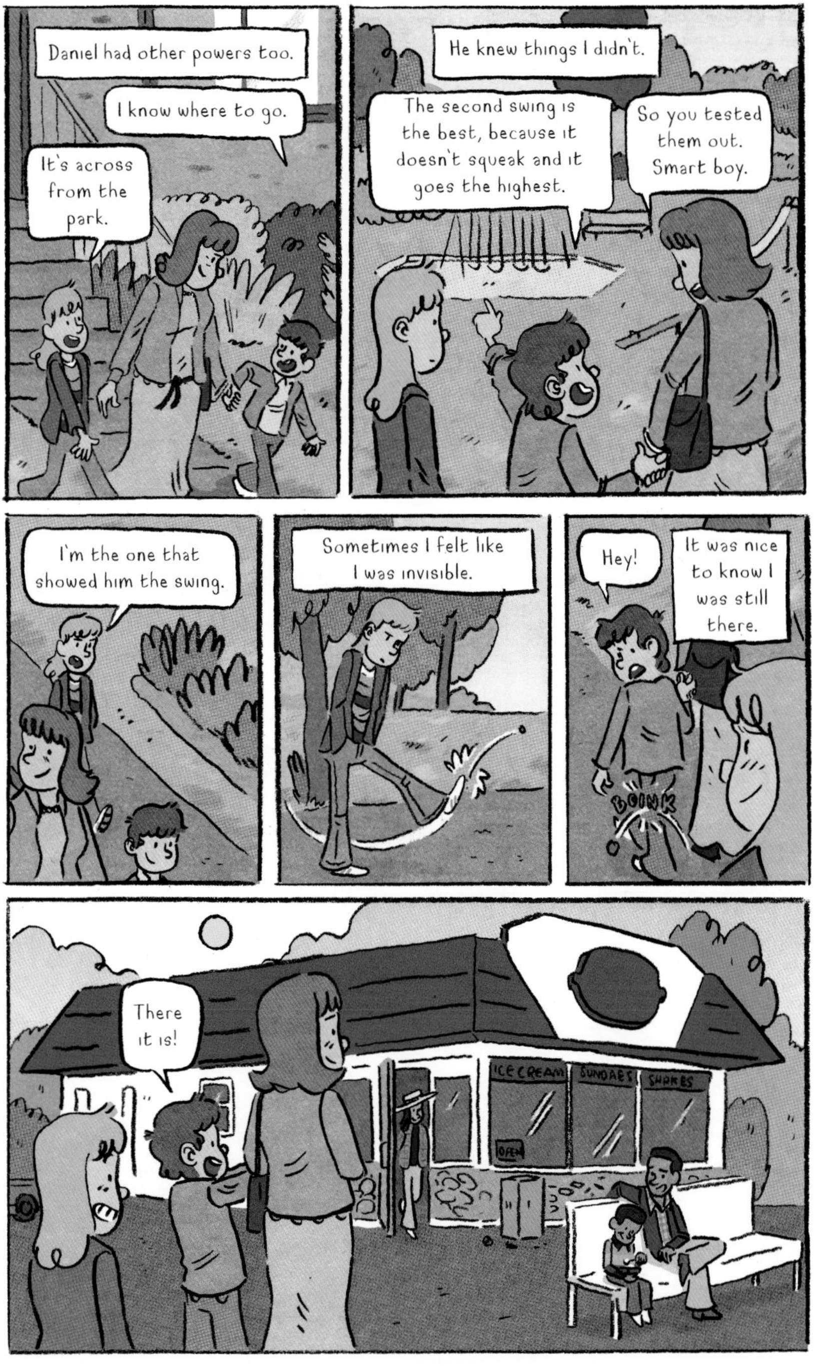
Daniel had other powers too.
I know where to go.
It's across from the park.
He knew things I didn't.
The second swing is the best, because it doesn't squeak and it goes the highest.
So you tested them out. Smart boy.
I'm the one that showed him the swing.
Sometimes I felt like I was invisible.
Hey!
It was nice to know I was still there.
BOINK
There it is!
ICE CREAM
SUNDAES
SHAKES
OPEN

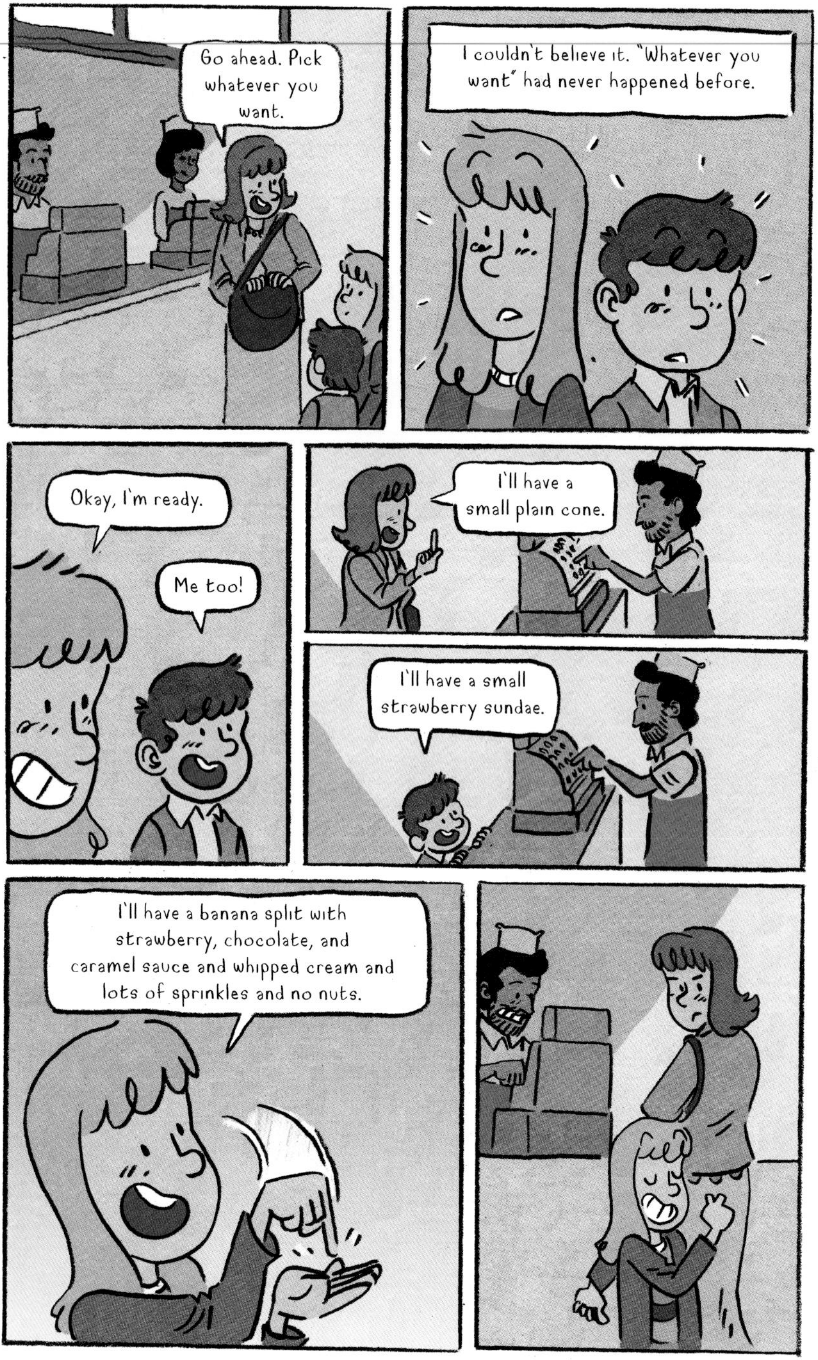
Go ahead. Pick whatever you want.
I couldn't believe it. "Whatever you want" had never happened before.
Okay, I'm ready.
Me too!
I'll have a small plain cone.
I'll have a small strawberry sundae.
I'll have a banana split with strawberry, chocolate, and caramel sauce and whipped cream and lots of sprinkles and no nuts.

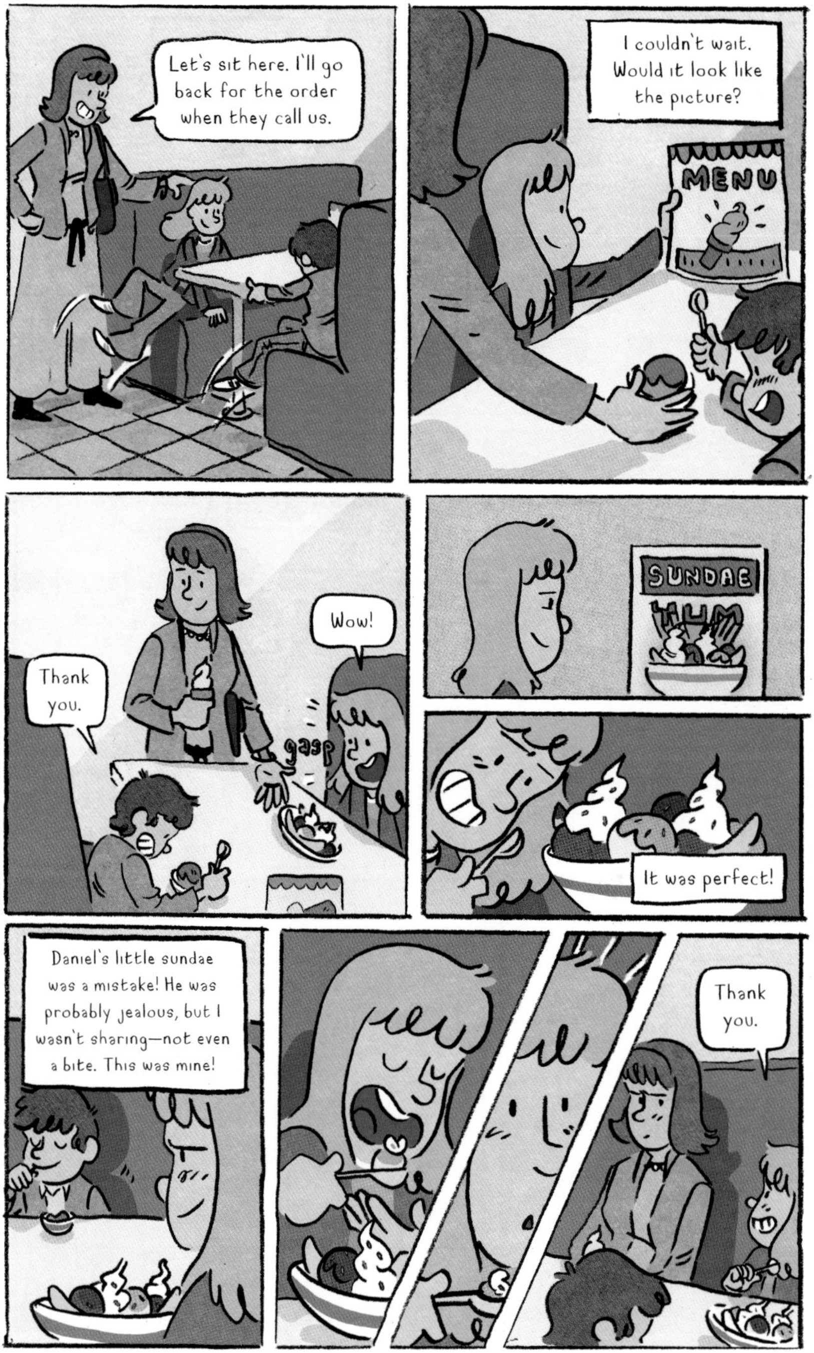
Let's sit here. I'll go back for the order when they call us.
I couldn't wait. Would it look like the picture?
MENU
Wow!
Thank you.
gasp
SUNDAE
It was perfect!
Daniel's little sundae was a mistake! He was probably jealous, but I wasn't sharing—not even a bite. This was mine!
Thank you.

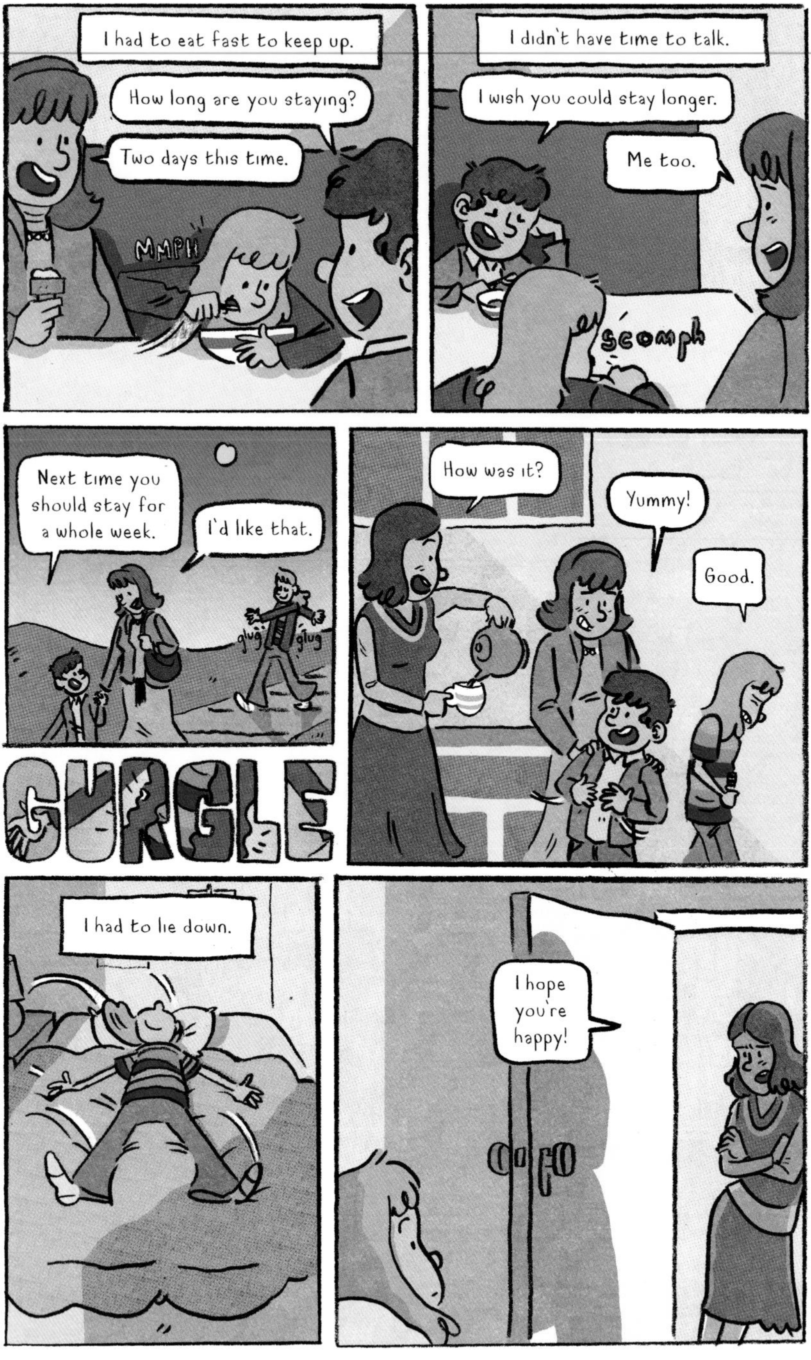
I had to eat fast to keep up.
How long are you staying?
Two days this time.
MMPH
I didn't have time to talk.
I wish you could stay longer.
Me too.
scomph
Next time you should stay for a whole week.
I'd like that.
glug glug
GURGLE
How was it?
Yummy!
Good.
I had to lie down.
I hope you're happy!

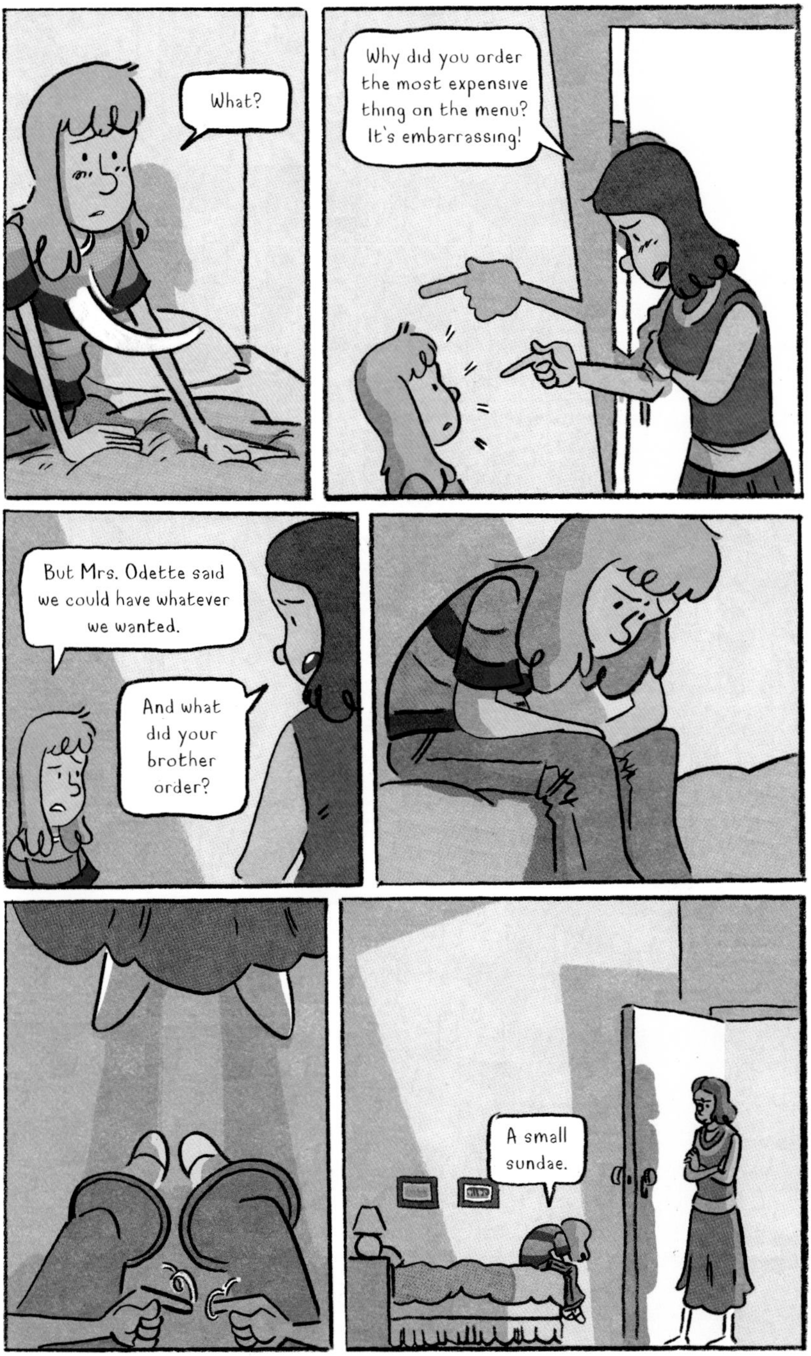
What?
Why did you order the most expensive thing on the menu? It's embarrassing!
But Mrs. Odette said we could have whatever we wanted.
And what did your brother order?
A small sundae.

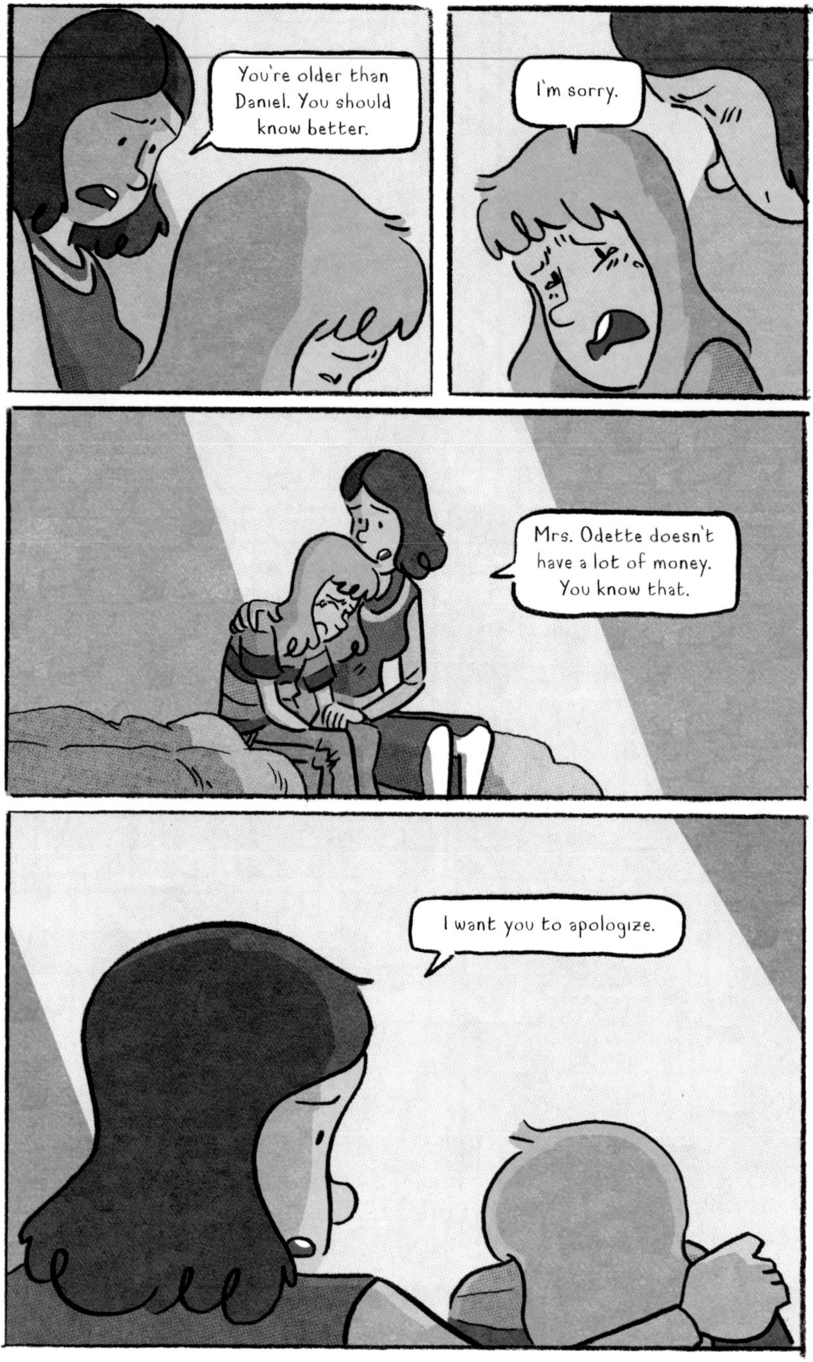
You're older than Daniel. You should know better.
I'm sorry.
Mrs. Odette doesn't have a lot of money. You know that.
I want you to apologize.

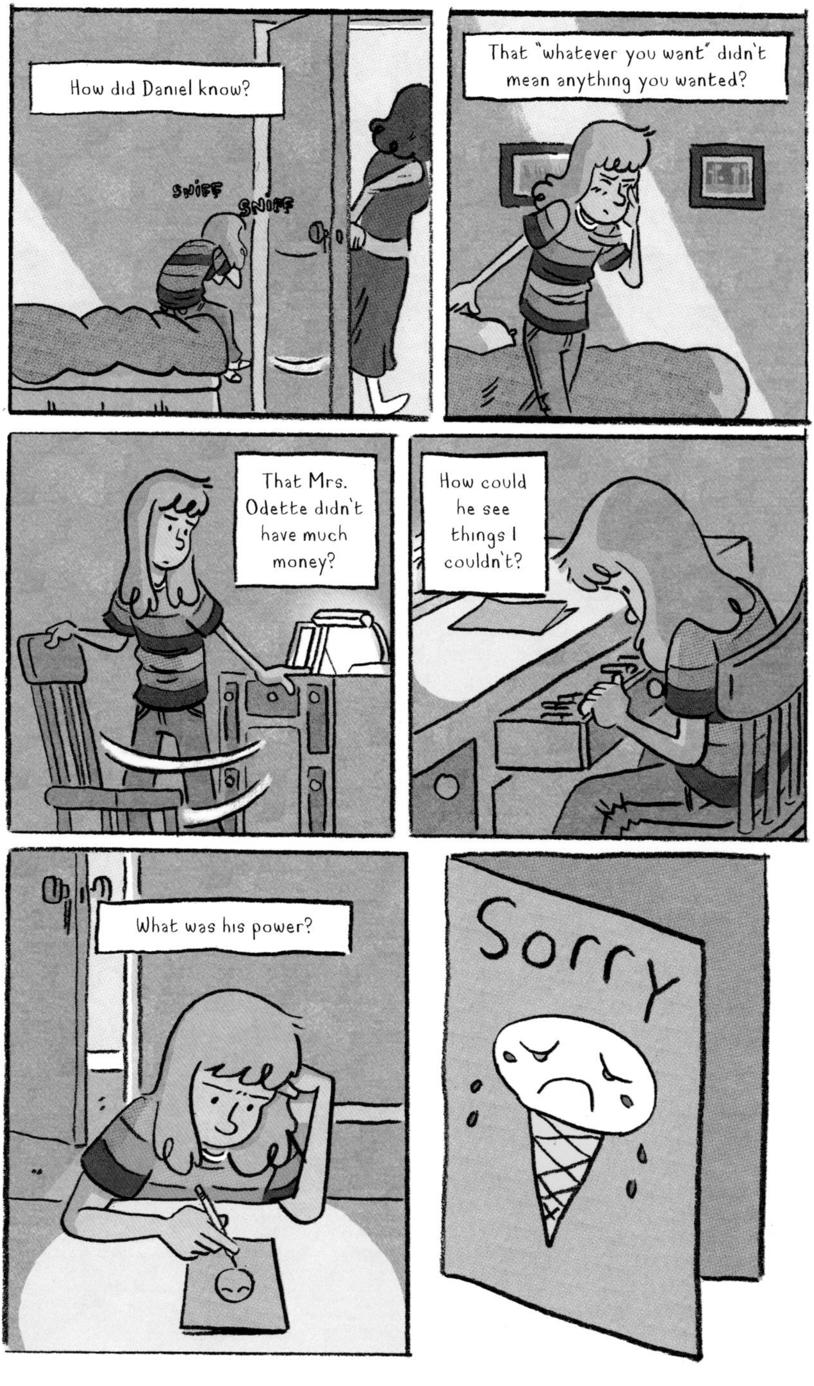
How did Daniel know?
SNIFF
SNIFF
That "whatever you want" didn't mean anything you wanted?
That Mrs. Odette didn't have much money?
How could he see things I couldn't?
What was his power?
Sorry

3

The Power of Games

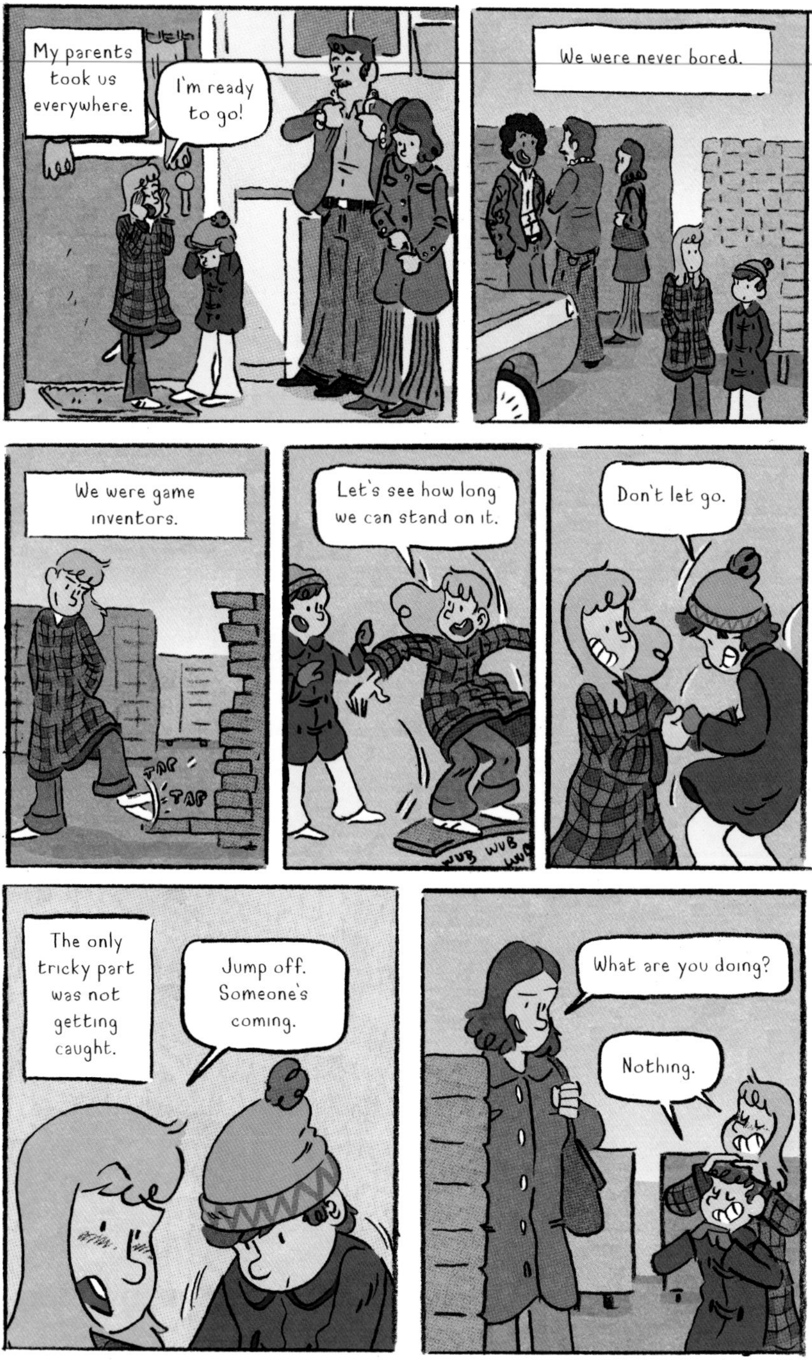
My parents took us everywhere.
I'm ready to go!
We were never bored.
We were game inventors.
TAP TAP
Let's see how long we can stand on it.
WUB WUB WUB
Don't let go.
The only tricky part was not getting caught.
Jump off. Someone's coming.
What are you doing?
Nothing.

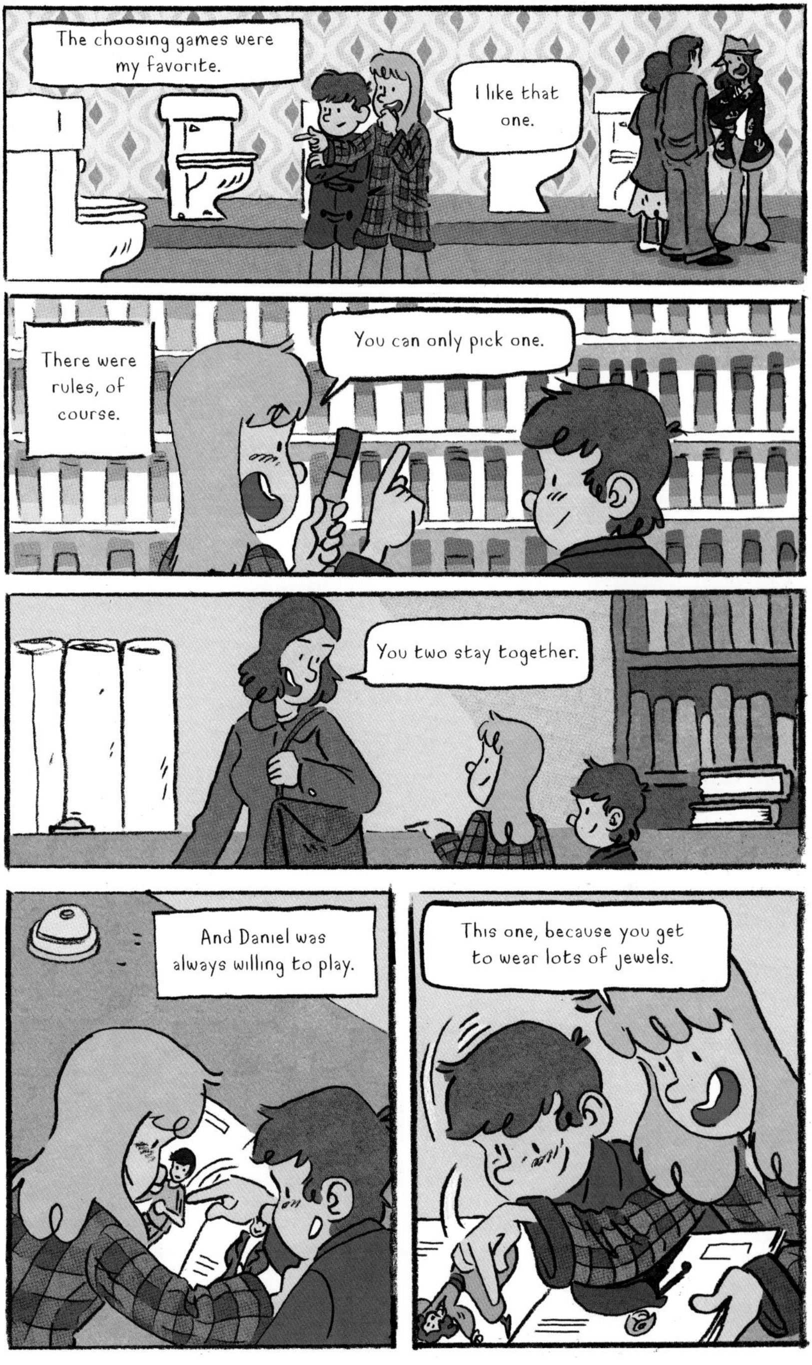

The choosing games were my favorite.
I like that one.
There were rules, of course.
You can only pick one.
You two stay together.
And Daniel was always willing to play.
This one, because you get to wear lots of jewels.

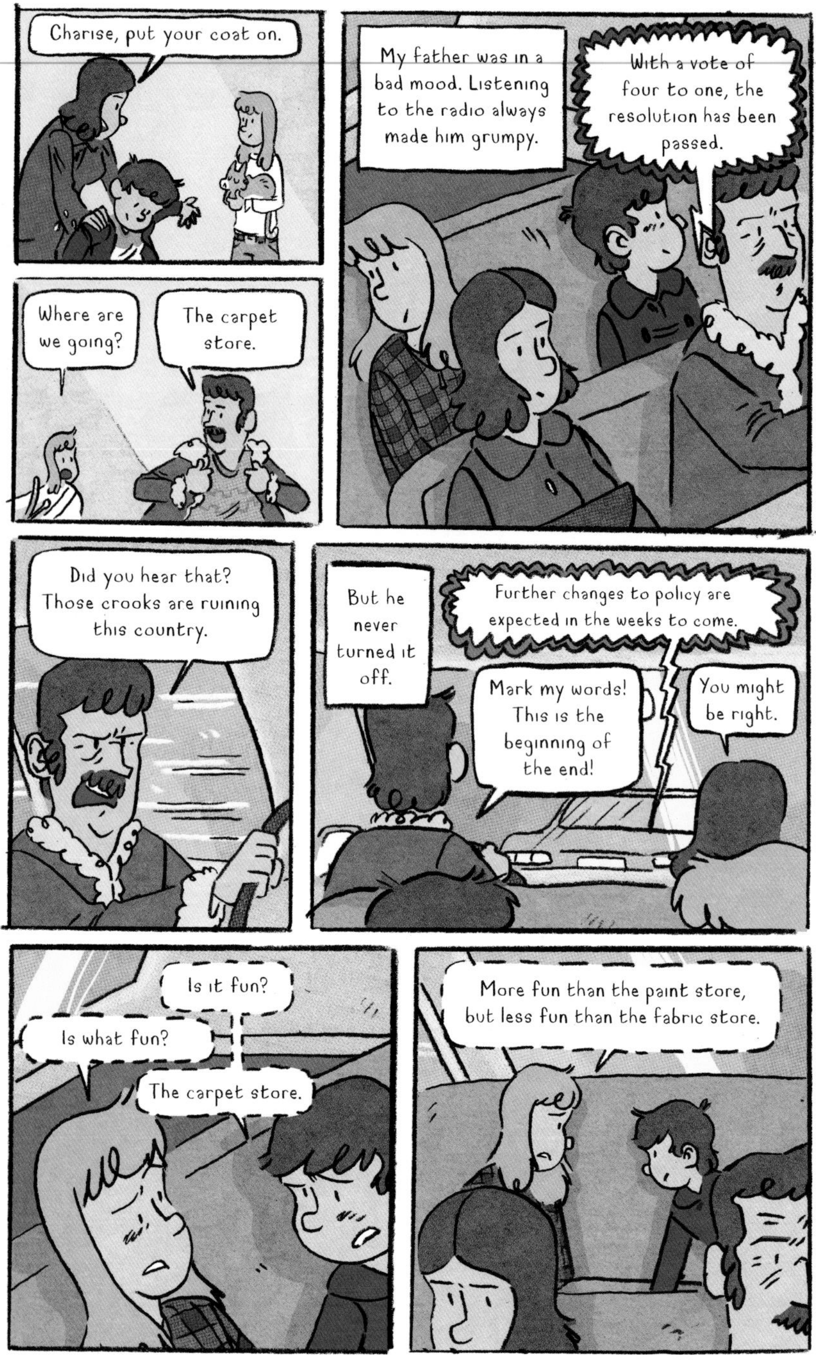
Charise, put your coat on.
Where are we going?
The carpet store.
My father was in a bad mood. Listening to the radio always made him grumpy.
With a vote of four to one, the resolution has been passed.
Did you hear that? Those crooks are ruining this country.
But he never turned it off.
Further changes to policy are expected in the weeks to come.
Mark my words! This is the beginning of the end!
You might be right.
Is it fun?
Is what fun?
The carpet store.
More fun than the paint store, but less fun than the fabric store.

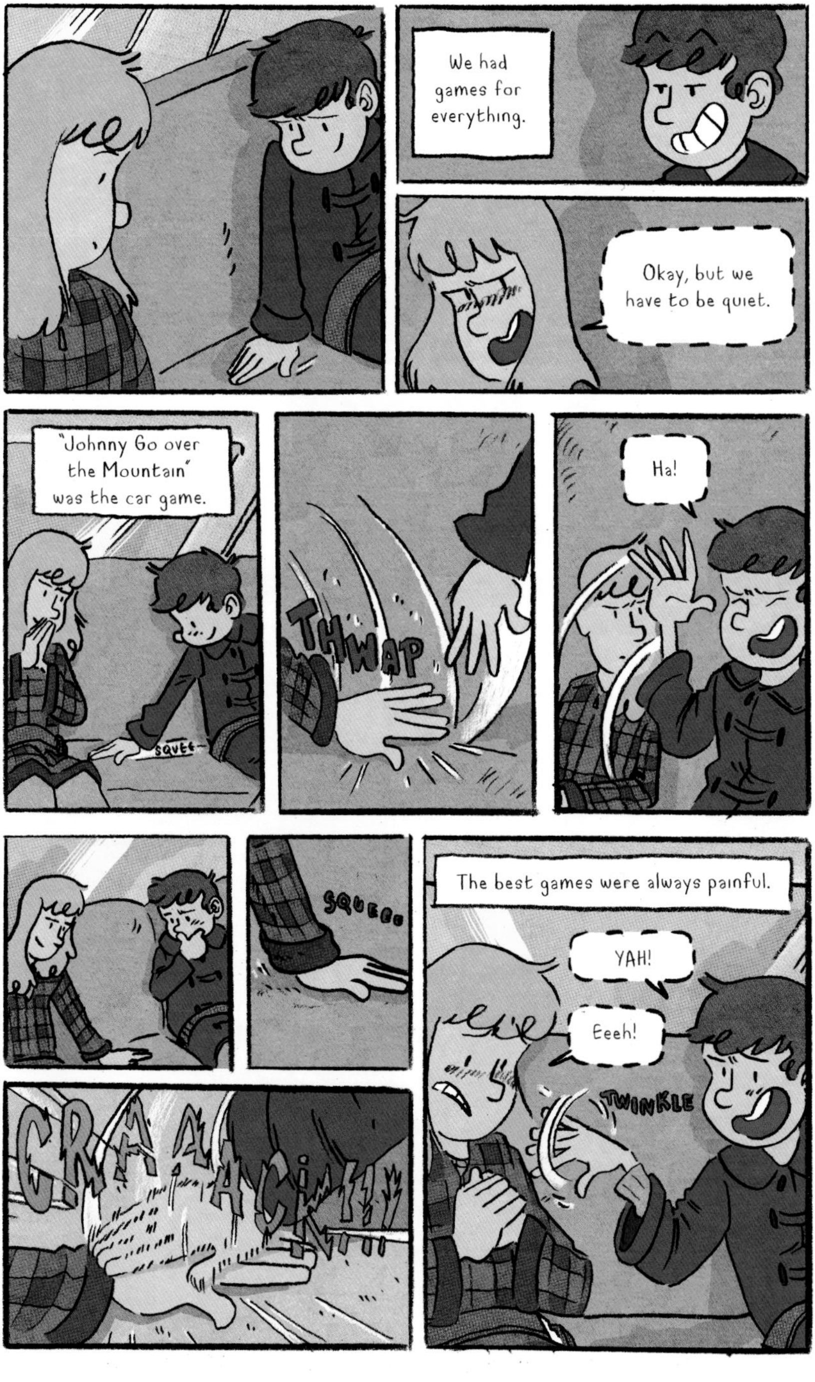

We had games for everything.
Okay, but we have to be quiet.
"Johnny Go over the Mountain" was the car game.
SQUEE
THWAP
Ha!
SQUEEE
The best games were always painful.
YAH!
Eeeh!
TWINKLE

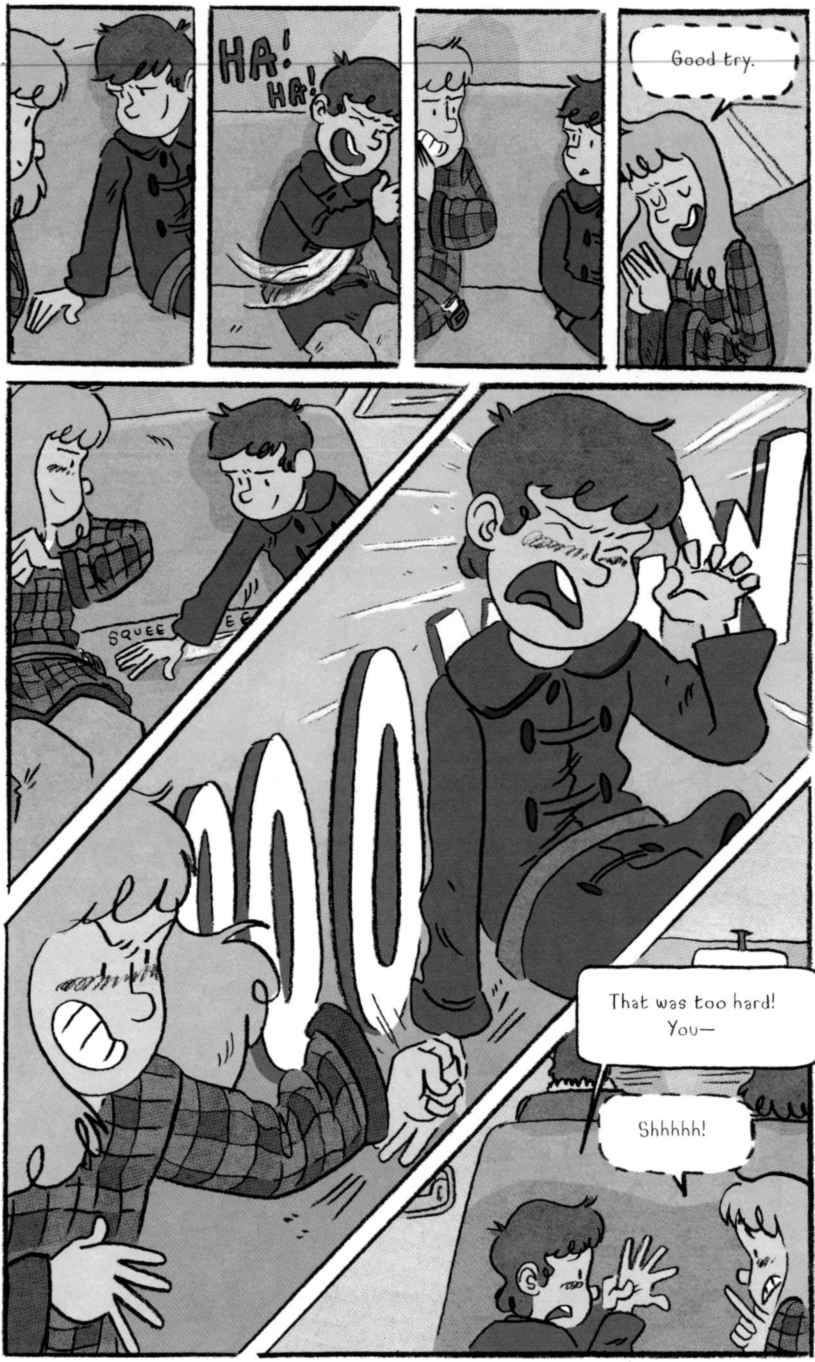
HA! HA!
Good try.
SQUEE
EE
That was too hard! You—
Shhhhh!

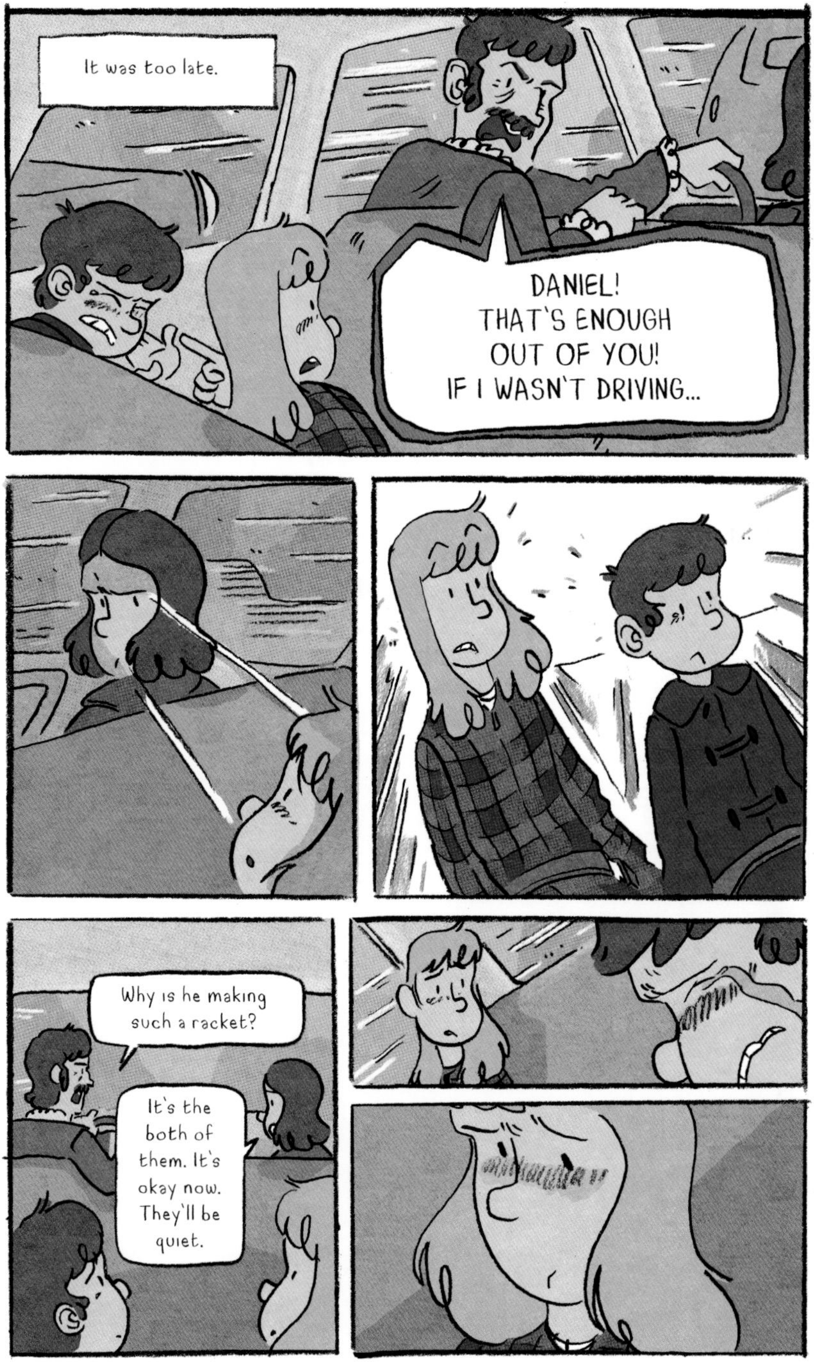
It was too late.
DANIEL! THAT'S ENOUGH OUT OF YOU! IF I WASN'T DRIVING...
Why is he making such a racket?
It's the both of them. It's okay now. They'll be quiet.

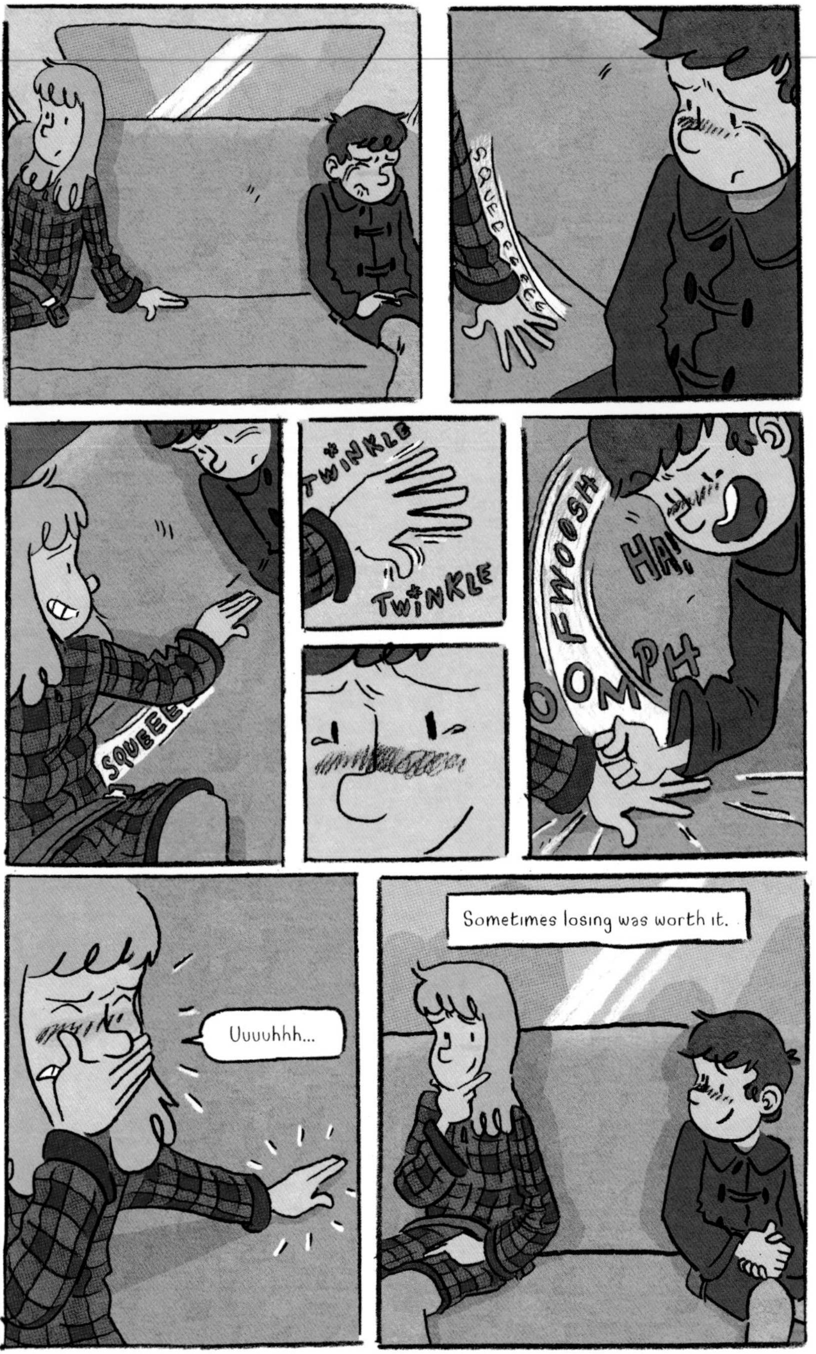
SQUEEEEEEE
SQUEEEE
TWINKLE
TWINKLE
FWOOSH
HA!
OOMPH
Uuuuhhh...
Sometimes losing was worth it.

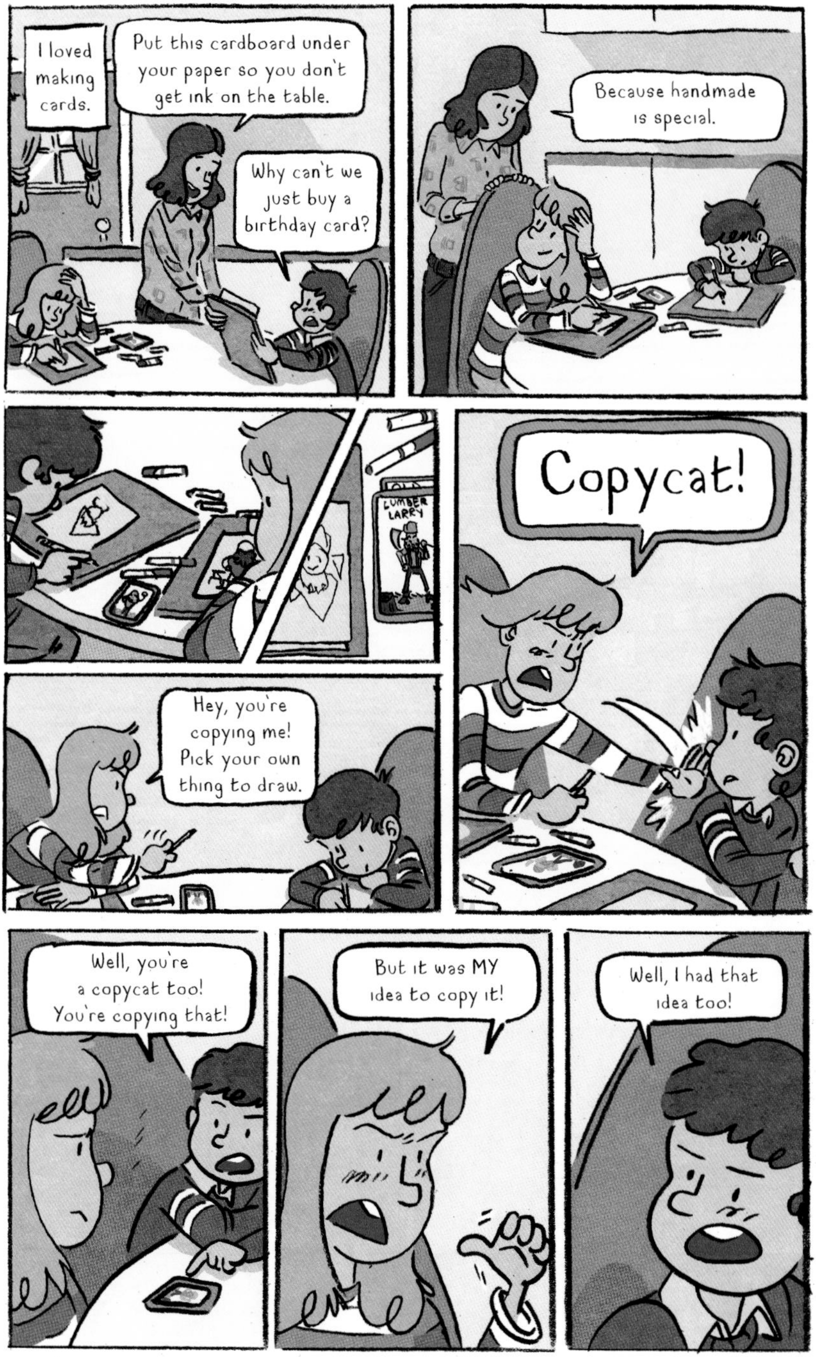
I loved making cards.
Put this cardboard under your paper so you don't get ink on the table.
Why can't we just buy a birthday card?
Because handmade is special.
LUMBER LARRY
Copycat!
Hey, you're copying me! Pick your own thing to draw.
Well, you're a copycat too! You're copying that!
But it was MY idea to copy it!
Well, I had that idea too!

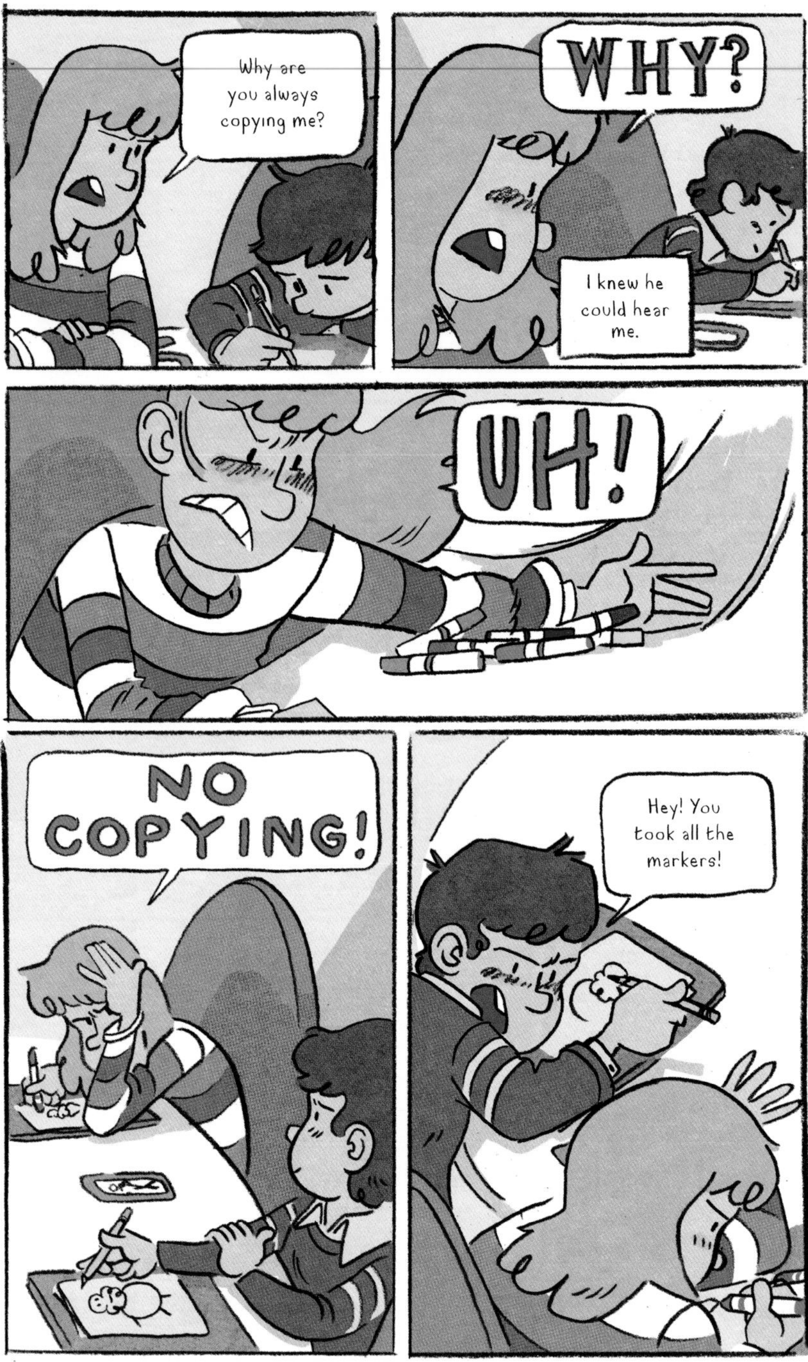

Why are you always copying me?
WHY?
I knew he could hear me.
UH!
NO COPYING!
Hey! You took all the markers!

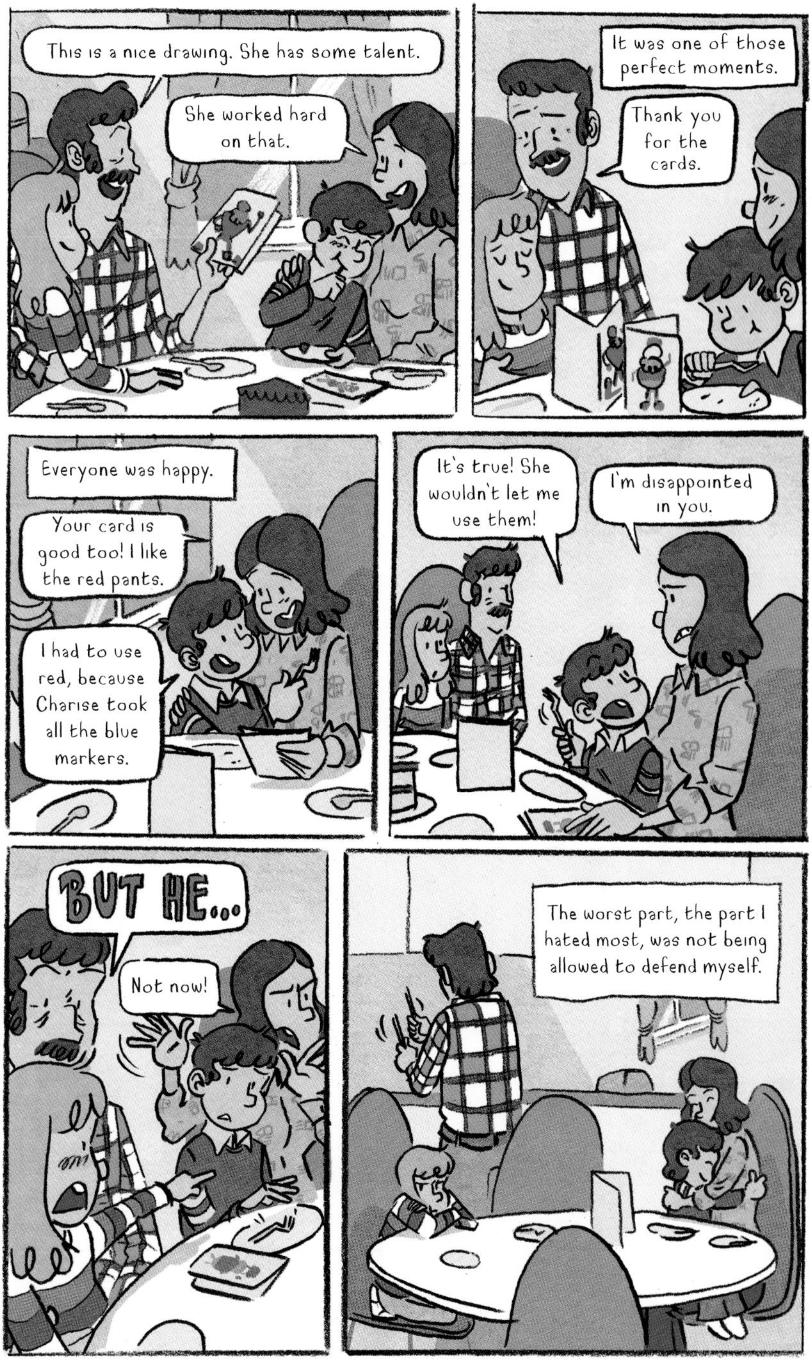
This is a nice drawing. She has some talent.
She worked hard on that.
It was one of those perfect moments.
Thank you for the cards.
Everyone was happy.
Your card is good too! I like the red pants.
I had to use red, because Charise took all the blue markers.
It's true! She wouldn't let me use them!
I'm disappointed in you.
BUT HE...
Not now!
The worst part, the part I hated most, was not being allowed to defend myself.

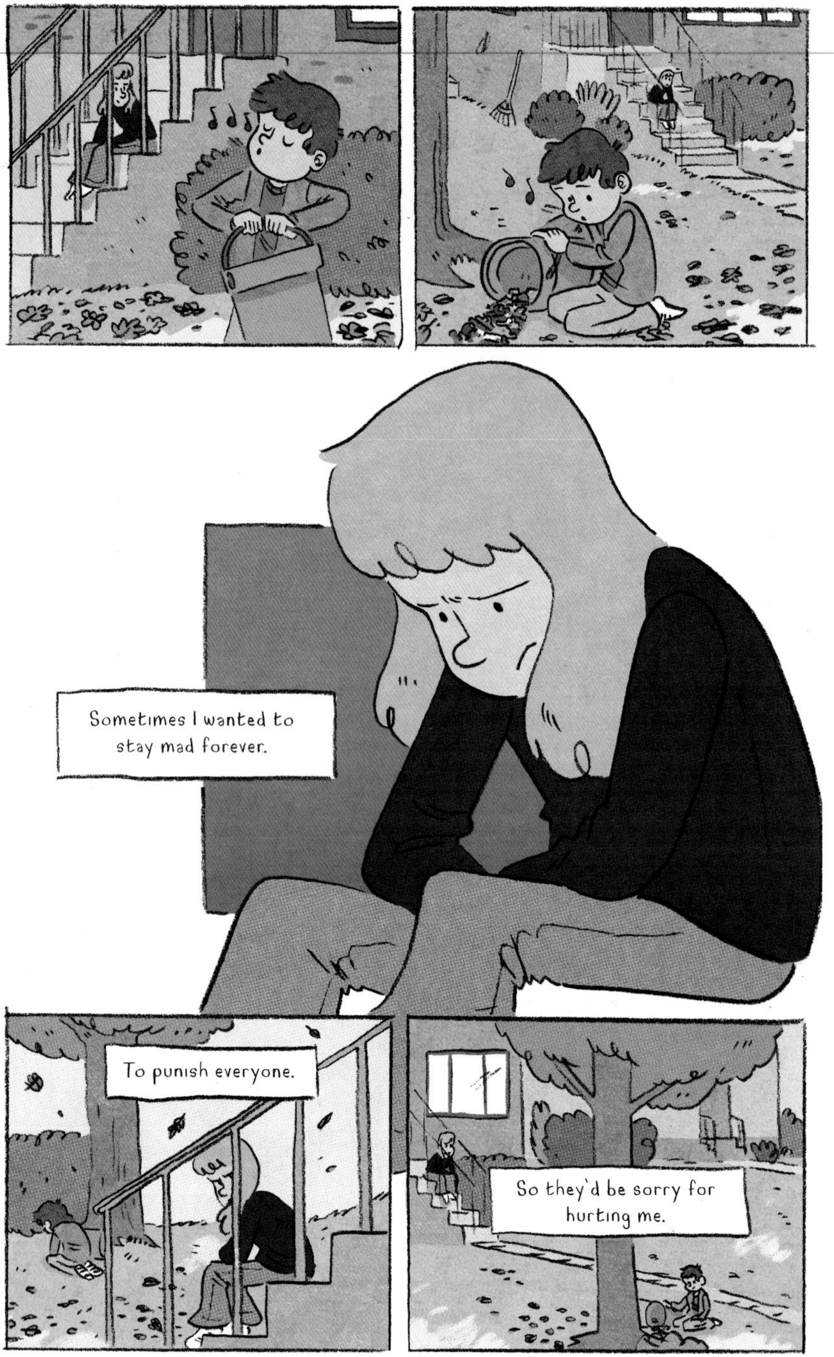
Sometimes I wanted to stay mad forever.
To punish everyone.
So they'd be sorry for hurting me.

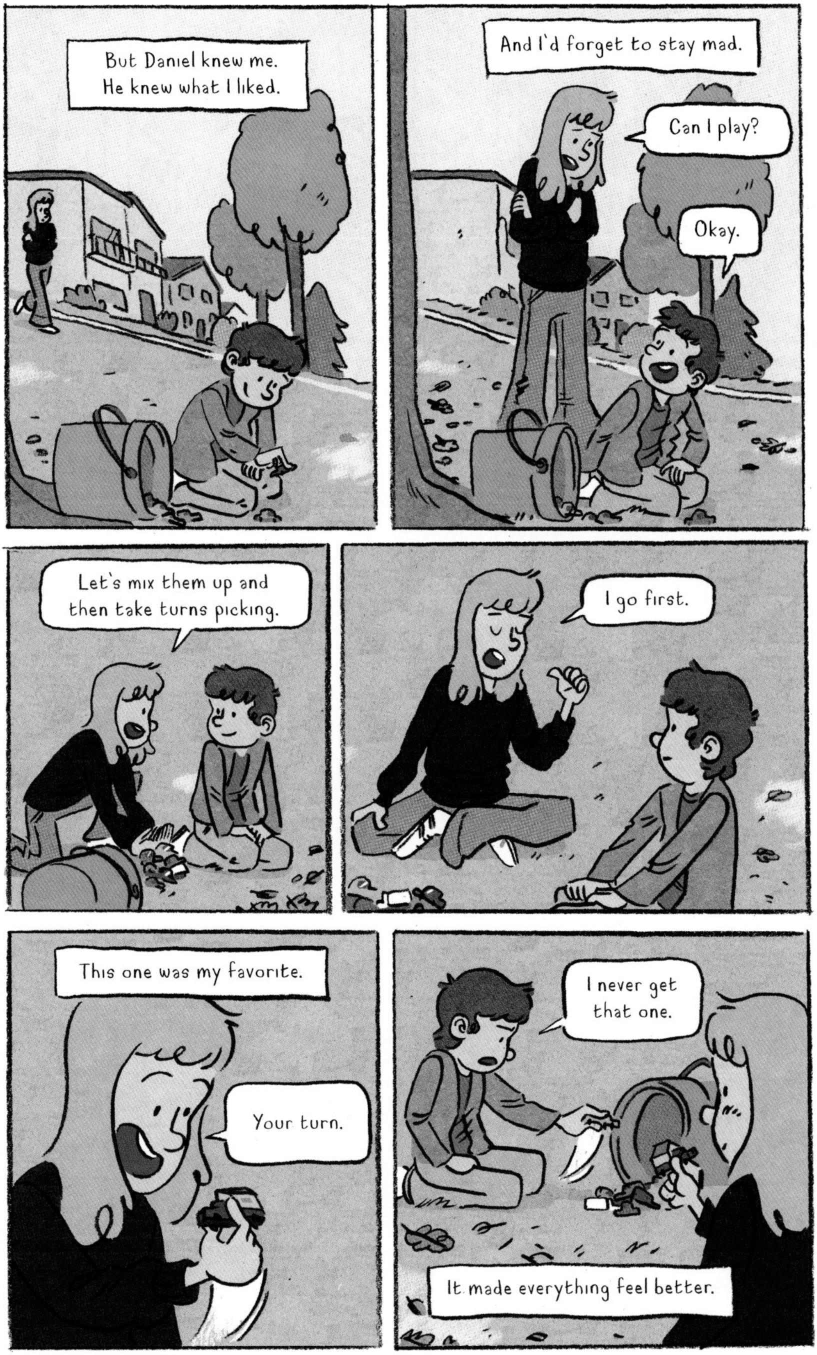
But Daniel knew me. He knew what I liked.
And I'd forget to stay mad.
Can I play?
Okay.
Let's mix them up and then take turns picking.
I go first.
This one was my favorite.
Your turn.
I never get that one.
It made everything feel better.

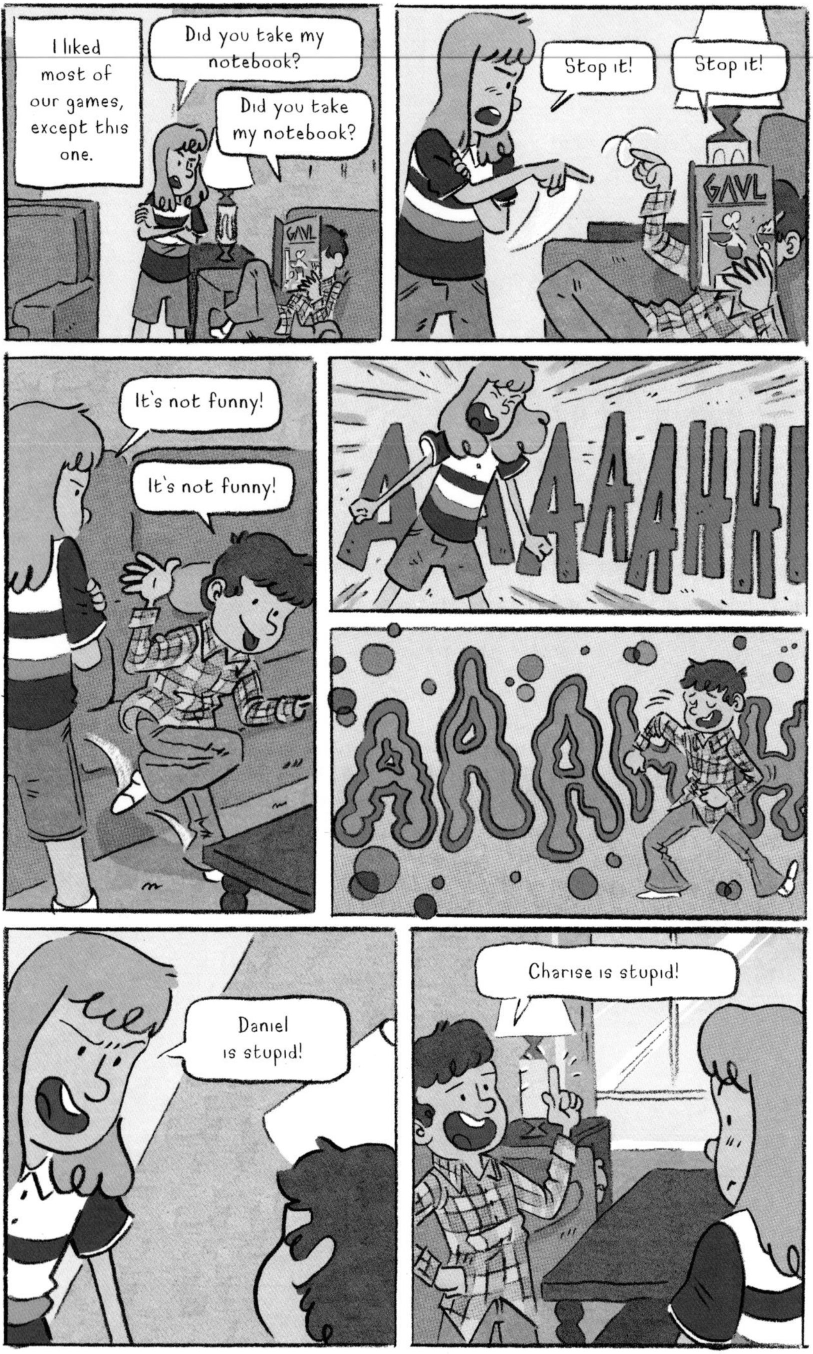
I liked most of our games, except this one.
Did you take my notebook?
Did you take my notebook?
Stop it!
Stop it!
It's not funny!
It's not funny!
AAAAHH
Daniel is stupid!
Charise is stupid!

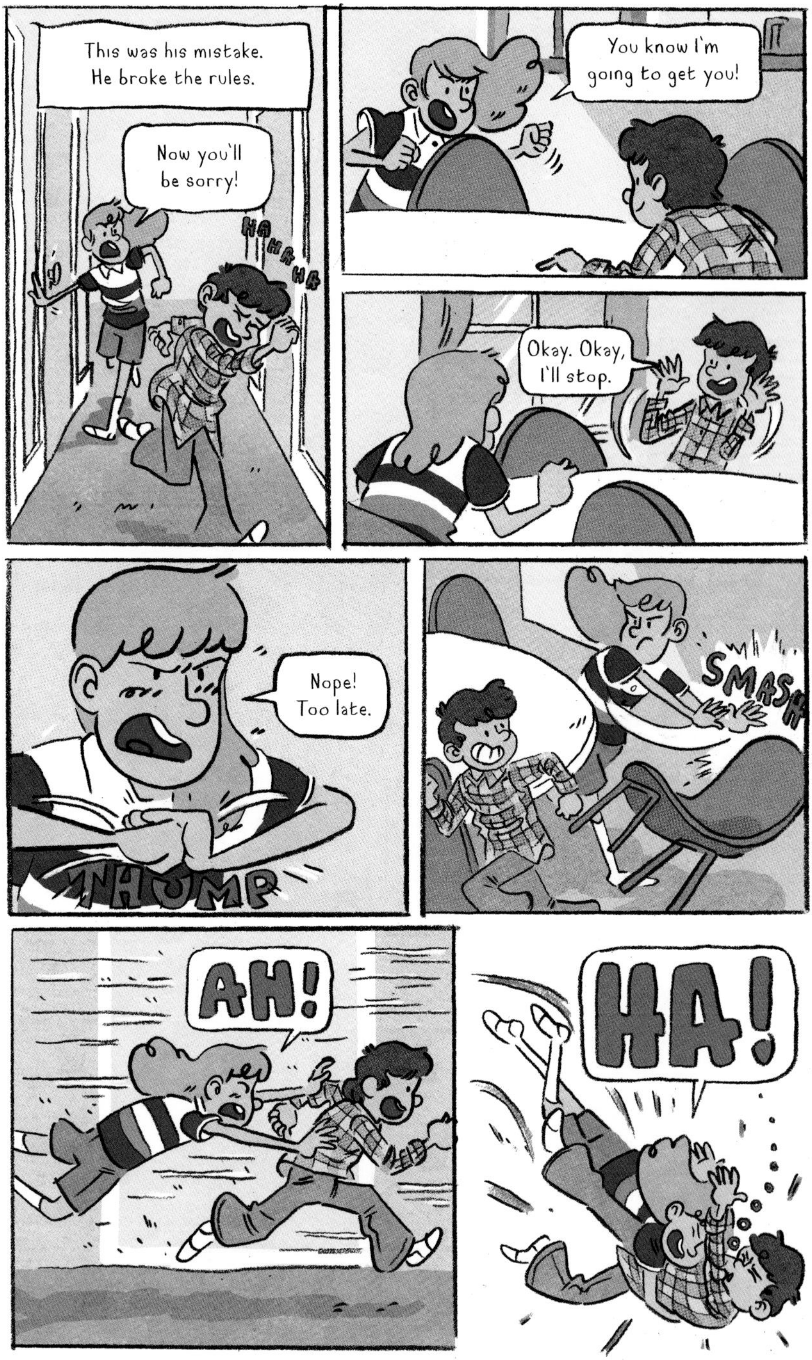
This was his mistake.
He broke the rules.
Now you'll be sorry!
HAHAHAHA
You know I'm going to get you!
Okay. Okay, I'll stop.
Nope! Too late.
THUMP
SMASH
AH!
HA!

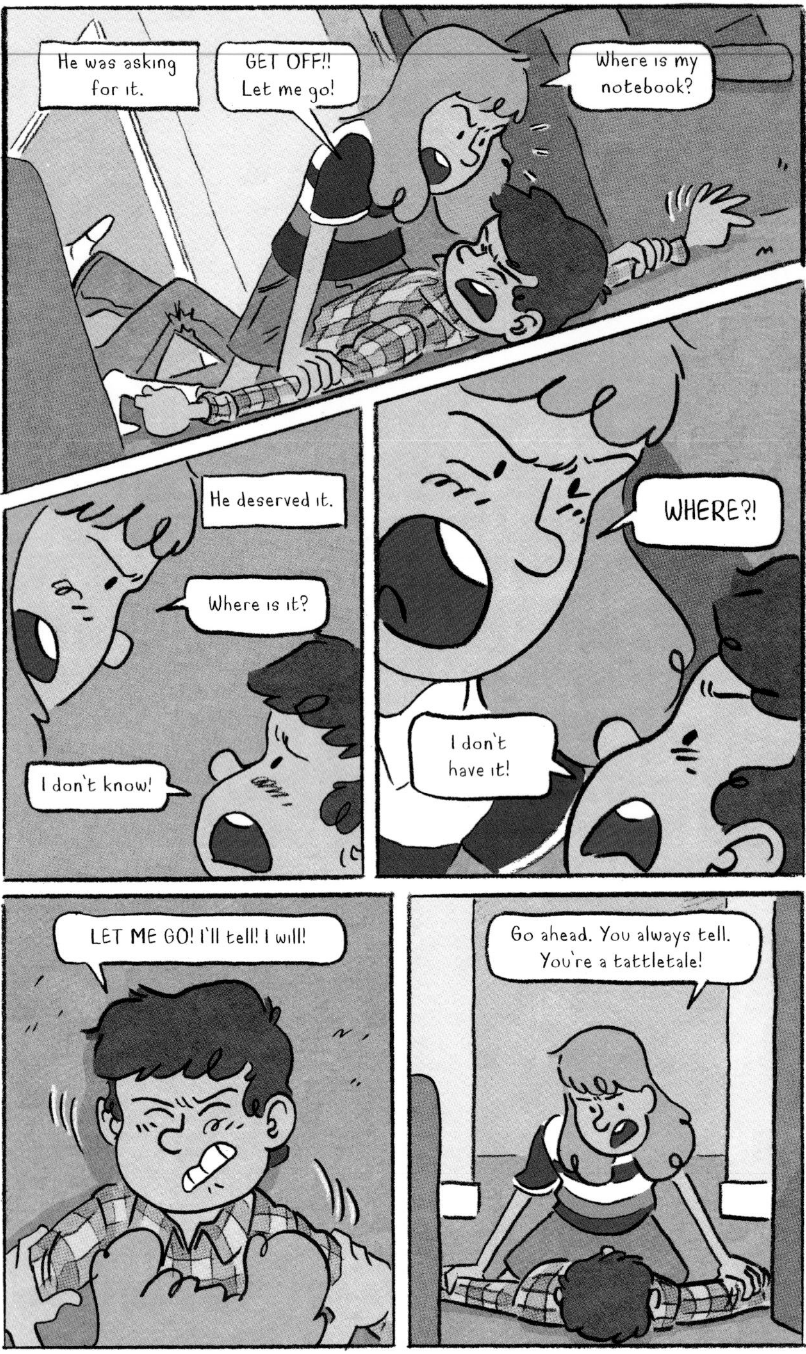
He was asking for it.
GET OFF!! Let me go!
Where is my notebook?
He deserved it.
Where is it?
I don't know!
WHERE?!
I don't have it!
LET ME GO! I'll tell! I will!
Go ahead. You always tell. You're a tattletale!

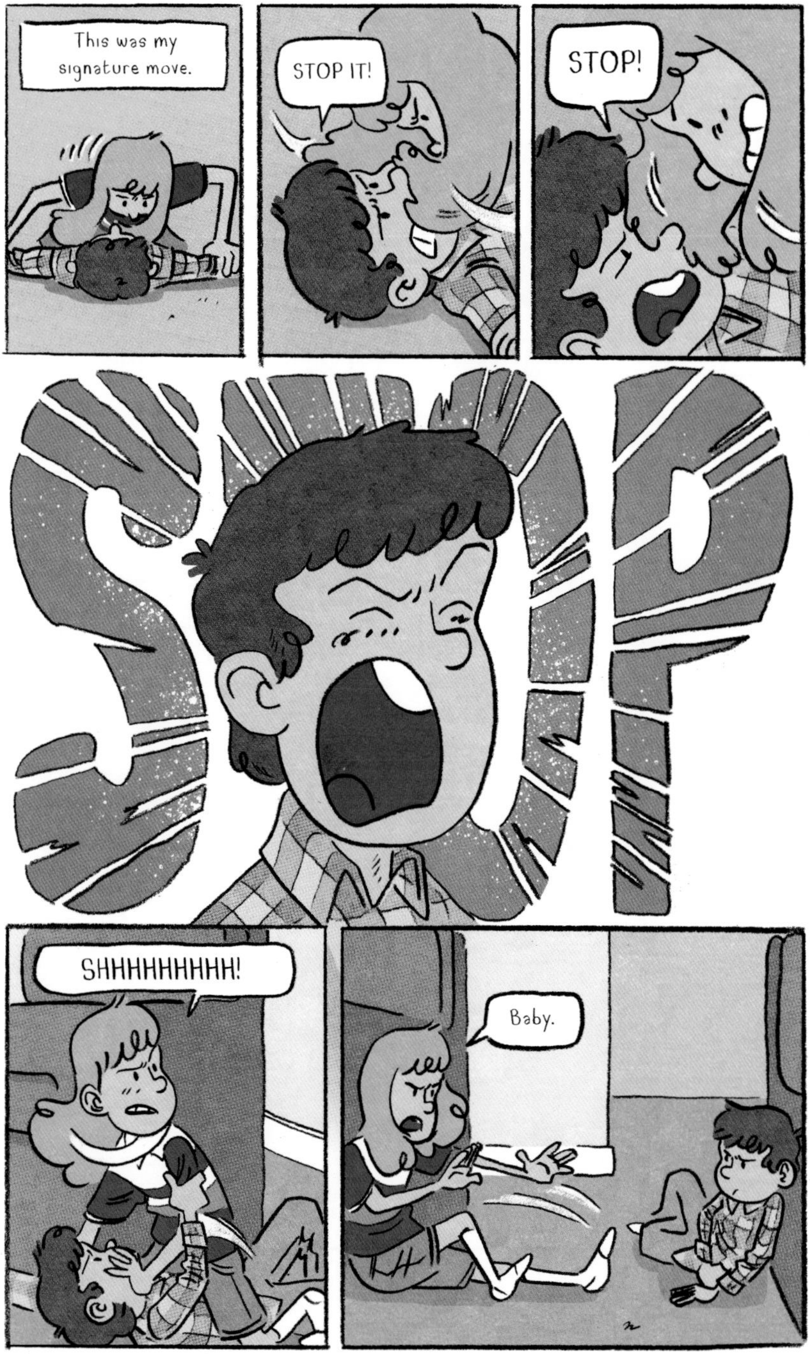
This was my signature move.
STOP IT!
STOP!
STOP
SHHHHHHHHH!
Baby.

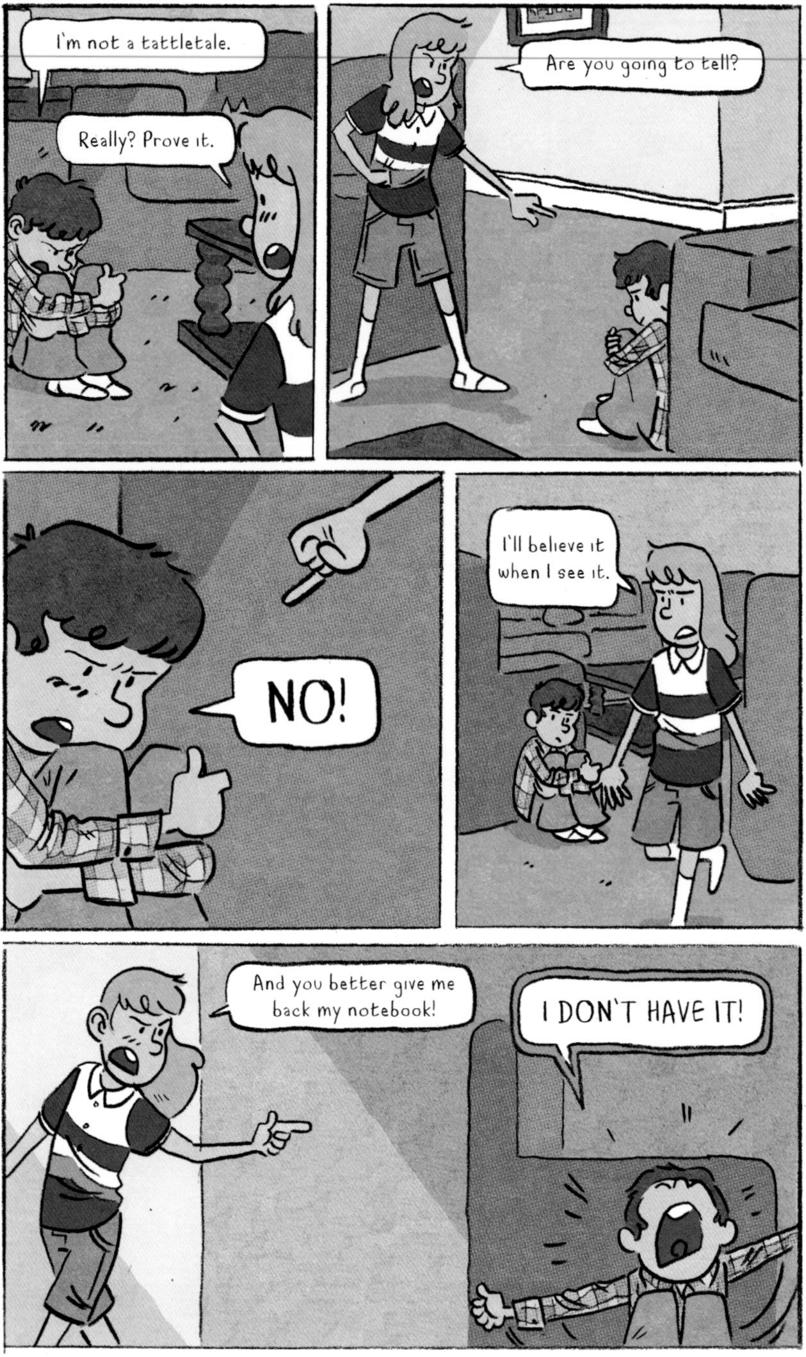
I'm not a tattletale.
Really? Prove it.
Are you going to tell?
NO!
I'll believe it when I see it.
And you better give me back my notebook!
I DON'T HAVE IT!

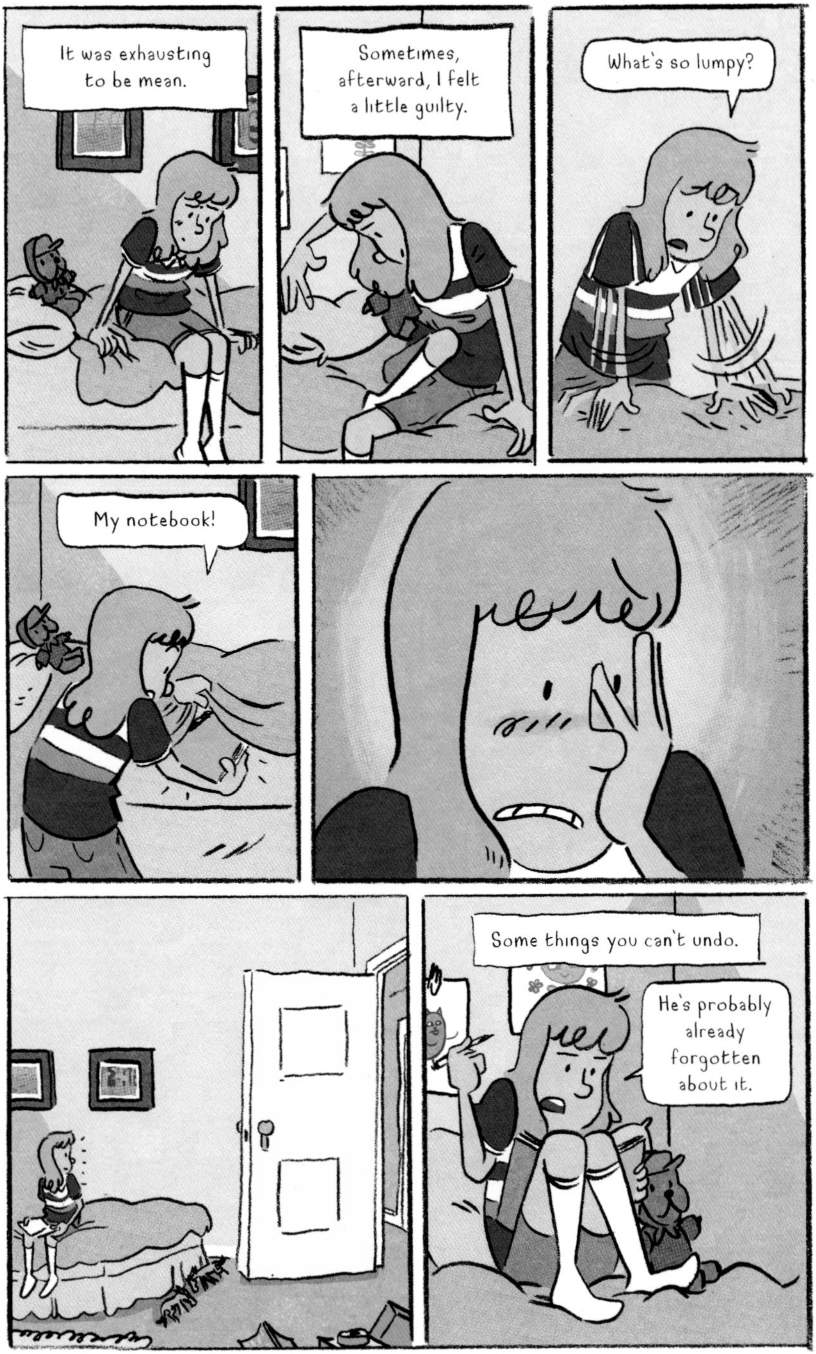
It was exhausting to be mean.
Sometimes, afterward, I felt a little guilty.
What's so lumpy?
My notebook!
Some things you can't undo.
He's probably already forgotten about it.

4

The Power of the Lie

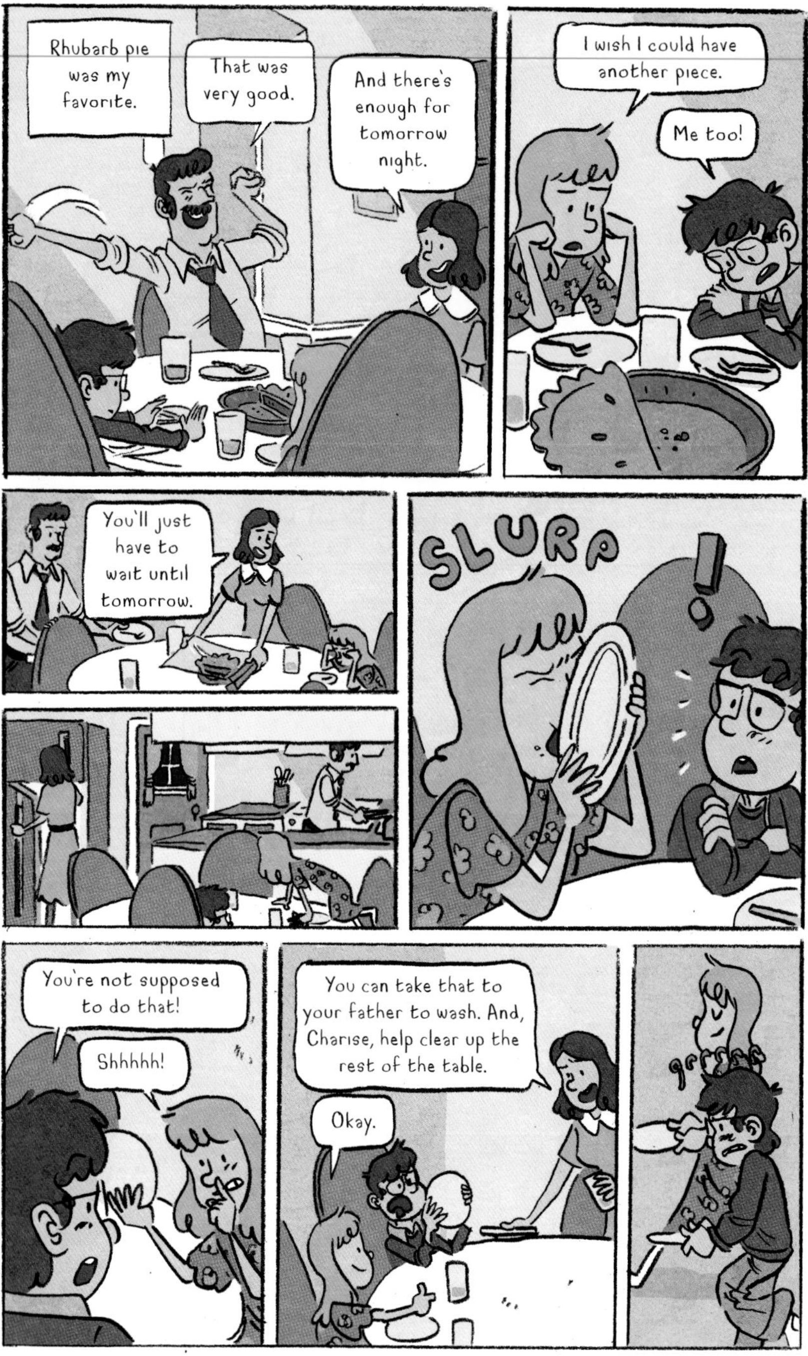
Rhubarb pie was my favorite.
That was very good.
And there's enough for tomorrow night.
I wish I could have another piece.
Me too!
You'll just have to wait until tomorrow.
SLURP
!
You're not supposed to do that!
Shhhhh!
You can take that to your father to wash. And, Charise, help clear up the rest of the table.
Okay.

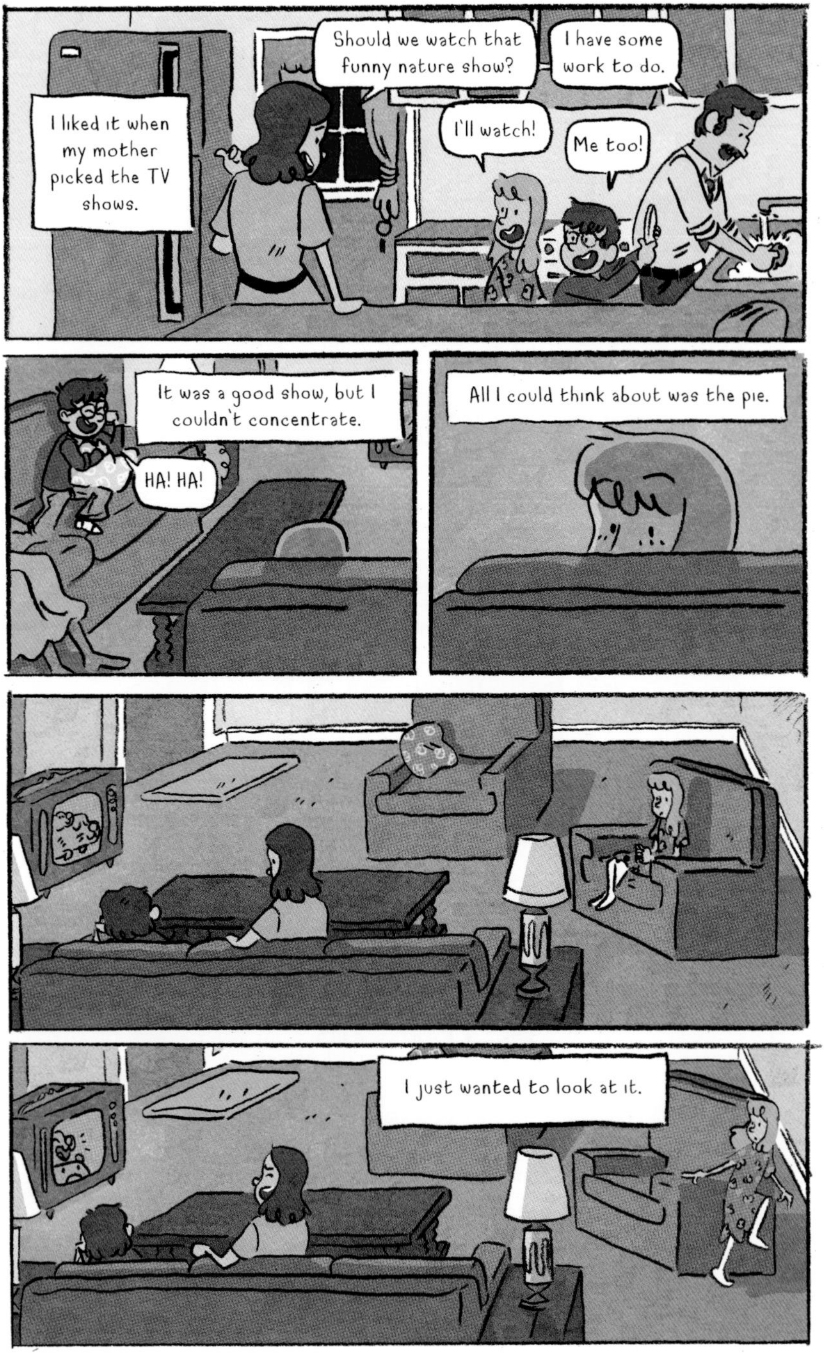
I liked it when my mother picked the TV shows.
Should we watch that funny nature show?
I have some work to do.
I'll watch!
Me too!
It was a good show, but I couldn't concentrate.
HA! HA!
All I could think about was the pie.
I just wanted to look at it.

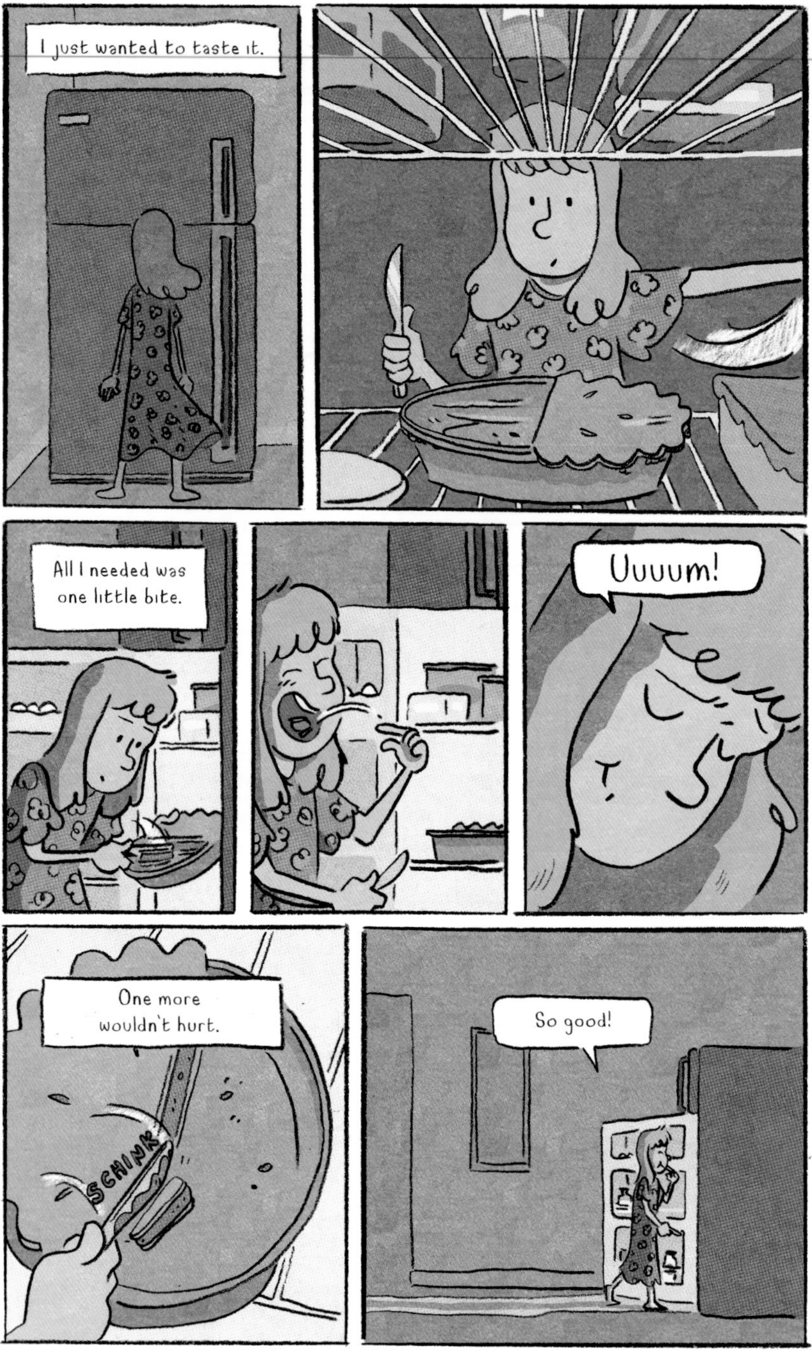
I just wanted to taste it.
All I needed was one little bite.
Uuuum!
One more wouldn't hurt.
SCHINK
So good!

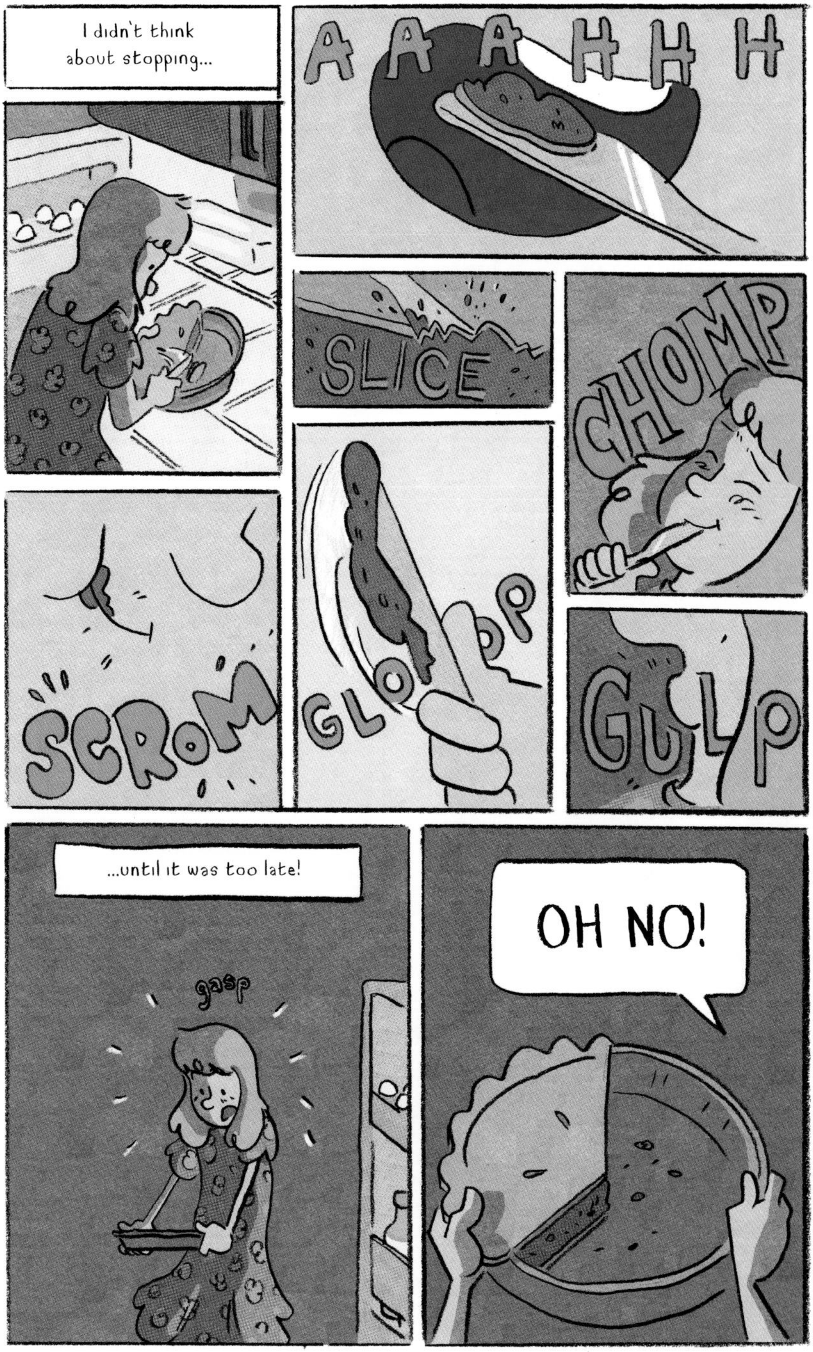
I didn't think about stopping...
AAAHHH
SLICE
CHOMP
SCROM
GLOOP
GULP
...until it was too late!
gasp
OH NO!

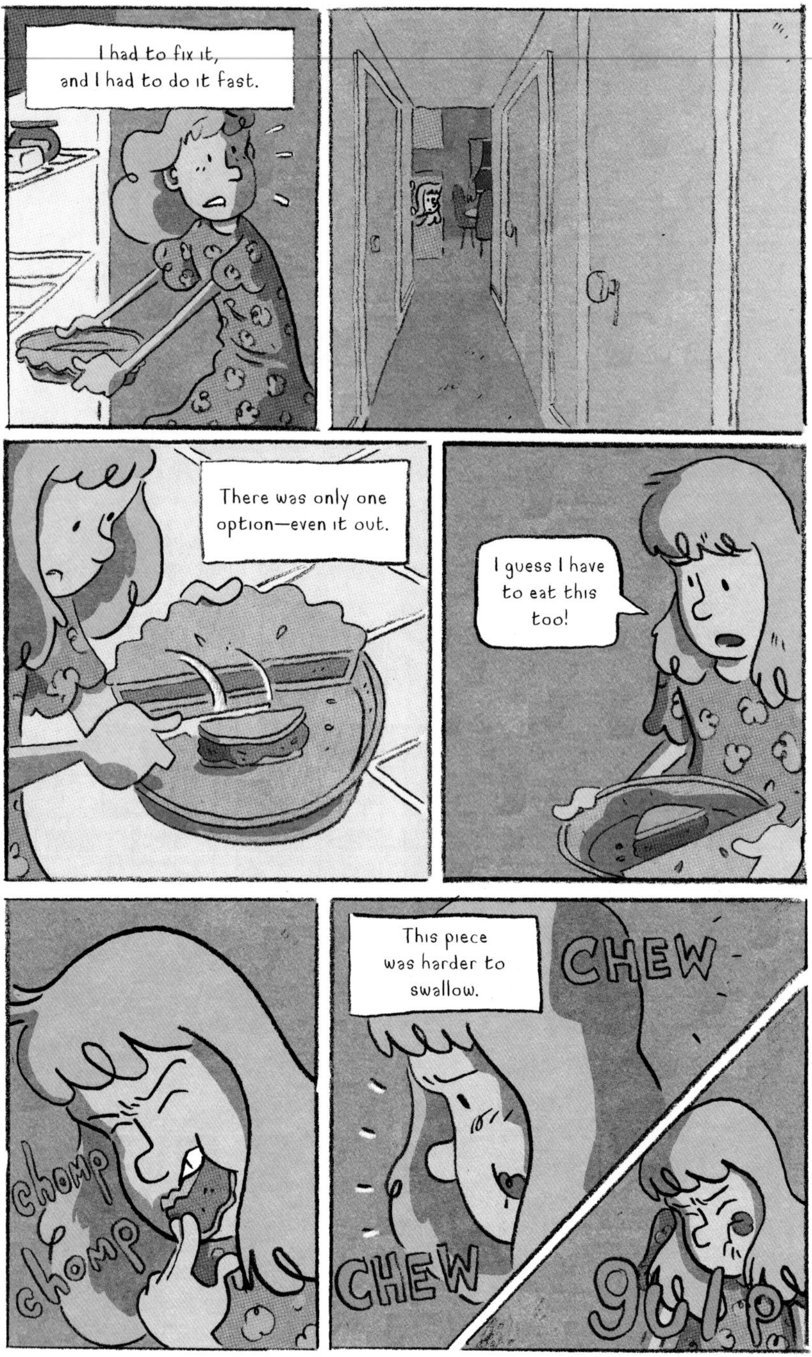
I had to fix it,
and I had to do it fast.
There was only one option—even it out.
I guess I have to eat this too!
chomp chomp chomp
This piece was harder to swallow.
CHEW
CHEW
gulp

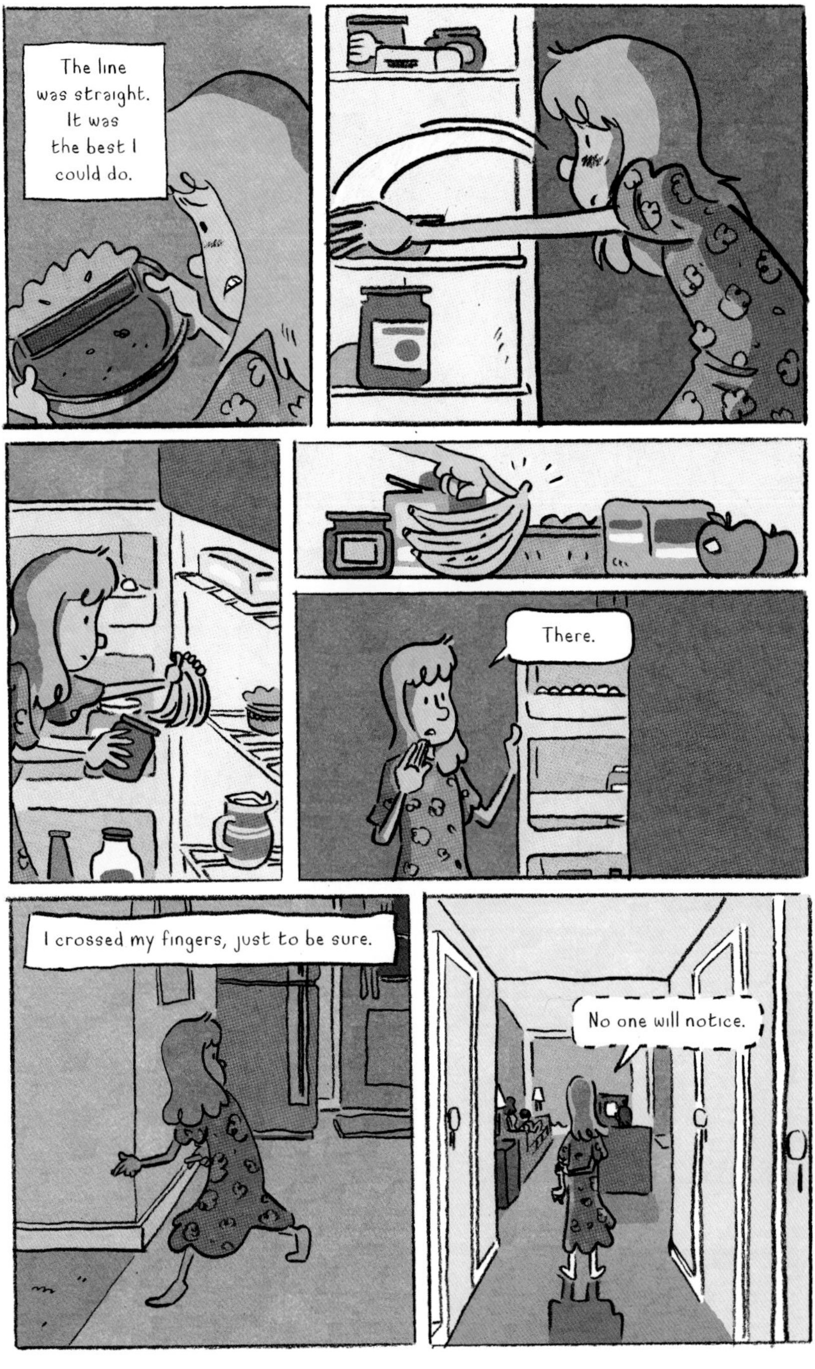

The line was straight. It was the best I could do.
There.
I crossed my fingers, just to be sure.
No one will notice.

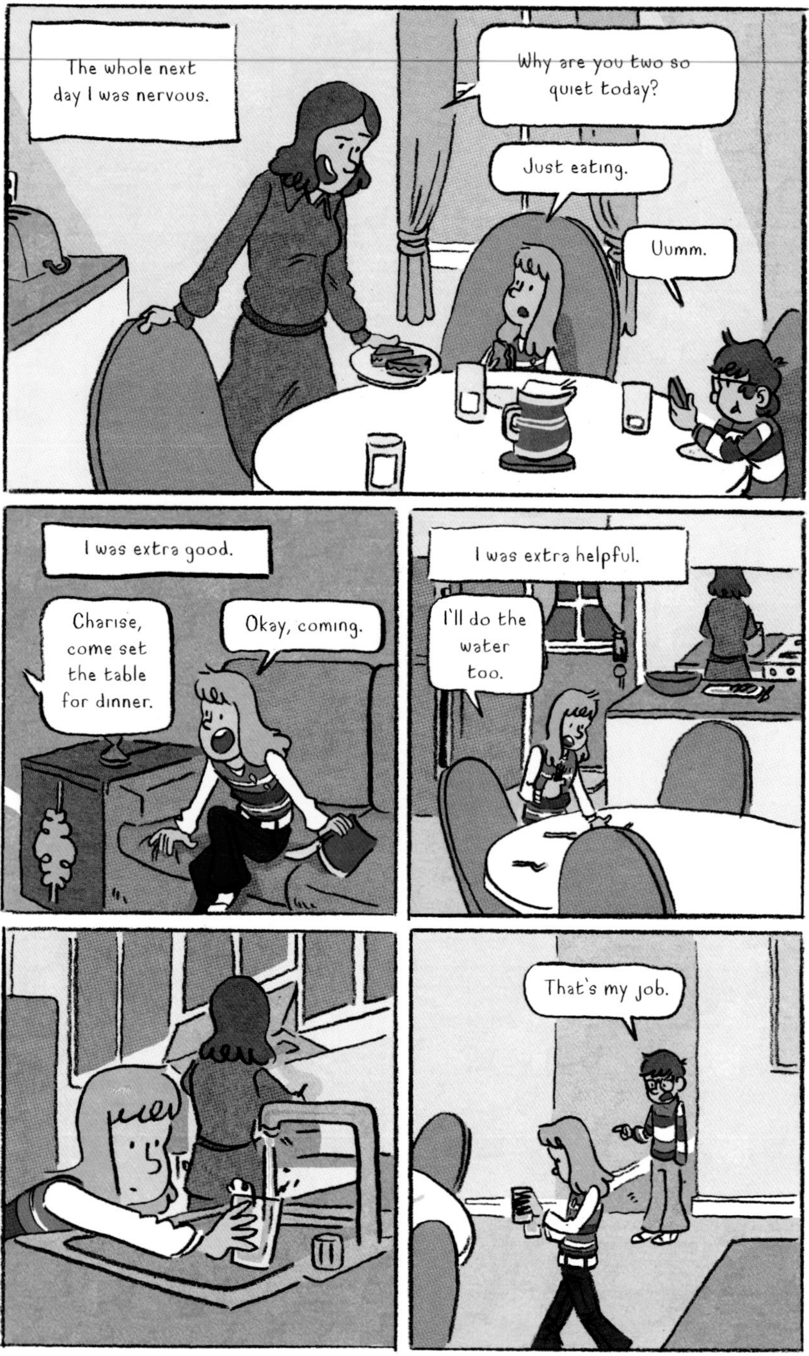
The whole next day I was nervous.
Why are you two so quiet today?
Just eating.
Uumm.
I was extra good.
Charise, come set the table for dinner.
Okay, coming.
I was extra helpful.
I'll do the water too.
That's my job.

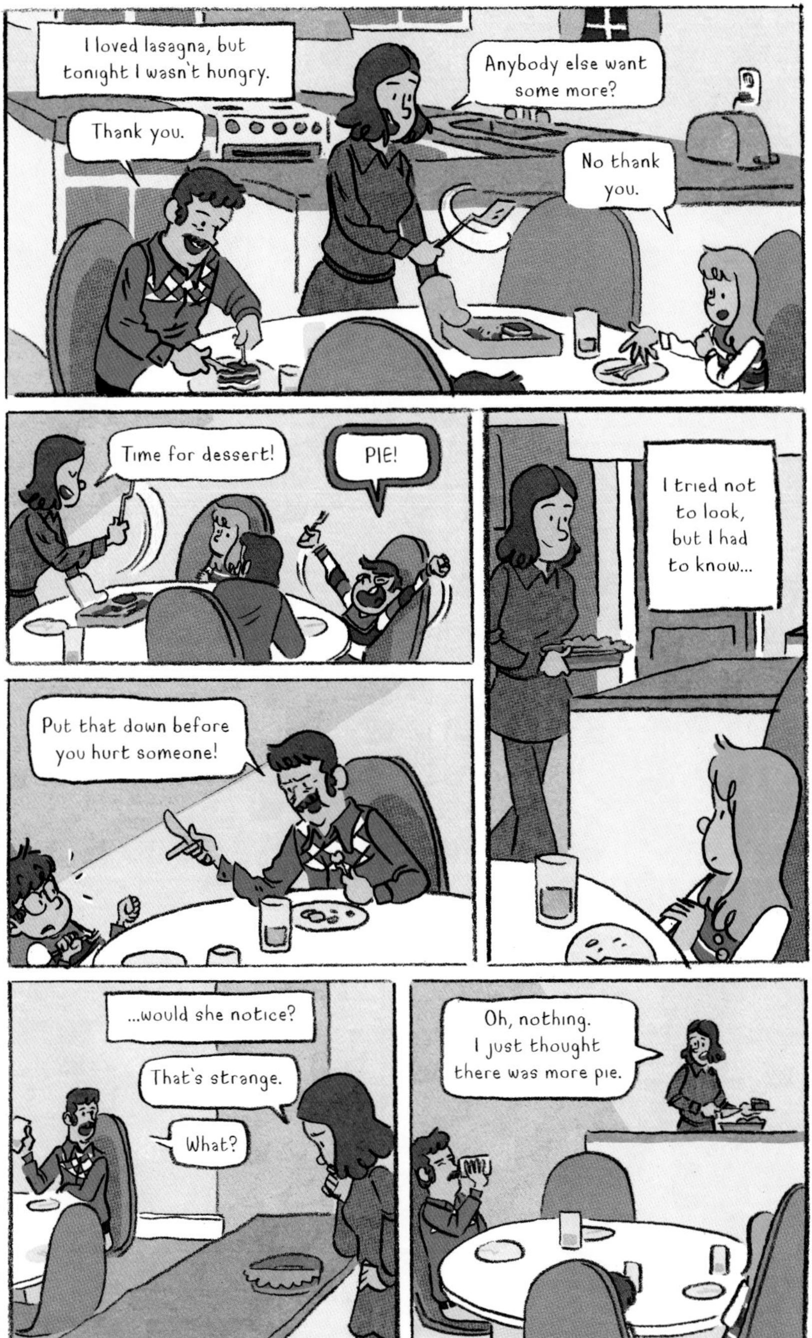
I loved lasagna, but tonight I wasn't hungry.
Anybody else want some more?
Thank you.
No thank you.
Time for dessert!
PIE!
I tried not to look, but I had to know...
Put that down before you hurt someone!
...would she notice?
That's strange.
What?
Oh, nothing. I just thought there was more pie.

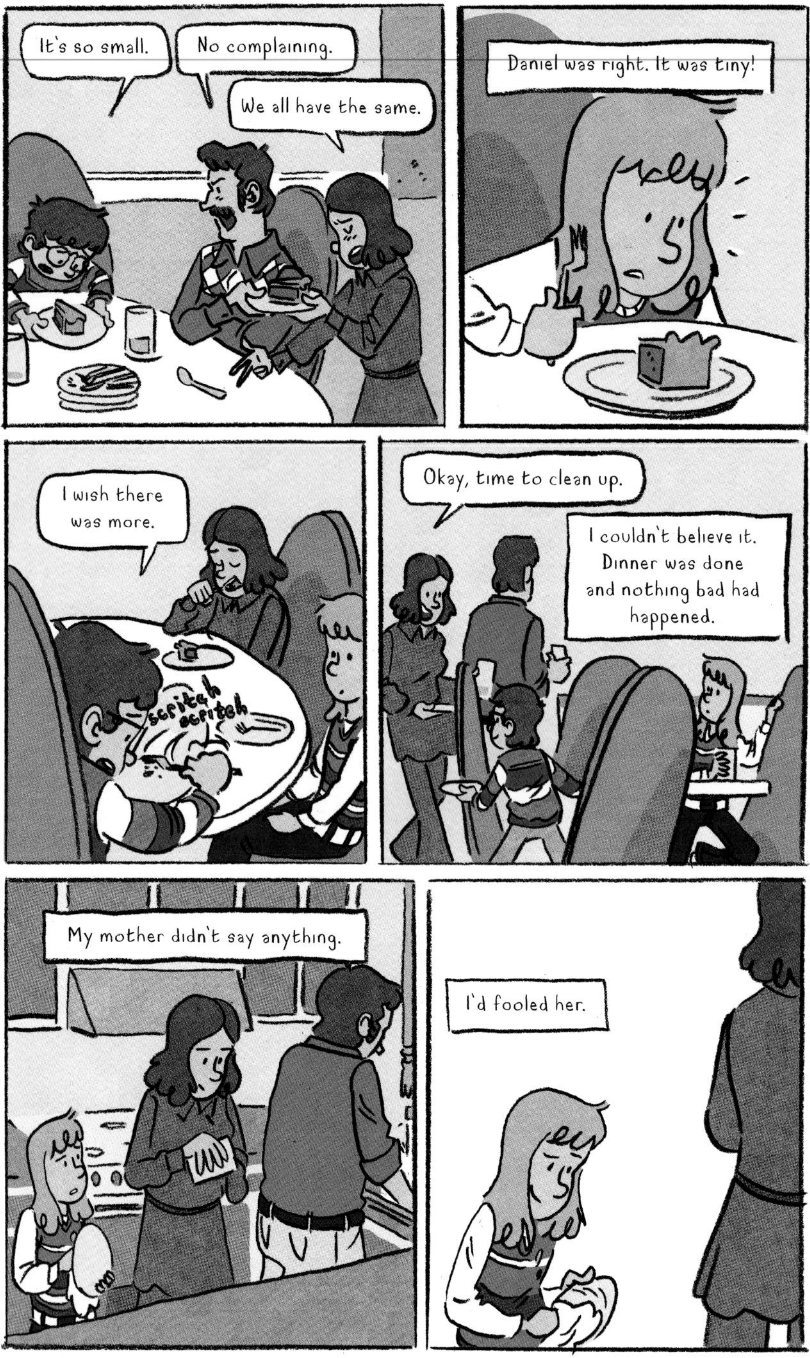
It's so small.
No complaining.
We all have the same.
Daniel was right. It was tiny!
I wish there was more.
scritch scritch
Okay, time to clean up.
I couldn't believe it. Dinner was done and nothing bad had happened.
My mother didn't say anything.
I'd fooled her.

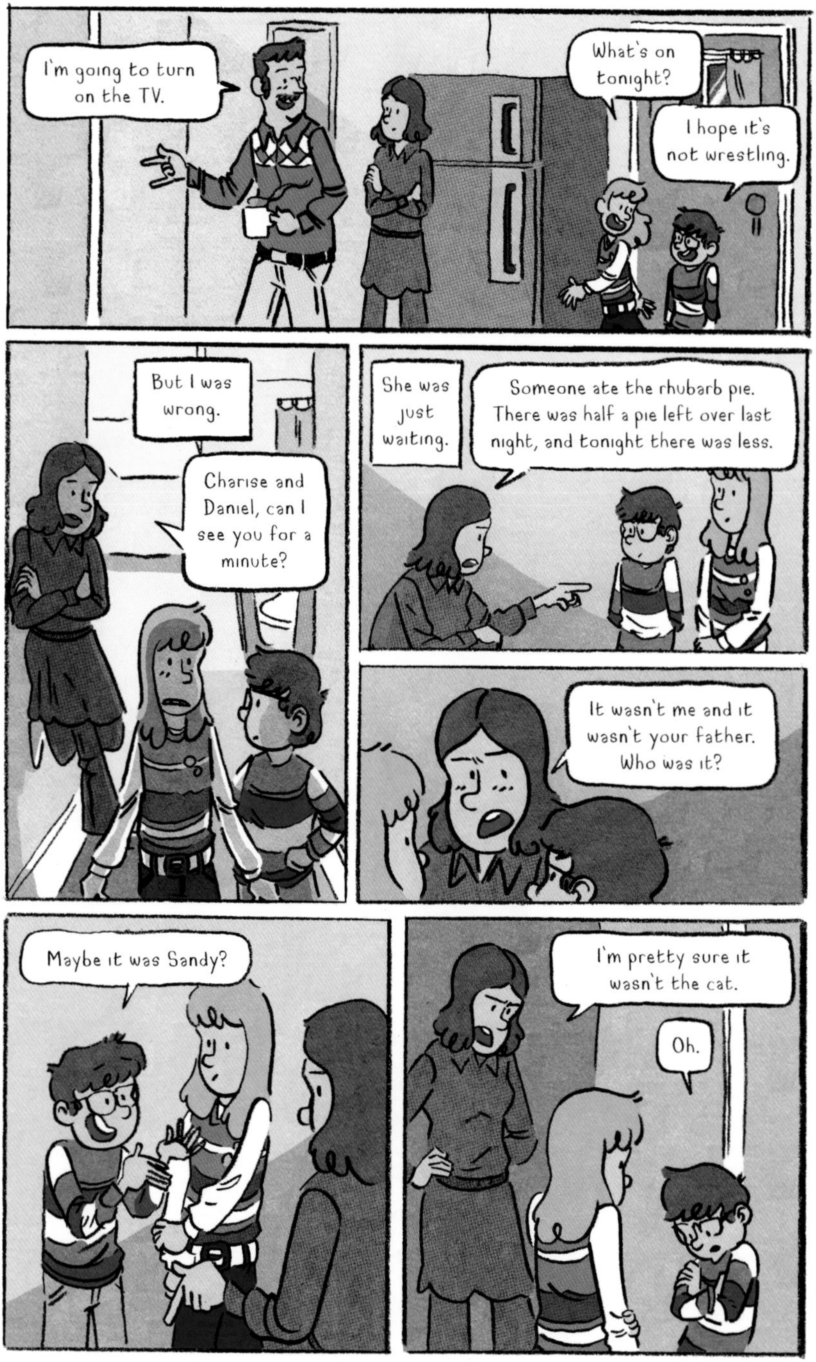
I'm going to turn on the TV.
What's on tonight?
I hope it's not wrestling.
But I was wrong.
Charise and Daniel, can I see you for a minute?
She was just waiting.
Someone ate the rhubarb pie. There was half a pie left over last night, and tonight there was less.
It wasn't me and it wasn't your father. Who was it?
Maybe it was Sandy?
I'm pretty sure it wasn't the cat.
Oh.

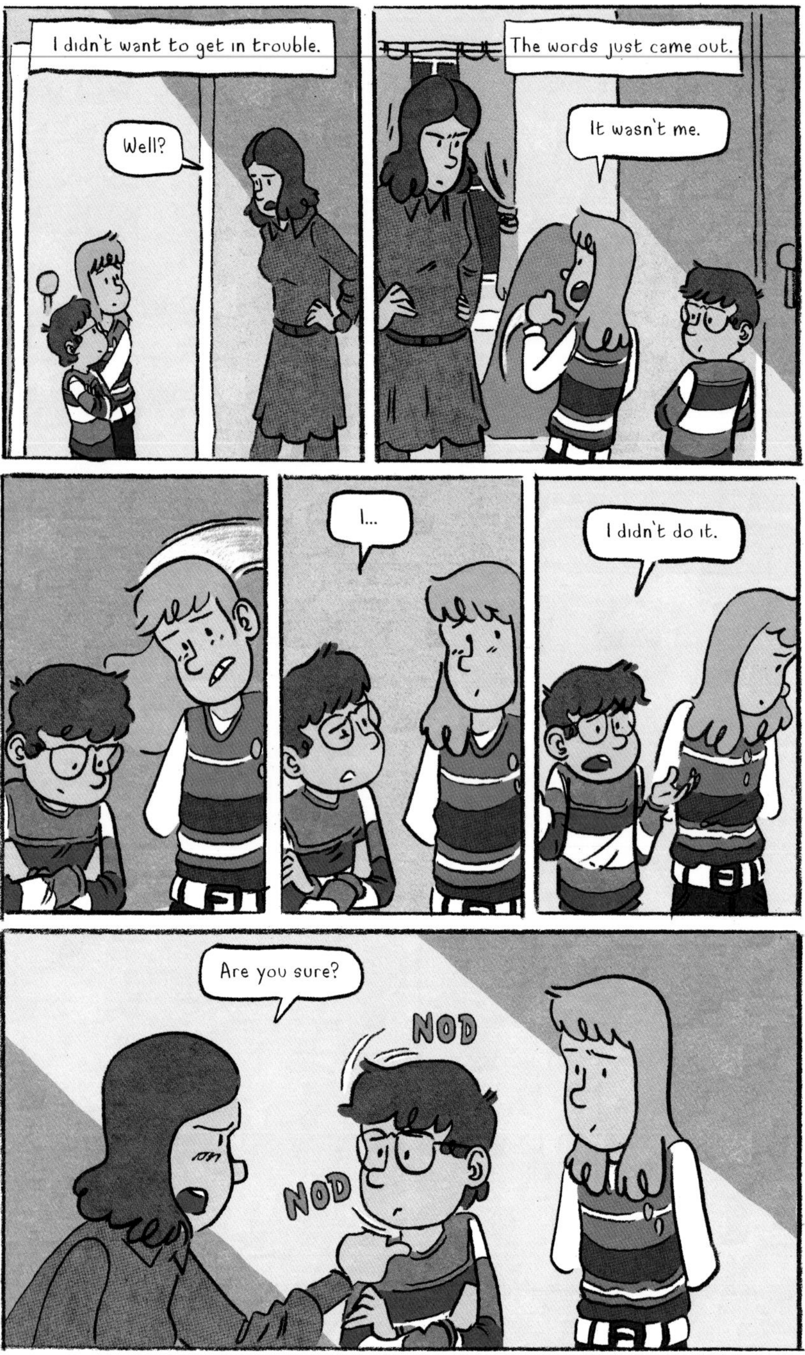
I didn't want to get in trouble.
Well?
The words just came out.
It wasn't me.
I...
I didn't do it.
Are you sure?
NOD
NOD

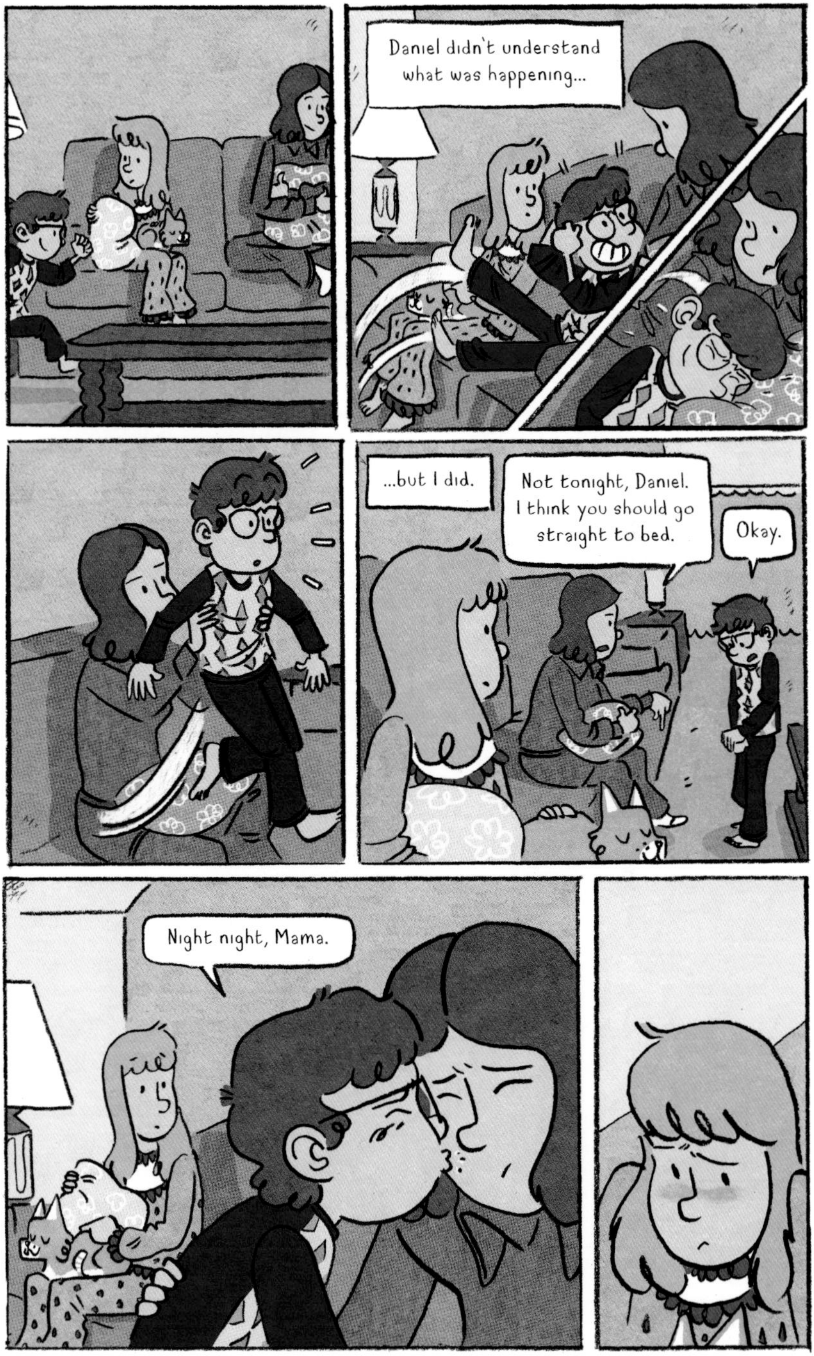
Daniel didn't understand what was happening...
...but I did.
Not tonight, Daniel. I think you should go straight to bed.
Okay.
Night night, Mama.

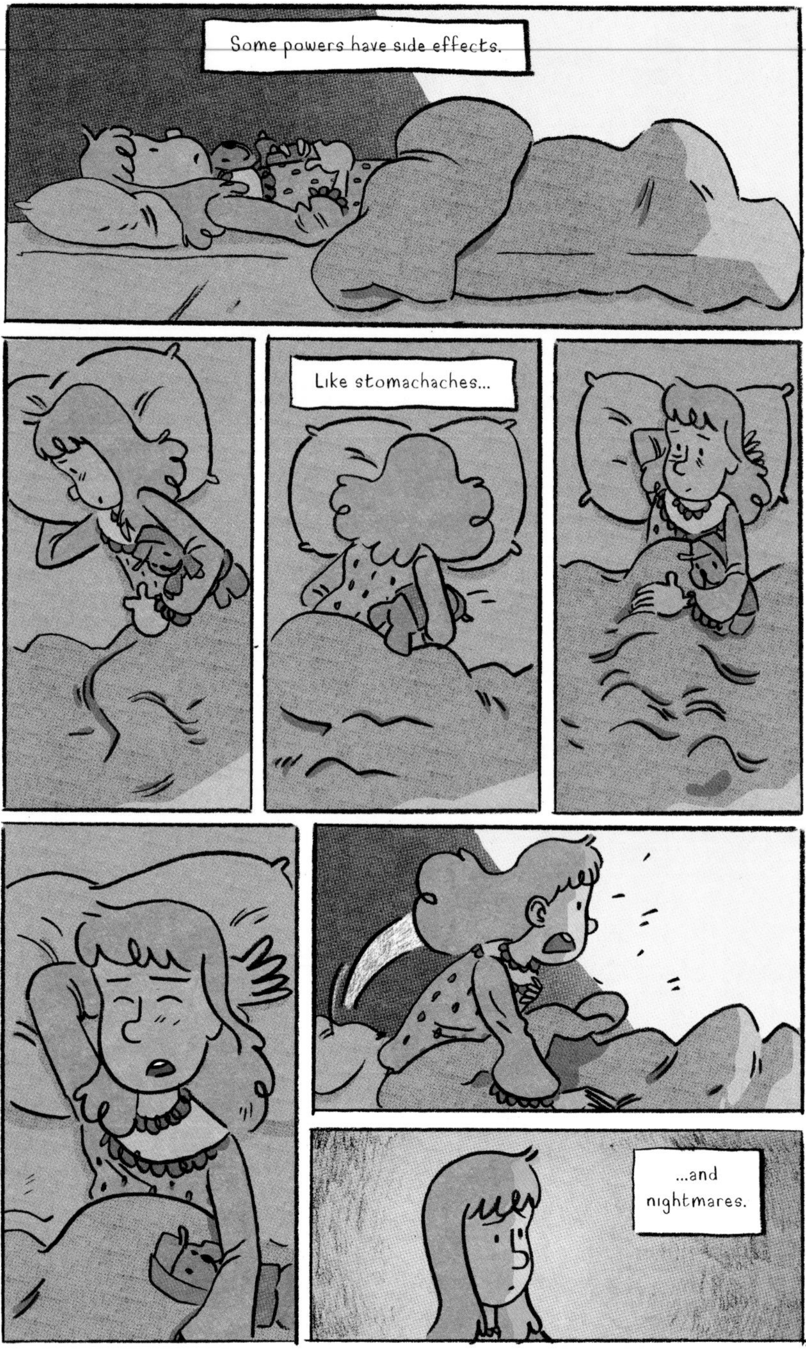
Some powers have side effects.
Like stomachaches...
...and nightmares.

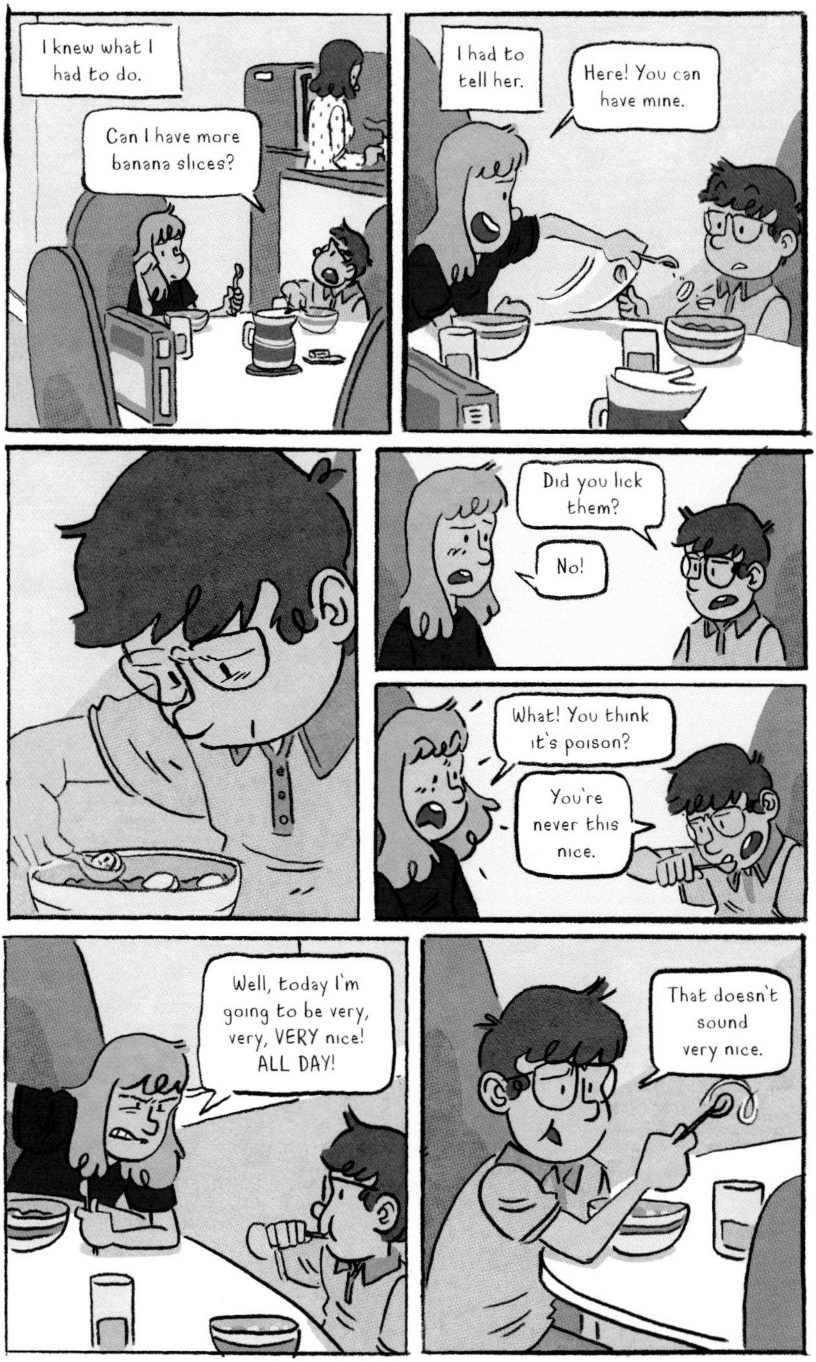
I knew what I had to do.
Can I have more banana slices?
I had to tell her.
Here! You can have mine.
Did you lick them?
No!
What! You think it's poison?
You're never this nice.
Well, today I'm going to be very, very, VERY nice! ALL DAY!
That doesn't sound very nice.

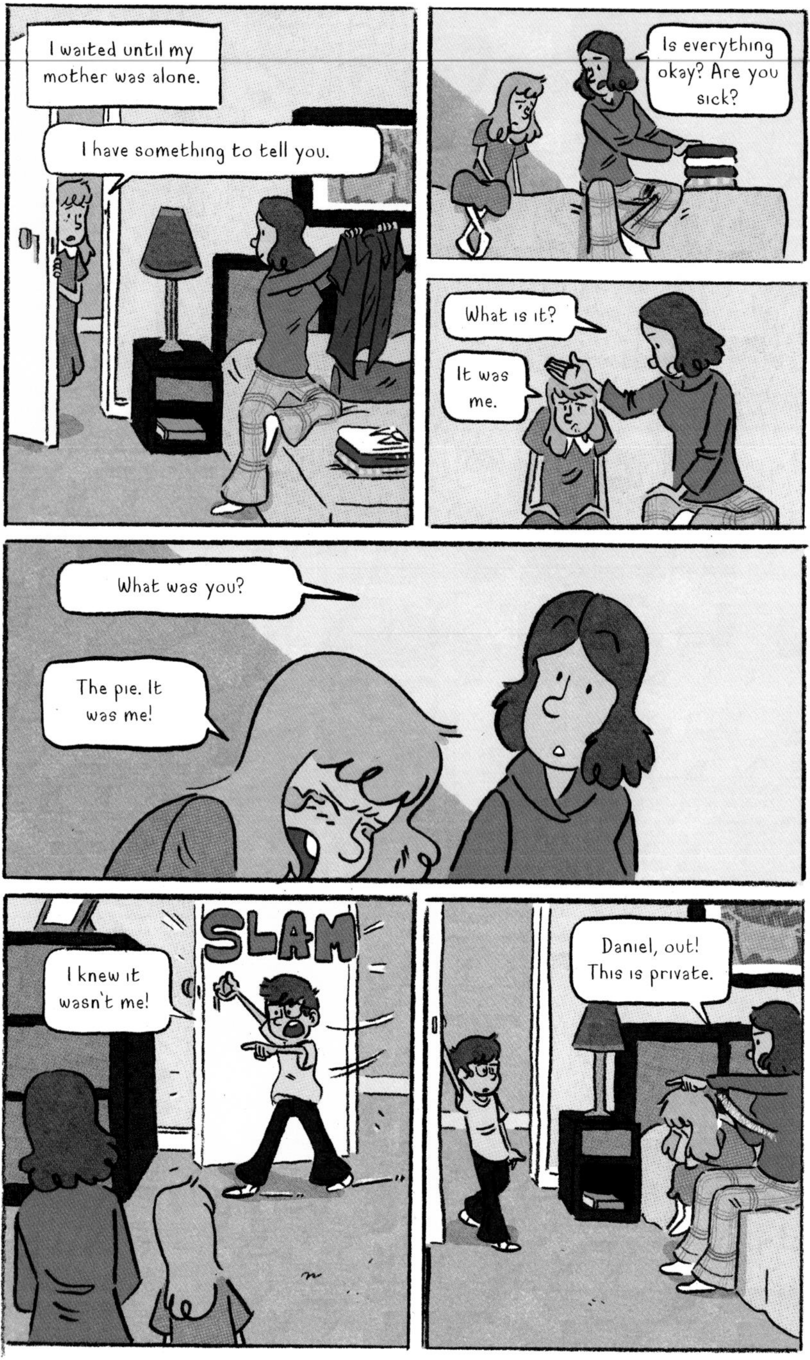
I waited until my mother was alone.
I have something to tell you.
Is everything okay? Are you sick?
What is it?
It was me.
What was you?
The pie. It was me!
SLAM
I knew it wasn't me!
Daniel, out! This is private.

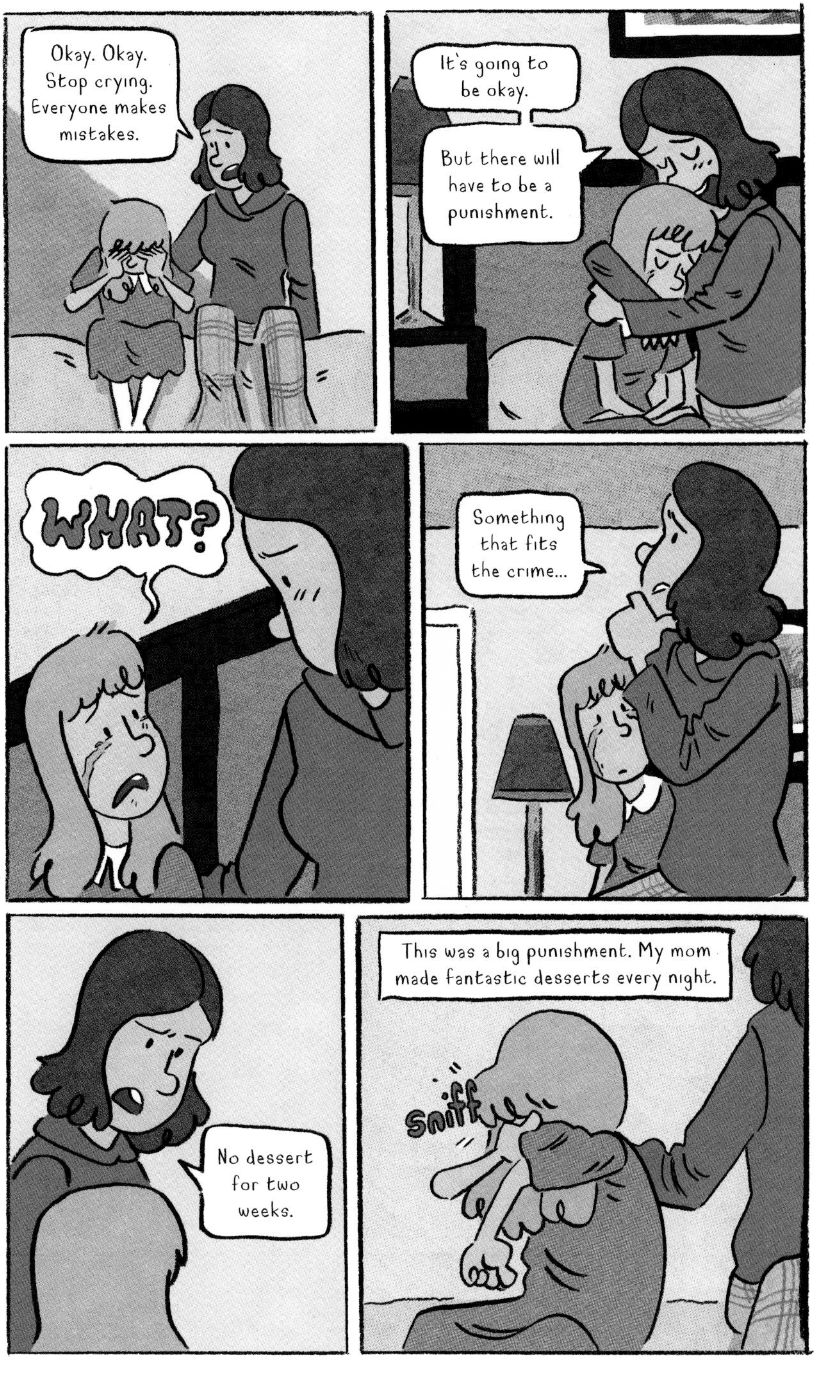
Okay. Okay. Stop crying. Everyone makes mistakes.
It's going to be okay.
But there will have to be a punishment.
WHAT?
Something that fits the crime...
No dessert for two weeks.
This was a big punishment. My mom made fantastic desserts every night.
sniff

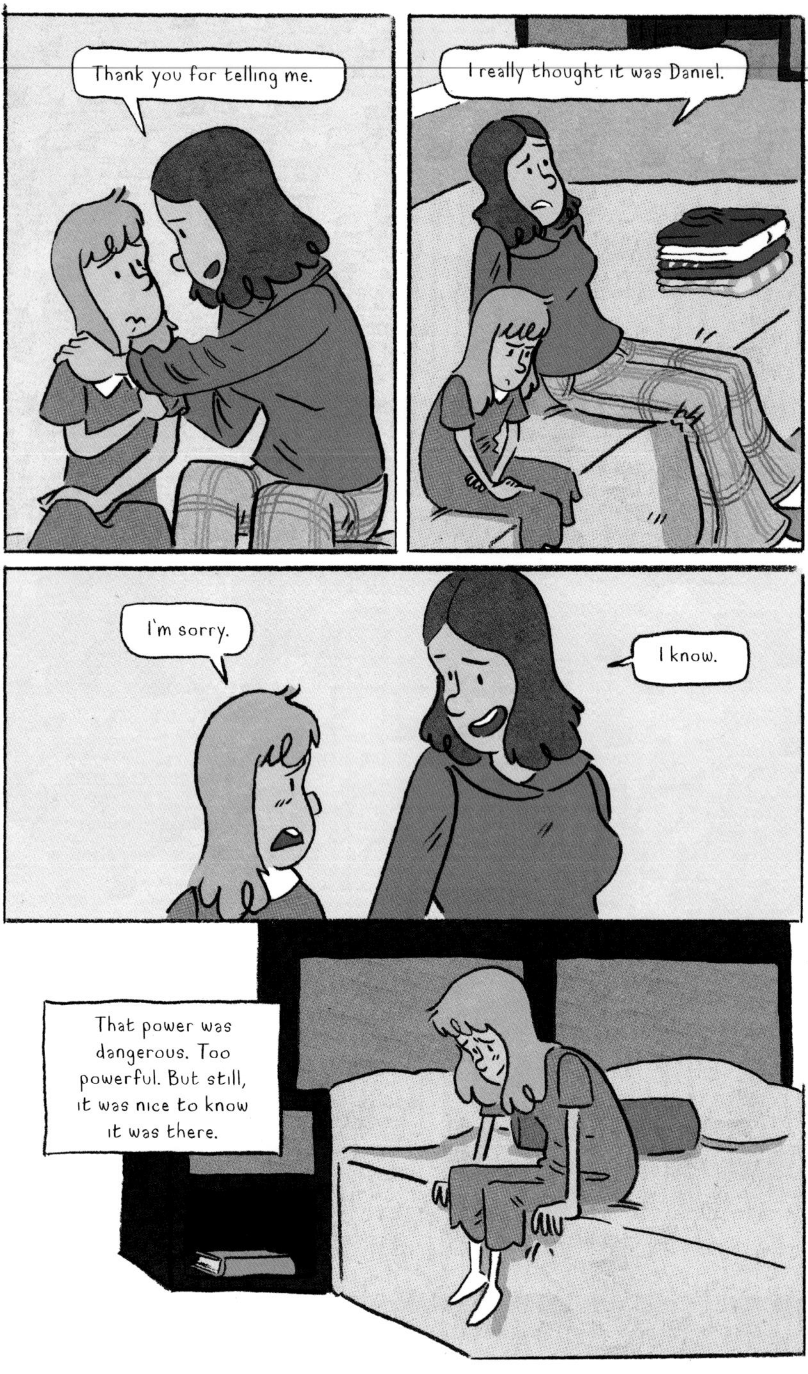
Thank you for telling me.
I really thought it was Daniel.
I'm sorry.
I know.
That power was dangerous. Too powerful. But still, it was nice to know it was there.

5

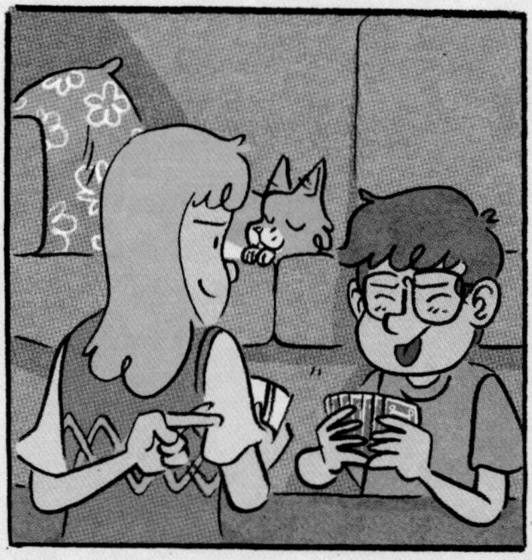

The Power to Fool

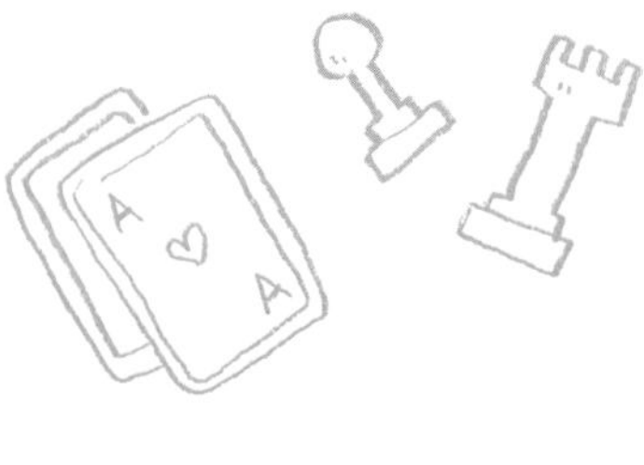
A
A

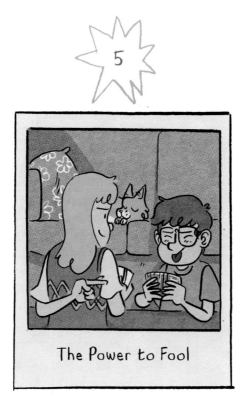

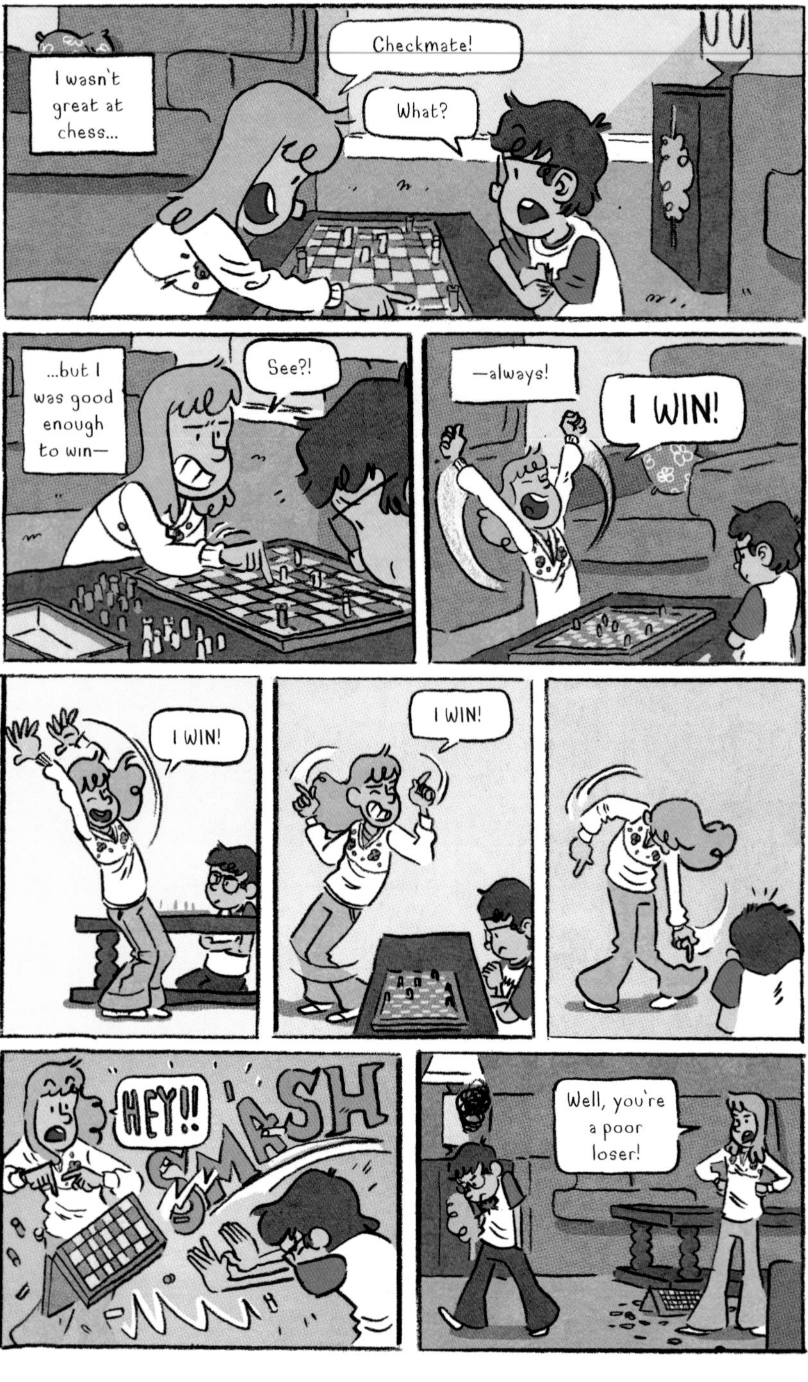
I wasn't great at chess...
Checkmate!
What?
...but I was good enough to win—
See?!
—always!
I WIN!
I WIN!
I WIN!
HEY!!
SMASH
Well, you're a poor loser!

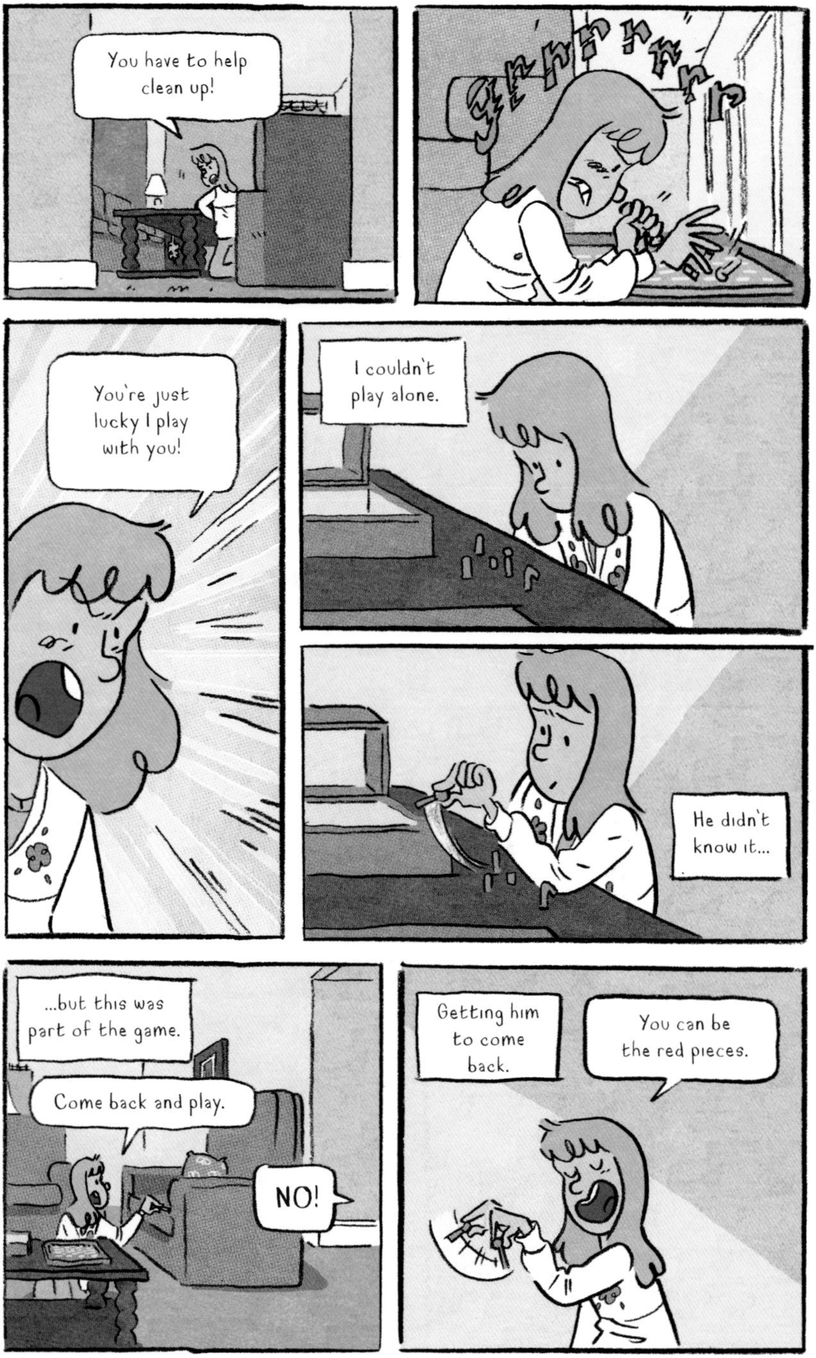
You have to help clean up!
You're just lucky I play with you!
I couldn't play alone.
He didn't know it...
...but this was part of the game.
Come back and play.
NO!
Getting him to come back.
You can be the red pieces.

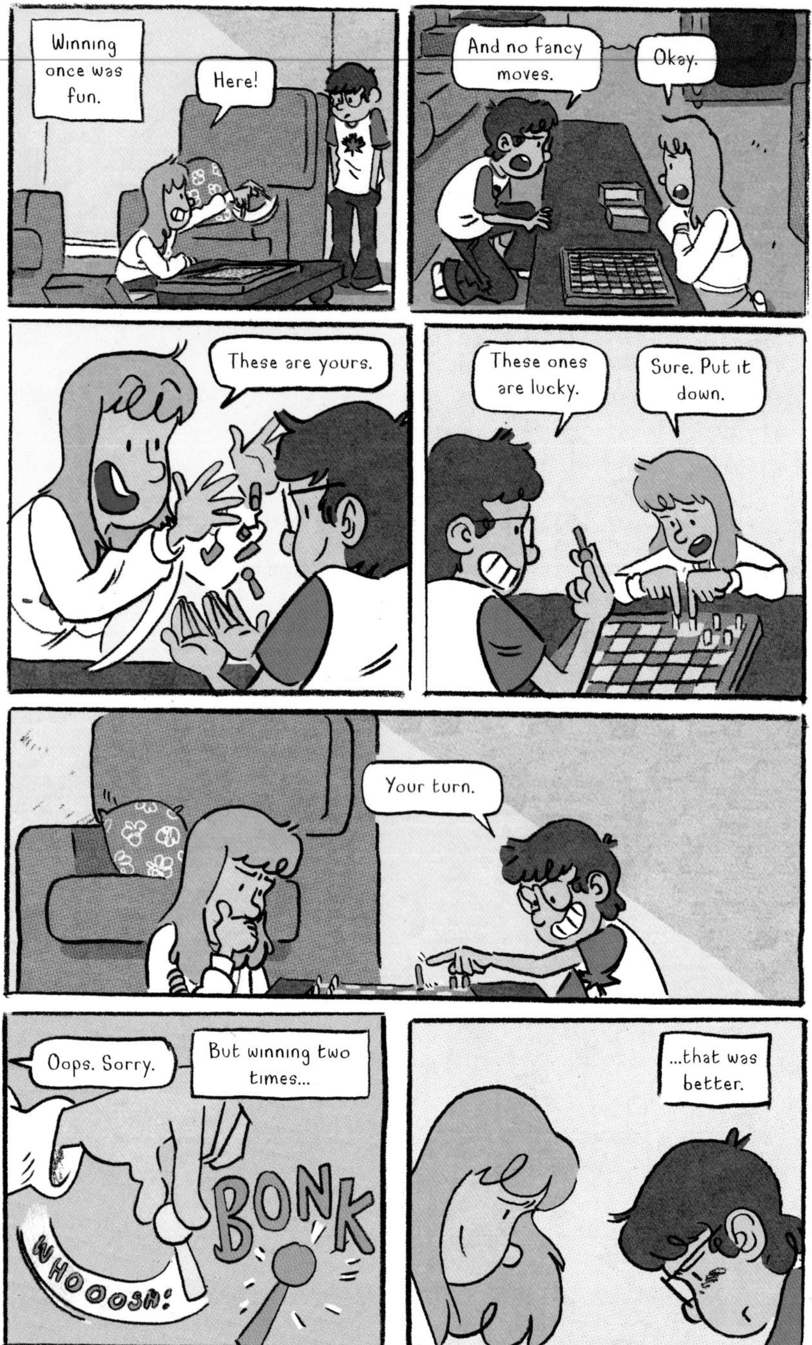

Winning once was fun.
Here!
And no fancy moves.
Okay.
These are yours.
These ones are lucky.
Sure. Put it down.
Your turn.
Oops. Sorry.
But winning two times...
WHOOOSH!
BONK
...that was better.

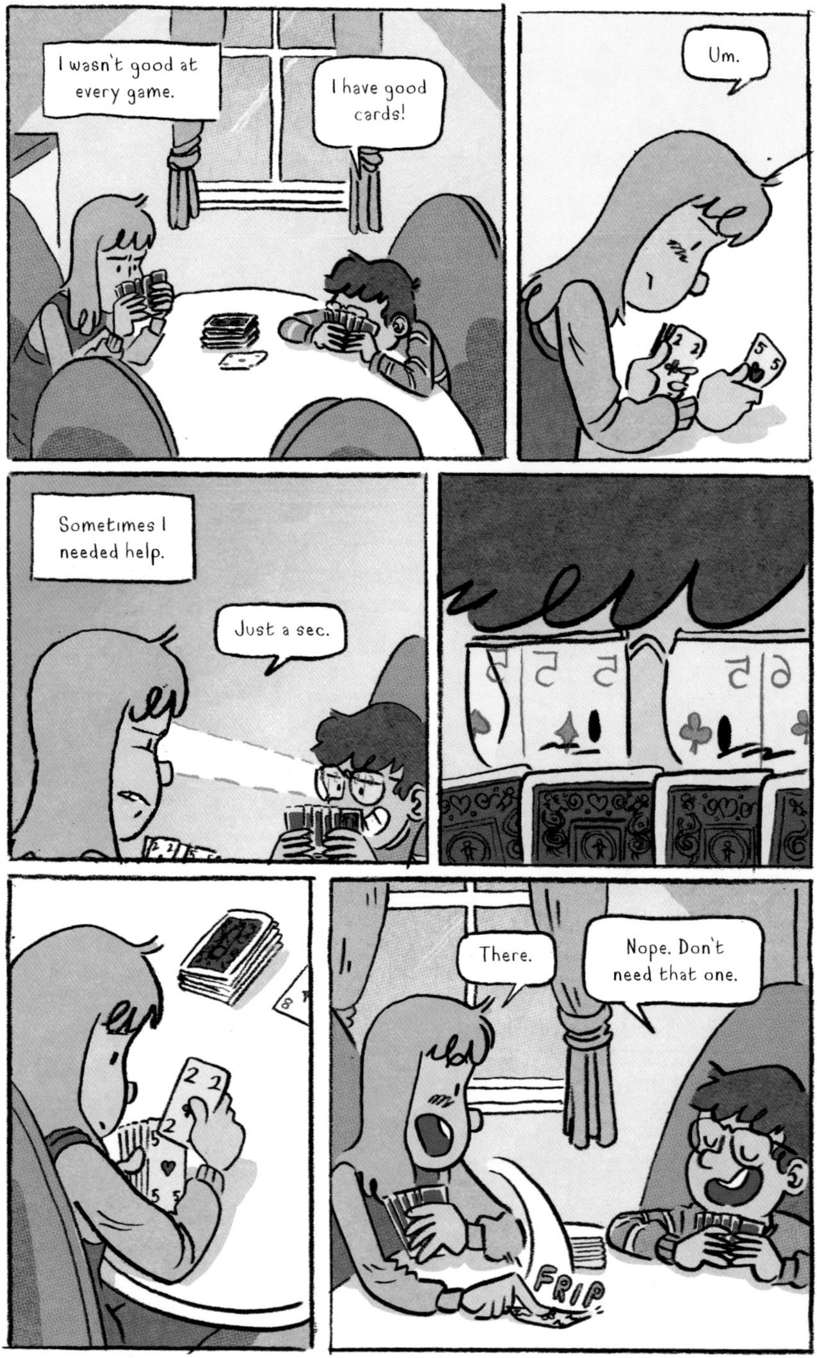
I wasn't good at every game.
I have good cards!
Um.
Sometimes I needed help.
Just a sec.
There.
Nope. Don't need that one.
FRIP

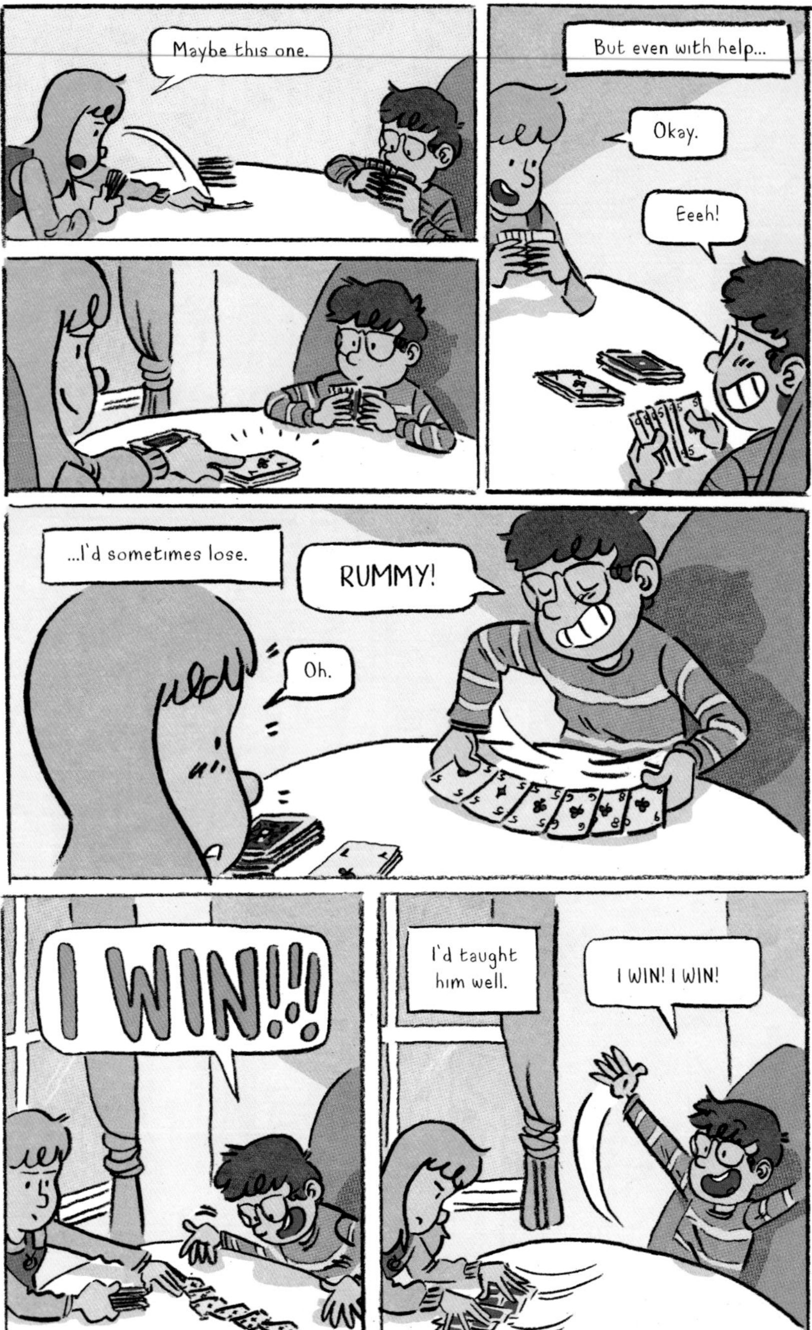

Maybe this one.
But even with help...
Okay.
Eeeh!
...I'd sometimes lose.
RUMMY!
Oh.
I WIN!!!
I'd taught him well.
I WIN! I WIN!

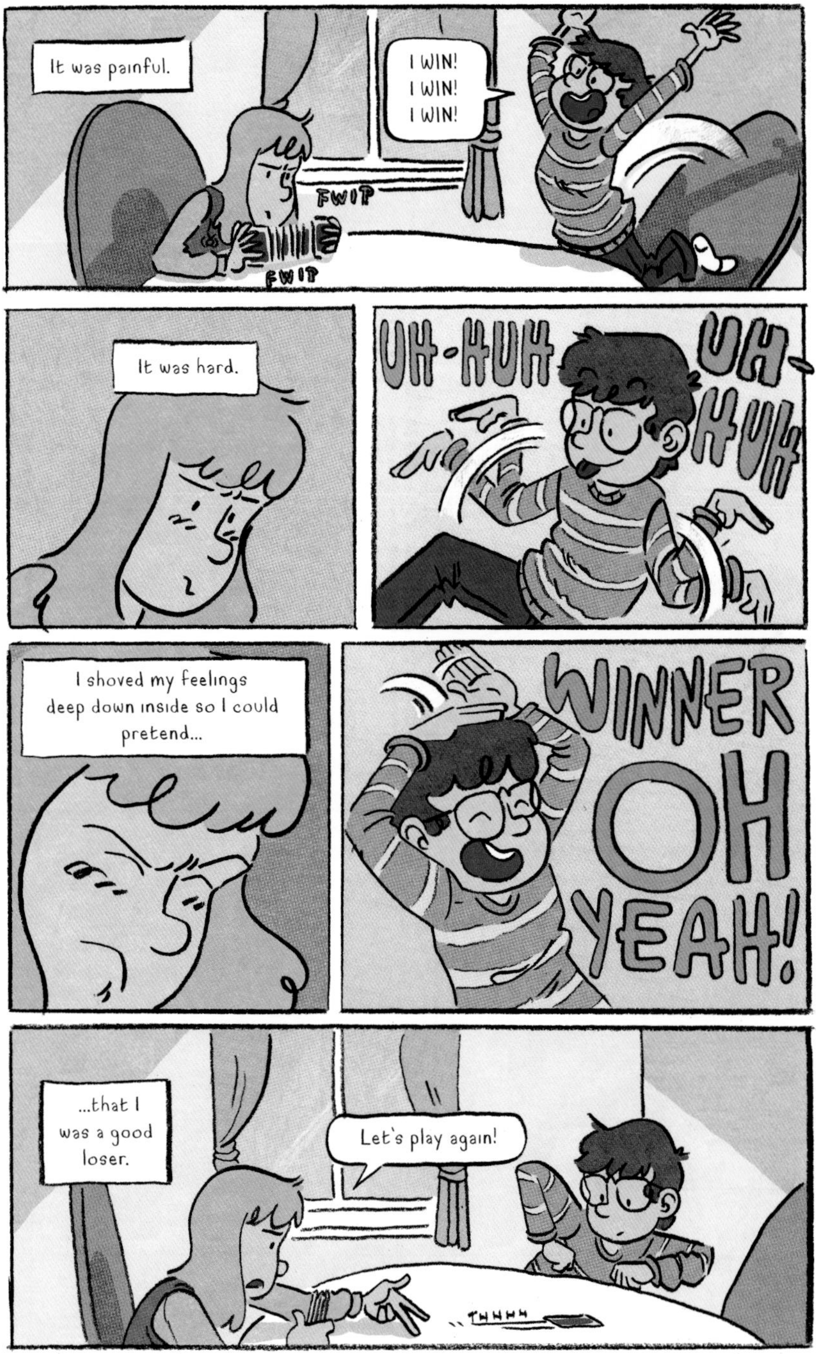
It was painful.
I WIN! I WIN! I WIN!
FWIP
FWIP
It was hard.
UH-HUH
UH-HUH
I shoved my feelings deep down inside so I could pretend...
WINNER
OH YEAH!
...that I was a good loser.
Let's play again!
THHHH

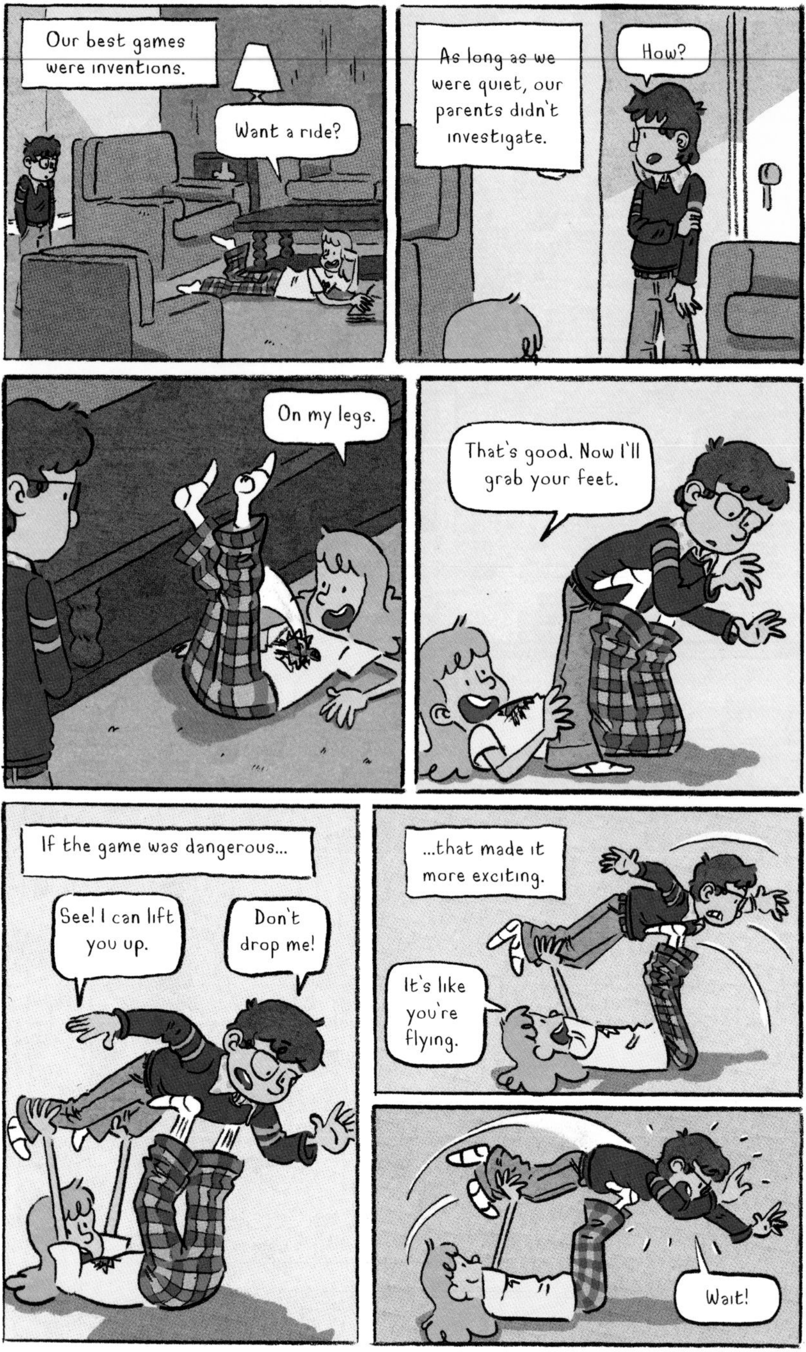
Our best games were inventions.
Want a ride?
As long as we were quiet, our parents didn't investigate.
How?
On my legs.
That's good. Now I'll grab your feet.
If the game was dangerous...
See! I can lift you up.
Don't drop me!
...that made it more exciting.
It's like you're flying.
Wait!

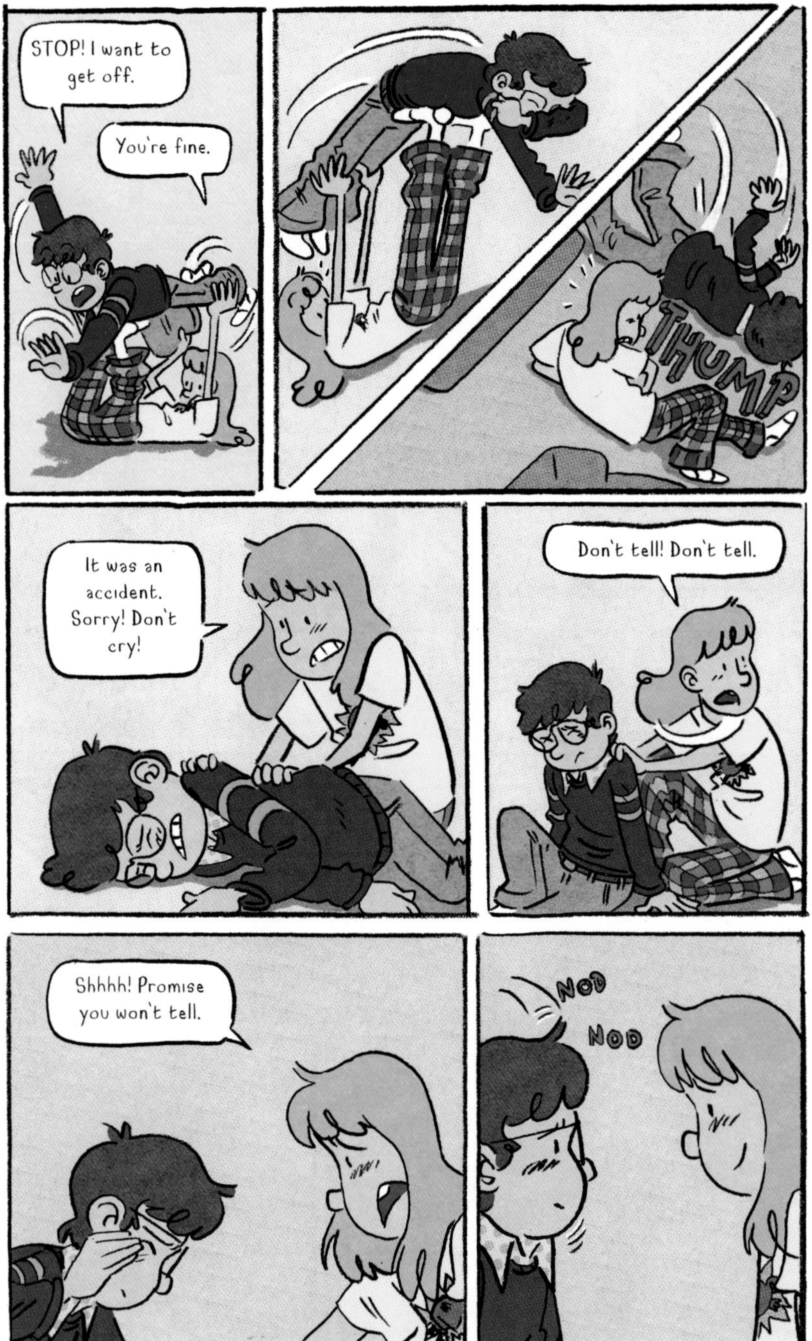
STOP! I want to get off.
You're fine.
THUMP
It was an accident. Sorry! Don't cry!
Don't tell! Don't tell.
Shhhh! Promise you won't tell.
NOD
NOD

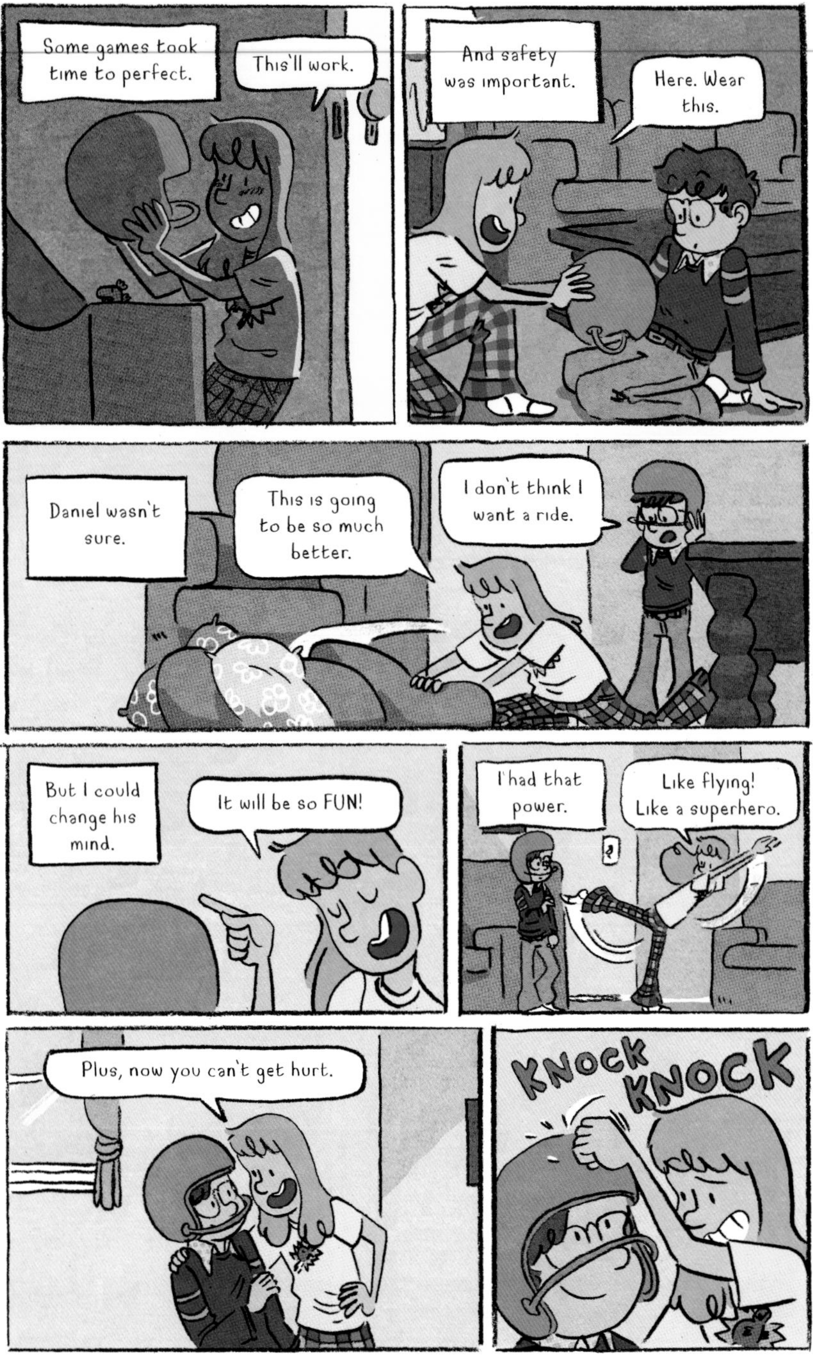
Some games took time to perfect.
This'll work.
And safety was important.
Here. Wear this.
Daniel wasn't sure.
This is going to be so much better.
I don't think I want a ride.
But I could change his mind.
It will be so FUN!
I had that power.
Like flying! Like a superhero.
Plus, now you can't get hurt.
KNOCK KNOCK

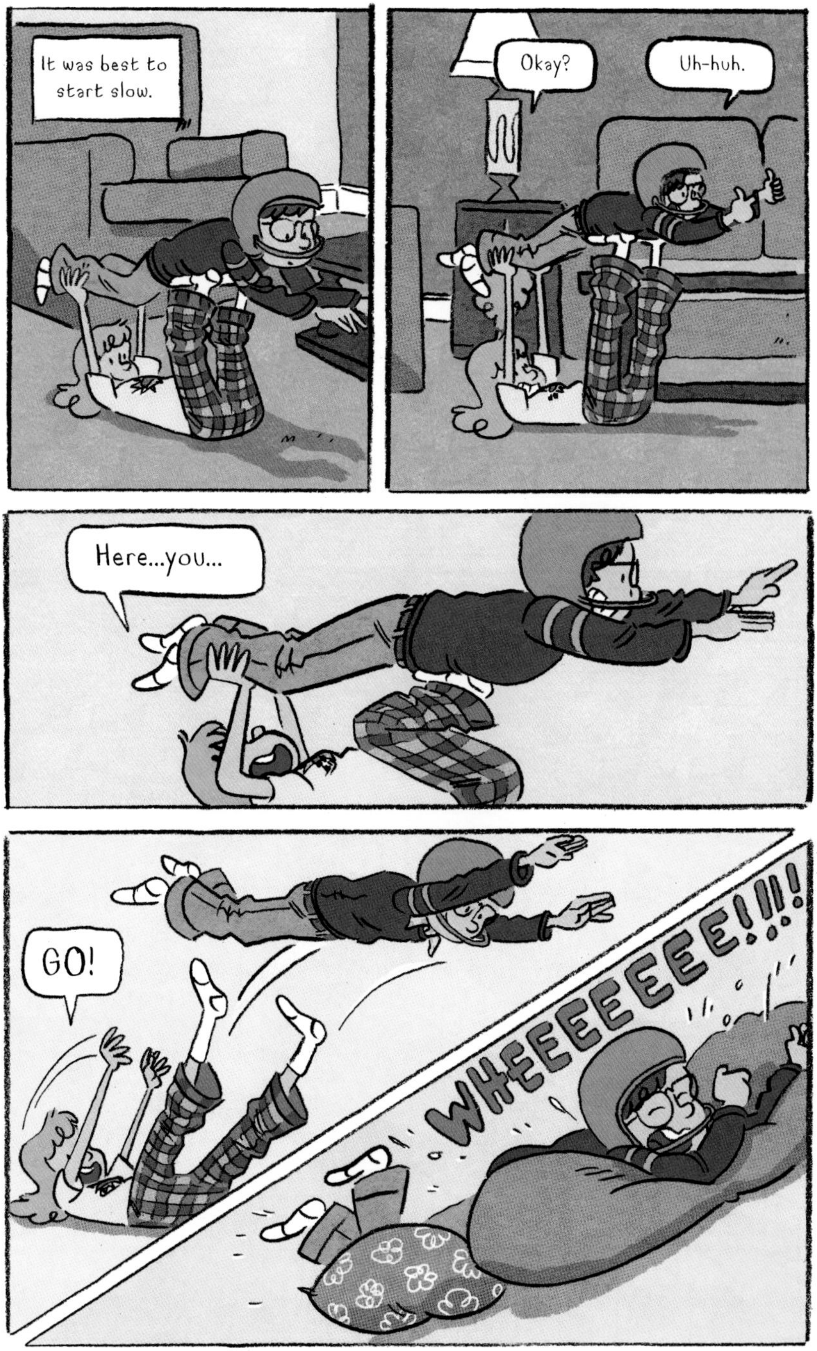
It was best to start slow.
Okay?
Uh-huh.
Here...you...
GO!
WHEEEEEEEE!!!!

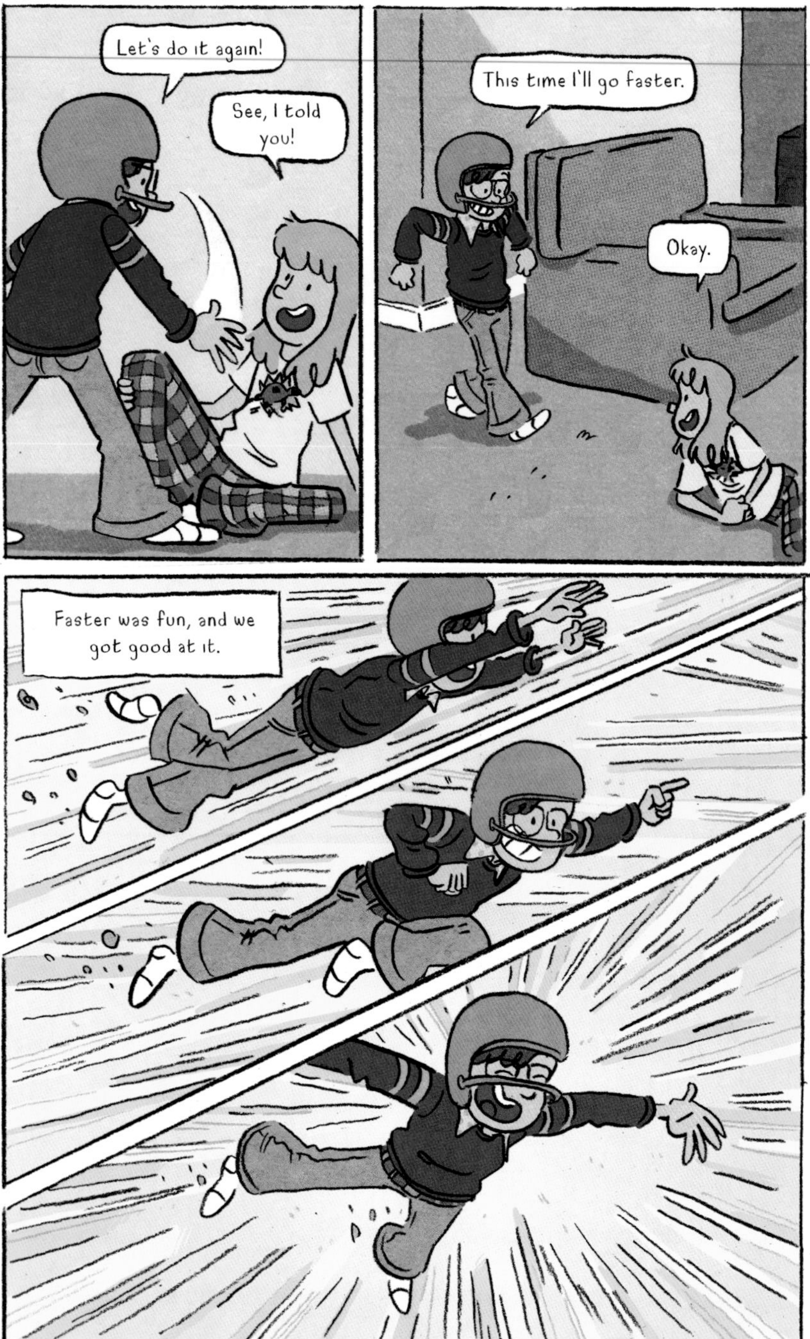
Let's do it again!
See, I told you!
This time I'll go faster.
Okay.
Faster was fun, and we got good at it.

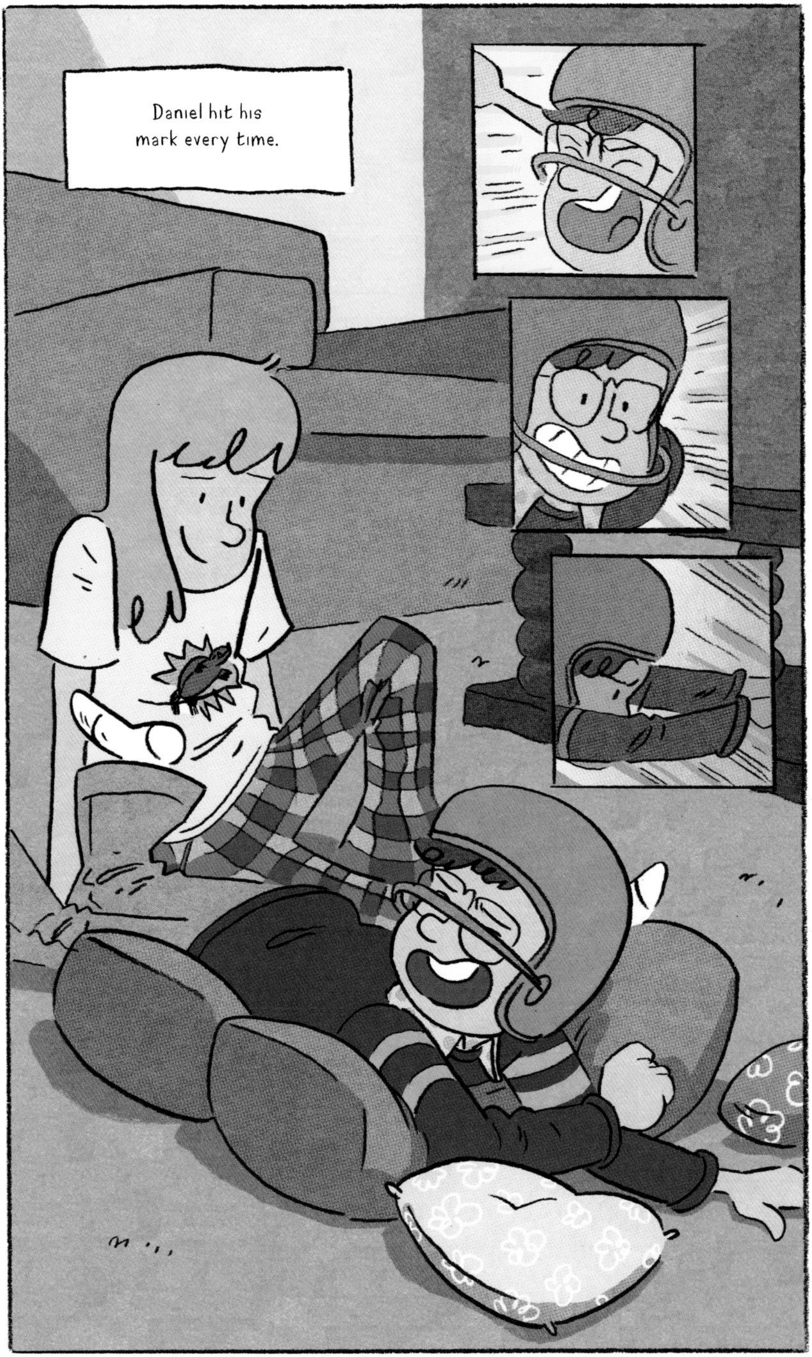
Daniel hit his mark every time.

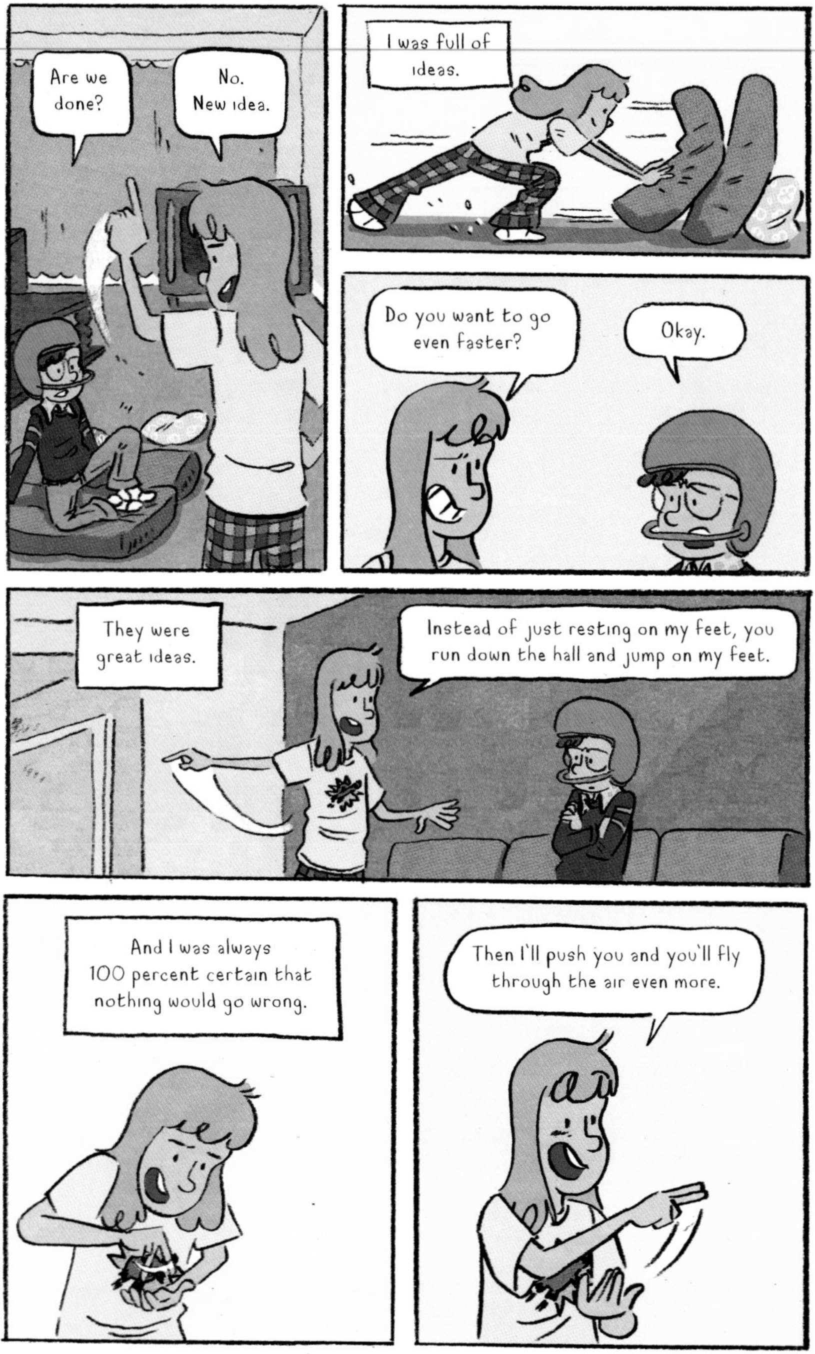
Are we done?
No. New idea.
I was full of ideas.
Do you want to go even faster?
Okay.
They were great ideas.
Instead of just resting on my feet, you run down the hall and jump on my feet.
And I was always 100 percent certain that nothing would go wrong.
Then I'll push you and you'll fly through the air even more.

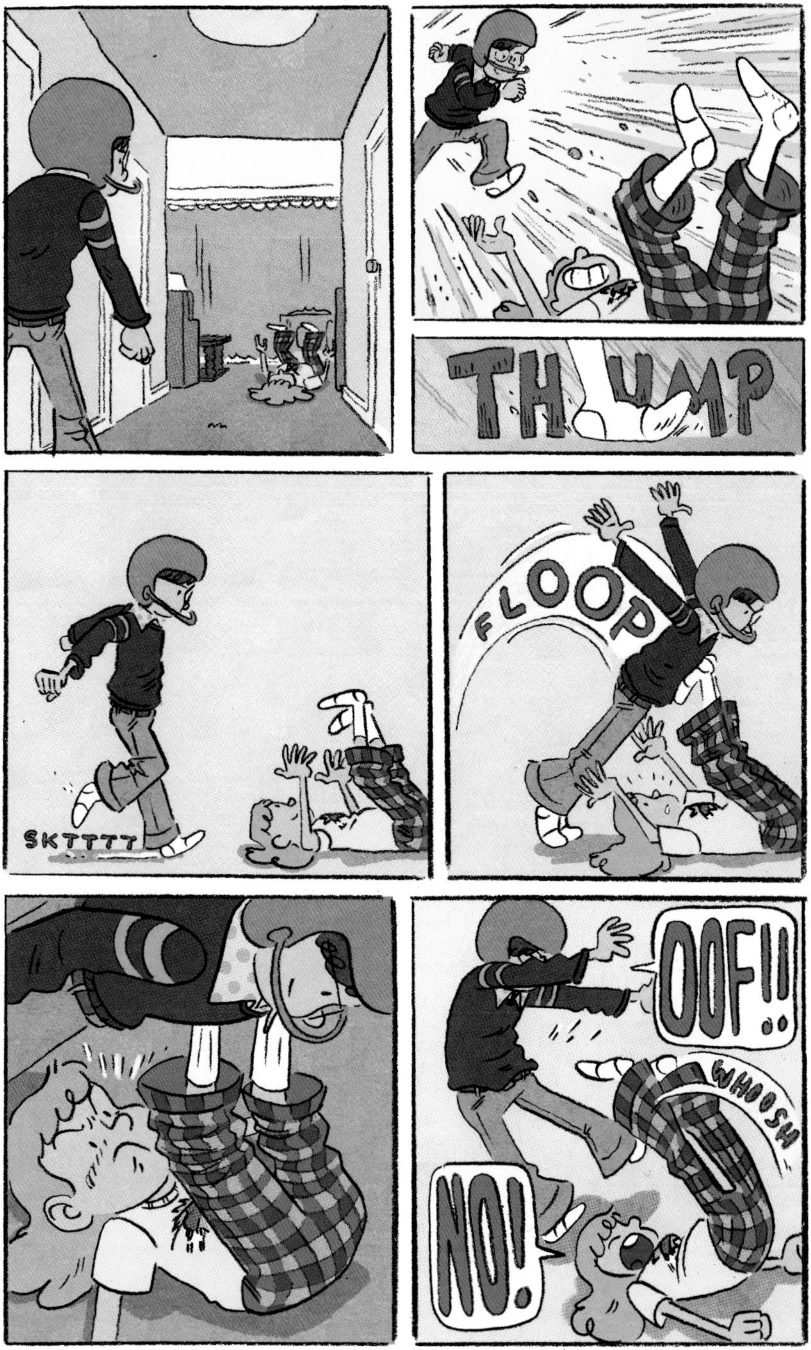
THUMP
SKTTTT
FLOOP
OOF!!
WHOOSH
NO!

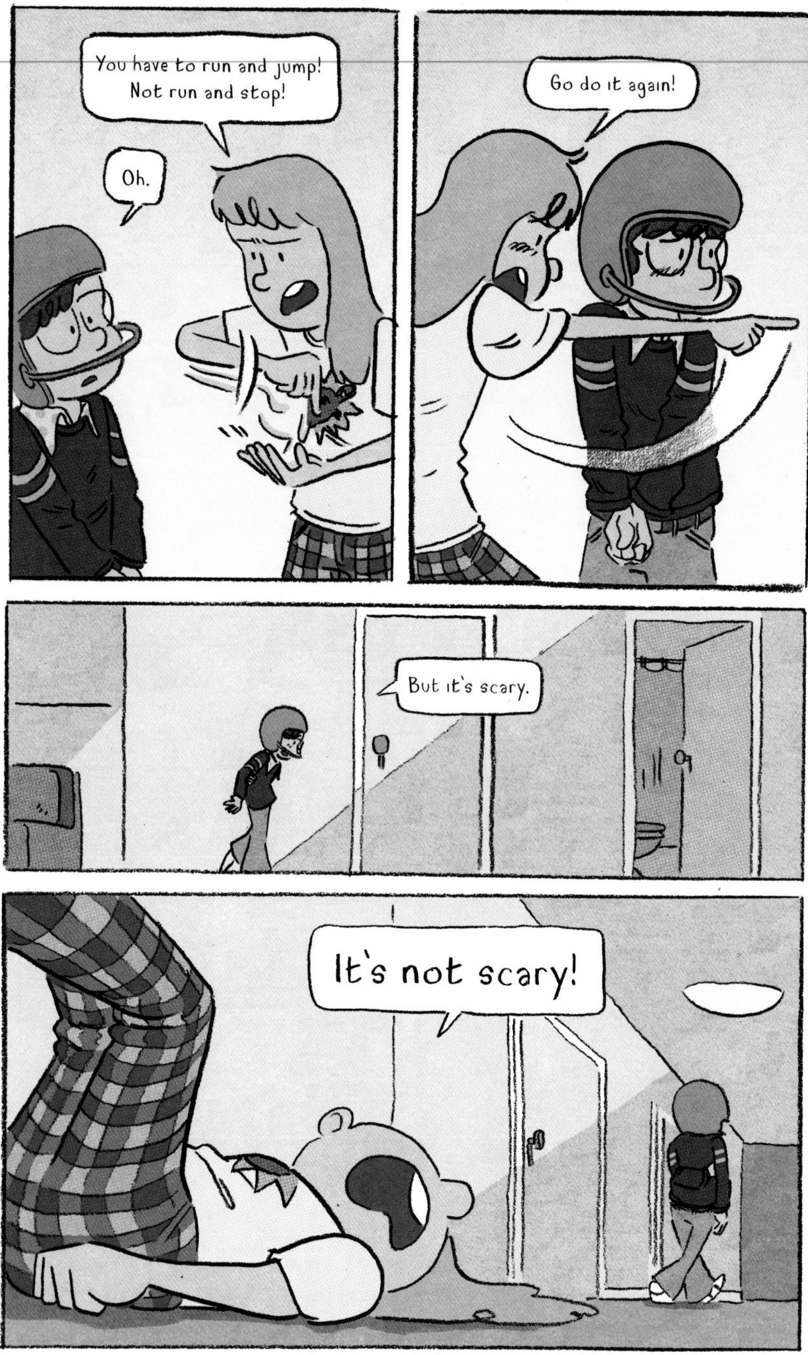
You have to run and jump! Not run and stop!
Oh.
Go do it again!
But it's scary.
It's not scary!

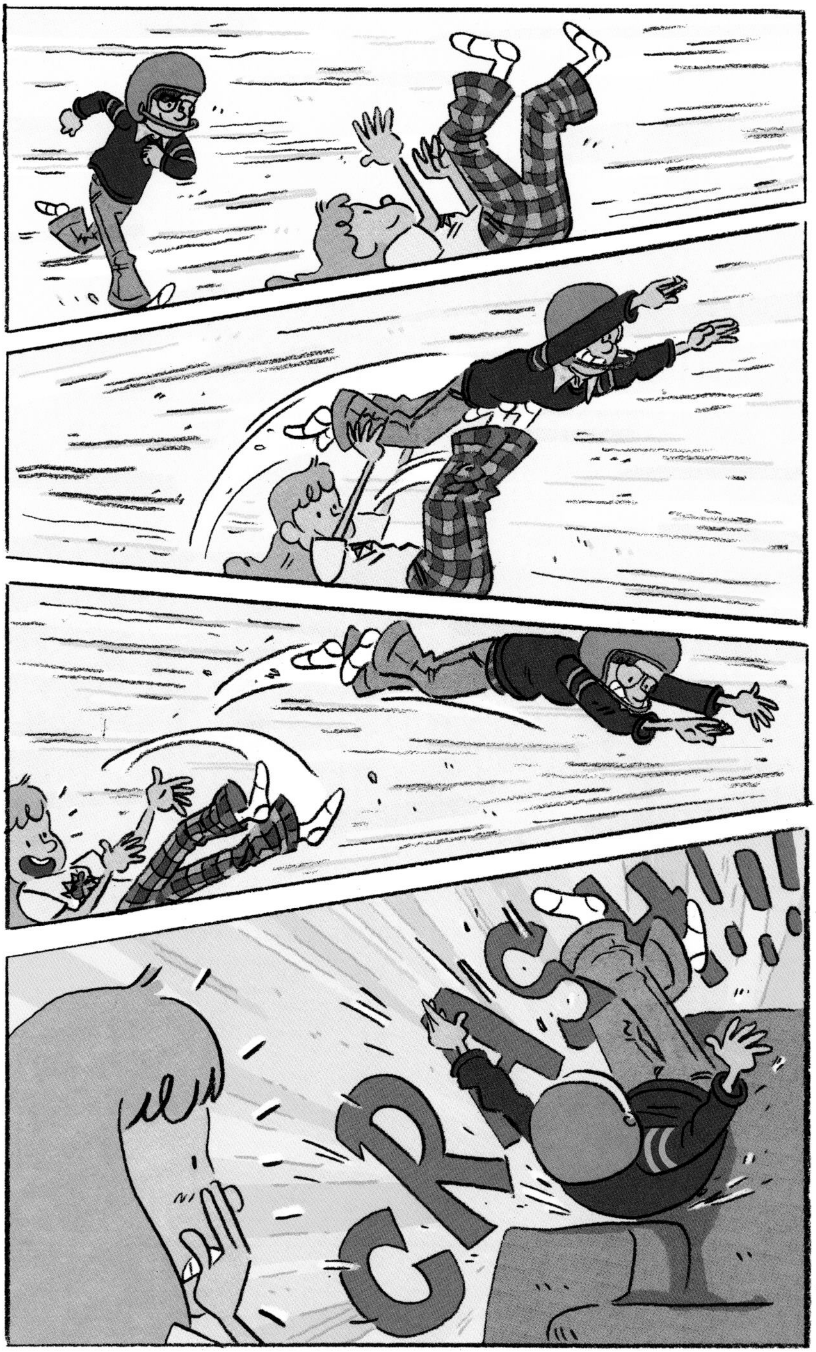
CRASH!!!

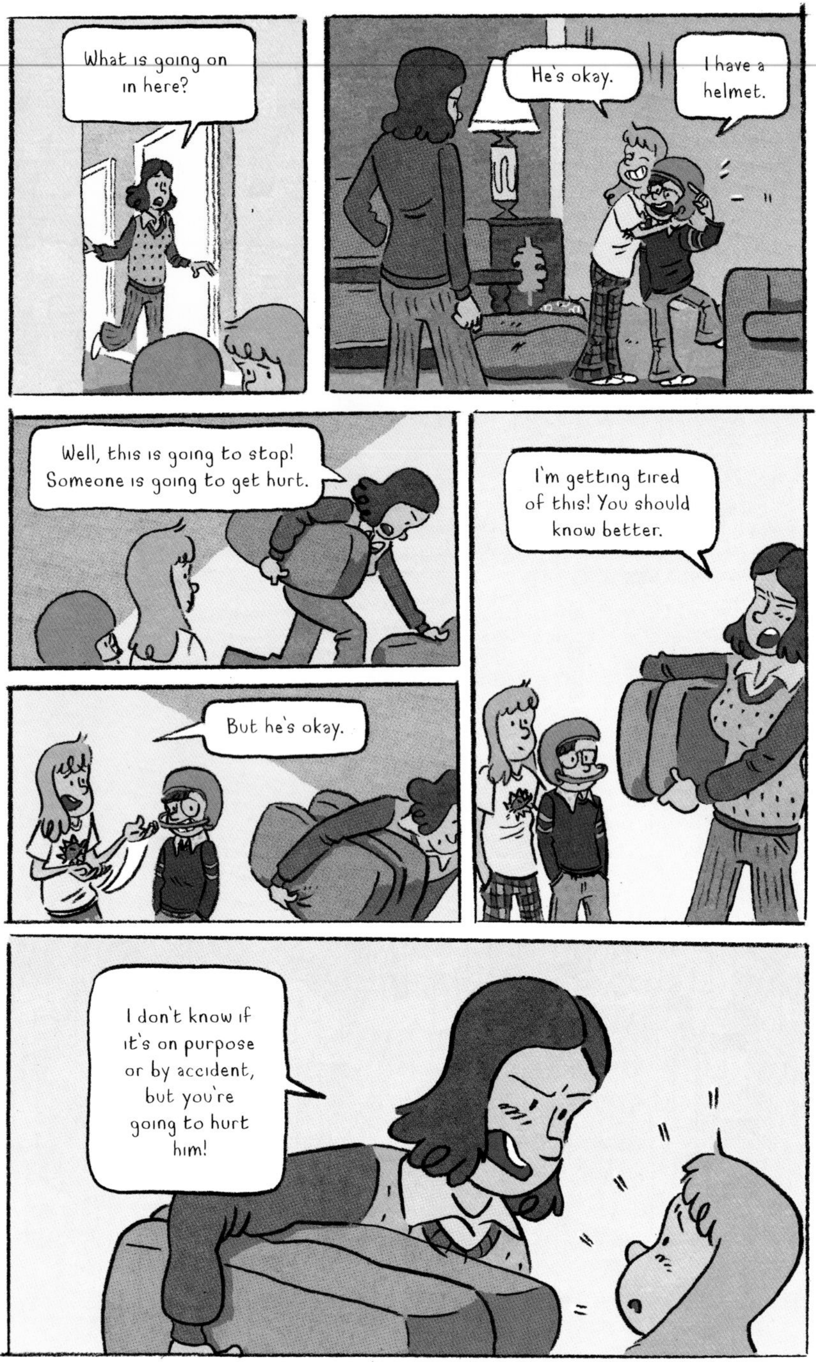

What is going on in here?
He's okay.
I have a helmet.
Well, this is going to stop! Someone is going to get hurt.
I'm getting tired of this! You should know better.
But he's okay.
I don't know if it's on purpose or by accident, but you're going to hurt him!

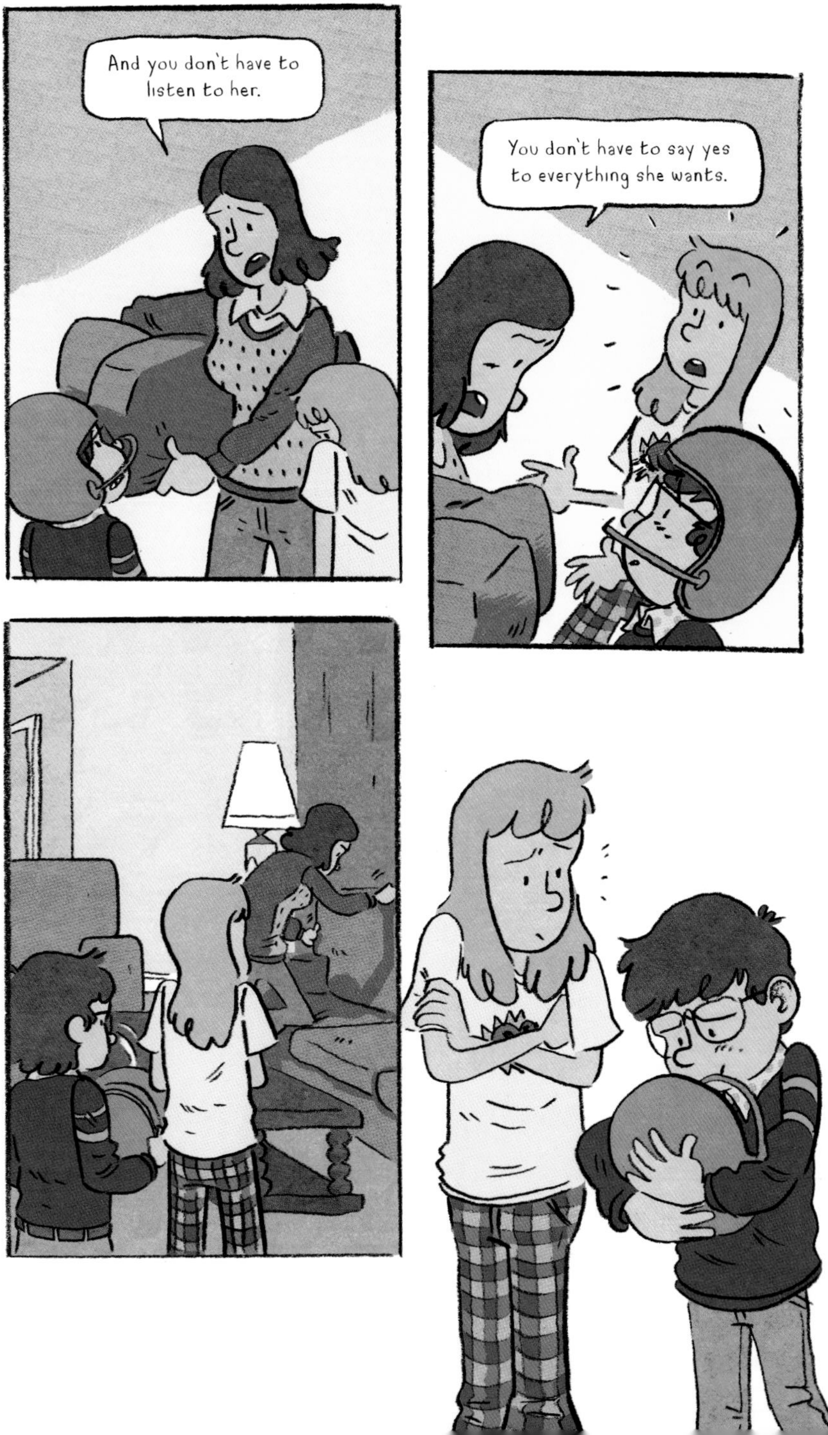
And you don't have to listen to her.
You don't have to say yes to everything she wants.

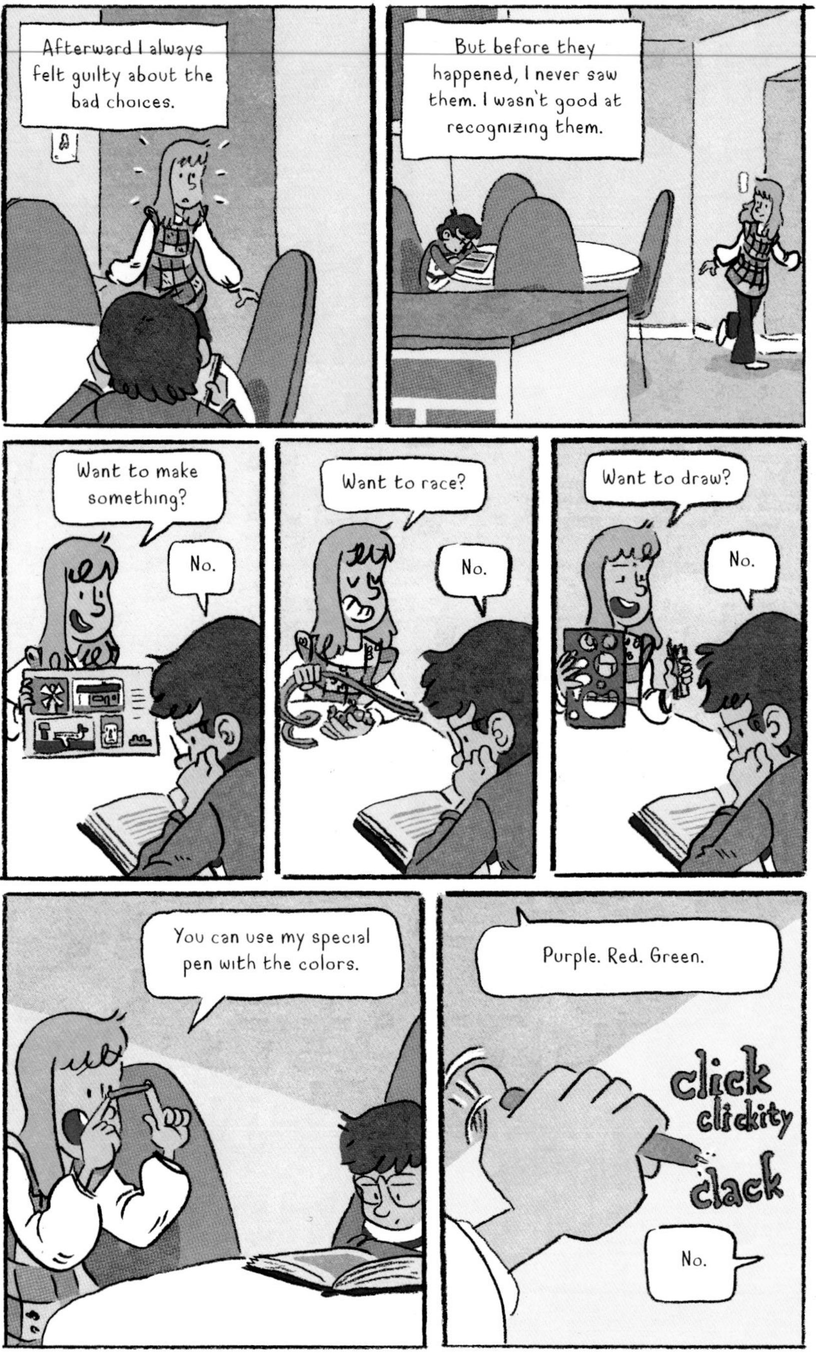

Afterward I always felt guilty about the bad choices.
But before they happened, I never saw them. I wasn't good at recognizing them.
Want to make something?
No.
Want to race?
No.
Want to draw?
No.
You can use my special pen with the colors.
Purple. Red. Green.
click clickity clack
No.

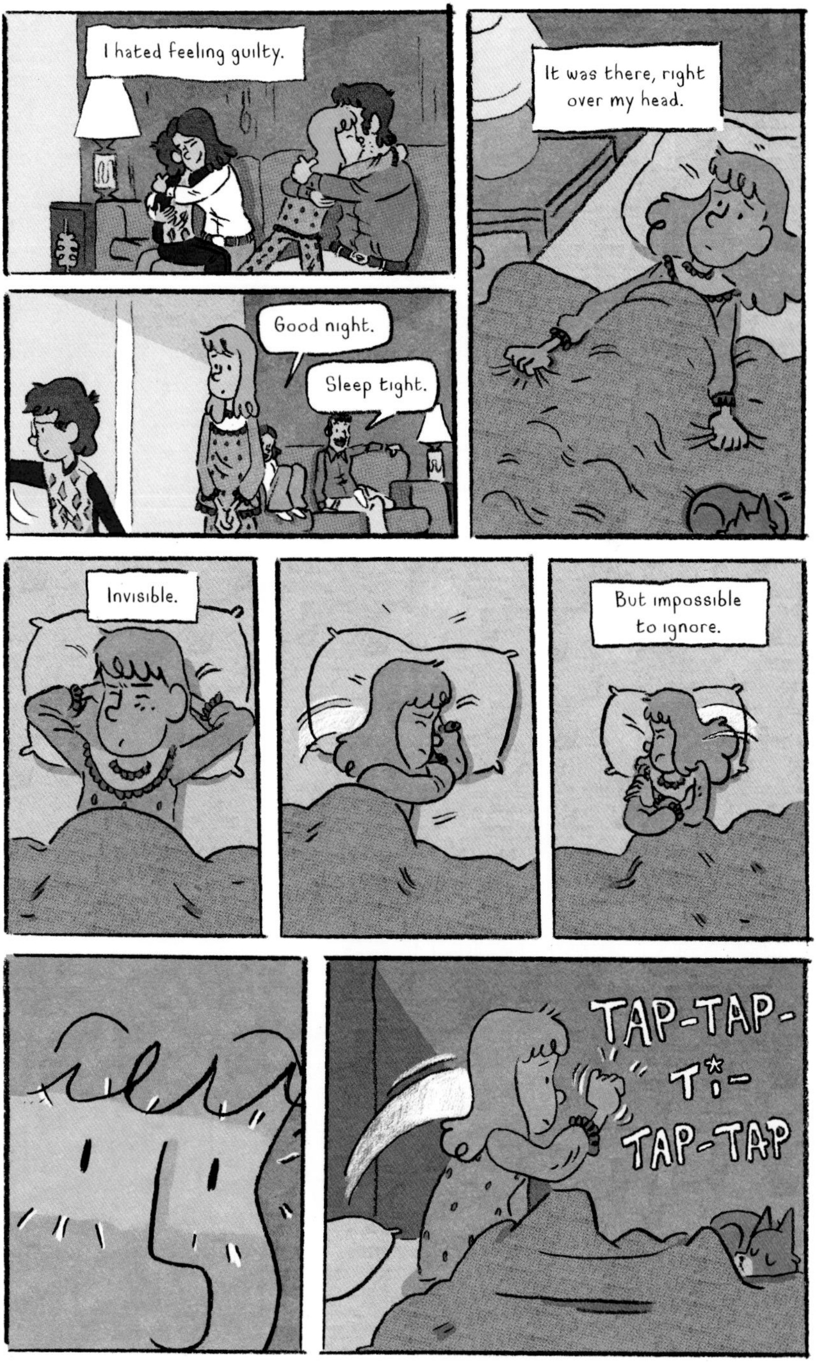
I hated feeling guilty.
It was there, right over my head.
Good night.
Sleep tight.
Invisible.
But impossible to ignore.
TAP-TAP-
T*i-
TAP-TAP

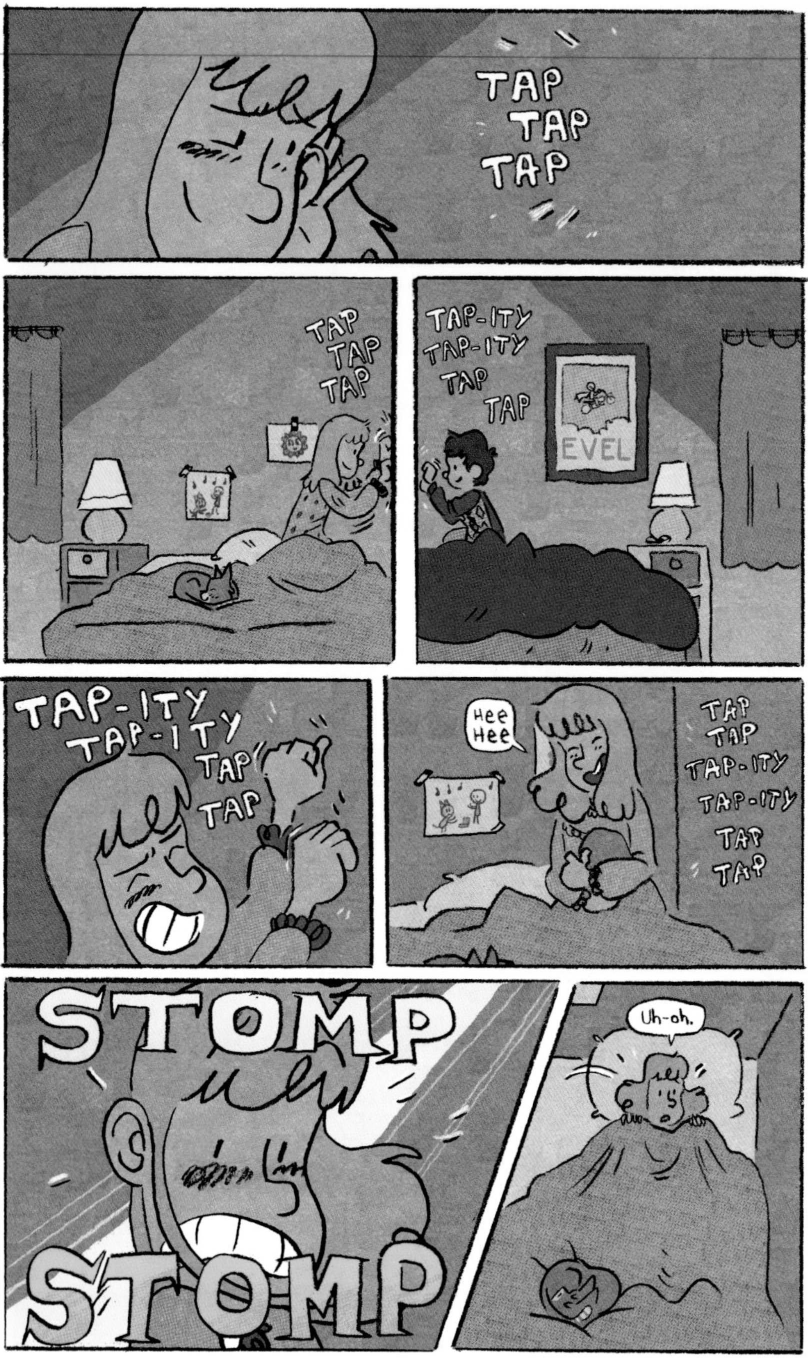
TAP
TAP
TAP
TAP
TAP
TAP
TAP-ITY
TAP-ITY
TAP
TAP
TAP-ITY
TAP-ITY
TAP
TAP
EVEL
Hee Hee
TAP
TAP
TAP-ITY
TAP-ITY
TAP
TAP
STOMP
STOMP
Uh-oh.

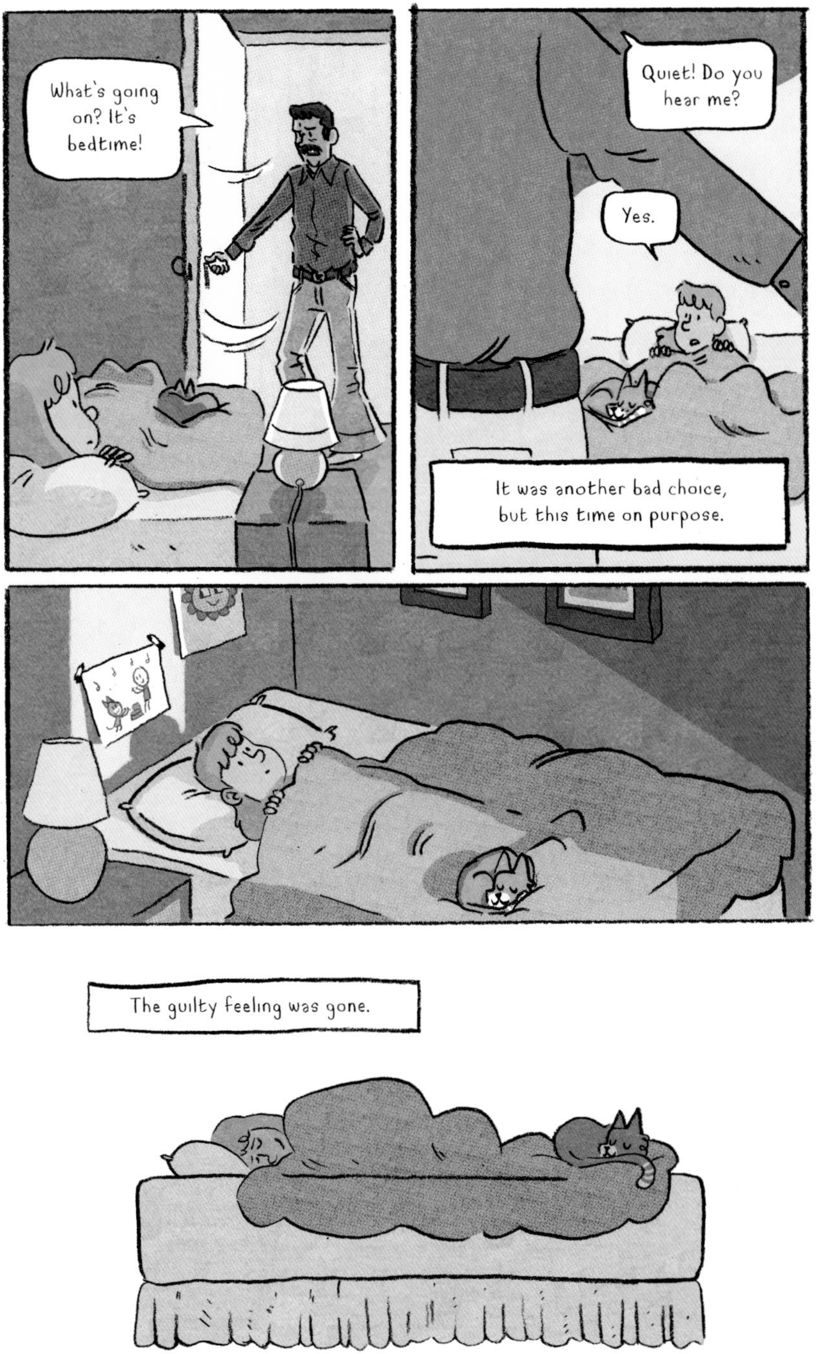
What's going on? It's bedtime!
Quiet! Do you hear me?
Yes.
It was another bad choice, but this time on purpose.
The guilty feeling was gone.

The Power of Blame

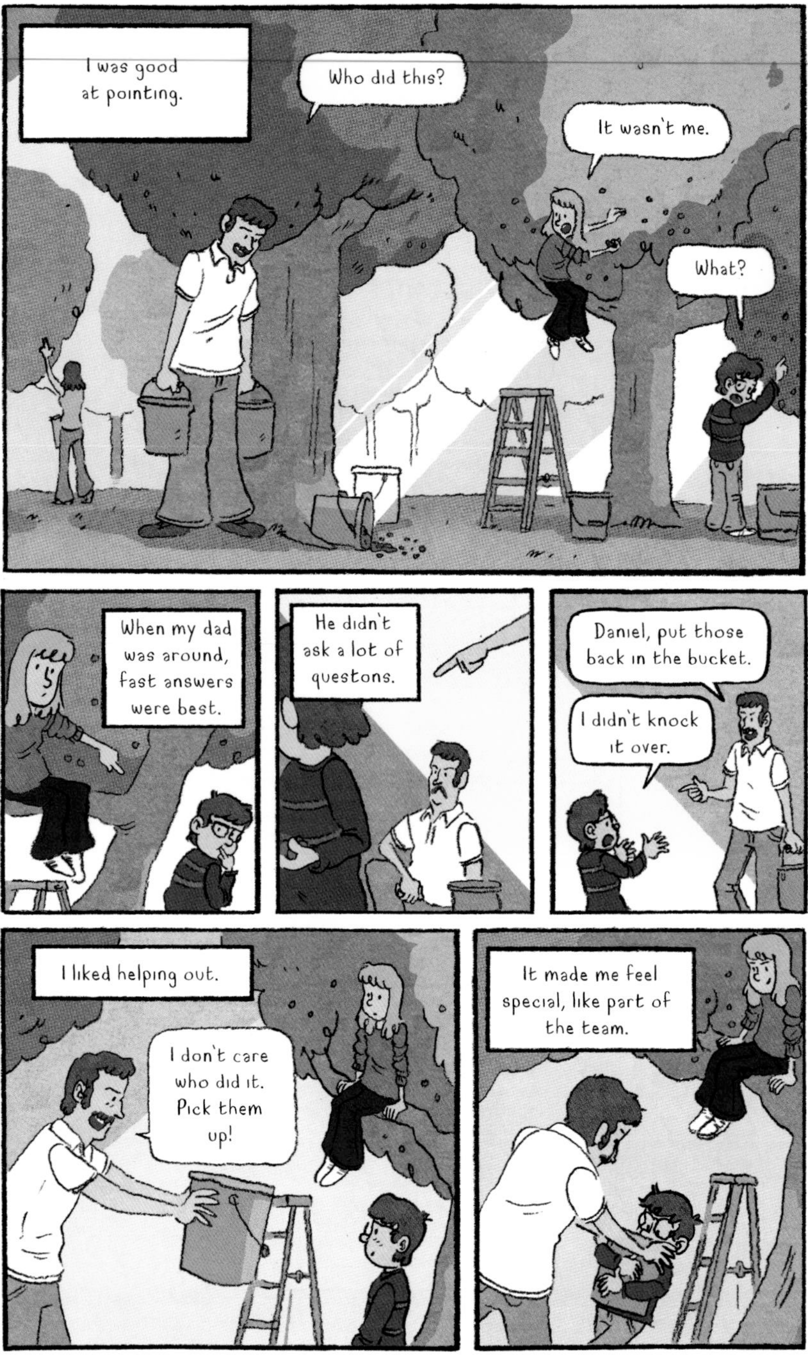
I was good at pointing.
Who did this?
It wasn't me.
What?
When my dad was around, fast answers were best.
He didn't ask a lot of questons.
Daniel, put those back in the bucket.
I didn't knock it over.
I liked helping out.
I don't care who did it. Pick them up!
It made me feel special, like part of the team.

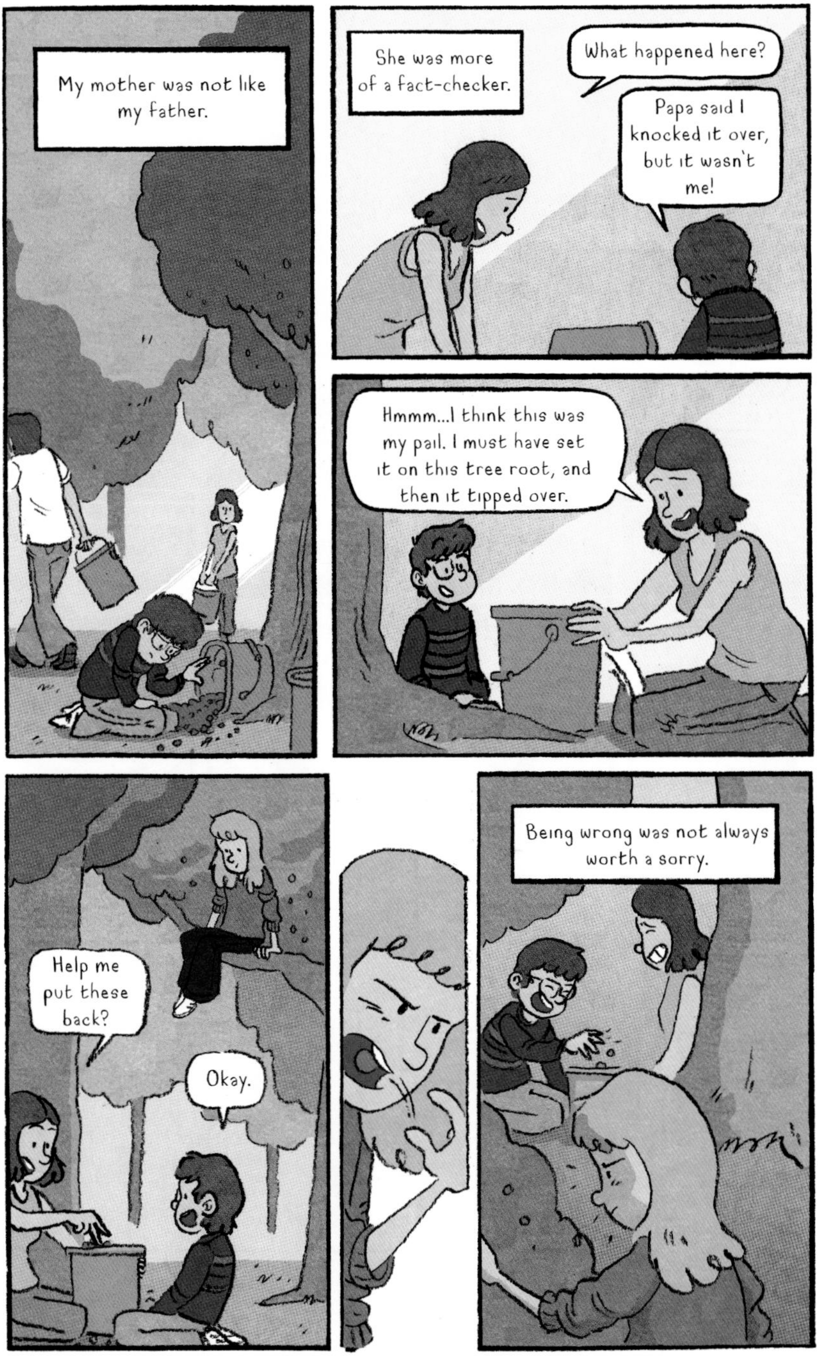
My mother was not like my father.
She was more of a fact-checker.
What happened here?
Papa said I knocked it over, but it wasn't me!
Hmmm...I think this was my pail. I must have set it on this tree root, and then it tipped over.
Help me put these back?
Okay.
Being wrong was not always worth a sorry.

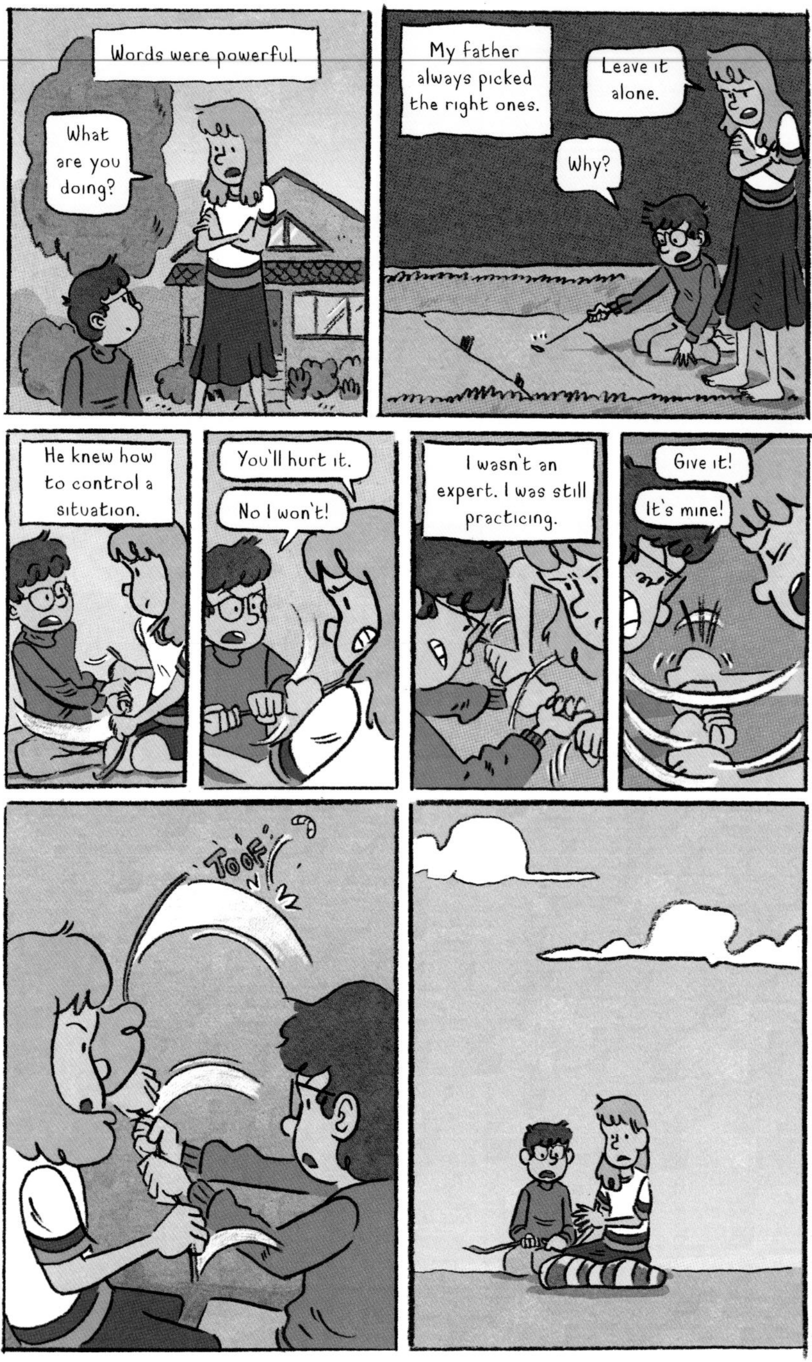
Words were powerful.
What are you doing?
My father always picked the right ones.
Leave it alone.
Why?
He knew how to control a situation.
You'll hurt it.
No I won't!
I wasn't an expert. I was still practicing.
Give it!
It's mine!
TOOF

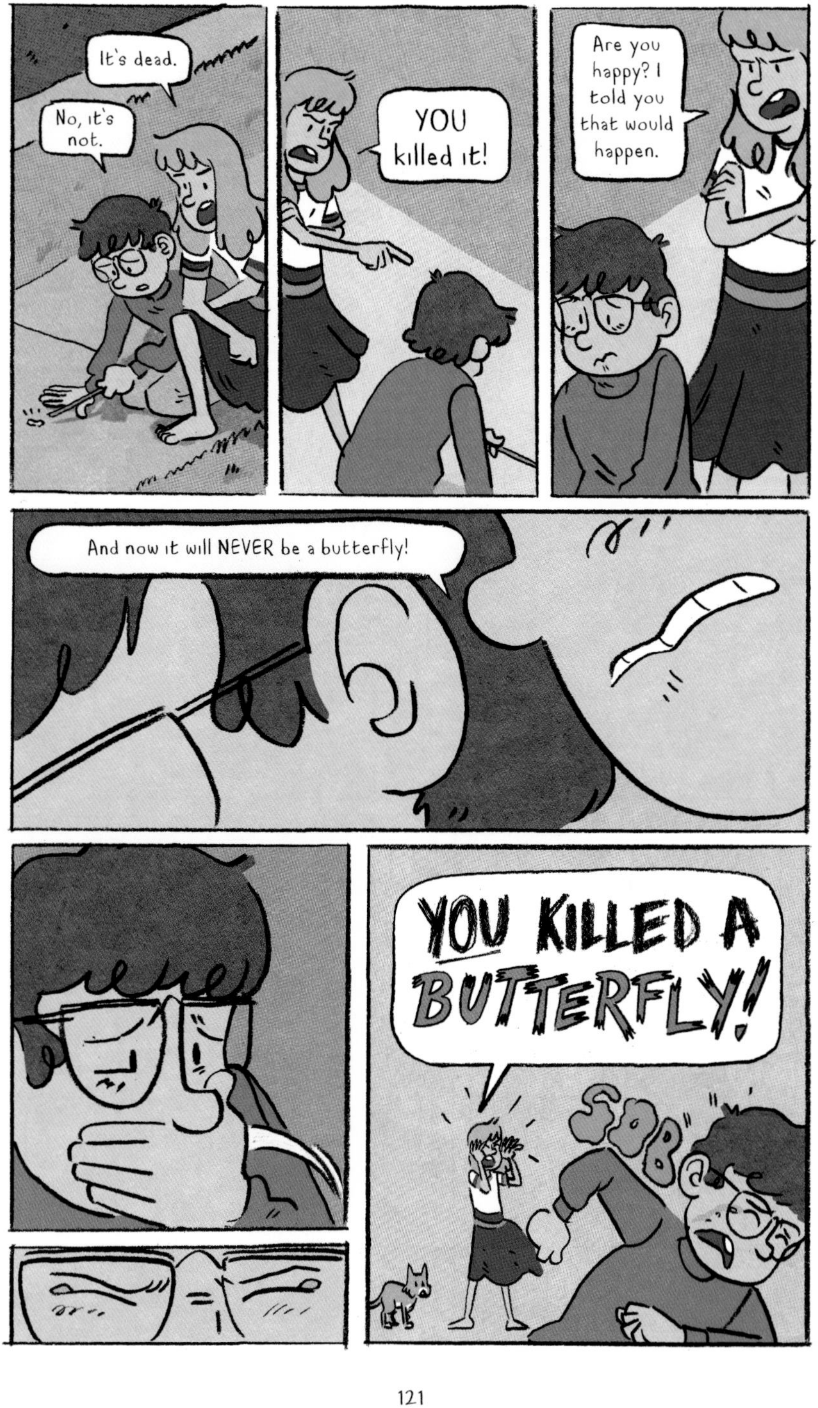
It's dead.
No, it's not.
YOU killed it!
Are you happy? I told you that would happen.
And now it will NEVER be a butterfly!
YOU KILLED A BUTTERFLY!
SOB

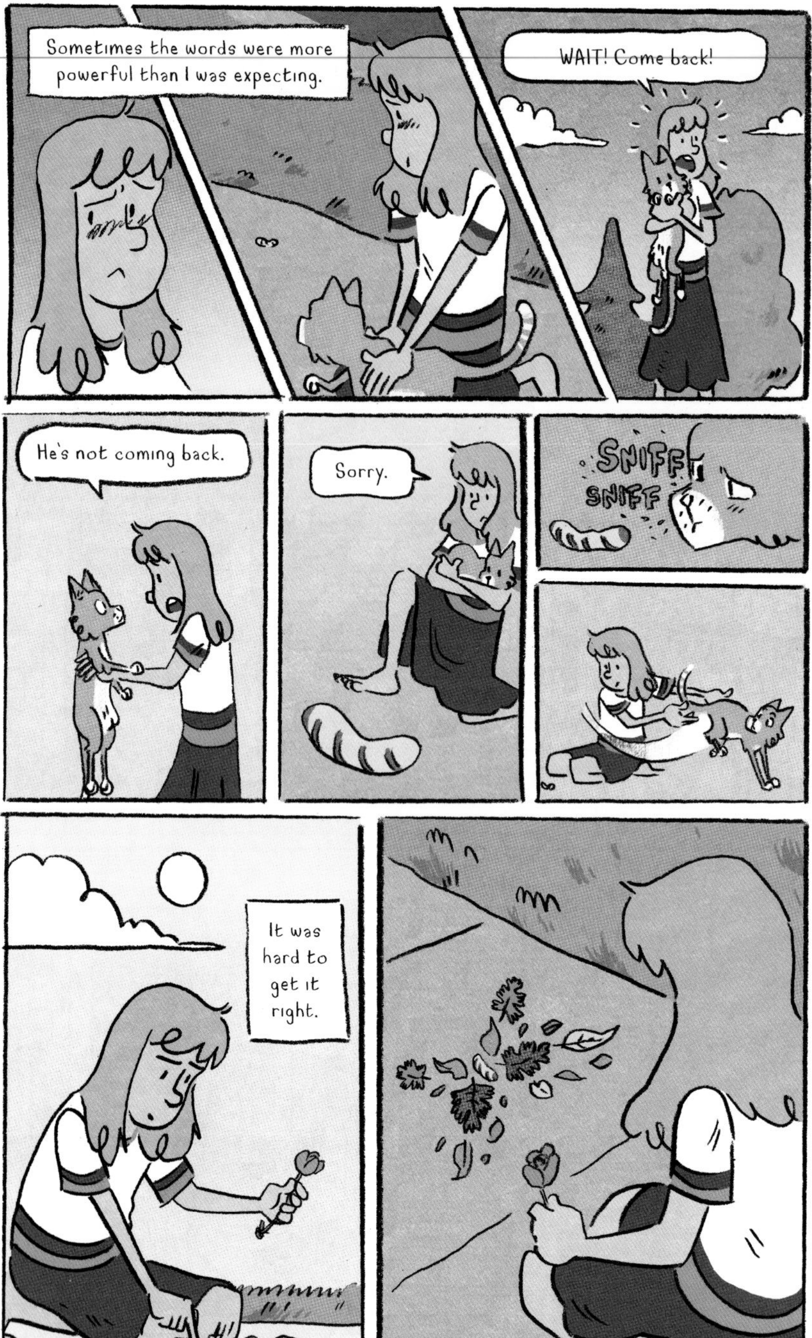
Sometimes the words were more powerful than I was expecting.
WAIT! Come back!
He's not coming back.
Sorry.
SNIFF
SNIFF
It was hard to get it right.

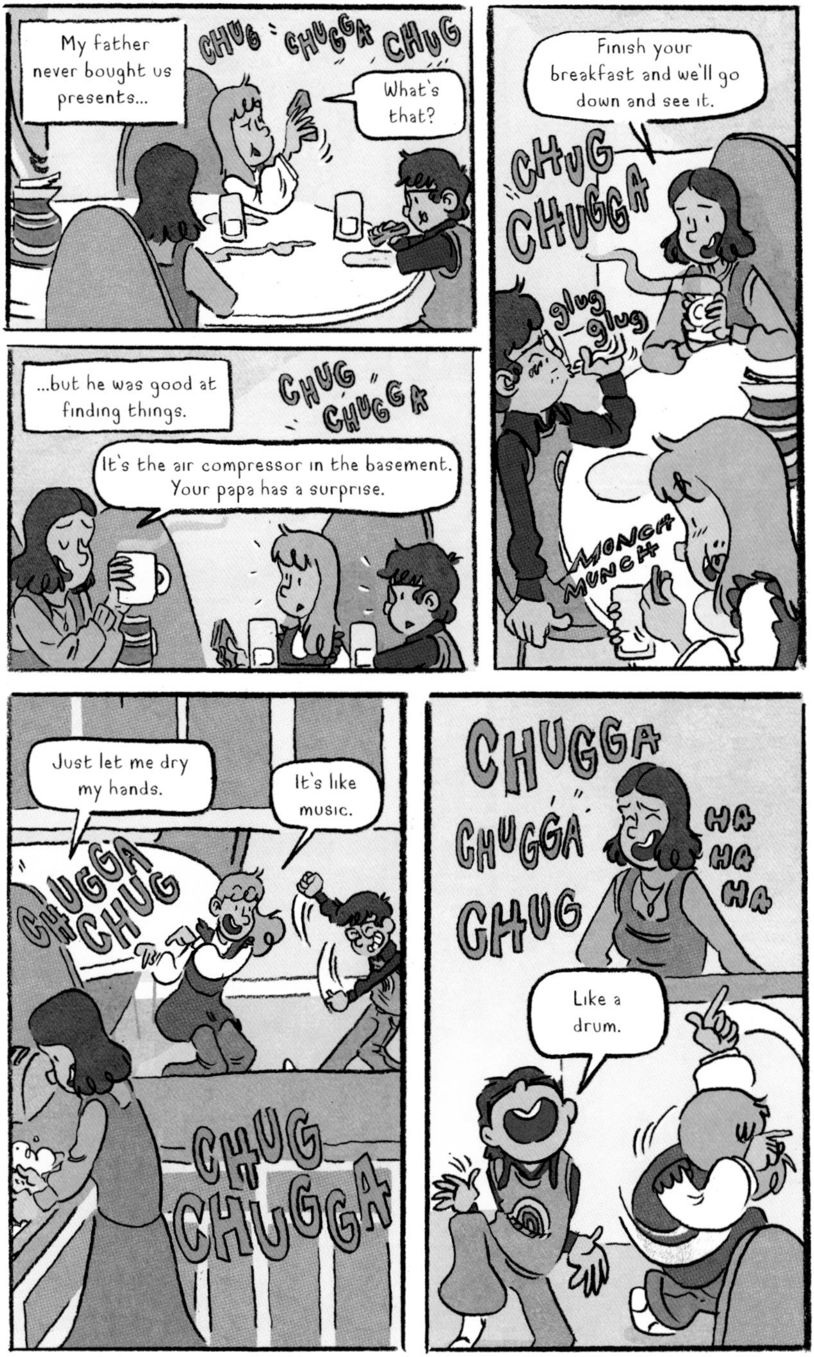
My father never bought us presents...
CHUG CHUGGA CHUG
What's that?
Finish your breakfast and we'll go down and see it.
CHUG CHUGGA
glug glug
MUNCH MUNCH
...but he was good at finding things.
CHUG CHUGGA
It's the air compressor in the basement. Your papa has a surprise.
Just let me dry my hands.
It's like music.
CHUGGA CHUG
CHUG CHUGGA
CHUGGA CHUGGA CHUG
HA HA HA
Like a drum.

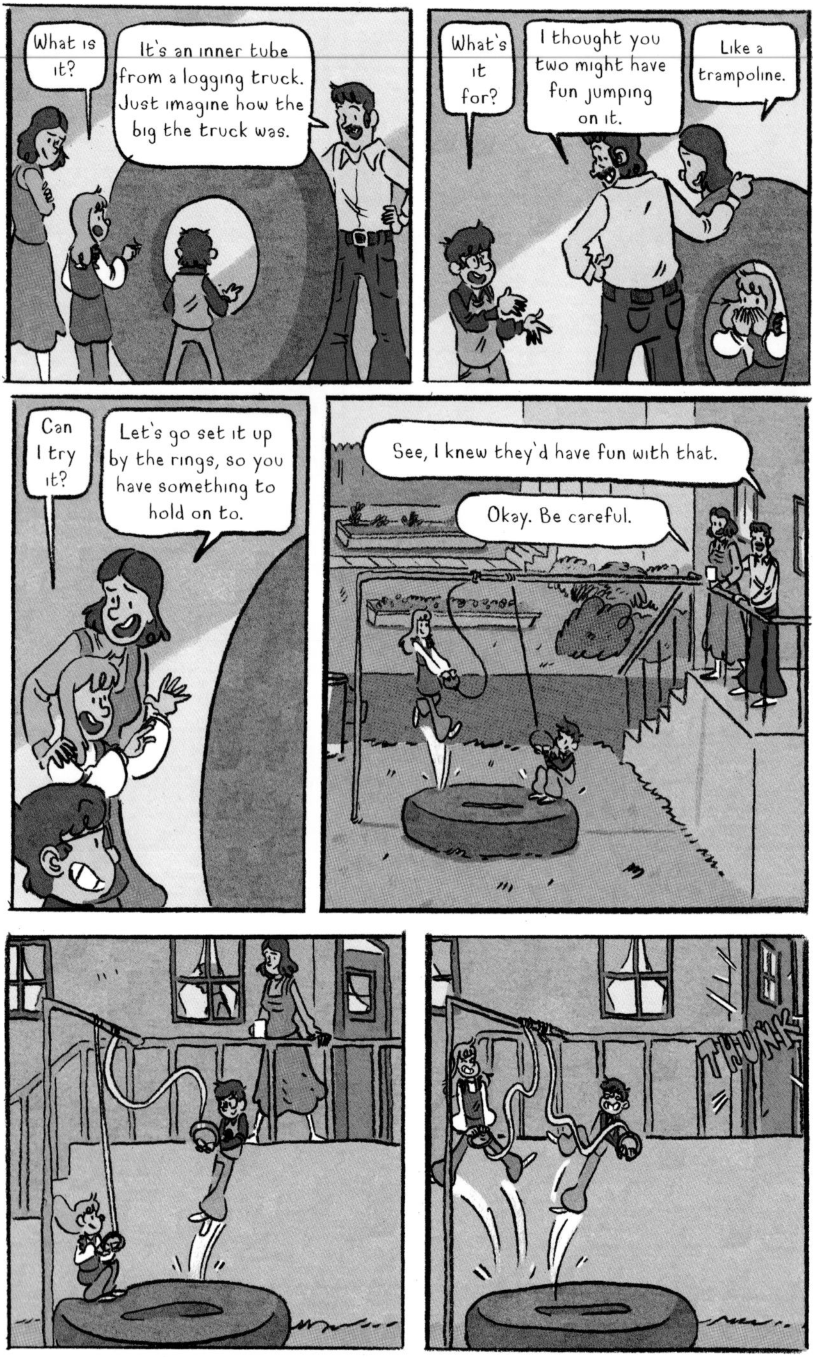
What is it?
It's an inner tube from a logging truck. Just imagine how the big the truck was.
What's it for?
I thought you two might have fun jumping on it.
Like a trampoline.
Can I try it?
Let's go set it up by the rings, so you have something to hold on to.
See, I knew they'd have fun with that.
Okay. Be careful.
THUNK

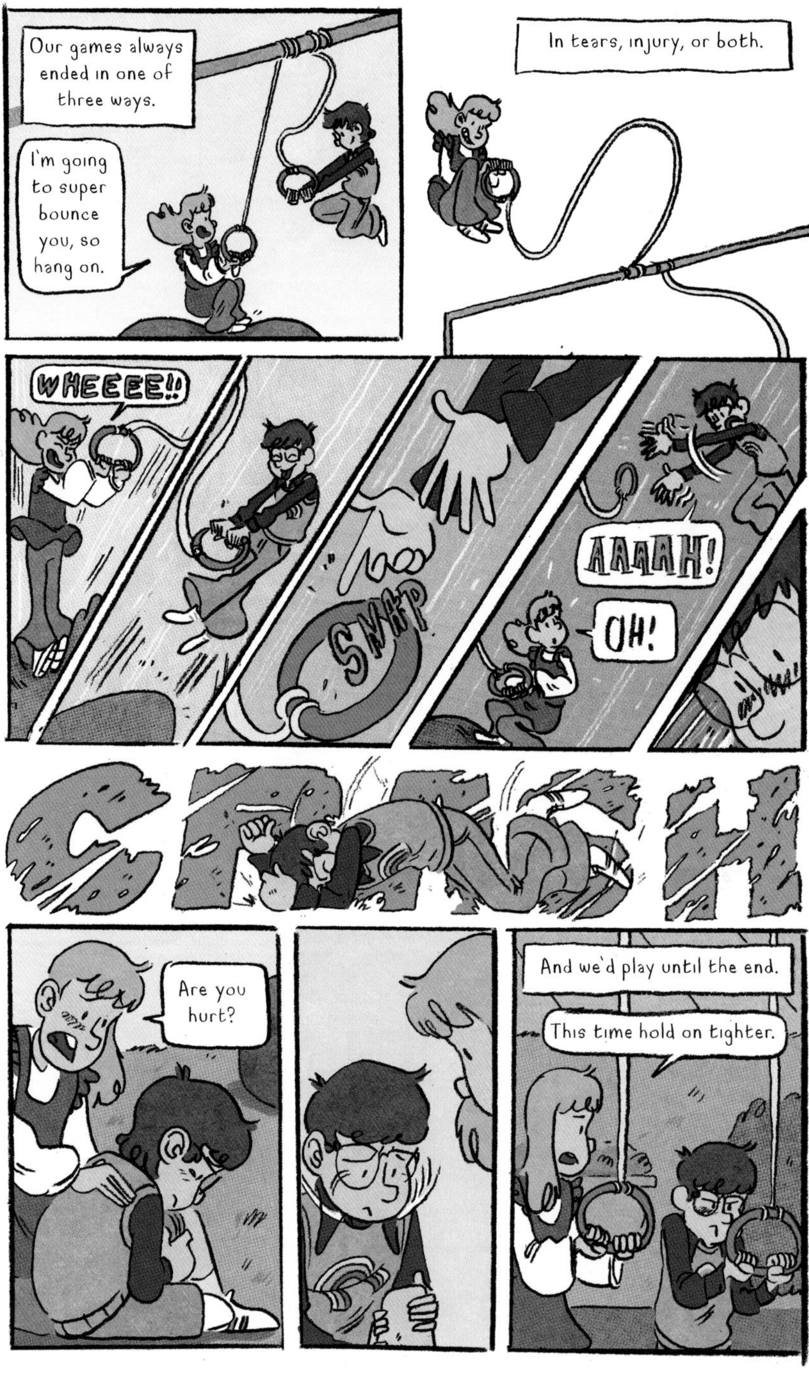
Our games always ended in one of three ways.
I'm going to super bounce you, so hang on.
In tears, injury, or both.
WHEEEE!!
SNAP
AAAAH!
OH!
CRASH
Are you hurt?
And we'd play until the end.
This time hold on tighter.

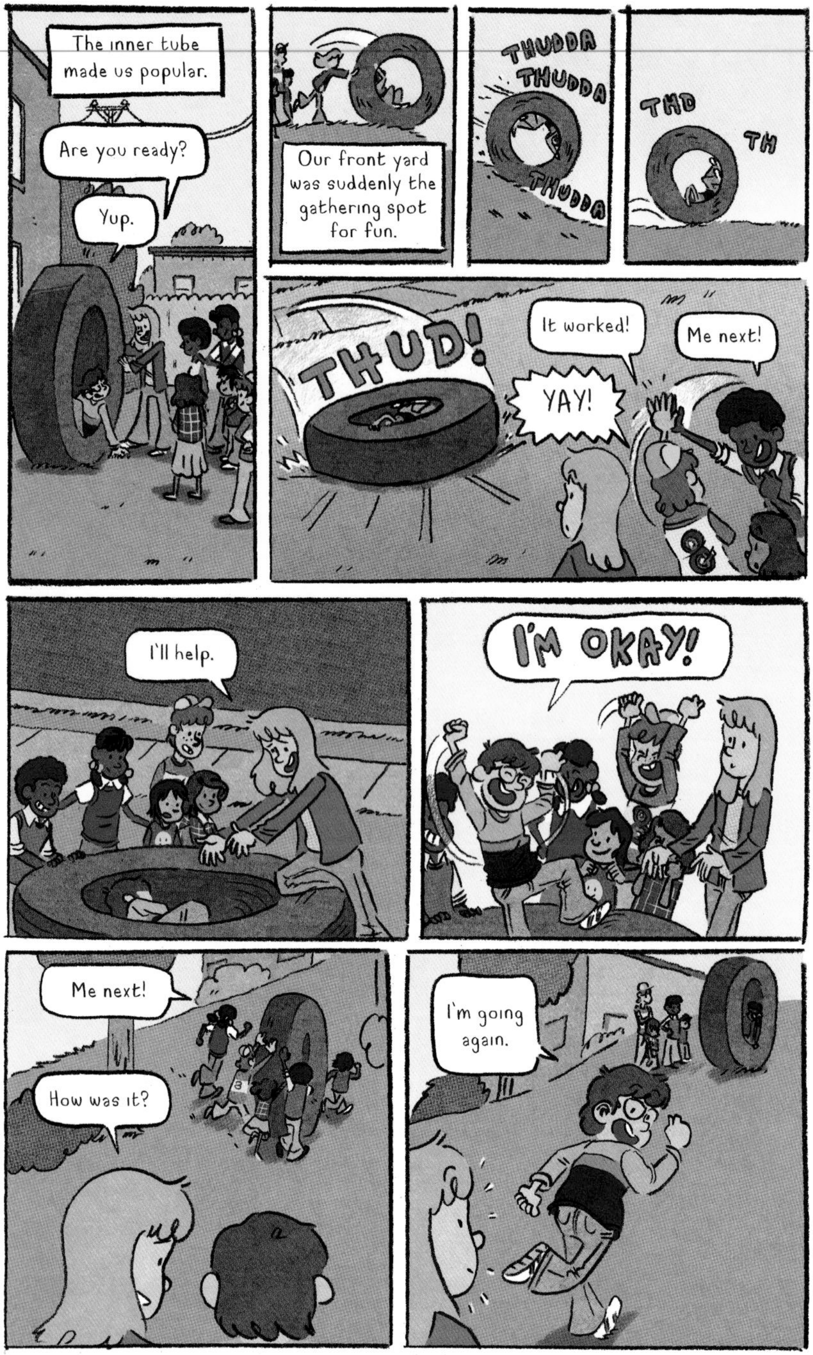
The inner tube made us popular.
Are you ready?
Yup.
Our front yard was suddenly the gathering spot for fun.
THUDDA
THUDDA
THUDDA
THD
TH
THUD!
It worked!
Me next!
YAY!
I'll help.
I'M OKAY!
Me next!
How was it?
I'm going again.

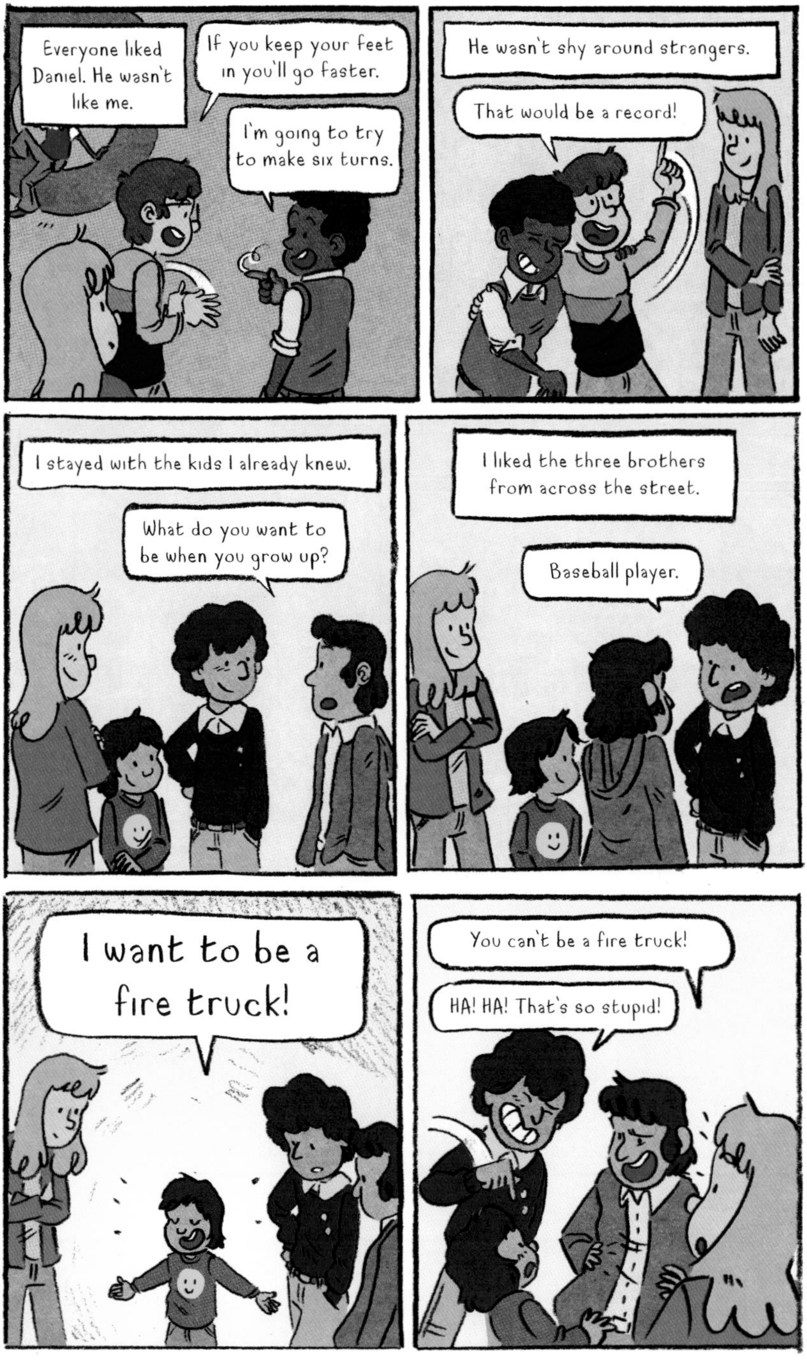
Everyone liked Daniel. He wasn't like me.
If you keep your feet in you'll go faster.
I'm going to try to make six turns.
He wasn't shy around strangers.
That would be a record!
I stayed with the kids I already knew.
What do you want to be when you grow up?
I liked the three brothers from across the street.
Baseball player.
I want to be a fire truck!
You can't be a fire truck!
HA! HA! That's so stupid!

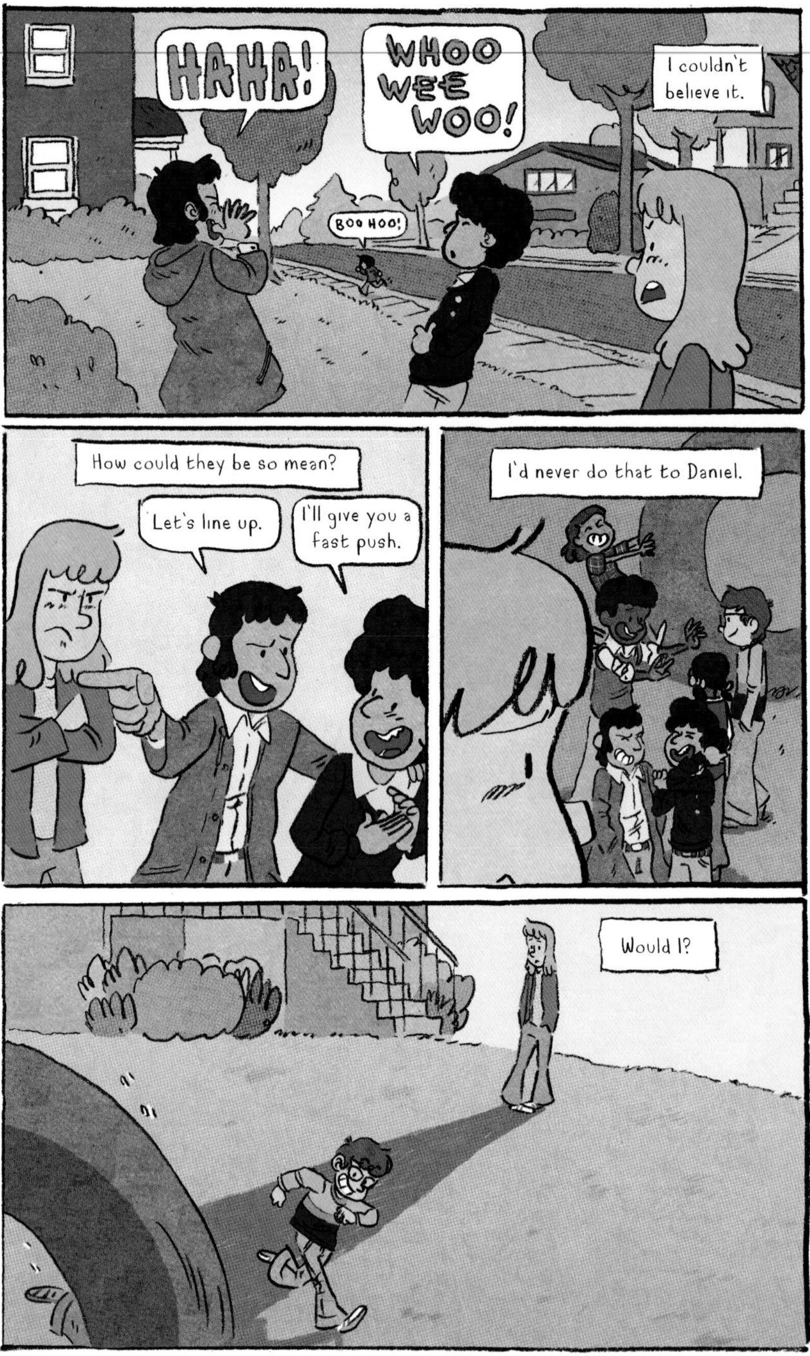
HAHA!
WHOO WEE WOO!
BOO HOO!
I couldn't believe it.
How could they be so mean?
Let's line up.
I'll give you a fast push.
I'd never do that to Daniel.
Would I?

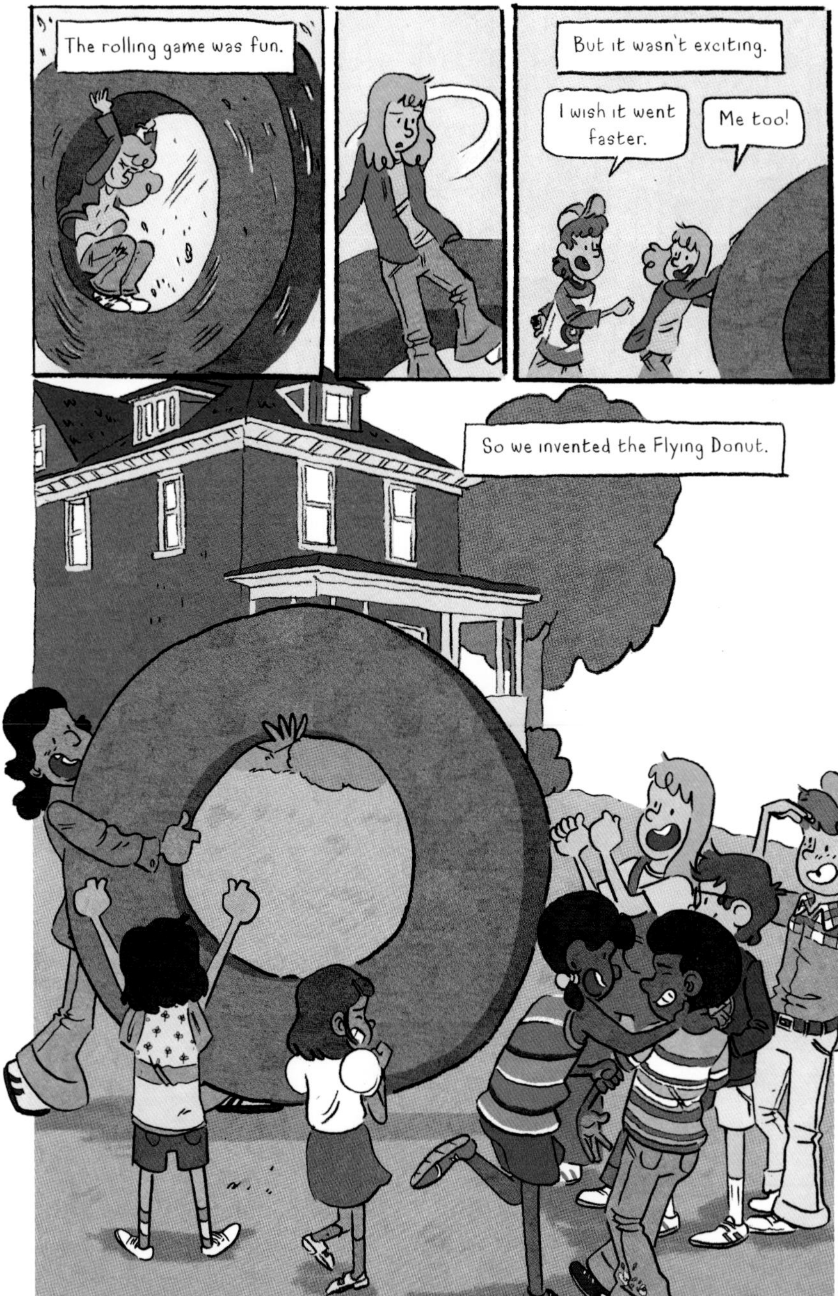
The rolling game was fun.
But it wasn't exciting.
I wish it went faster.
Me too!
So we invented the Flying Donut.

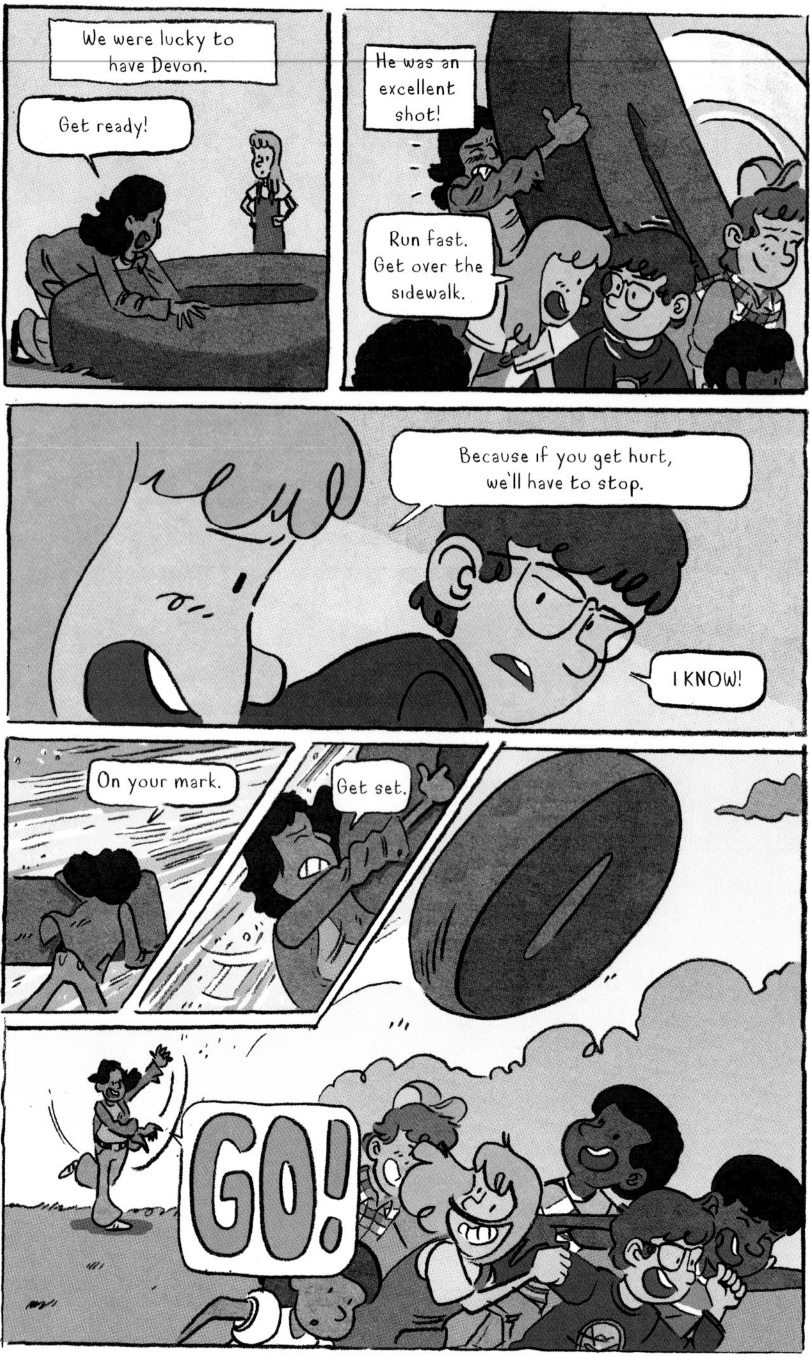
We were lucky to have Devon.
Get ready!
He was an excellent shot!
Run fast. Get over the sidewalk.
Because if you get hurt, we'll have to stop.
I KNOW!
On your mark.
Get set.
GO!

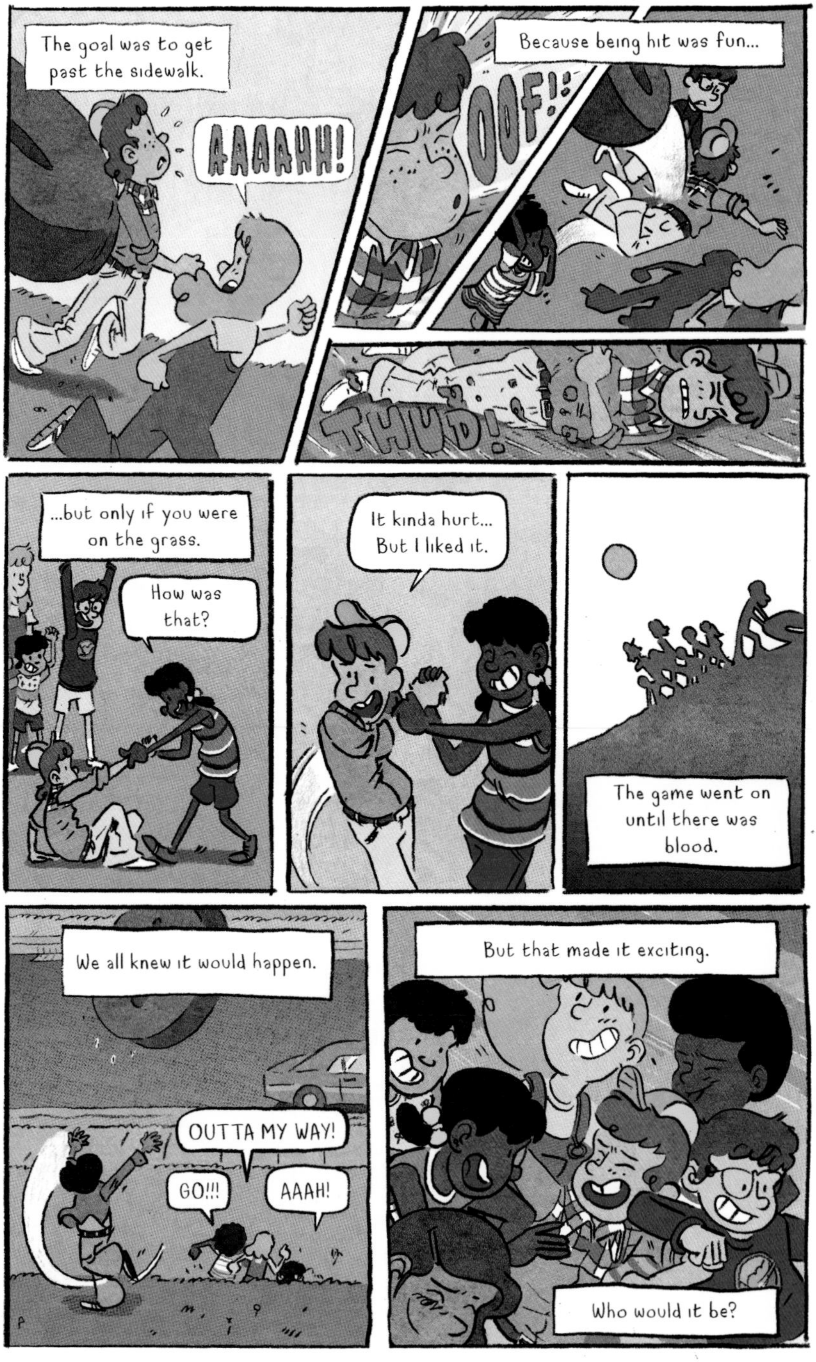
The goal was to get past the sidewalk.
AAAAHH!
Because being hit was fun...
OOF!!
THUD!
...but only if you were on the grass.
How was that?
It kinda hurt... But I liked it.
The game went on until there was blood.
We all knew it would happen.
OUTTA MY WAY!
GO!!!
AAAH!
But that made it exciting.
Who would it be?

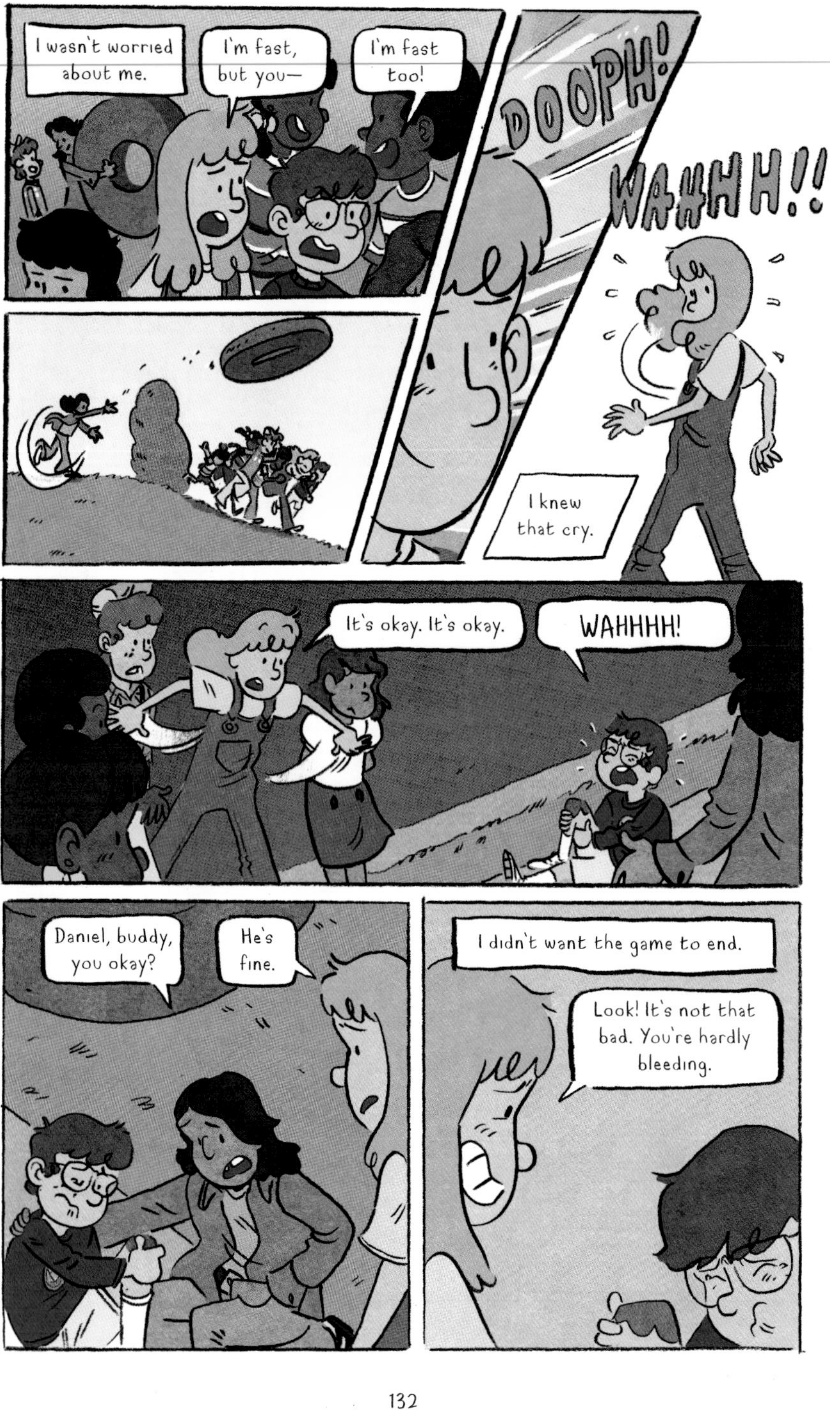
I wasn't worried about me.
I'm fast, but you—
I'm fast too!
DOOPH!
WAHHH!!
I knew that cry.
It's okay. It's okay.
WAHHHH!
Daniel, buddy, you okay?
He's fine.
I didn't want the game to end.
Look! It's not that bad. You're hardly bleeding.

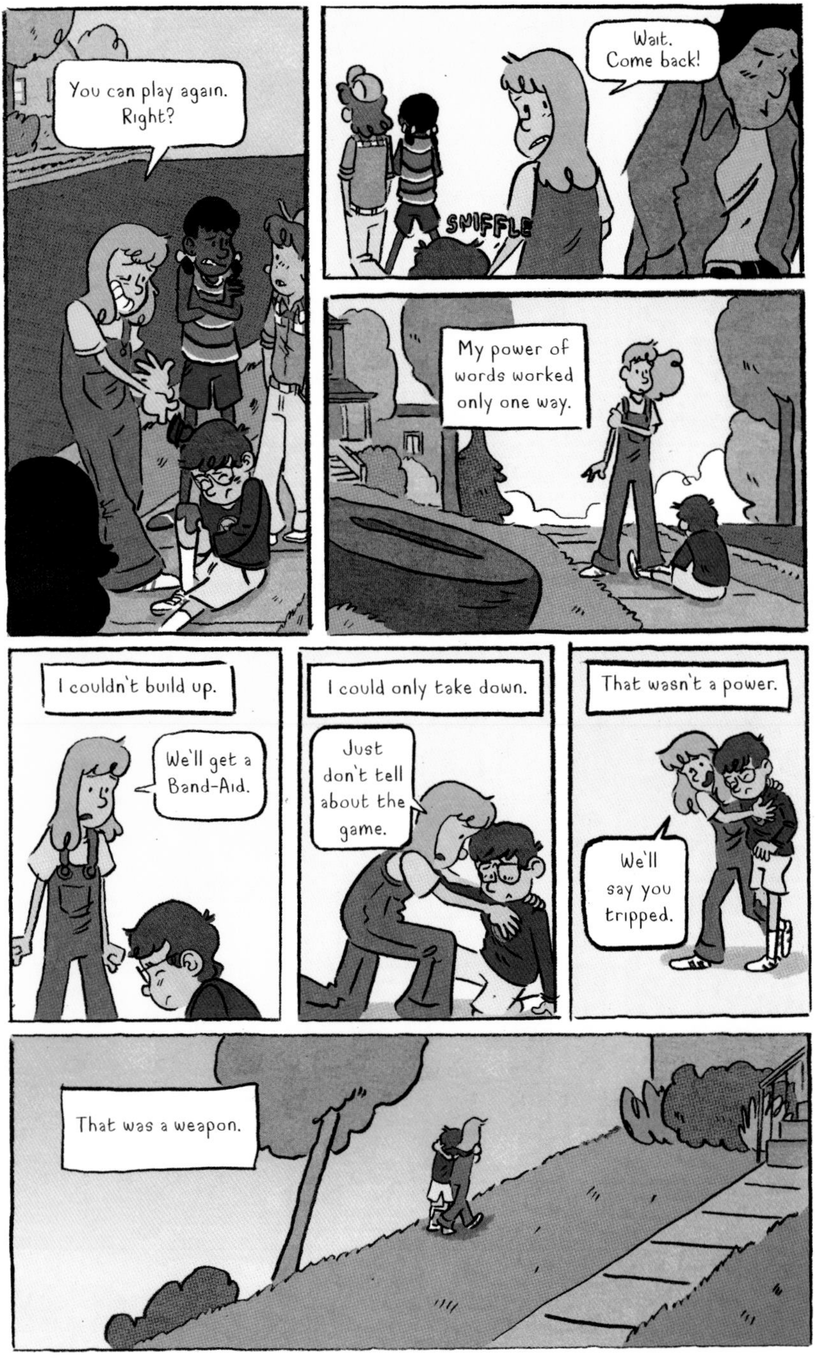

You can play again. Right?
Wait. Come back!
SNIFFLE
My power of words worked only one way.
I couldn't build up.
We'll get a Band-Aid.
I could only take down.
Just don't tell about the game.
That wasn't a power.
We'll say you tripped.
That was a weapon.

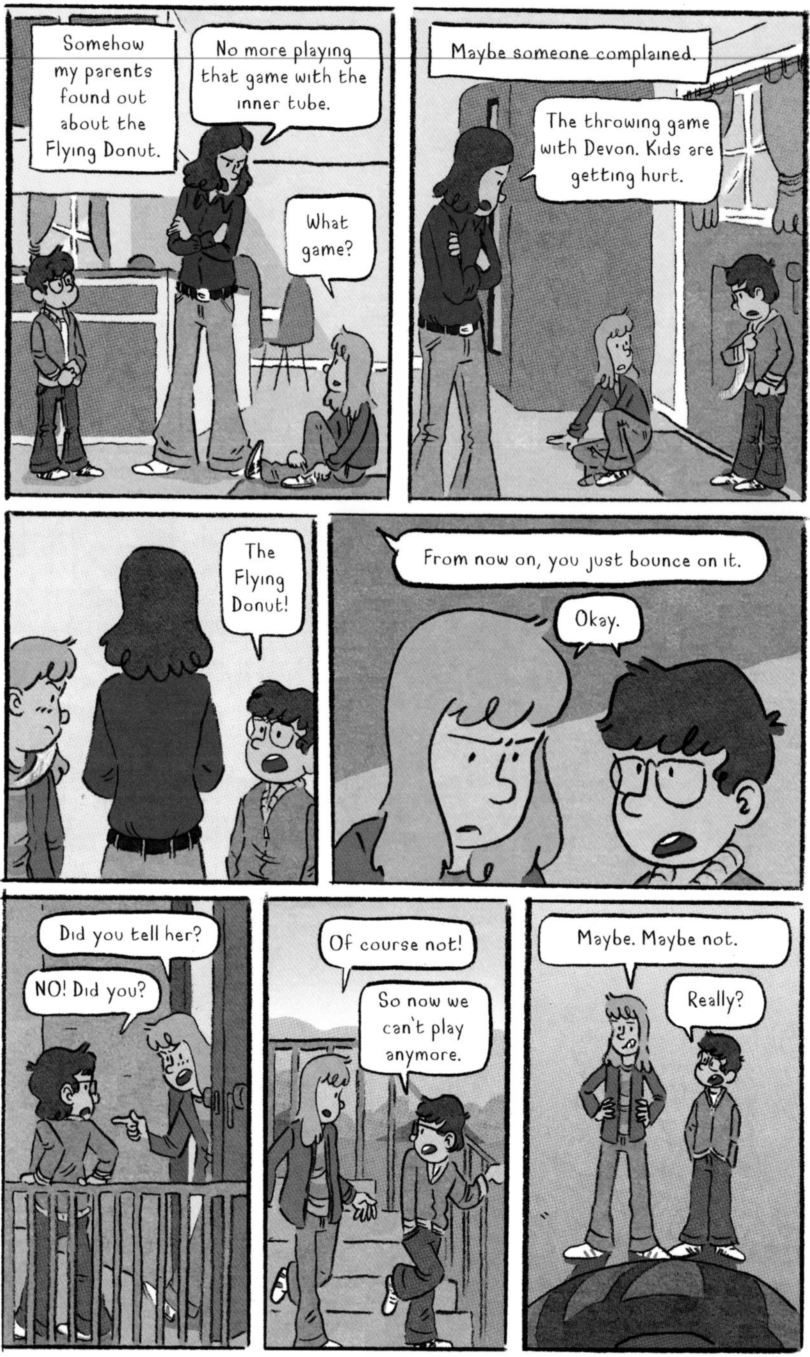
Somehow my parents found out about the Flying Donut.
No more playing that game with the inner tube.
What game?
Maybe someone complained.
The throwing game with Devon. Kids are getting hurt.
The Flying Donut!
From now on, you just bounce on it.
Okay.
Did you tell her?
NO! Did you?
Of course not!
So now we can't play anymore.
Maybe. Maybe not.
Really?

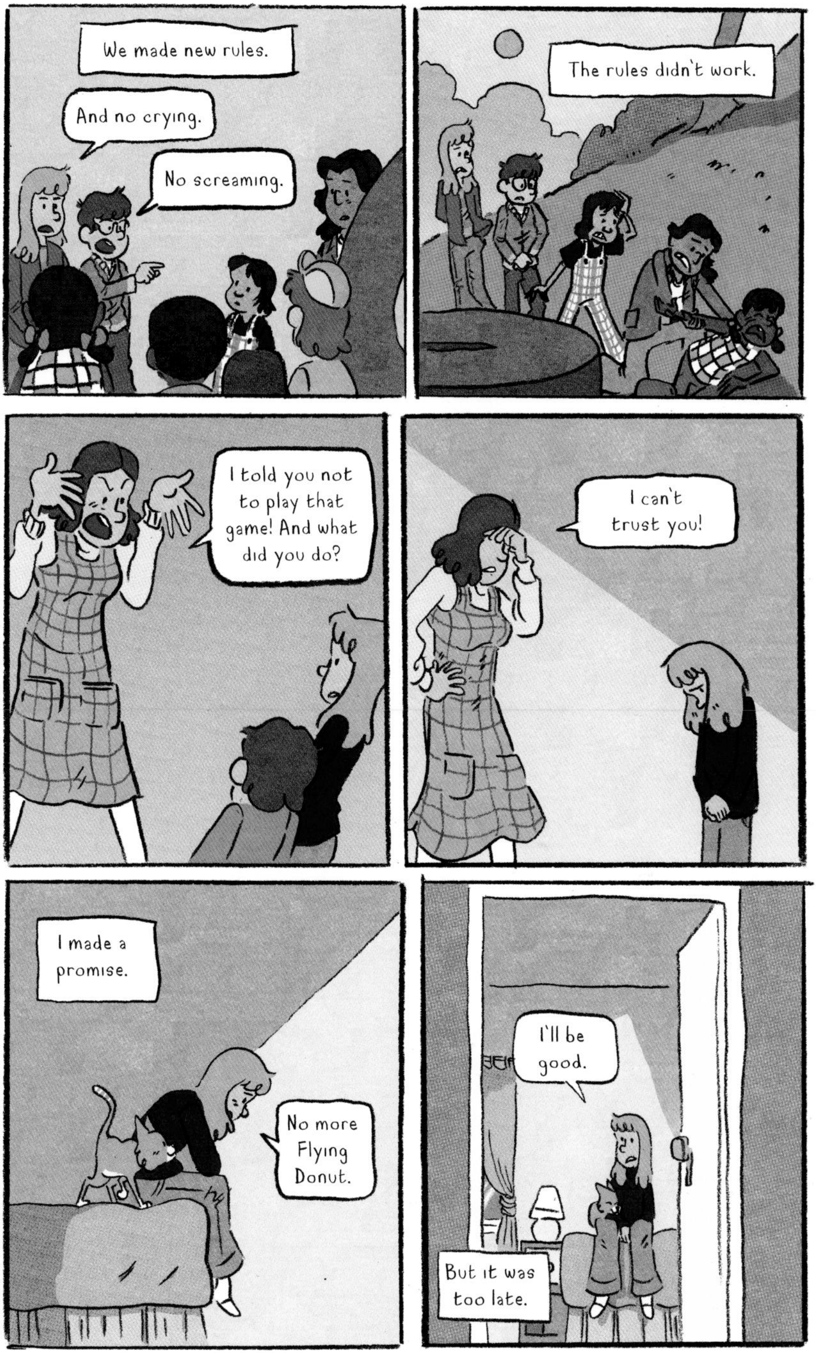
We made new rules.
And no crying.
No screaming.
The rules didn't work.
I told you not to play that game! And what did you do?
I can't trust you!
I made a promise.
No more Flying Donut.
I'll be good.
But it was too late.

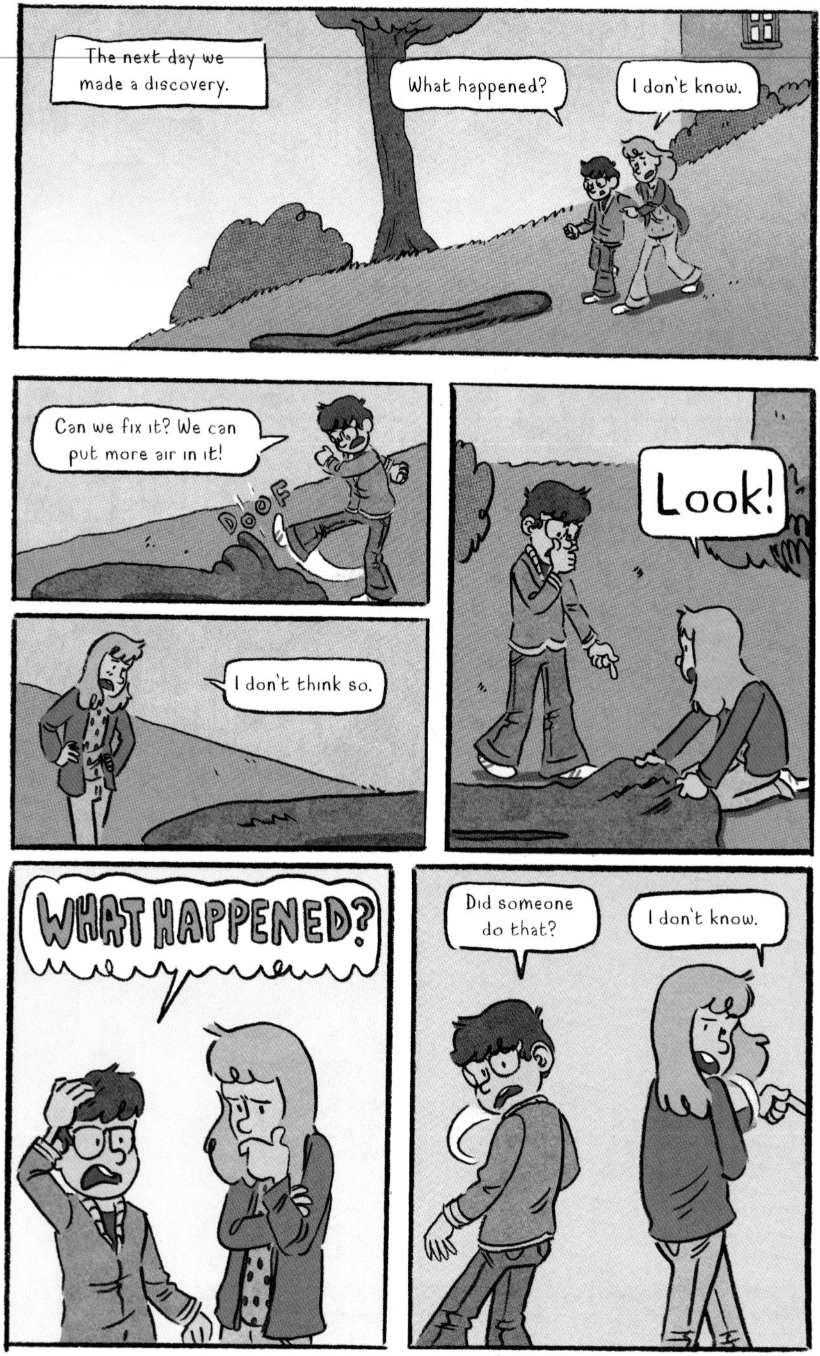
The next day we made a discovery.
What happened?
I don't know.
Can we fix it? We can put more air in it!
DOOF
I don't think so.
Look!
WHAT HAPPENED?
Did someone do that?
I don't know.

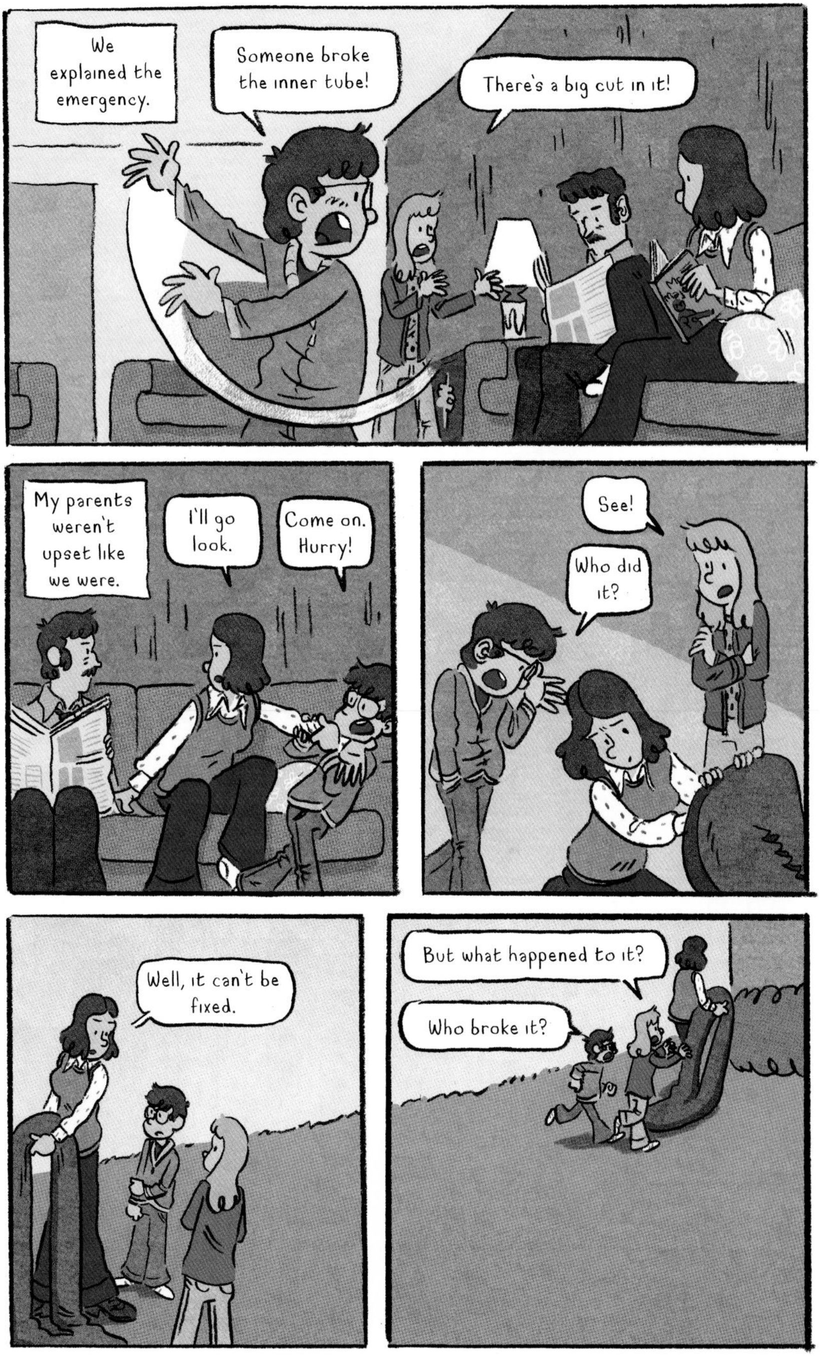
We explained the emergency.
Someone broke the inner tube!
There's a big cut in it!
My parents weren't upset like we were.
I'll go look.
Come on. Hurry!
See!
Who did it?
Well, it can't be fixed.
But what happened to it?
Who broke it?

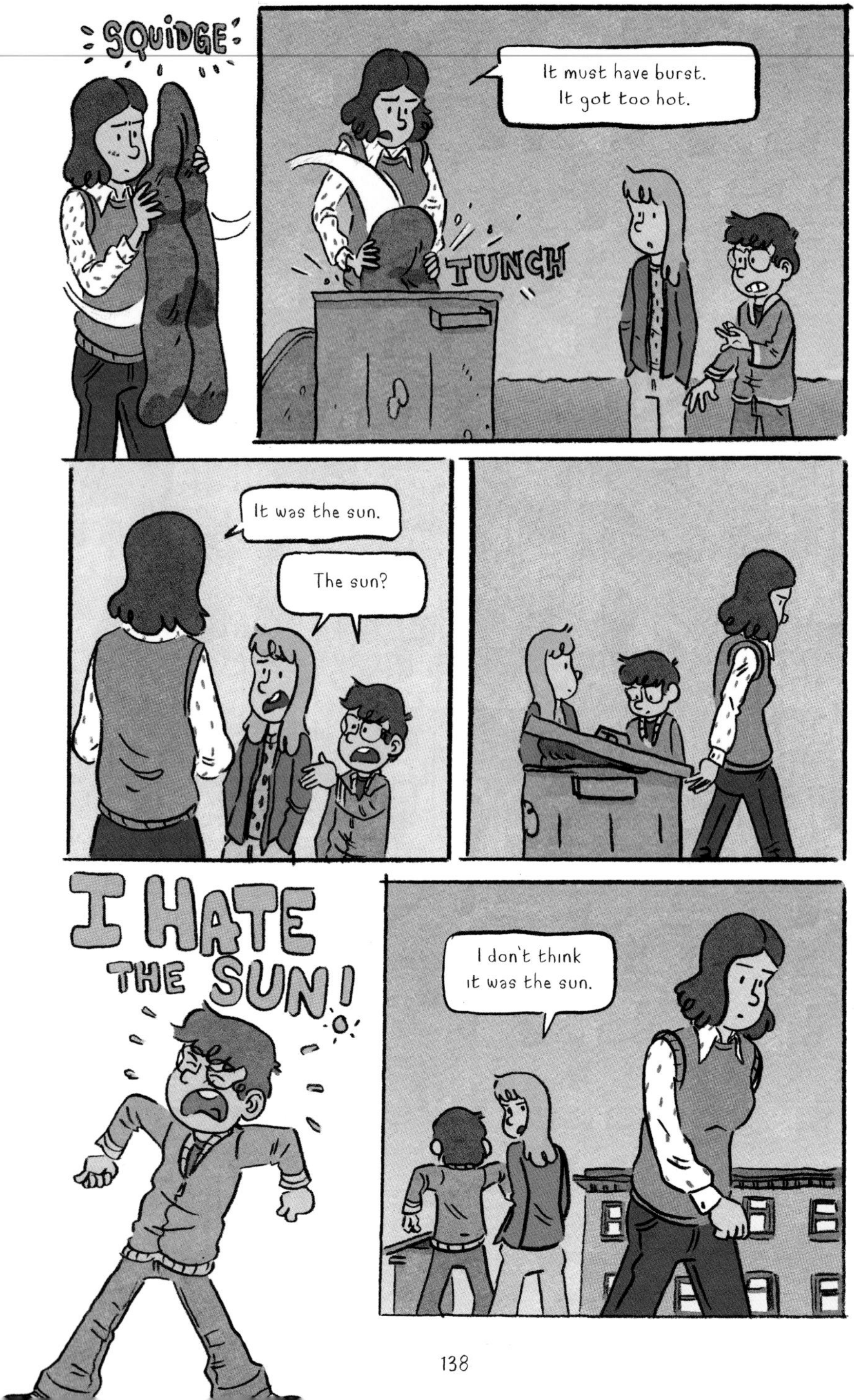
SQUIDGE
It must have burst.
It got too hot.
TUNCH
It was the sun.
The sun?
I HATE THE SUN!
I don't think
it was the sun.

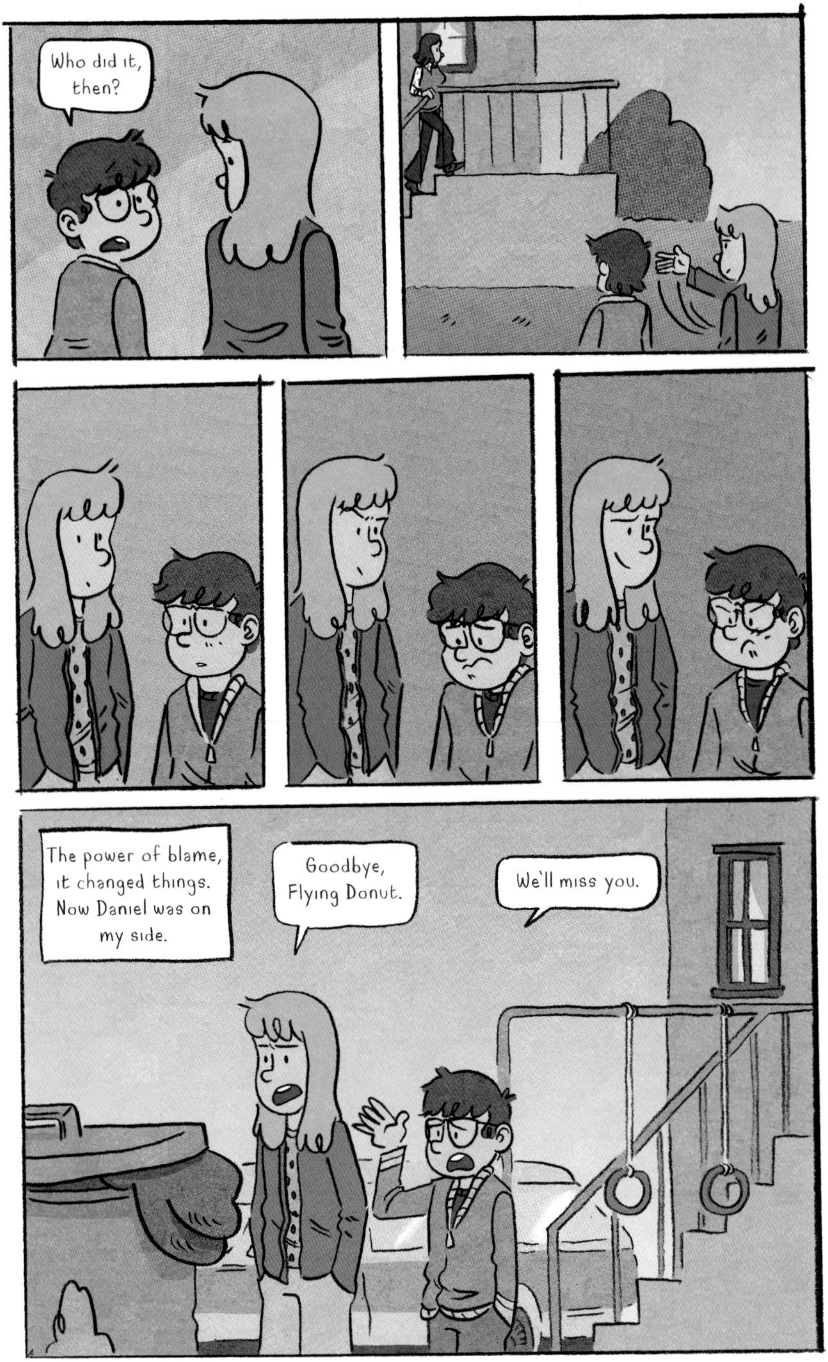

Who did it, then?
The power of blame, it changed things. Now Daniel was on my side.
Goodbye, Flying Donut.
We'll miss you.

The Power of the Boss

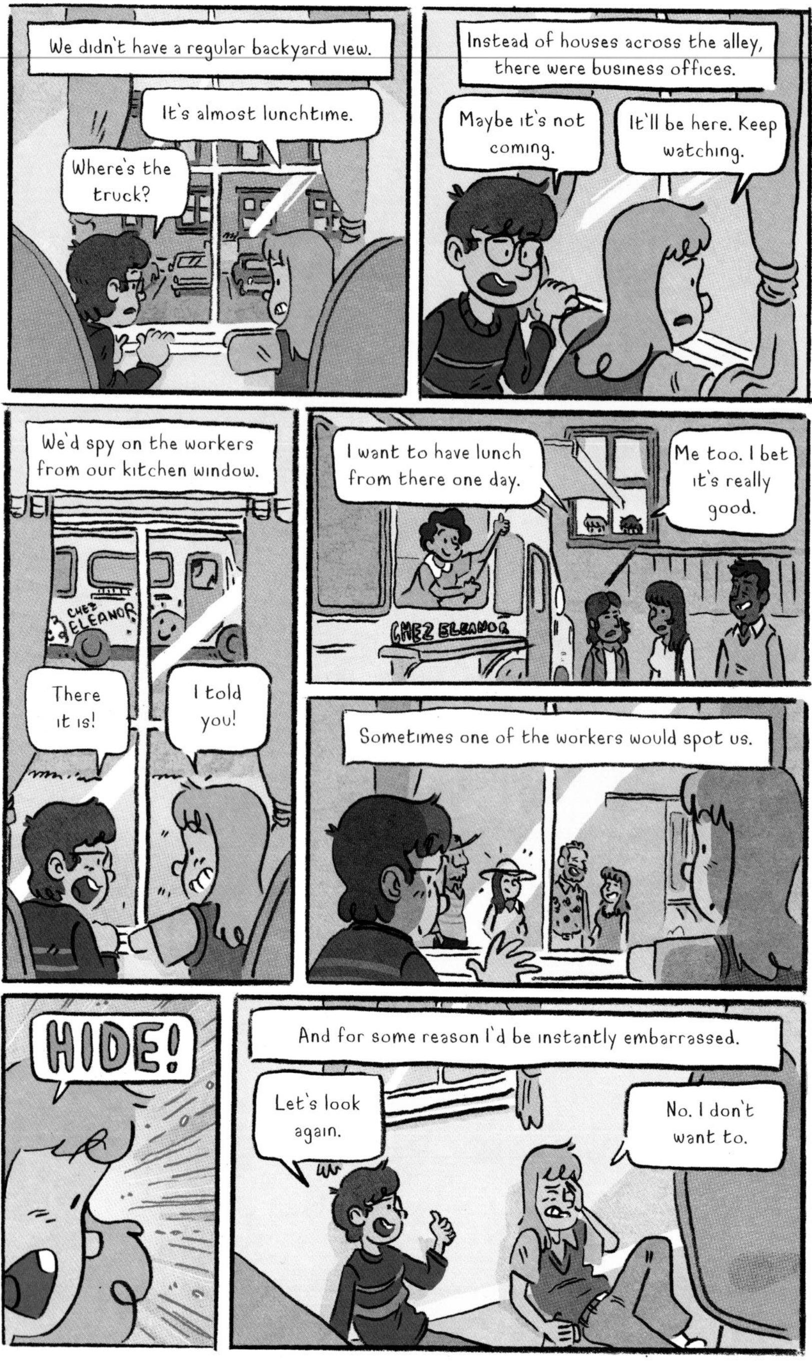
We didn't have a regular backyard view.
It's almost lunchtime.
Where's the truck?
Instead of houses across the alley, there were business offices.
Maybe it's not coming.
It'll be here. Keep watching.
We'd spy on the workers from our kitchen window.
CHEZ ELEANOR
There it is!
I told you!
I want to have lunch from there one day.
Me too. I bet it's really good.
CHEZ ELEANOR
Sometimes one of the workers would spot us.
HIDE!
And for some reason I'd be instantly embarrassed.
Let's look again.
No. I don't want to.

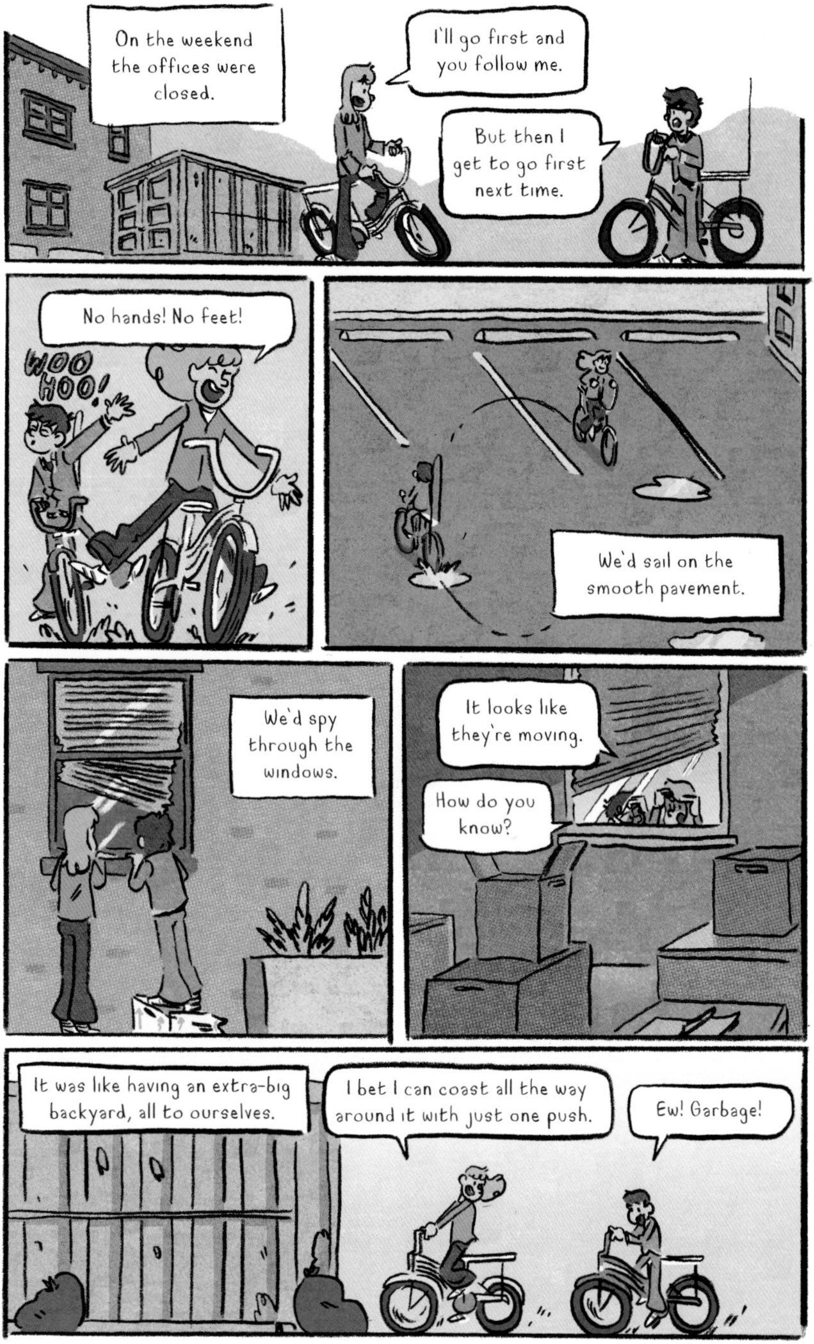
On the weekend the offices were closed.
I'll go first and you follow me.
But then I get to go first next time.
No hands! No feet!
WOO HOO!
We'd sail on the smooth pavement.
We'd spy through the windows.
It looks like they're moving.
How do you know?
It was like having an extra-big backyard, all to ourselves.
I bet I can coast all the way around it with just one push.
Ew! Garbage!

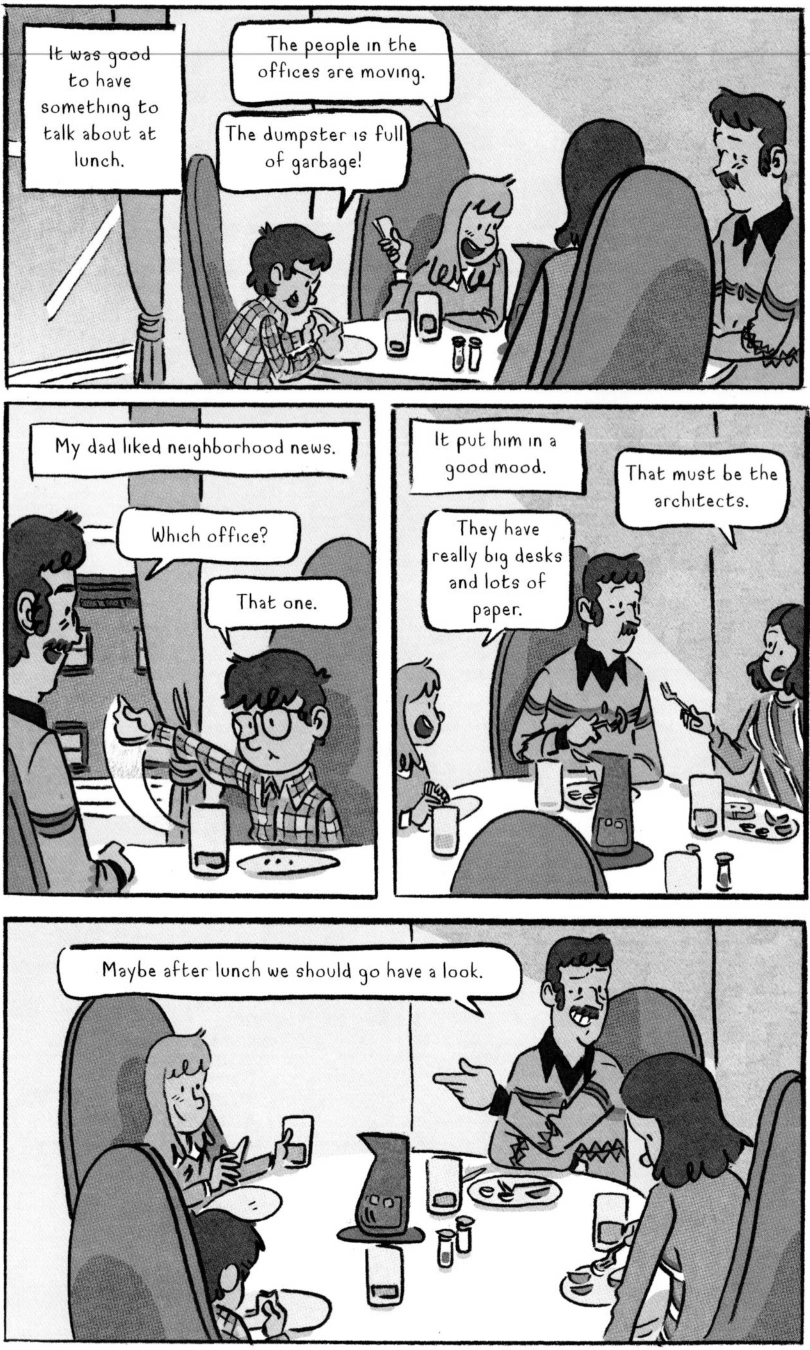
It was good to have something to talk about at lunch.
The people in the offices are moving.
The dumpster is full of garbage!
My dad liked neighborhood news.
Which office?
That one.
It put him in a good mood.
That must be the architects.
They have really big desks and lots of paper.
Maybe after lunch we should go have a look.

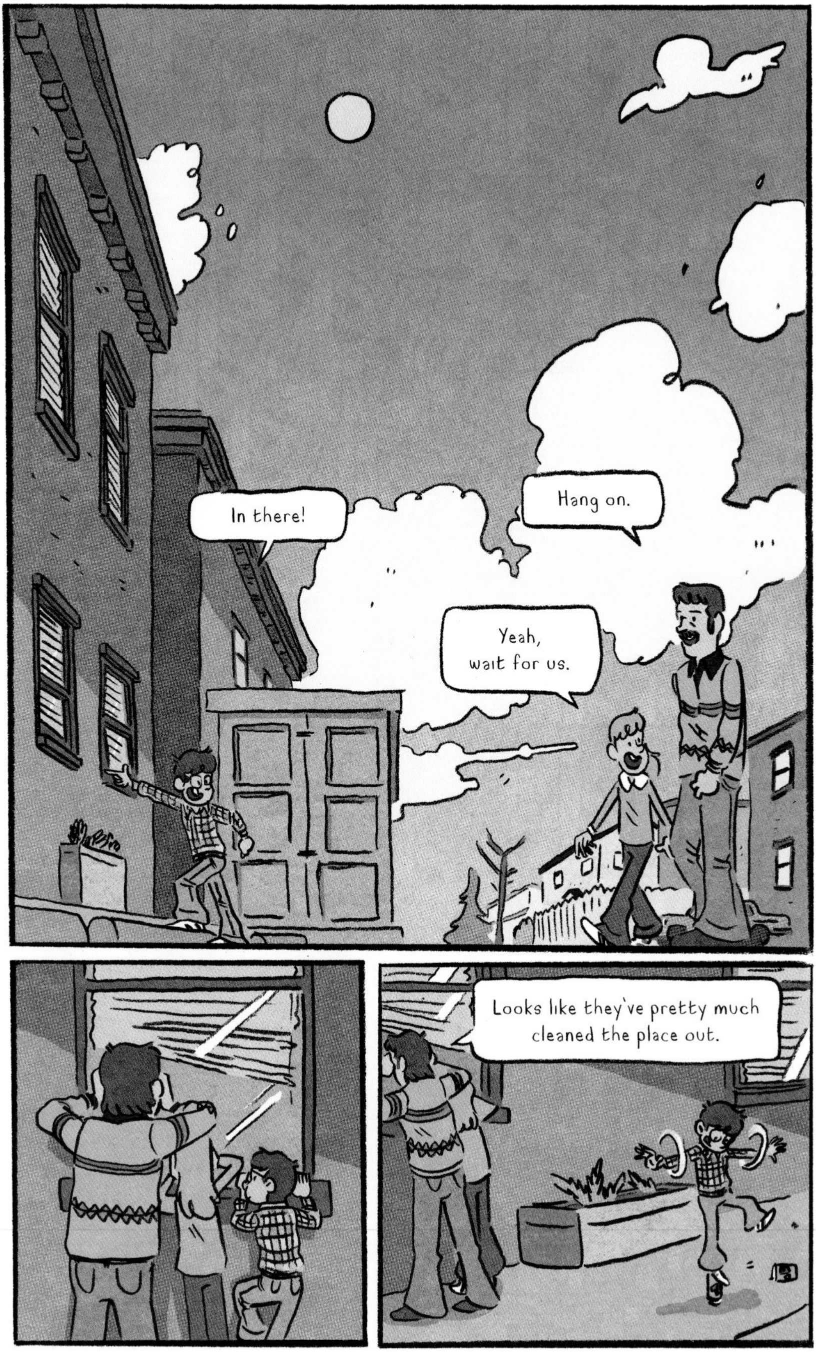
In there!
Hang on.
Yeah, wait for us.
Looks like they've pretty much cleaned the place out.

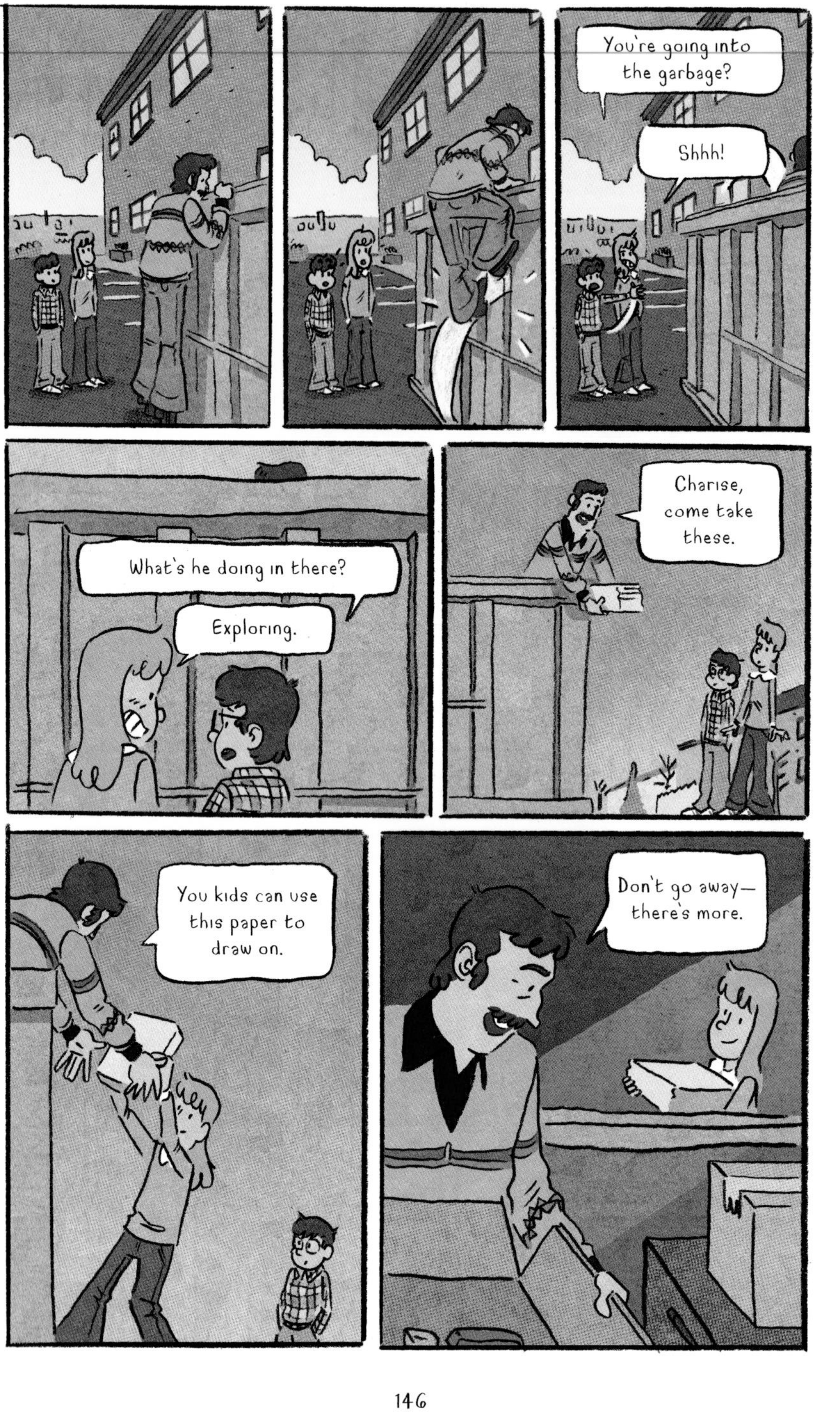
You're going into the garbage?
Shhh!
What's he doing in there?
Exploring.
Charise, come take these.
You kids can use this paper to draw on.
Don't go away— there's more.

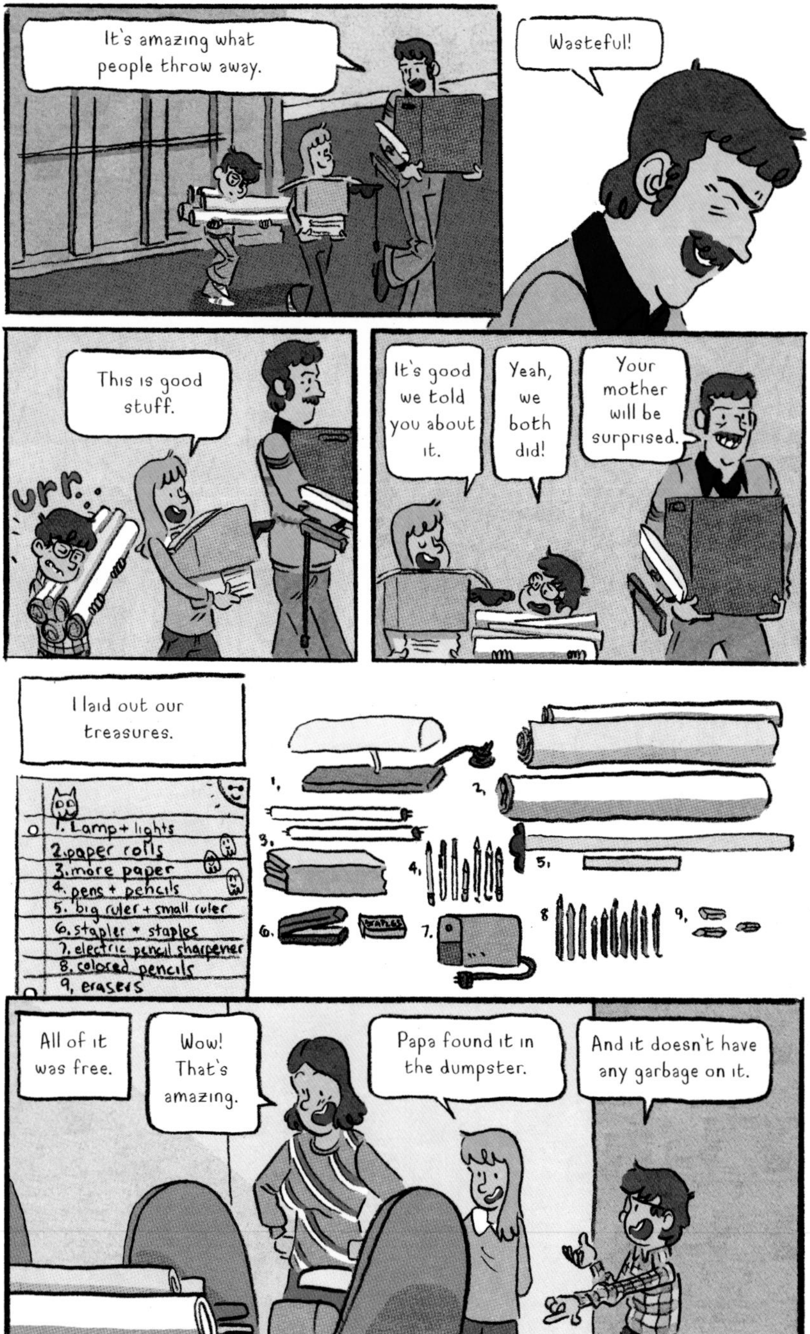
It's amazing what people throw away.
Wasteful!
This is good stuff.
urr..
It's good we told you about it.
Yeah, we both did!
Your mother will be surprised.
I laid out our treasures.
1. Lamp + lights
2. paper rolls
3. more paper
4. pens + pencils
5. big ruler + small ruler
6. stapler + staples
7. electric pencil sharpener
8. colored pencils
9. erasers
STAPLES
All of it was free.
Wow! That's amazing.
Papa found it in the dumpster.
And it doesn't have any garbage on it.

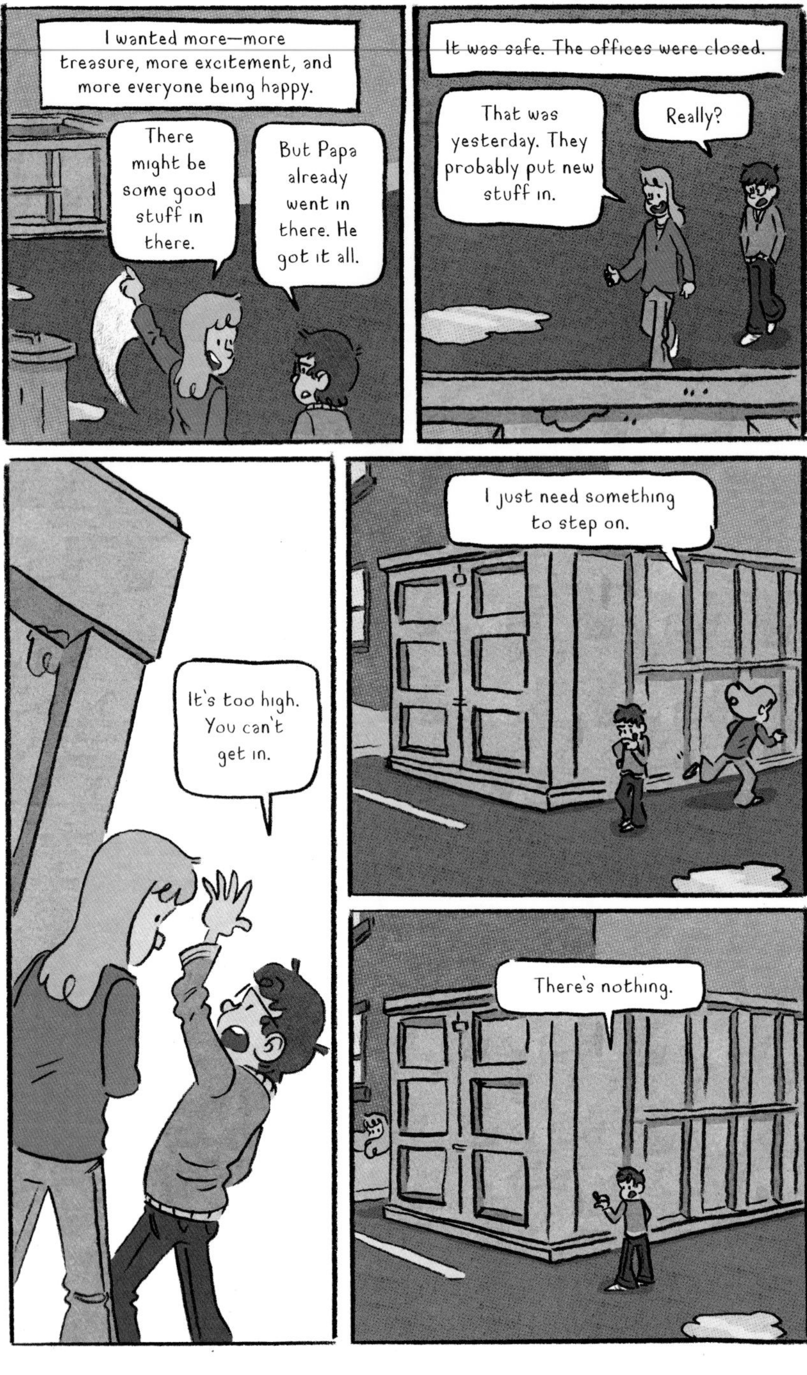
I wanted more—more treasure, more excitement, and more everyone being happy.
There might be some good stuff in there.
But Papa already went in there. He got it all.
It was safe. The offices were closed.
That was yesterday. They probably put new stuff in.
Really?
It's too high. You can't get in.
I just need something to step on.
There's nothing.

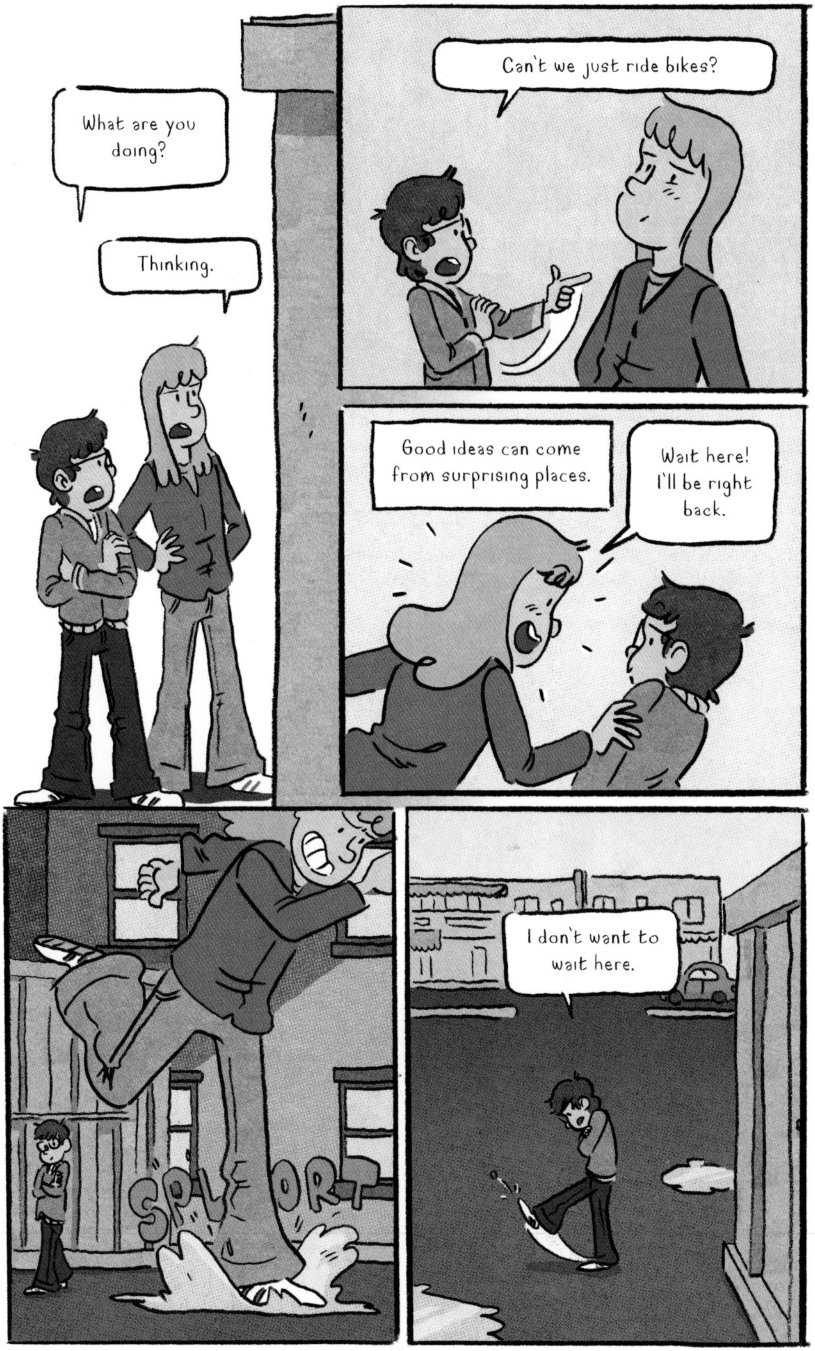
What are you doing?
Thinking.
Can't we just ride bikes?
Good ideas can come from surprising places.
Wait here! I'll be right back.
SPLORT
I don't want to wait here.

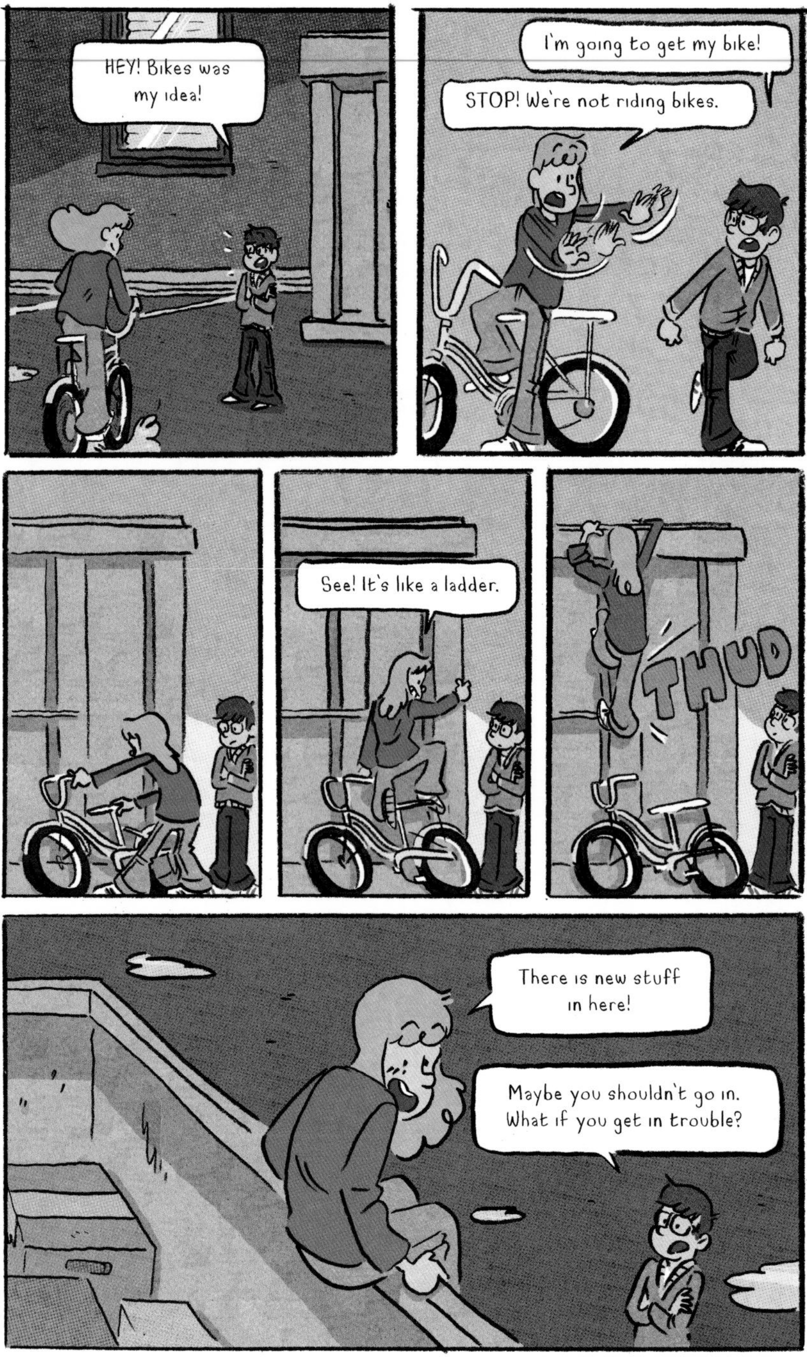
HEY! Bikes was my idea!
I'm going to get my bike!
STOP! We're not riding bikes.
See! It's like a ladder.
THUD
There is new stuff in here!
Maybe you shouldn't go in. What if you get in trouble?

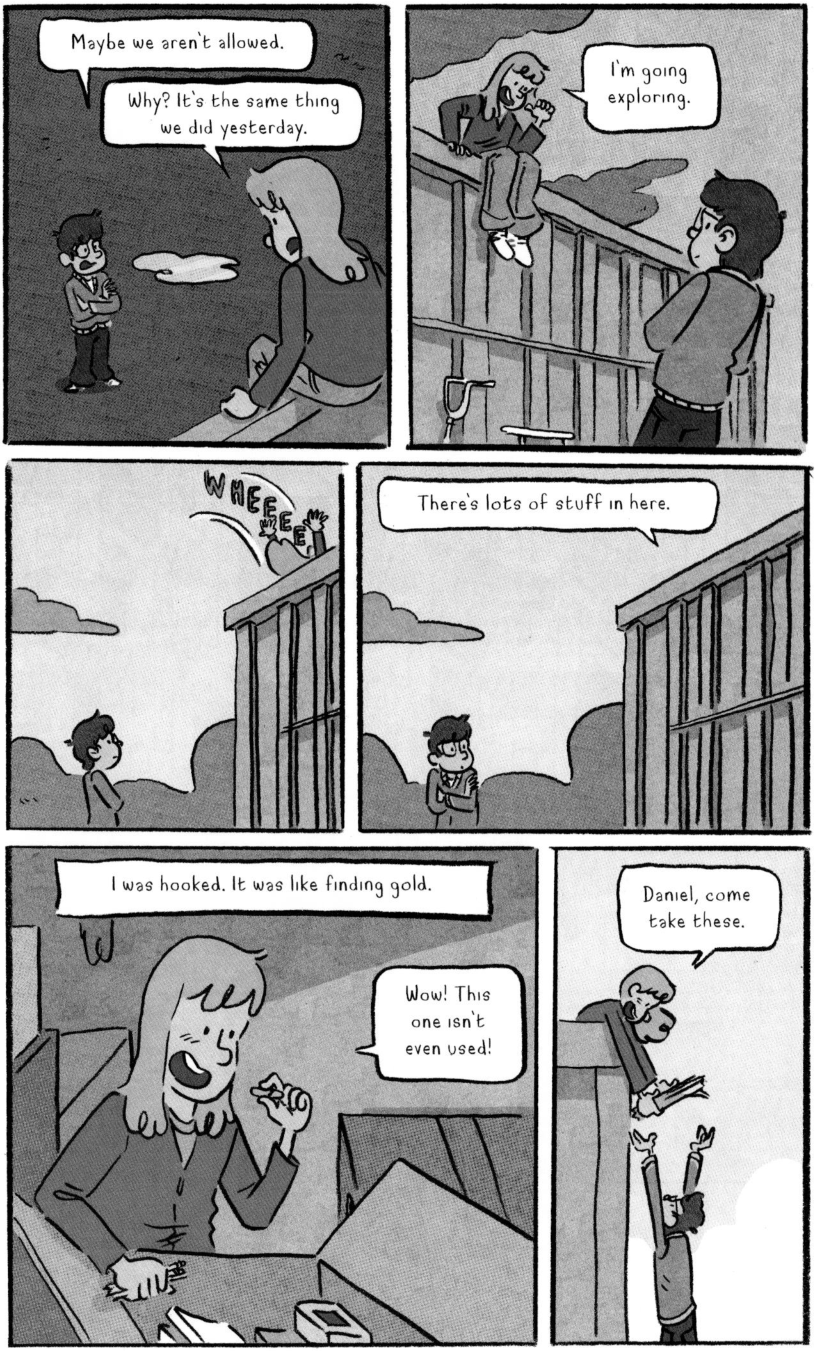
Maybe we aren't allowed.
Why? It's the same thing we did yesterday.
I'm going exploring.
WHEEEEE
There's lots of stuff in here.
I was hooked. It was like finding gold.
Wow! This one isn't even used!
Daniel, come take these.

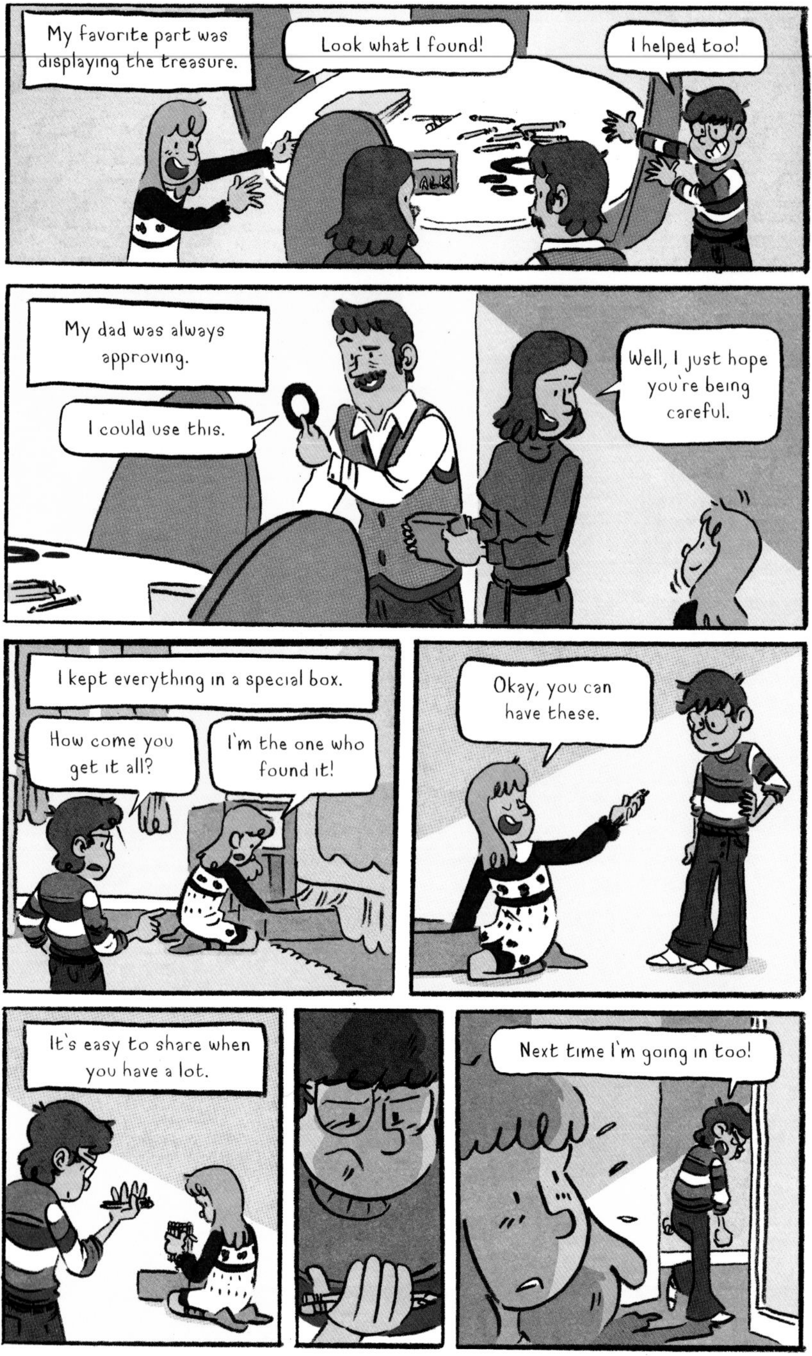
My favorite part was displaying the treasure.
Look what I found!
I helped too!
My dad was always approving.
I could use this.
Well, I just hope you're being careful.
I kept everything in a special box.
How come you get it all?
I'm the one who found it!
Okay, you can have these.
It's easy to share when you have a lot.
Next time I'm going in too!

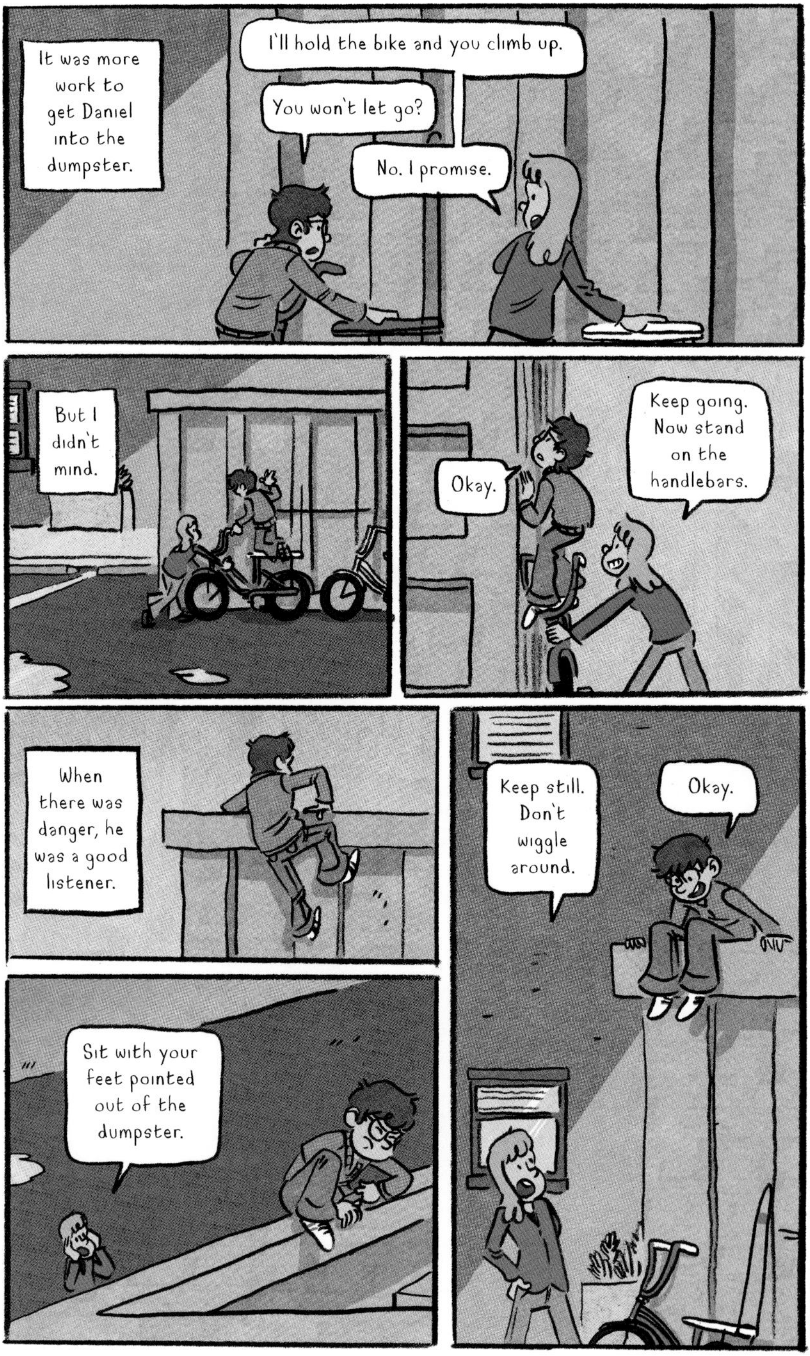
It was more work to get Daniel into the dumpster.
I'll hold the bike and you climb up.
You won't let go?
No. I promise.
But I didn't mind.
Okay.
Keep going. Now stand on the handlebars.
When there was danger, he was a good listener.
Sit with your feet pointed out of the dumpster.
Keep still. Don't wiggle around.
Okay.

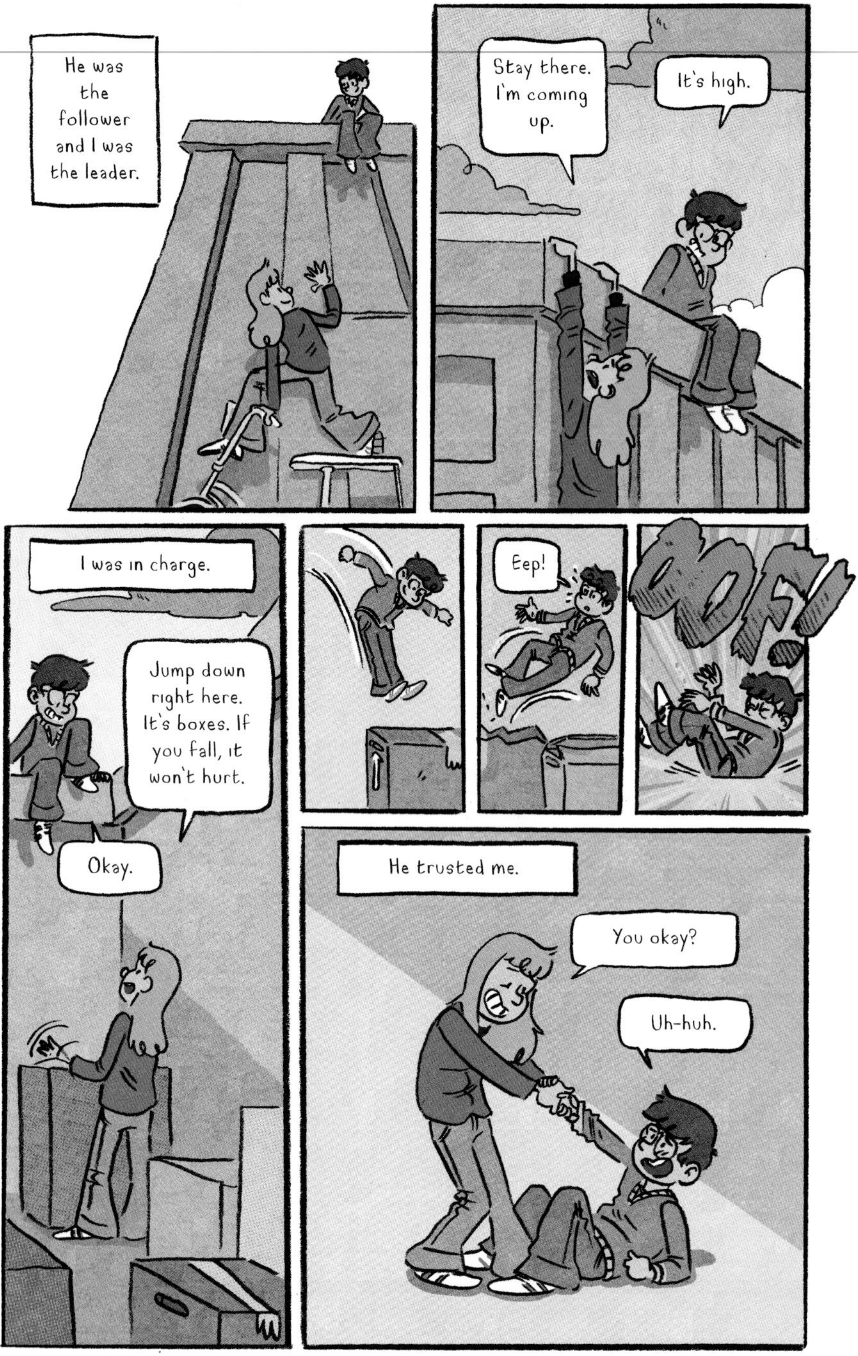
He was the follower and I was the leader.
Stay there. I'm coming up.
It's high.
I was in charge.
Jump down right here. It's boxes. If you fall, it won't hurt.
Okay.
Eep!
OOF!
He trusted me.
You okay?
Uh-huh.

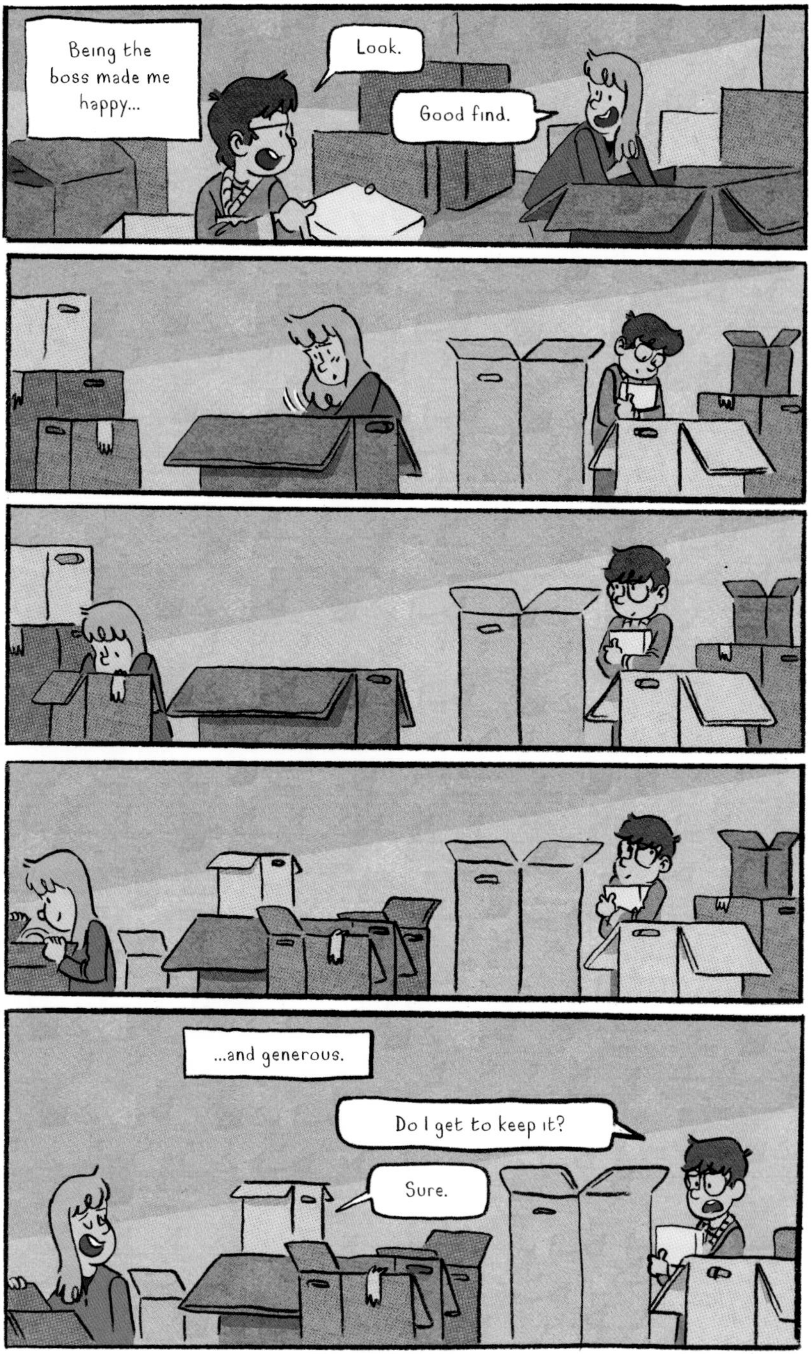
Being the boss made me happy...
Look.
Good find.
...and generous.
Do I get to keep it?
Sure.

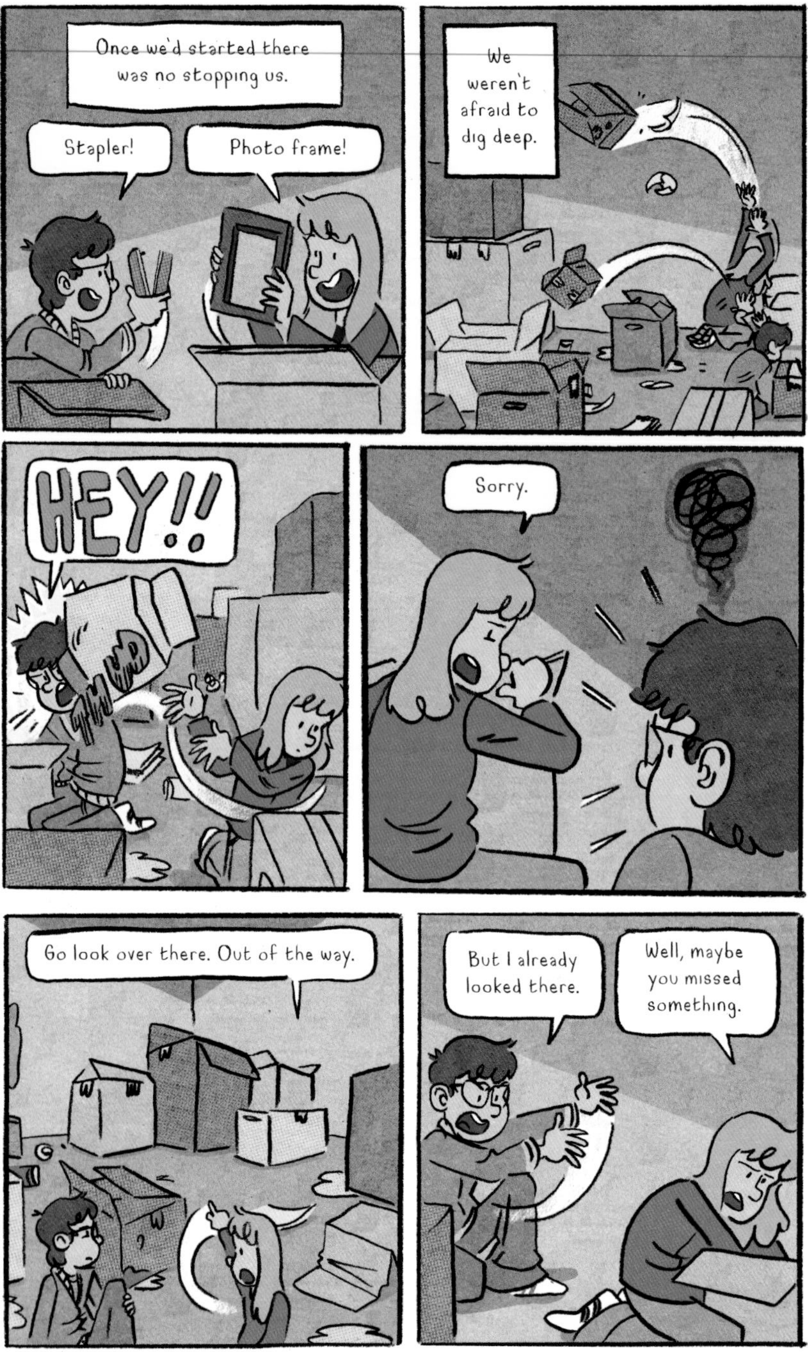
Once we'd started there was no stopping us.
Stapler!
Photo frame!
We weren't afraid to dig deep.
HEY!!
Sorry.
Go look over there. Out of the way.
But I already looked there.
Well, maybe you missed something.

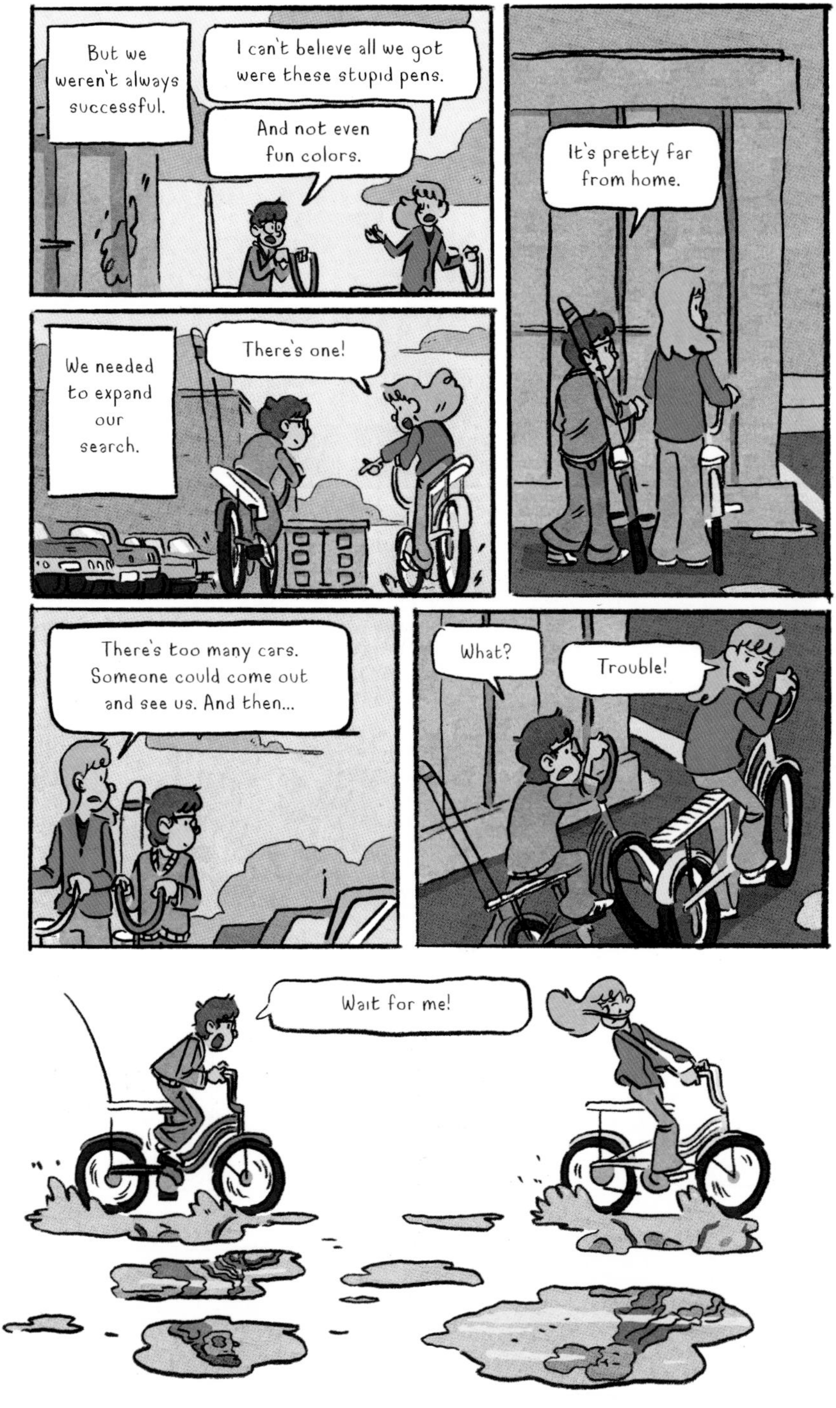

But we weren't always successful.
I can't believe all we got were these stupid pens.
And not even fun colors.
It's pretty far from home.
We needed to expand our search.
There's one!
There's too many cars. Someone could come out and see us. And then...
What?
Trouble!
Wait for me!

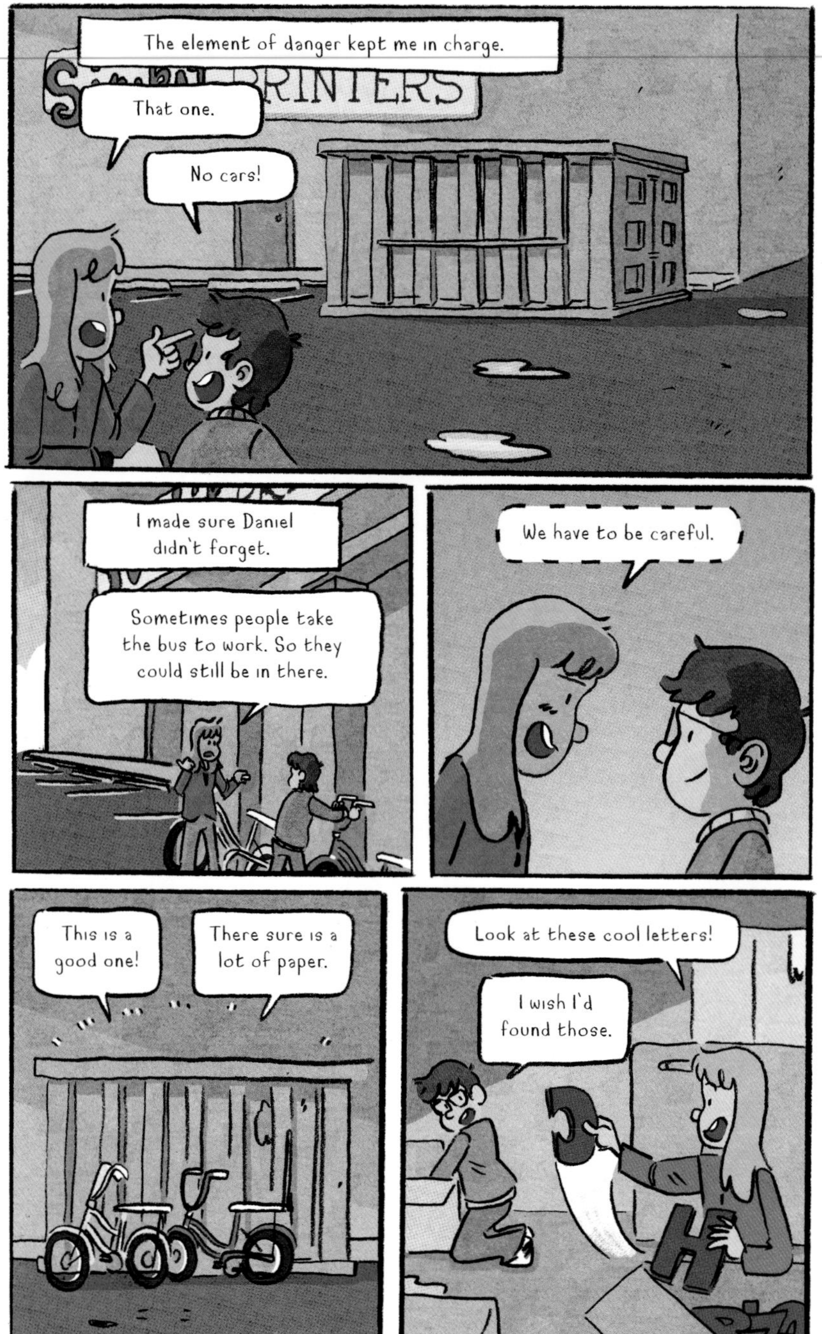

The element of danger kept me in charge.
PRINTERS
That one.
No cars!
I made sure Daniel didn't forget.
Sometimes people take the bus to work. So they could still be in there.
We have to be careful.
This is a good one!
There sure is a lot of paper.
Look at these cool letters!
I wish I'd found those.

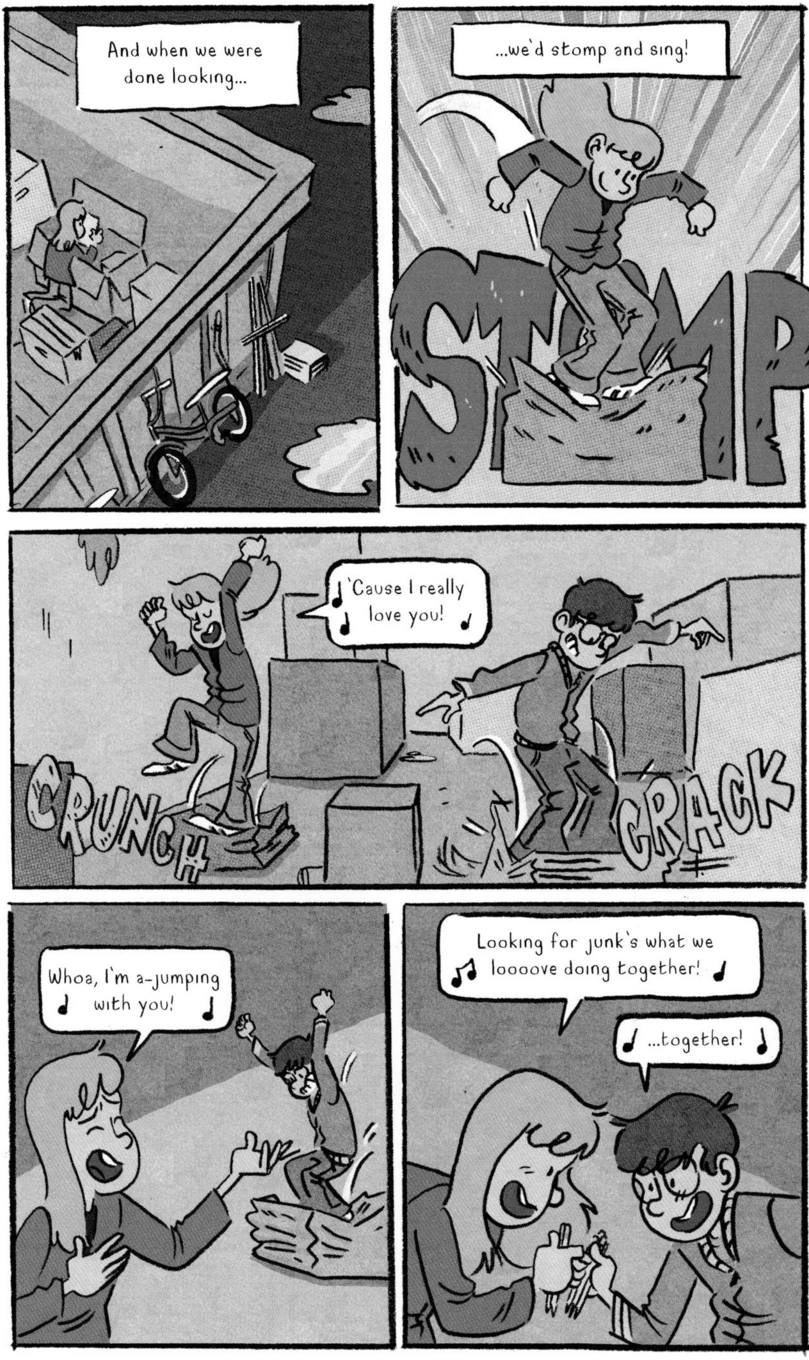
And when we were done looking...
...we'd stomp and sing!
STOMP
'Cause I really love you!
CRUNCH
CRACK
Whoa, I'm a-jumping with you!
Looking for junk's what we loooove doing together!
...together!

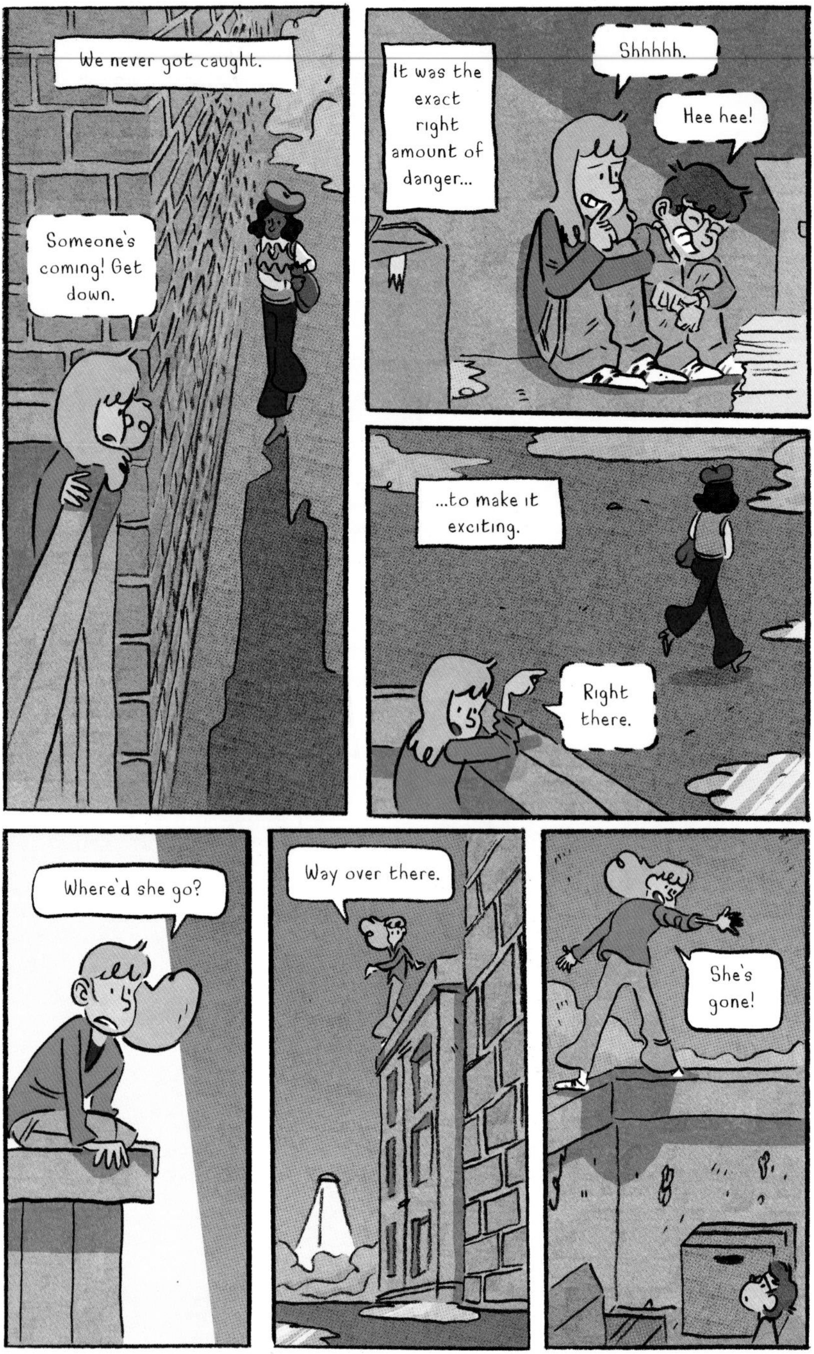
We never got caught.
Someone's coming! Get down.
It was the exact right amount of danger...
Shhhhh.
Hee hee!
...to make it exciting.
Right there.
Where'd she go?
Way over there.
She's gone!

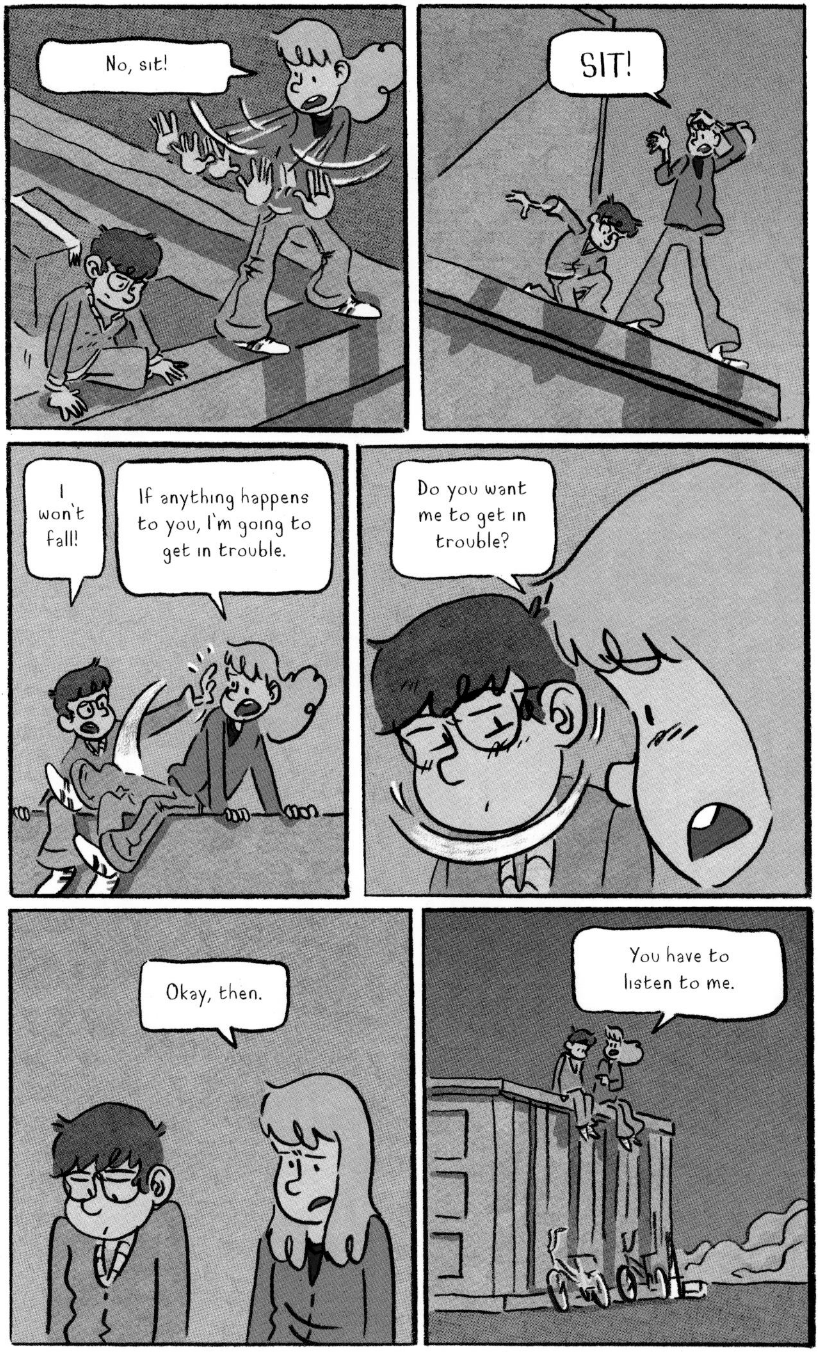
No, sit!
SIT!
I won't fall!
If anything happens to you, I'm going to get in trouble.
Do you want me to get in trouble?
Okay, then.
You have to listen to me.

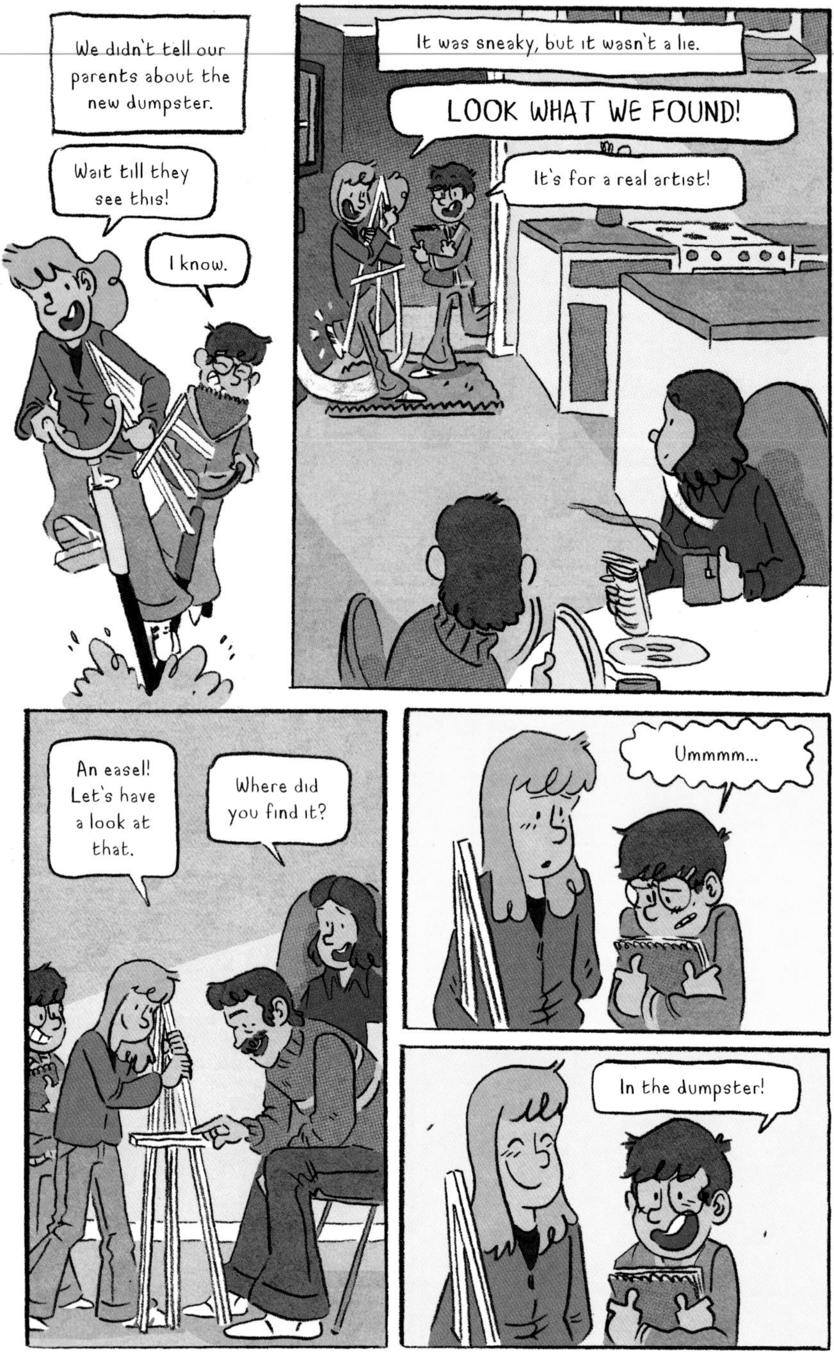
We didn't tell our parents about the new dumpster.
Wait till they see this!
I know.
It was sneaky, but it wasn't a lie.
LOOK WHAT WE FOUND!
It's for a real artist!
An easel! Let's have a look at that.
Where did you find it?
Ummmm...
In the dumpster!

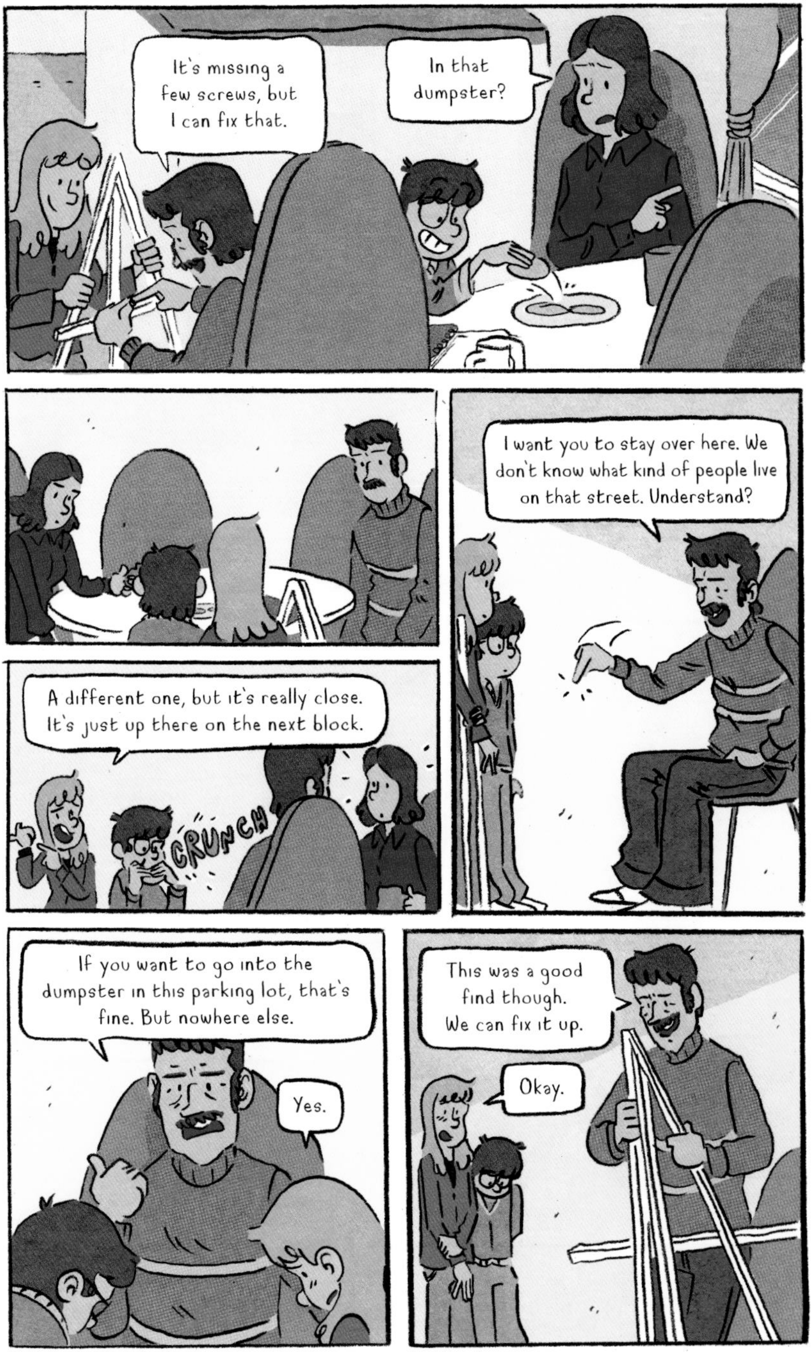
It's missing a few screws, but I can fix that.
In that dumpster?
A different one, but it's really close. It's just up there on the next block.
CRUNCH
I want you to stay over here. We don't know what kind of people live on that street. Understand?
If you want to go into the dumpster in this parking lot, that's fine. But nowhere else.
Yes.
This was a good find though. We can fix it up.
Okay.

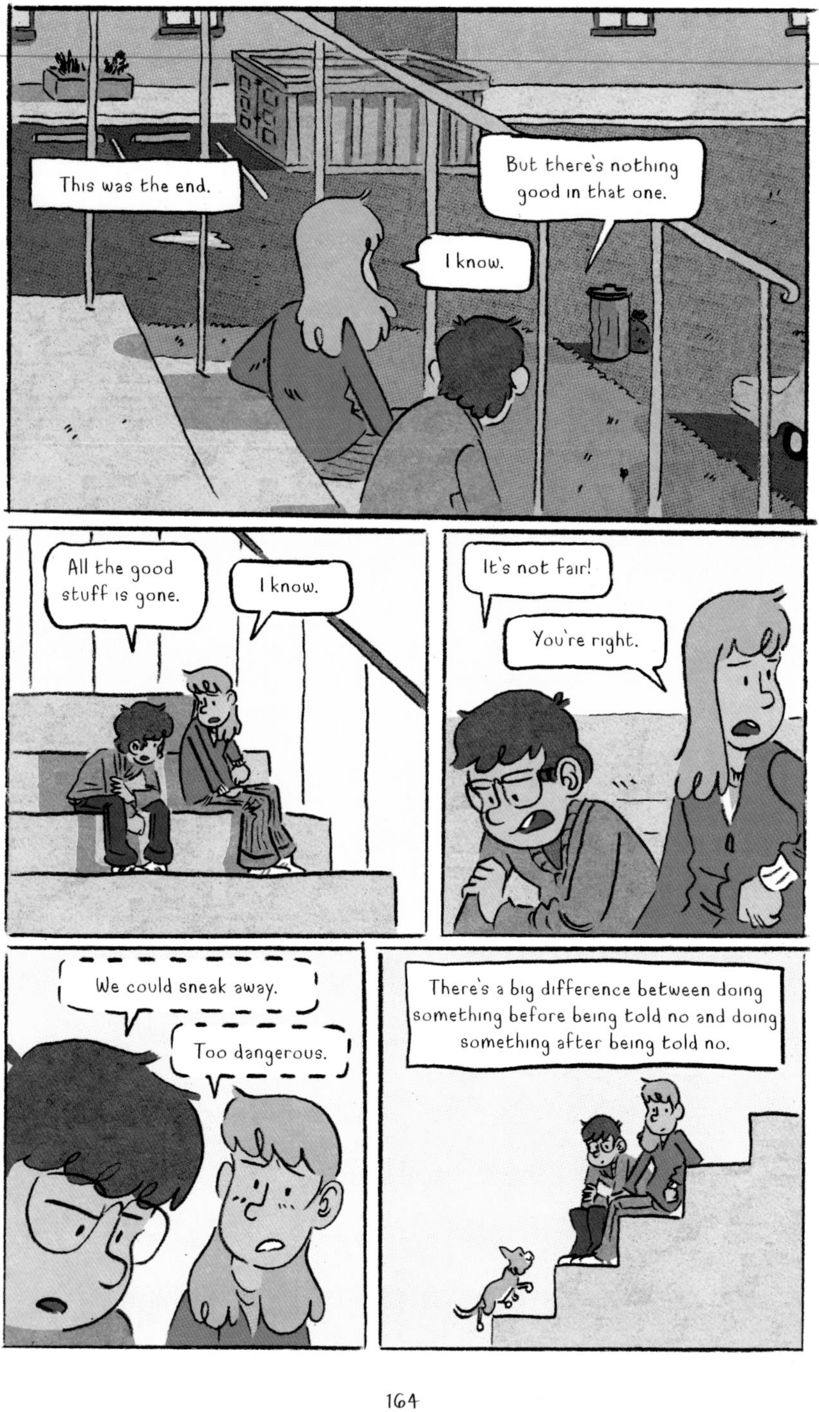
This was the end.
But there's nothing good in that one.
I know.
All the good stuff is gone.
I know.
It's not fair!
You're right.
We could sneak away.
Too dangerous.
There's a big difference between doing something before being told no and doing something after being told no.

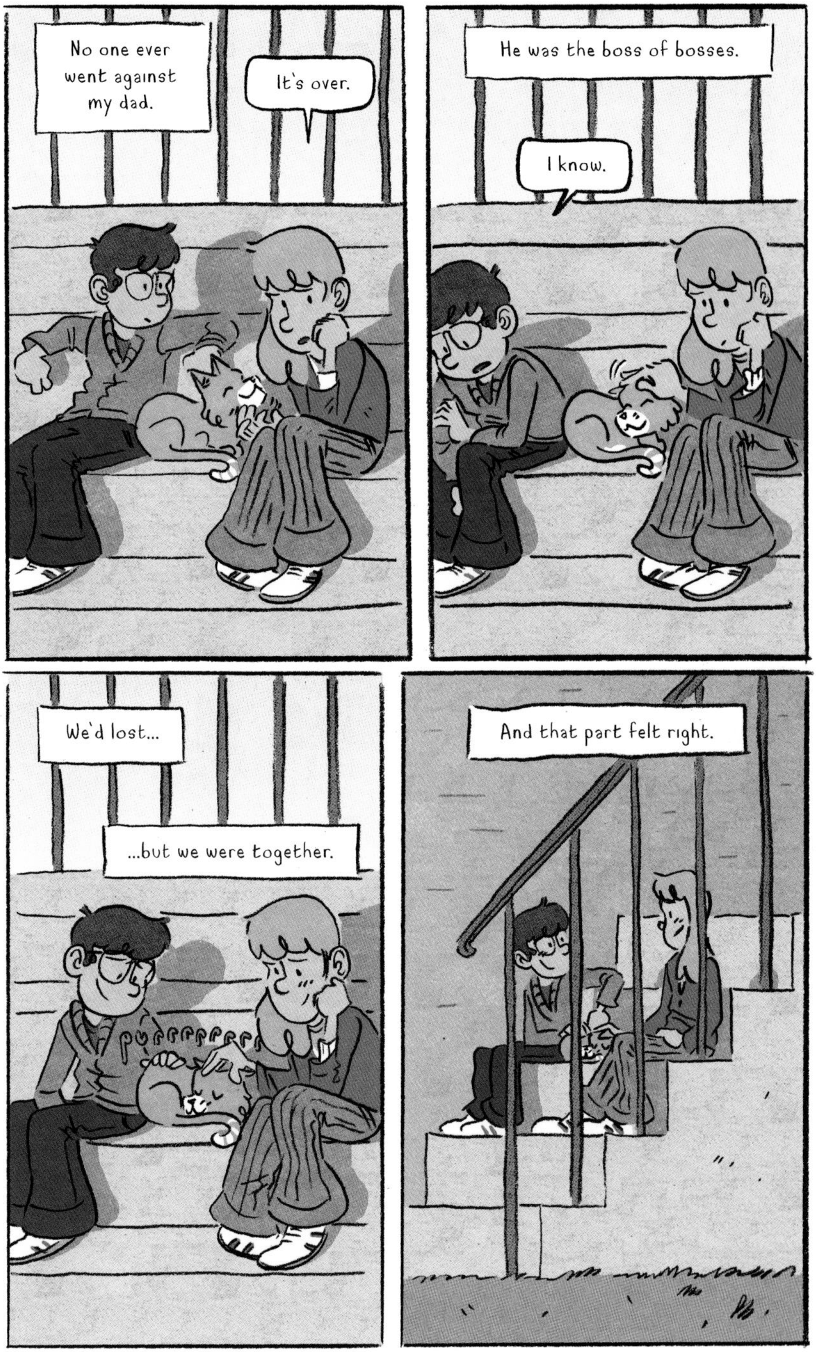
No one ever went against my dad.
It's over.
He was the boss of bosses.
I know.
We'd lost...
...but we were together.
purrrrrrrr
And that part felt right.

8

The Power to Dare

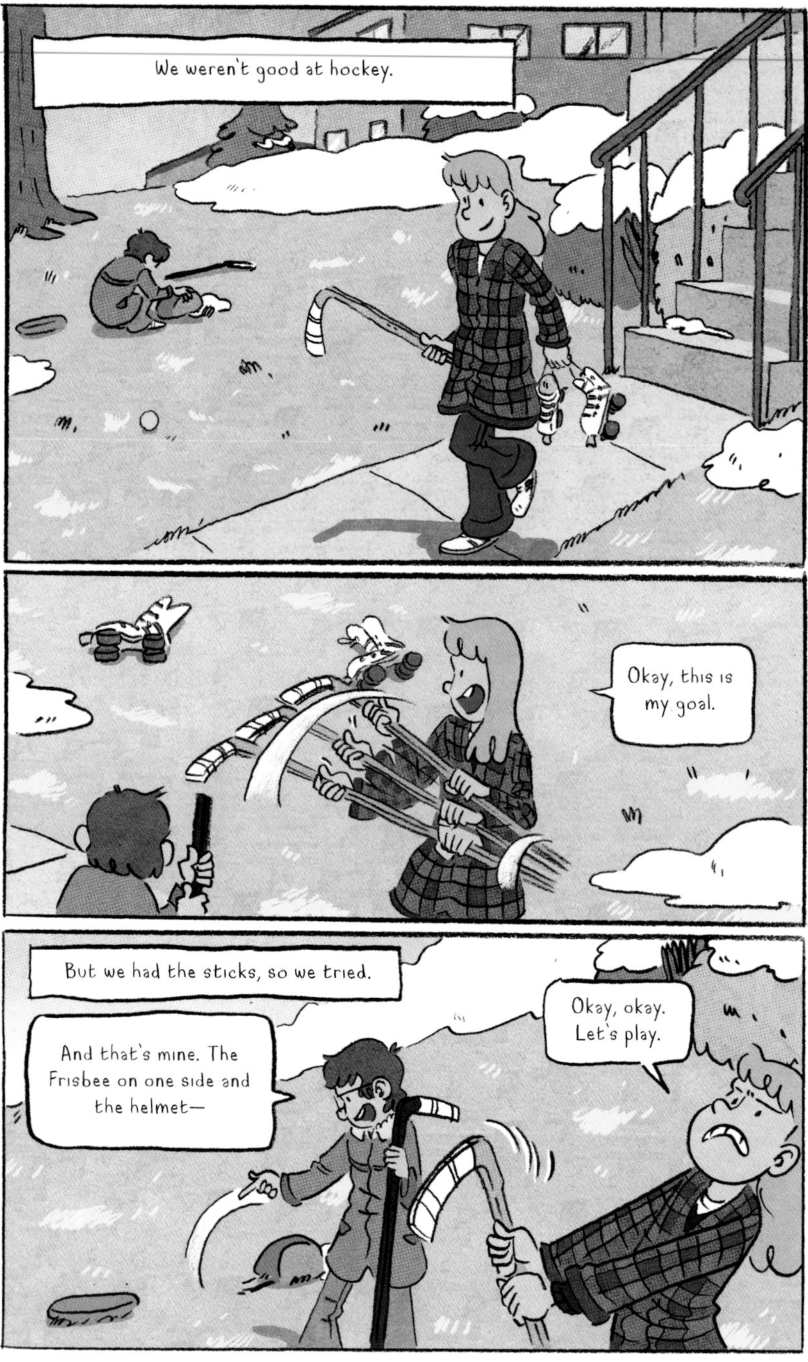
We weren't good at hockey.
Okay, this is my goal.
But we had the sticks, so we tried.
And that's mine. The Frisbee on one side and the helmet—
Okay, okay. Let's play.

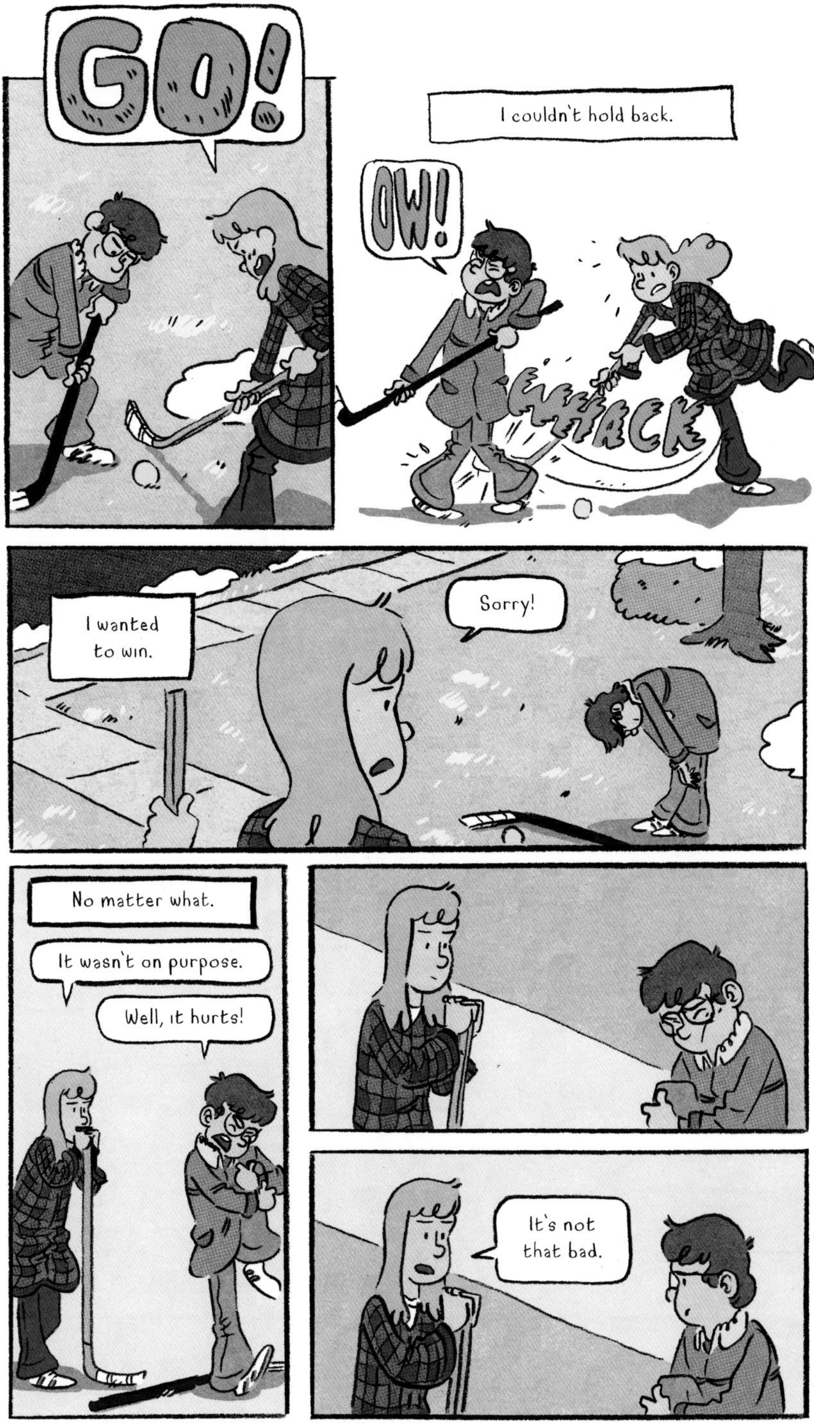
GO!
I couldn't hold back.
OW!
WHACK
I wanted to win.
Sorry!
No matter what.
It wasn't on purpose.
Well, it hurts!
It's not that bad.

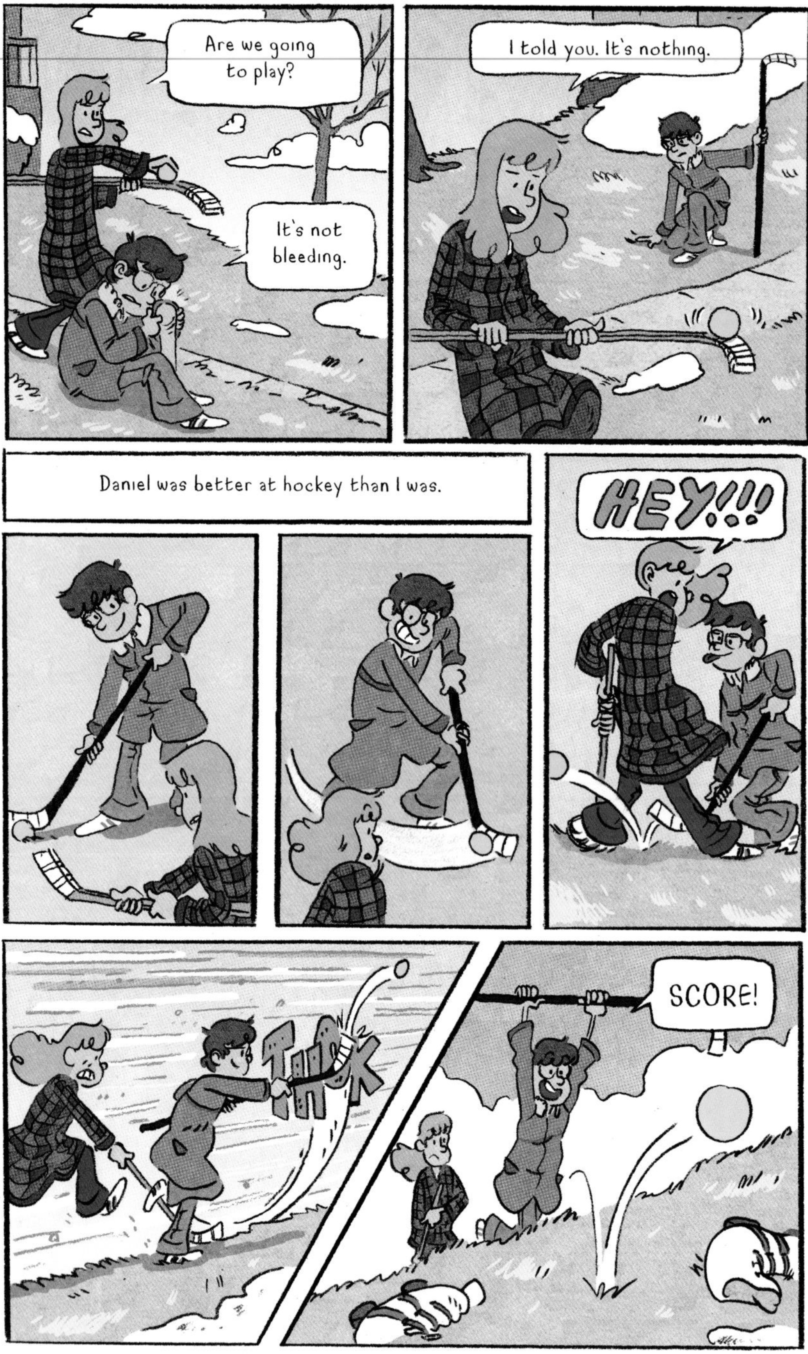
Are we going to play?
It's not bleeding.
I told you. It's nothing.
Daniel was better at hockey than I was.
HEY!!!
THOK
SCORE!

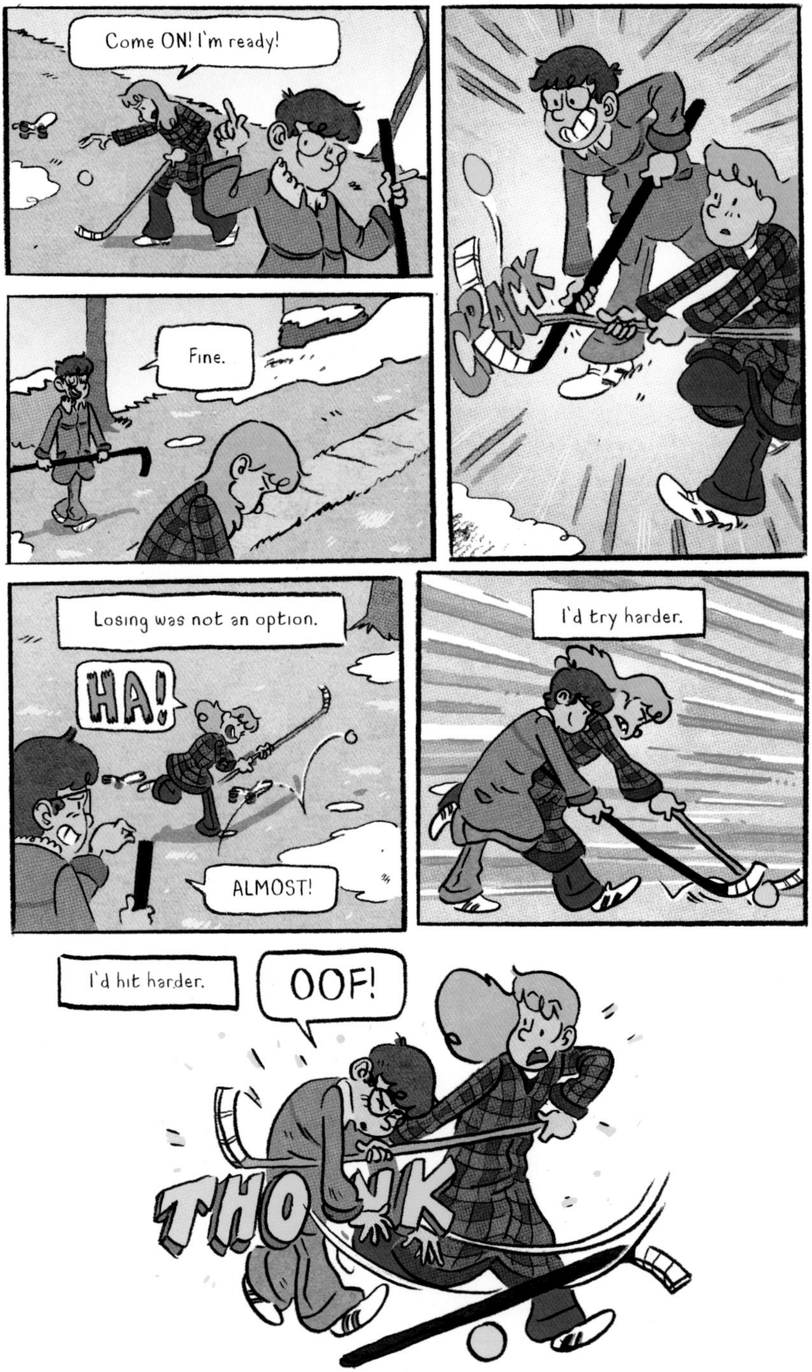

Come ON! I'm ready!
Fine.
CRACK
Losing was not an option.
HA!
ALMOST!
I'd try harder.
I'd hit harder.
OOF!
THONK

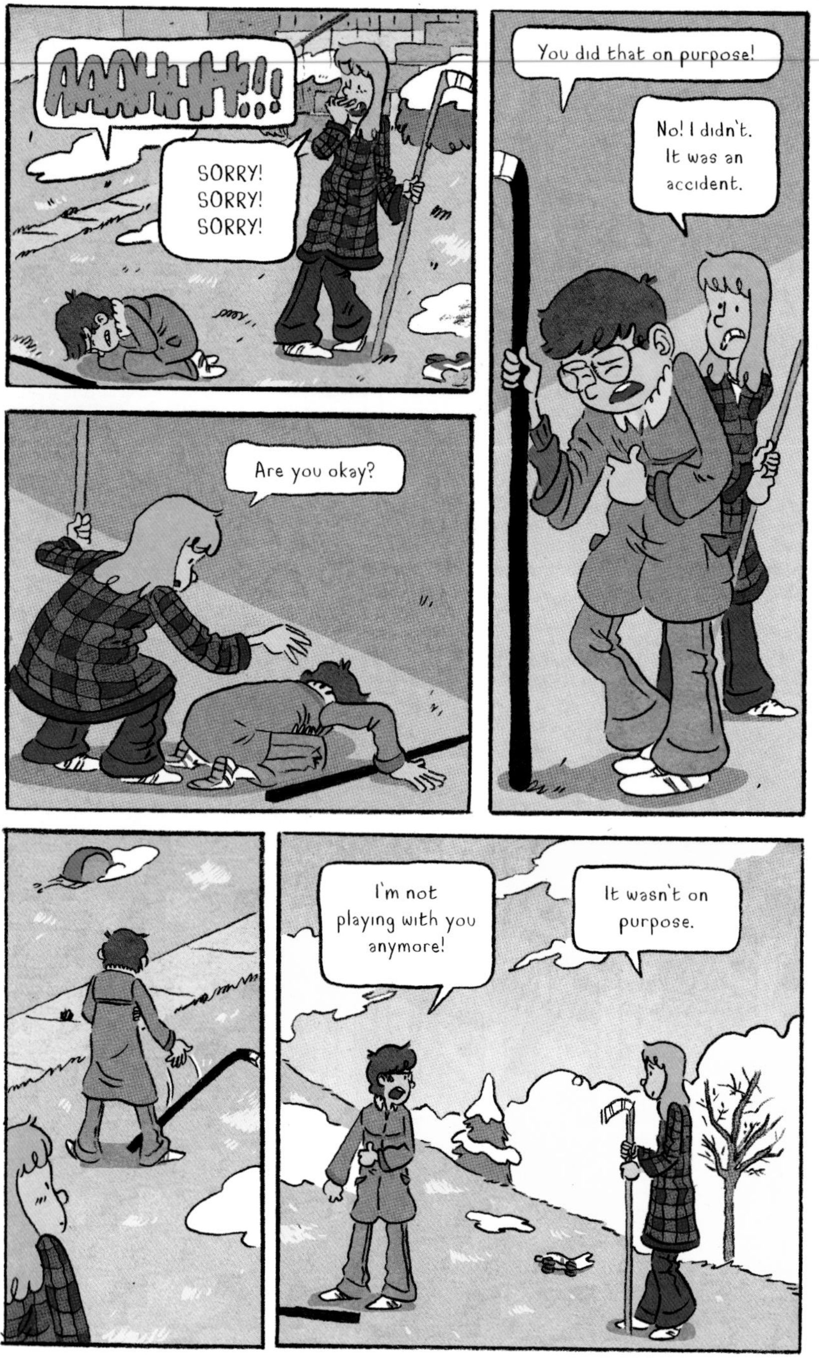
AAAHHH!!!
SORRY! SORRY! SORRY!
You did that on purpose!
No! I didn't. It was an accident.
Are you okay?
I'm not playing with you anymore!
It wasn't on purpose.

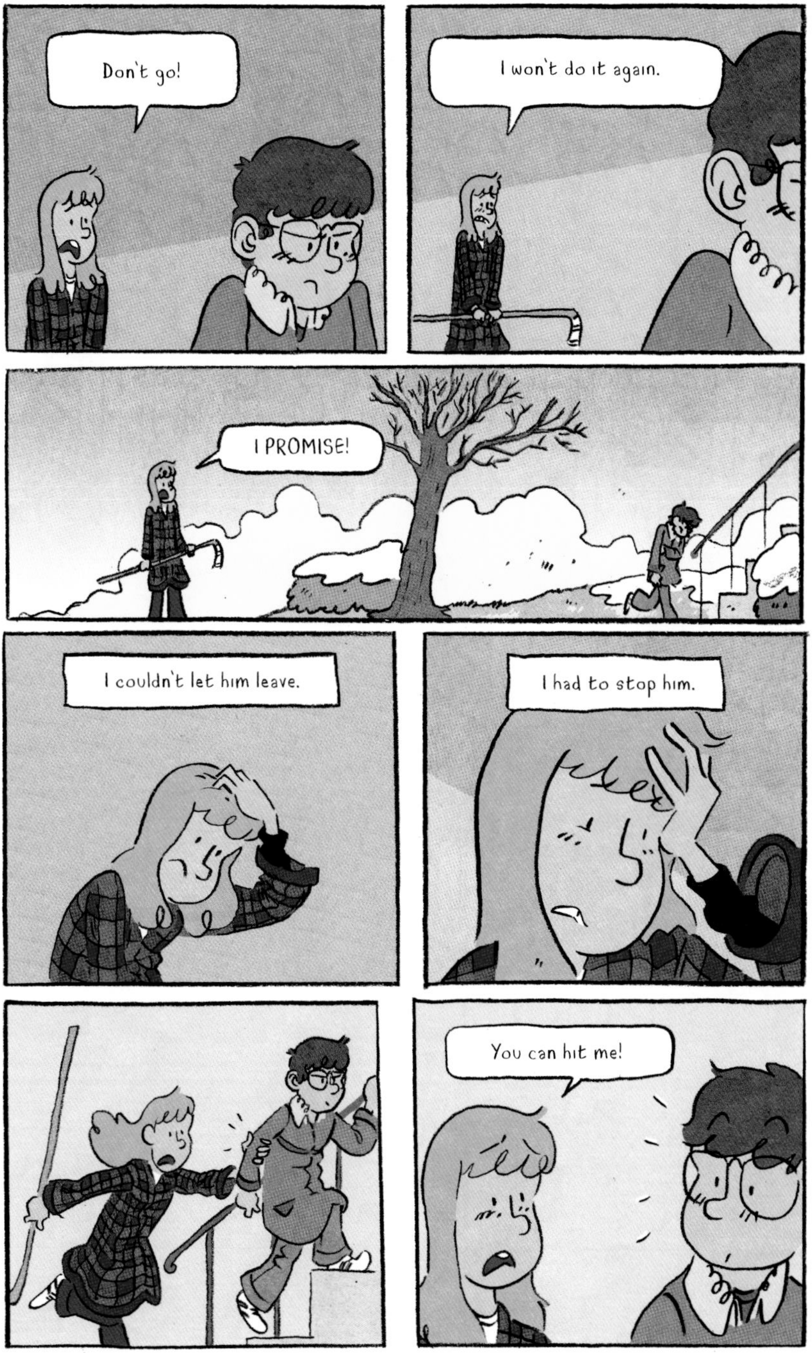
Don't go!
I won't do it again.
I PROMISE!
I couldn't let him leave.
I had to stop him.
You can hit me!

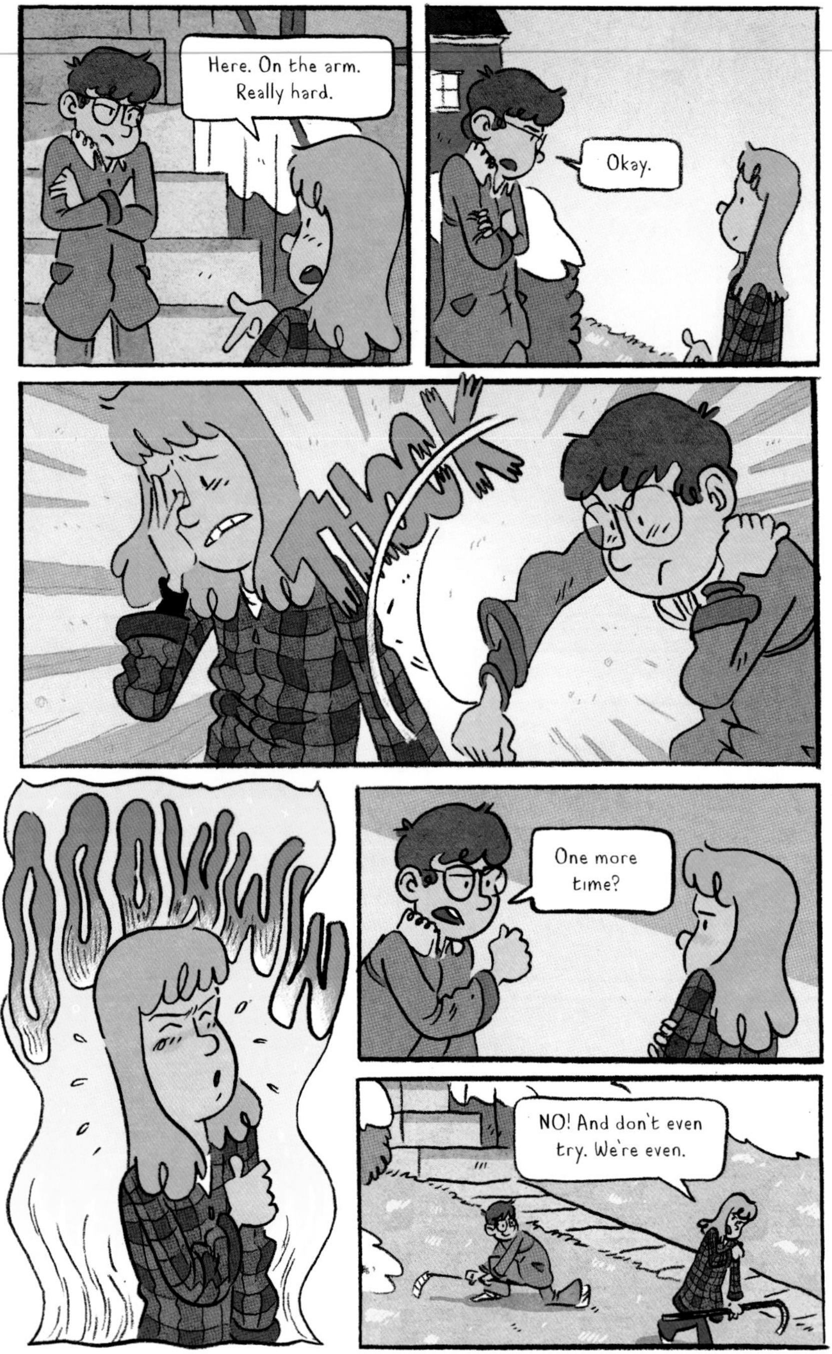
Here. On the arm. Really hard.
Okay.
One more time?
NO! And don't even try. We're even.

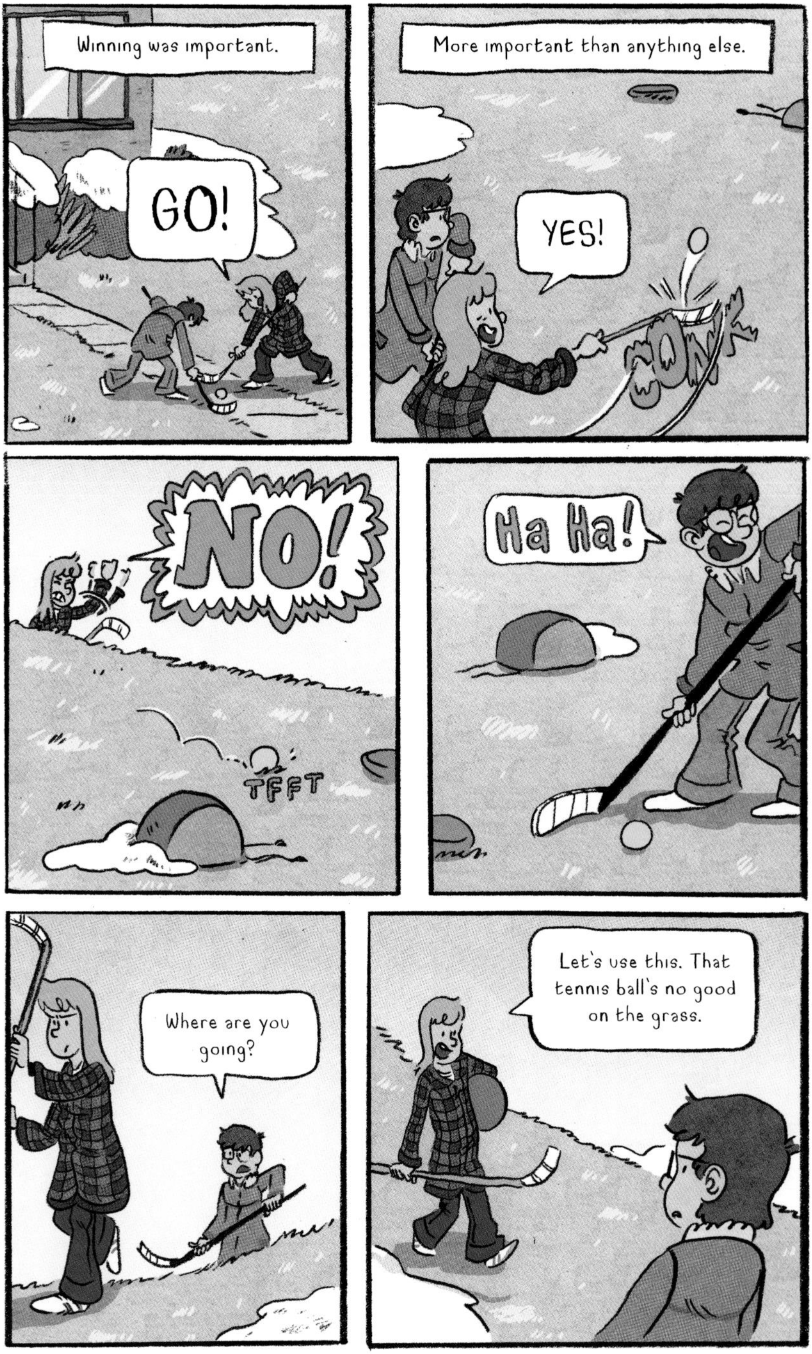
Winning was important.
GO!
More important than anything else.
YES!
NO!
TFFT
Ha Ha!
Where are you going?
Let's use this. That tennis ball's no good on the grass.

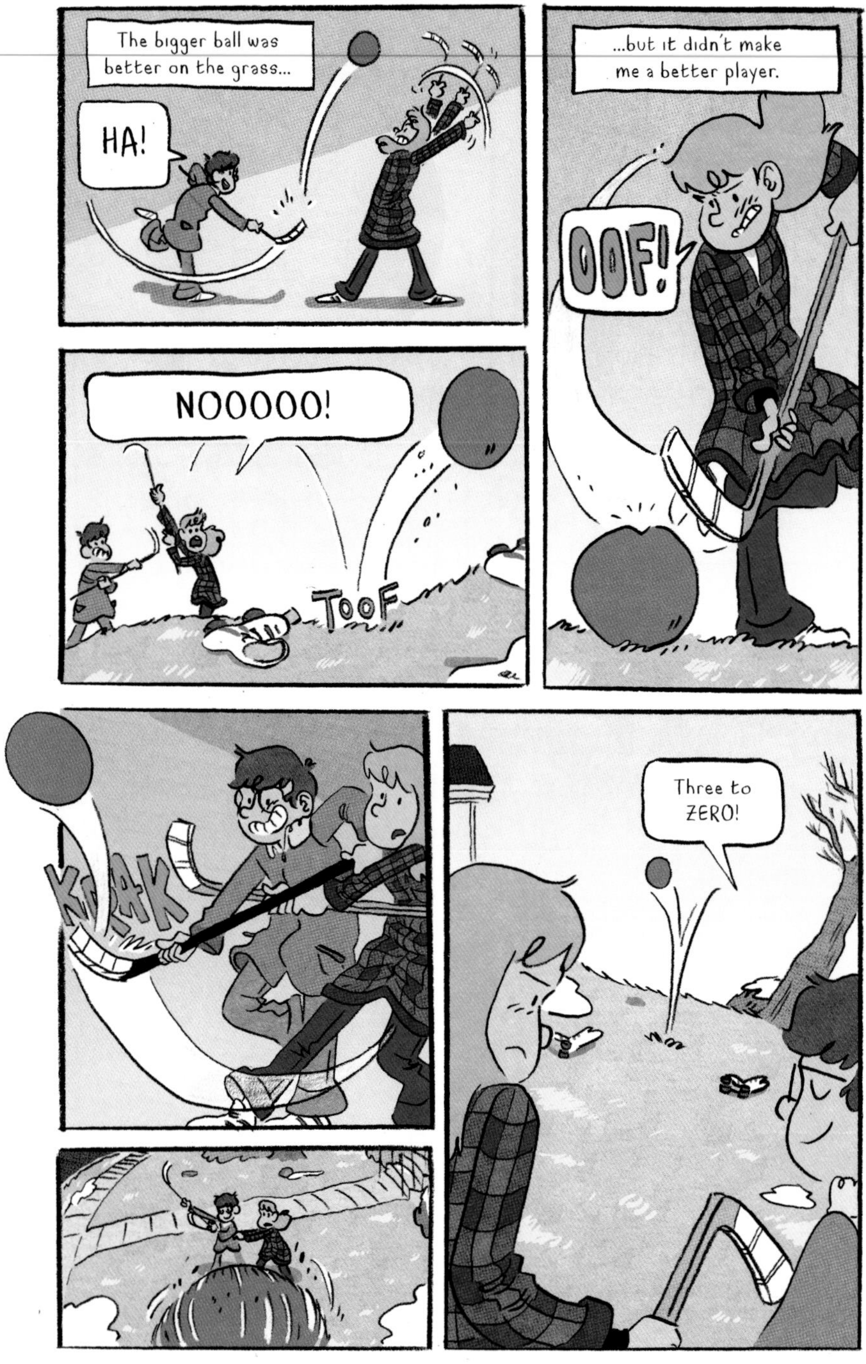
The bigger ball was better on the grass...
HA!
...but it didn't make me a better player.
OOF!
NOOOOO!
TOOF
Three to ZERO!

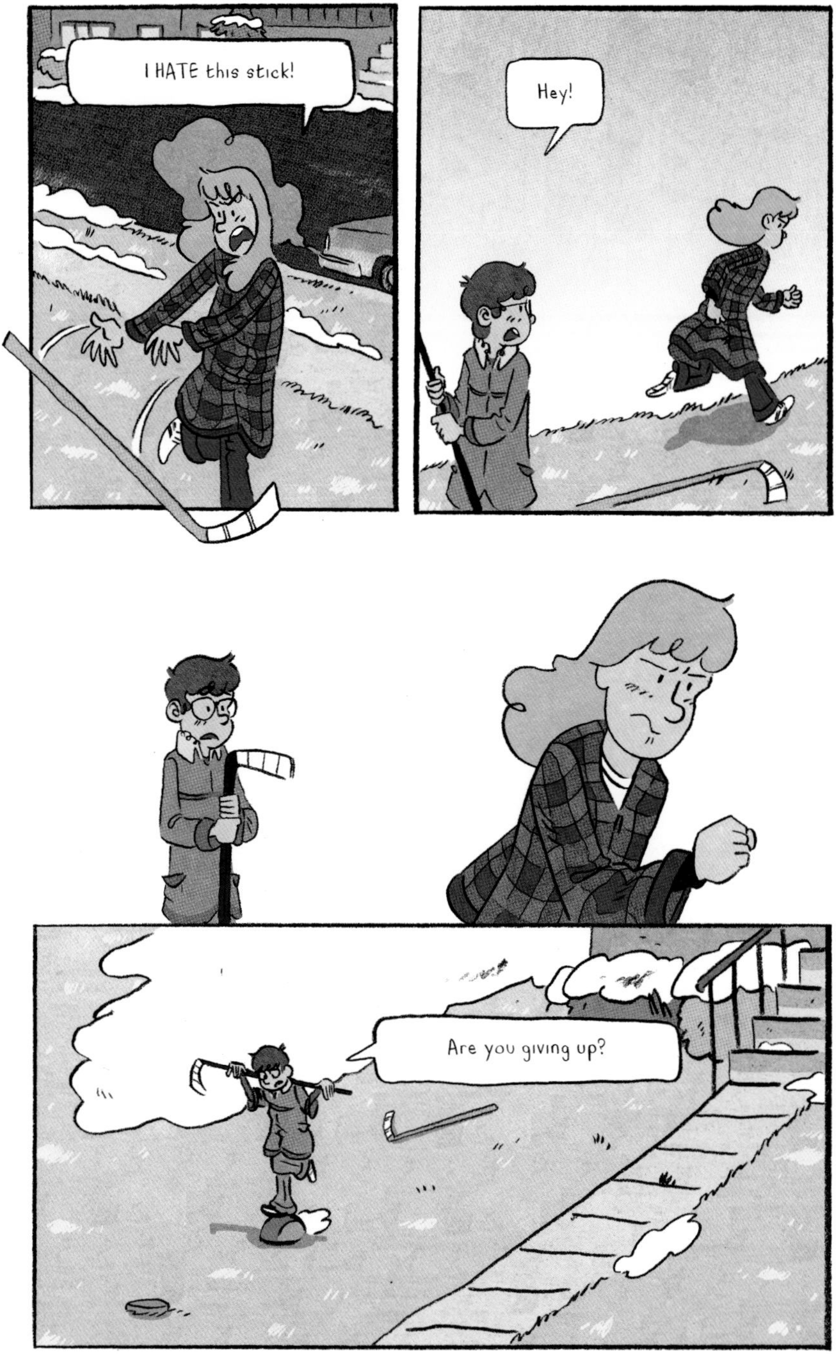
I HATE this stick!
Hey!
Are you giving up?

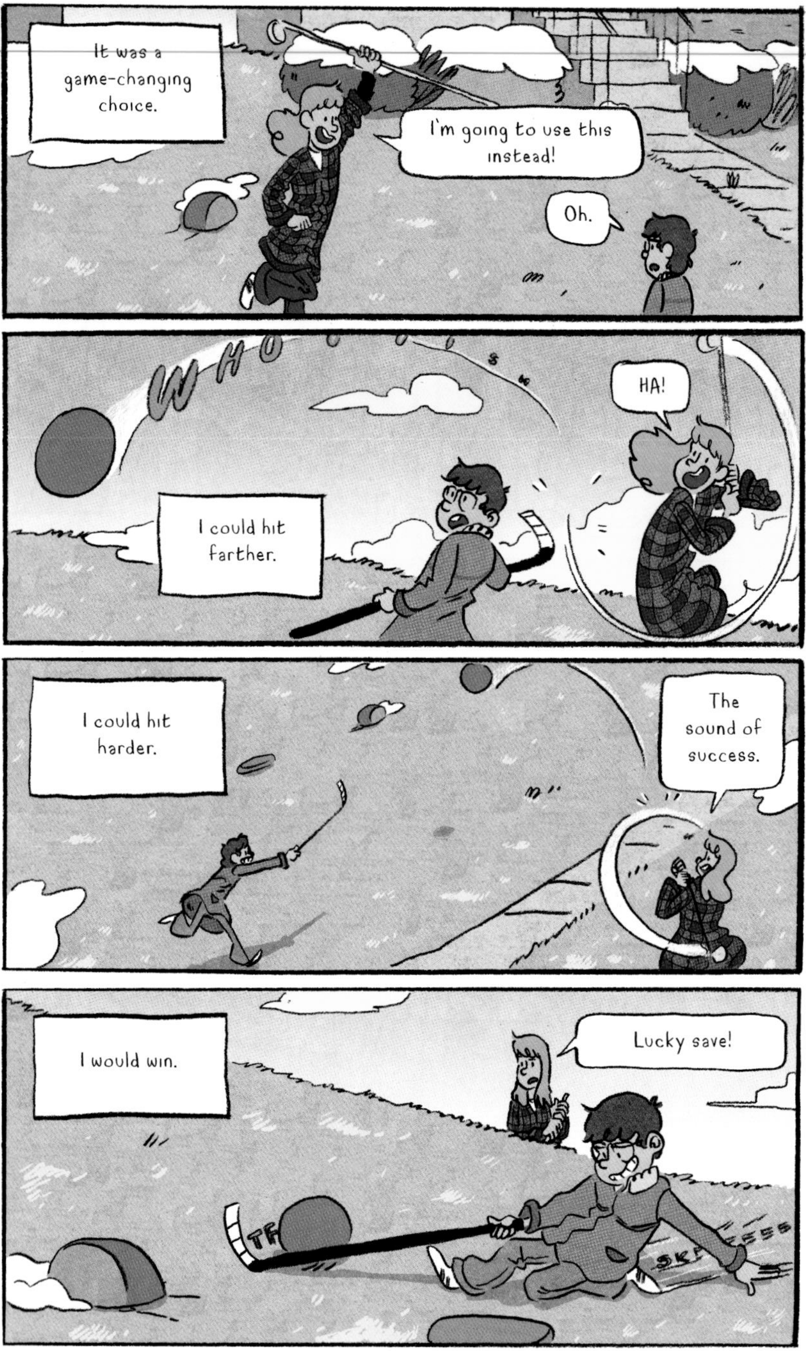
It was a game-changing choice.
I'm going to use this instead!
Oh.
WHOOOOSH
HA!
I could hit farther.
I could hit harder.
The sound of success.
I would win.
Lucky save!

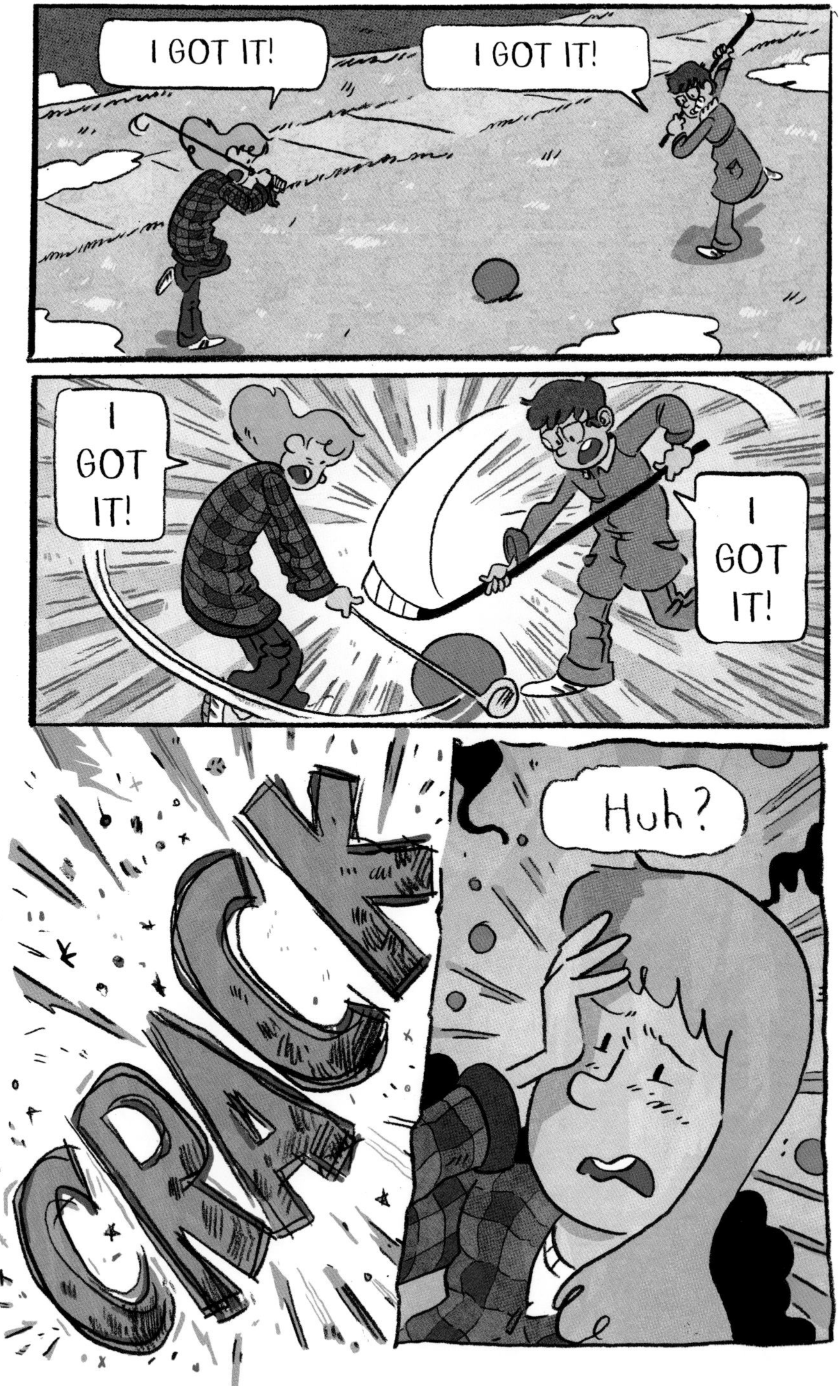
I GOT IT!
I GOT IT!
I GOT IT!
I GOT IT!
CRACK
Huh?

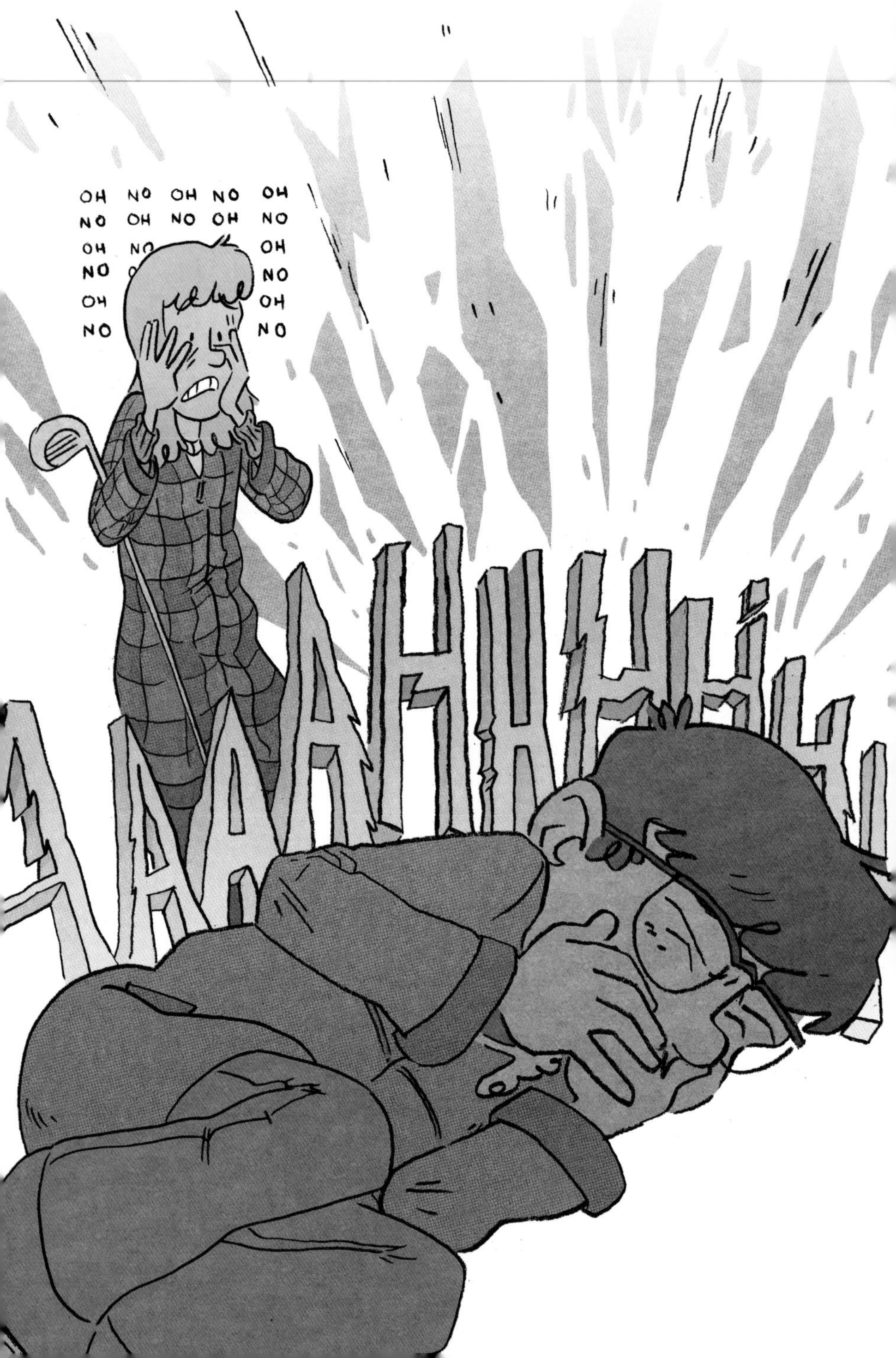
OH NO OH NO OH NO OH NO OH NO OH NO OH NO OH NO OH NO OH NO
AAAHHHHHH

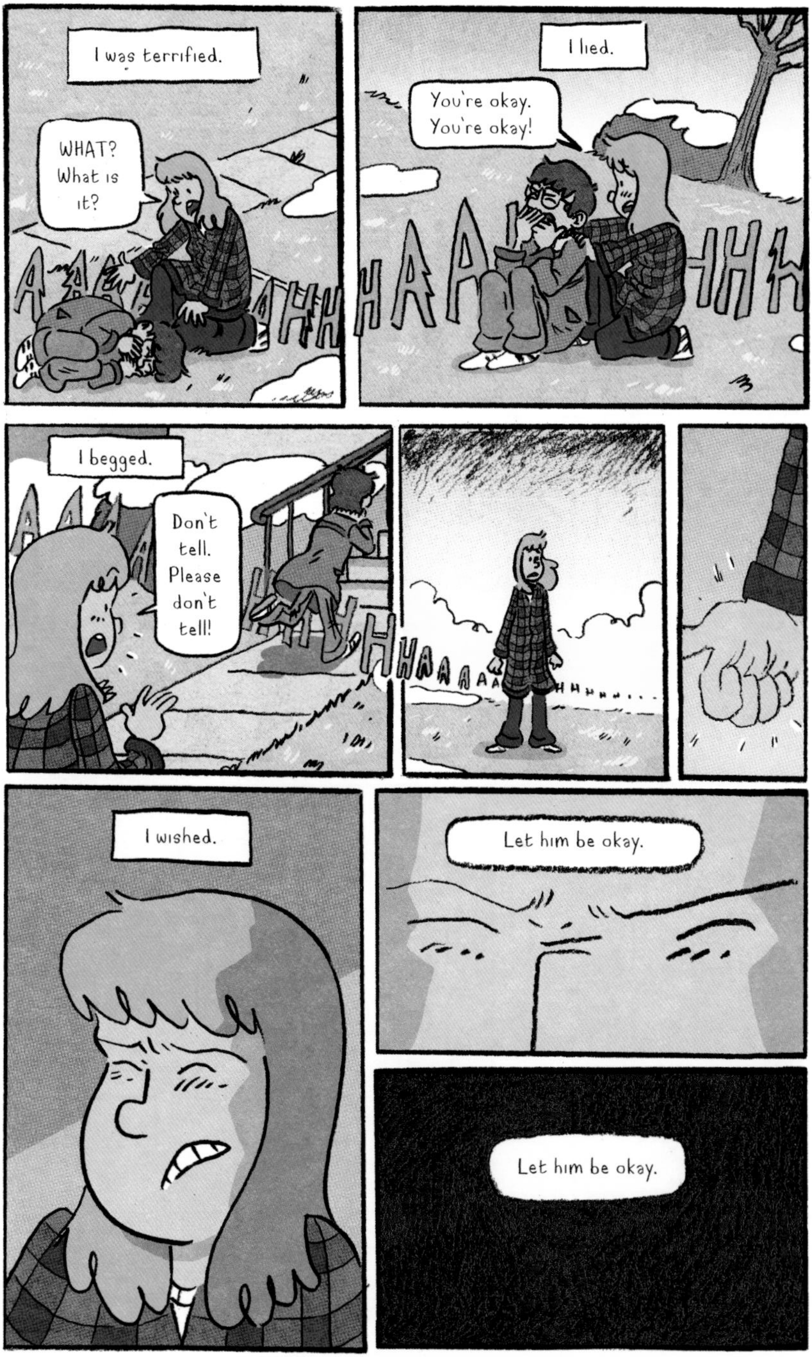
I was terrified.
WHAT? What is it?
AAAHHHHAAAHHH
I lied.
You're okay. You're okay!
I begged.
Don't tell. Please don't tell!
HHAAAAAHHHHH...
I wished.
Let him be okay.
Let him be okay.

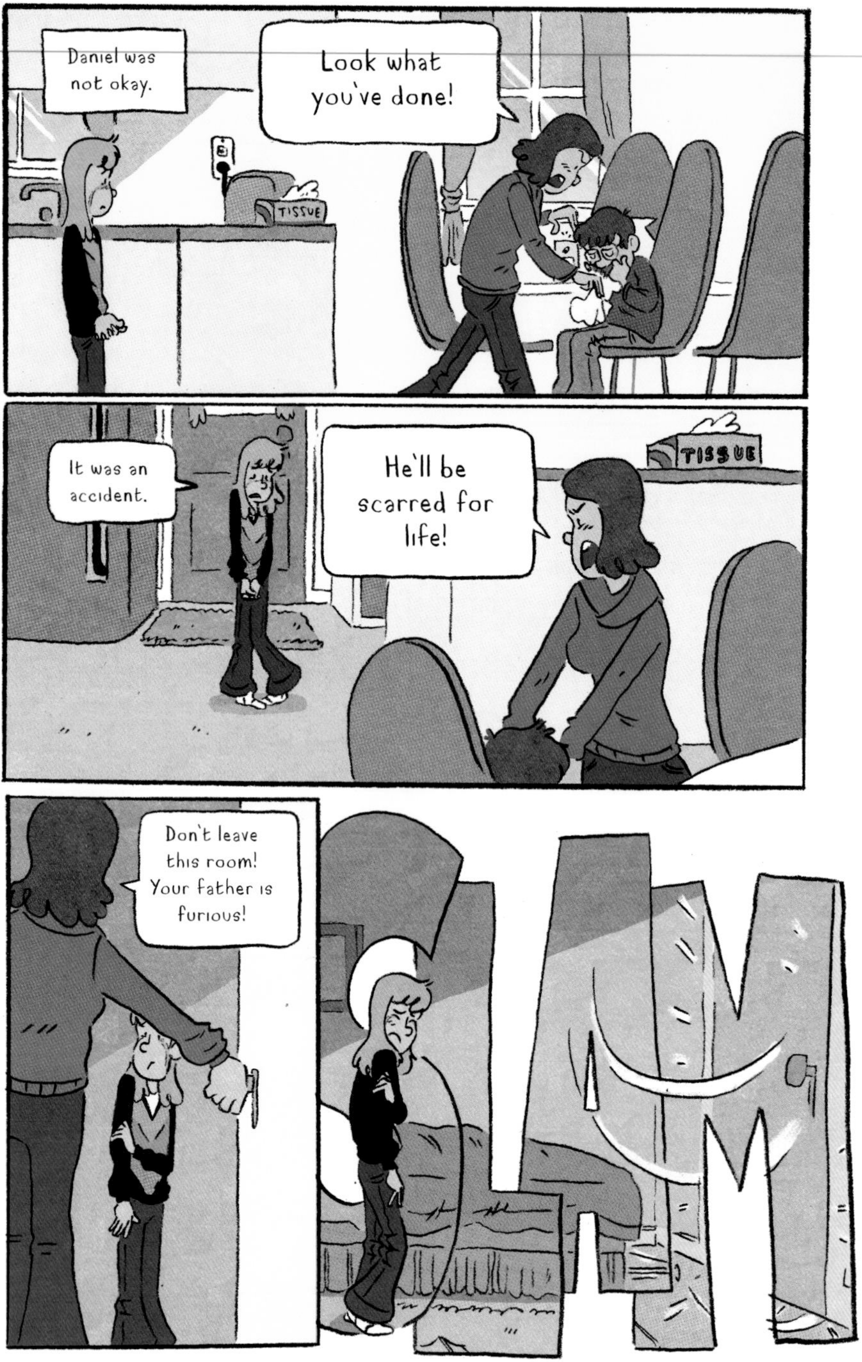
Daniel was not okay.
Look what you've done!
TISSUE
It was an accident.
He'll be scarred for life!
TISSUE
Don't leave this room! Your father is furious!
SLAM

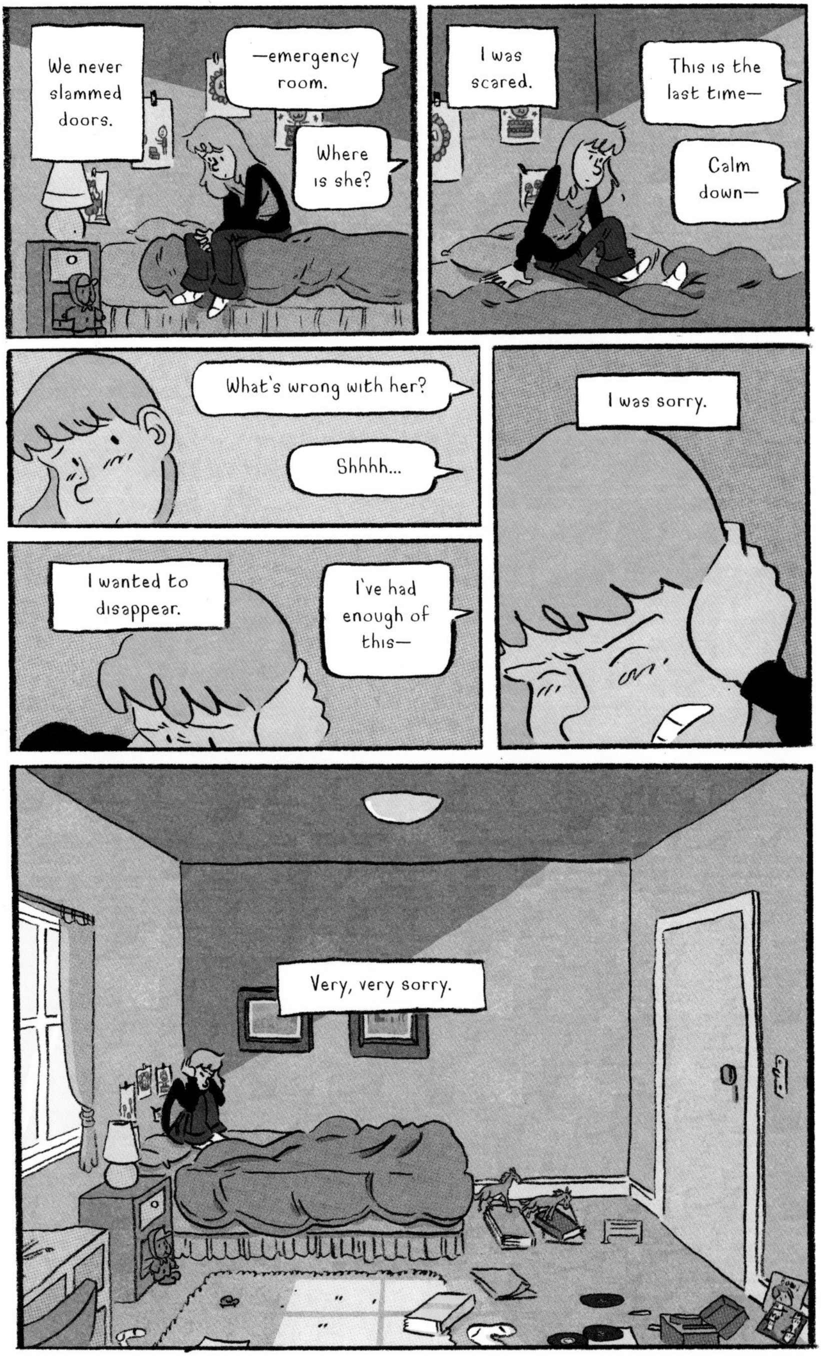
We never slammed doors.
—emergency room.
Where is she?
I was scared.
This is the last time—
Calm down—
What's wrong with her?
Shhhh...
I wanted to disappear.
I've had enough of this—
I was sorry.
Very, very sorry.

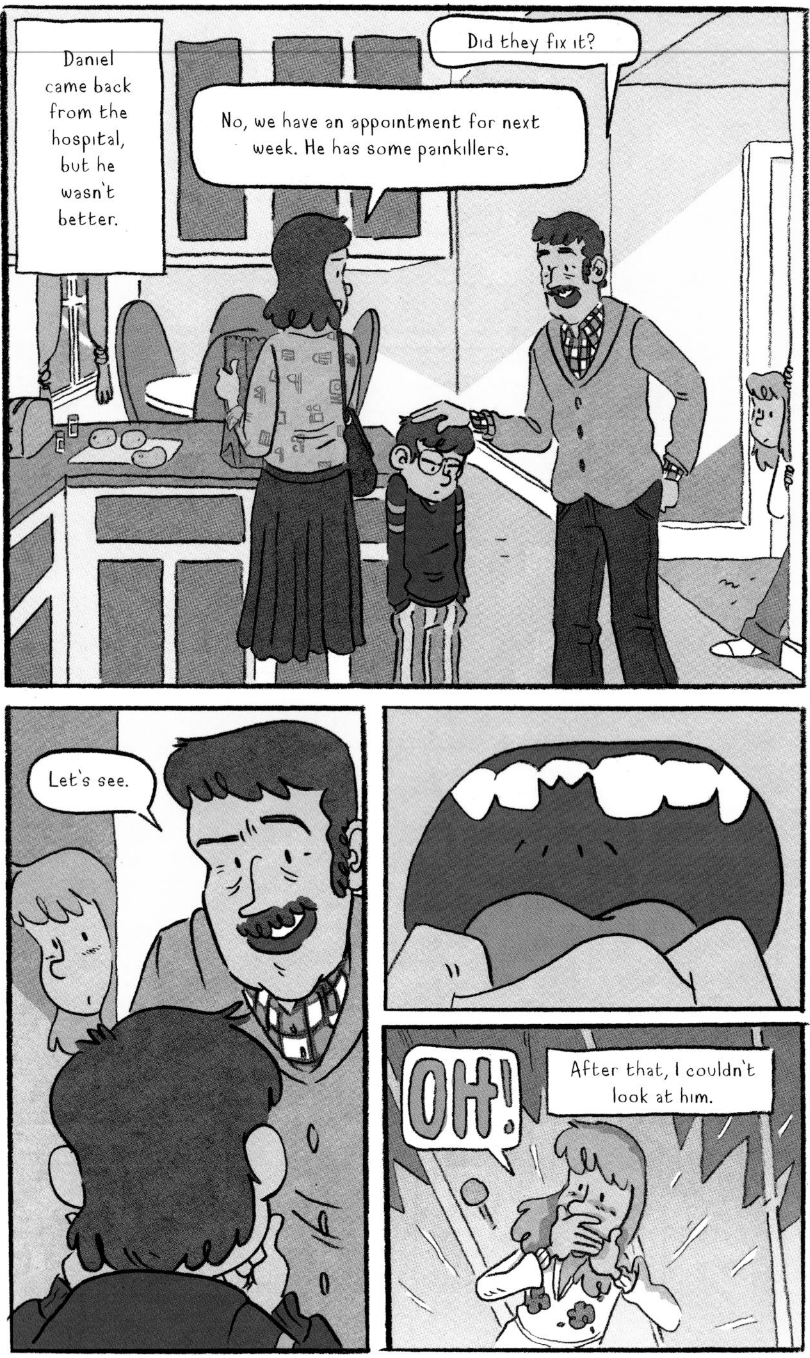

Daniel came back from the hospital, but he wasn't better.
Did they fix it?
No, we have an appointment for next week. He has some painkillers.
Let's see.
OH!
After that, I couldn't look at him.

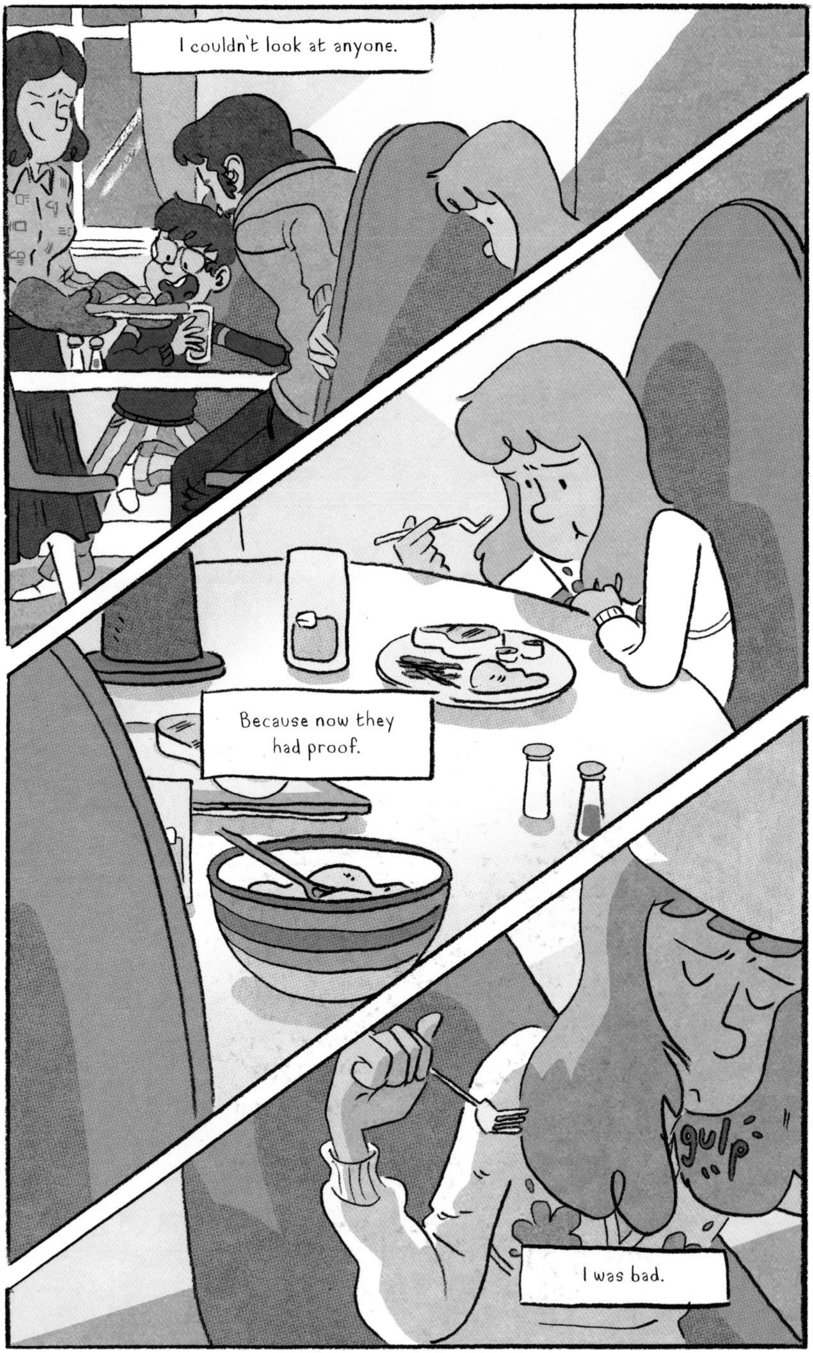
I couldn't look at anyone.
Because now they had proof.
gulp
I was bad.

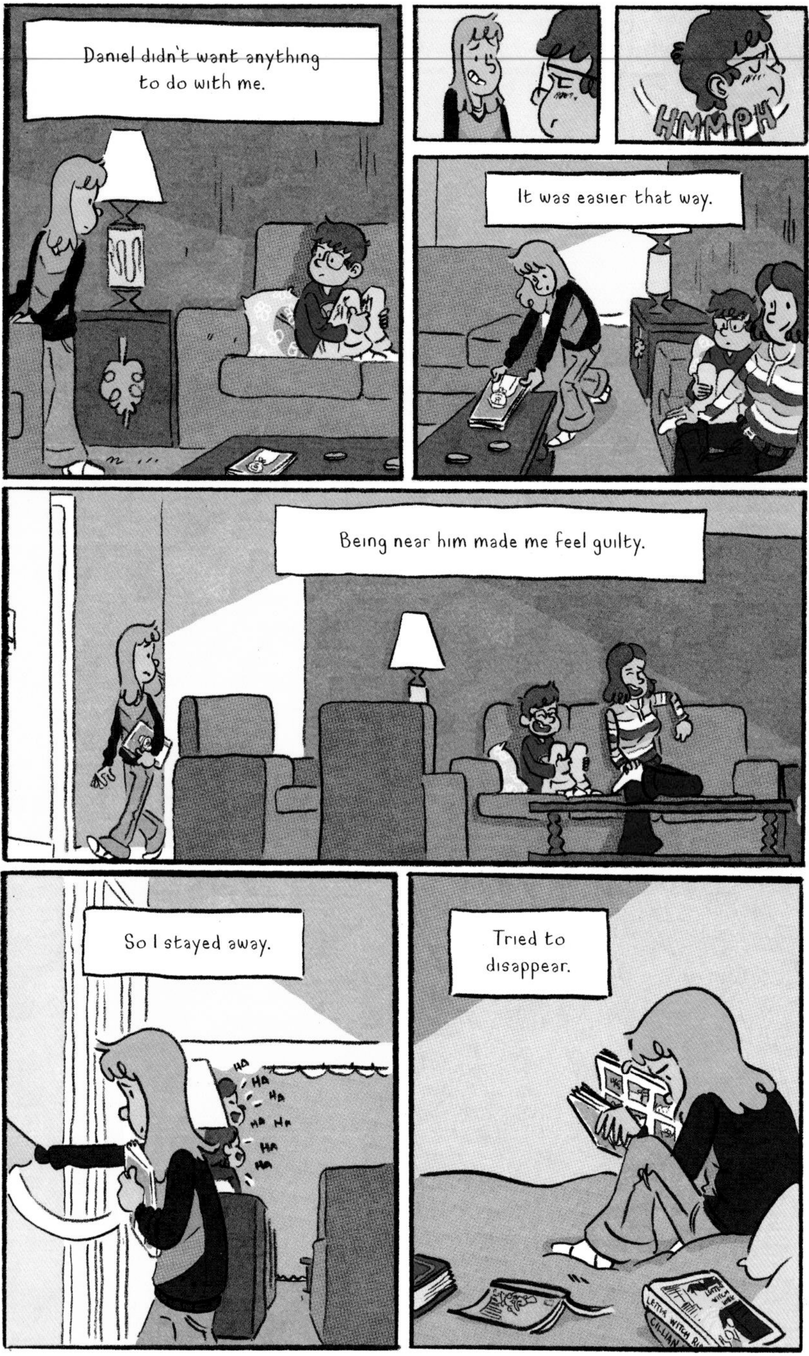
Daniel didn't want anything to do with me.
HMMPH
It was easier that way.
Being near him made me feel guilty.
So I stayed away.
HA HA HA HA HA HA HA
Tried to disappear.

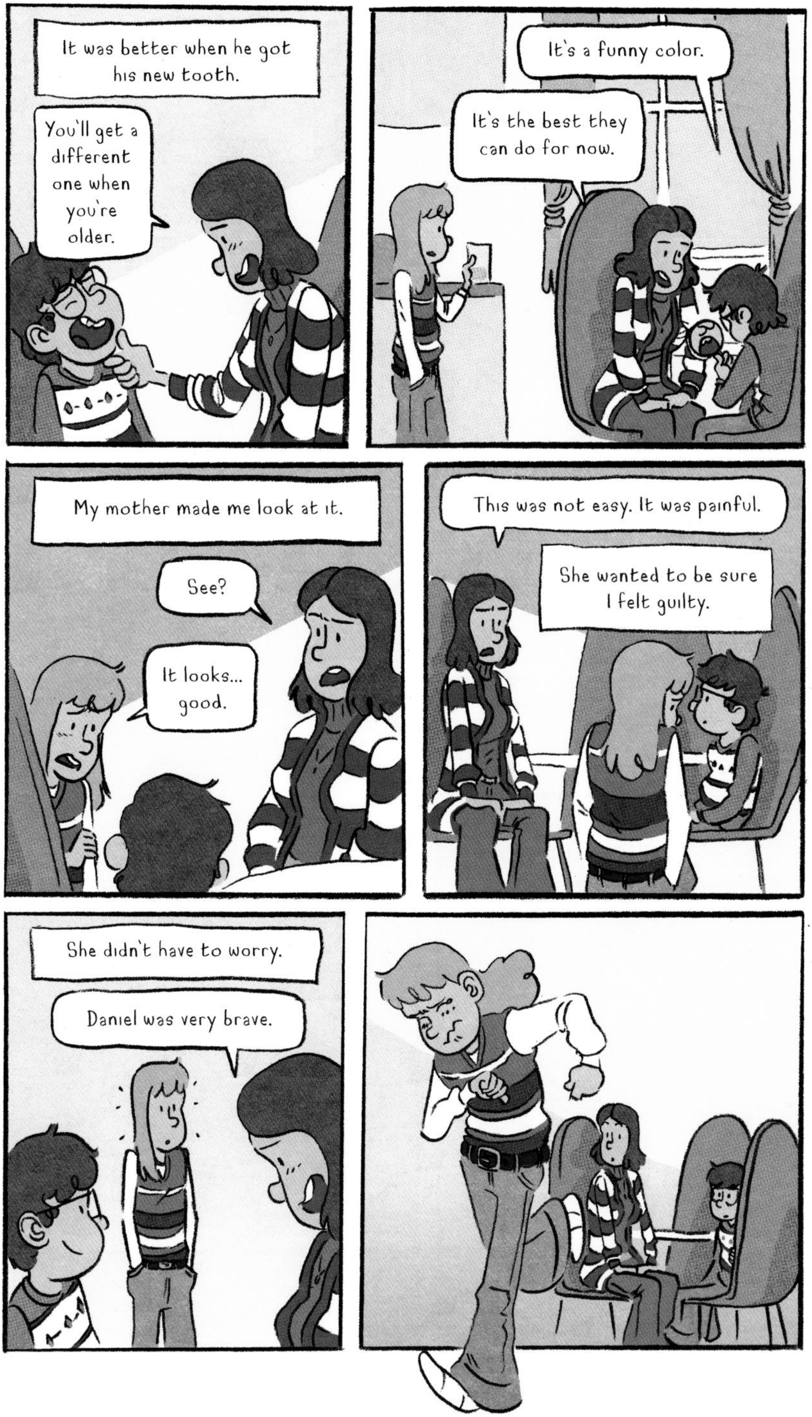
It was better when he got his new tooth.
You'll get a different one when you're older.
It's a funny color.
It's the best they can do for now.
My mother made me look at it.
See?
It looks... good.
This was not easy. It was painful.
She wanted to be sure I felt guilty.
She didn't have to worry.
Daniel was very brave.

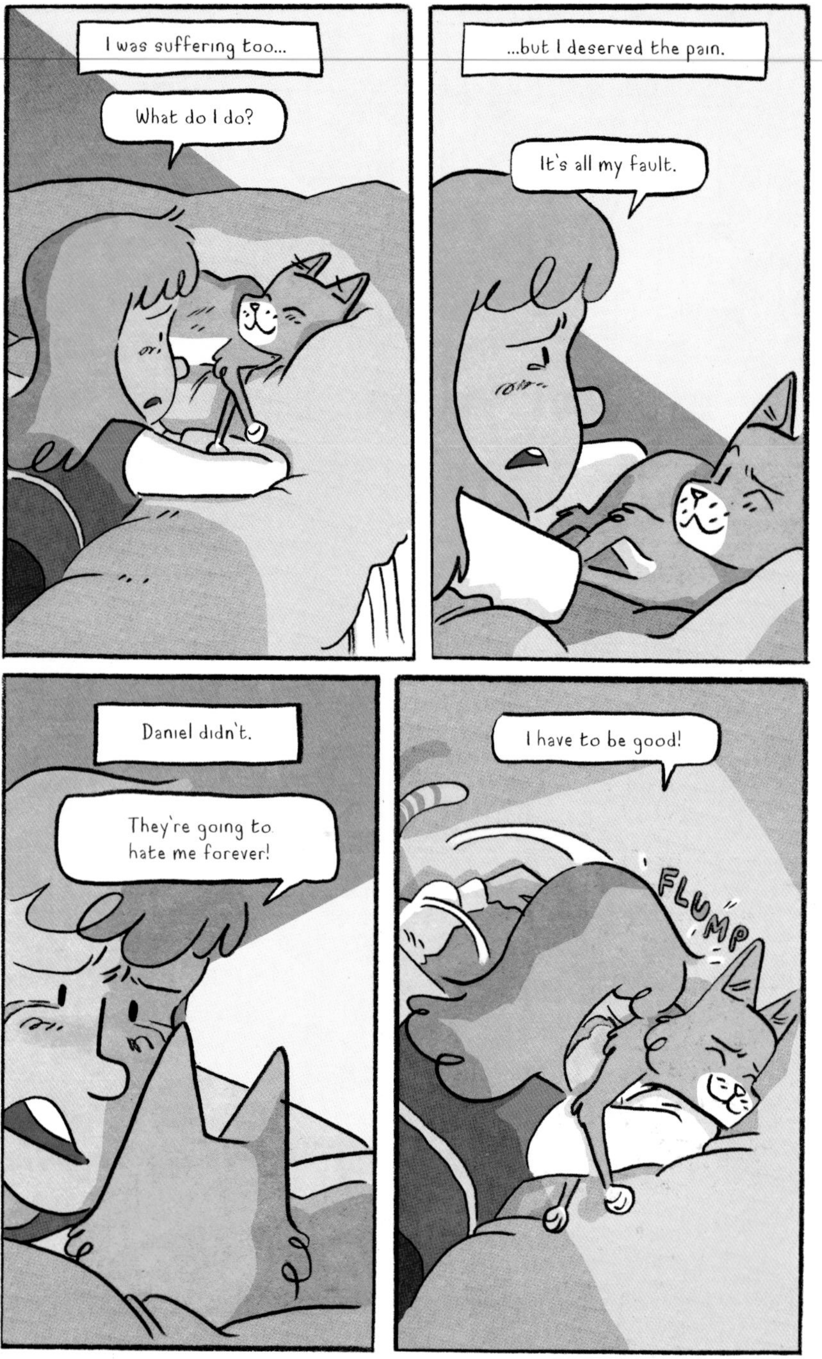
I was suffering too...
What do I do?
...but I deserved the pain.
It's all my fault.
Daniel didn't.
They're going to hate me forever!
I have to be good!
FLUMP

9

The Power to Lead

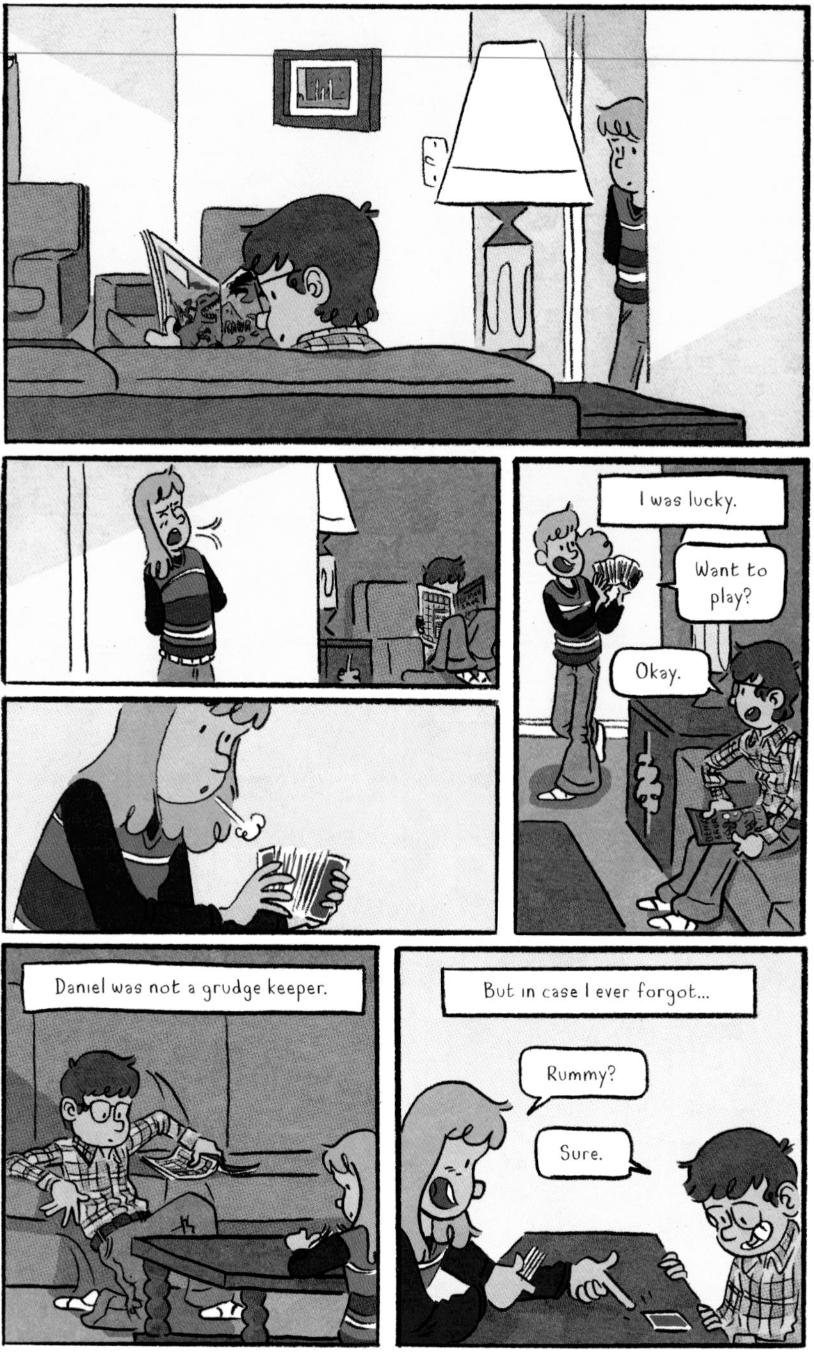
I was lucky.
Want to play?
Okay.
Daniel was not a grudge keeper.
But in case I ever forgot...
Rummy?
Sure.

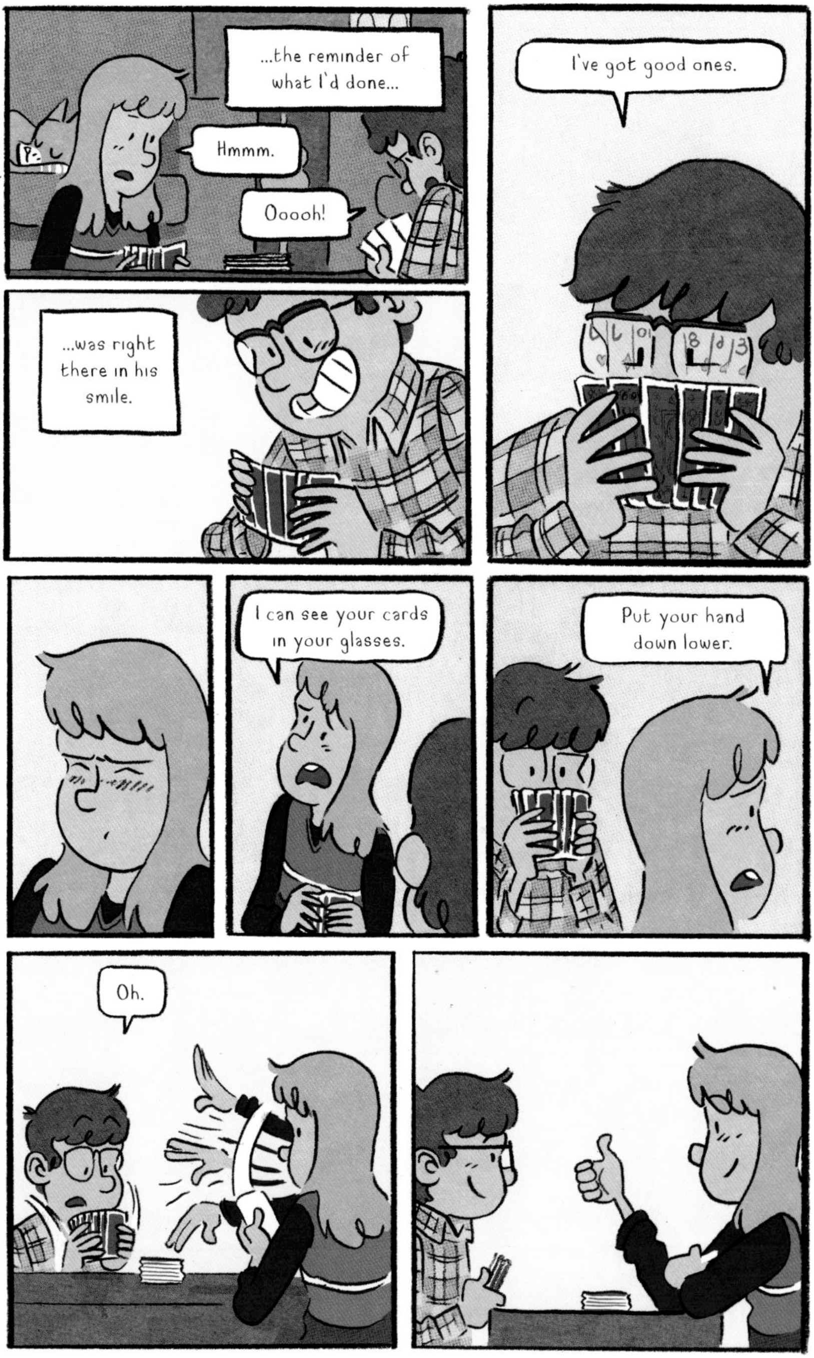
...the reminder of what I'd done...
Hmmm.
Ooooh!
I've got good ones.
...was right there in his smile.
I can see your cards in your glasses.
Put your hand down lower.
Oh.

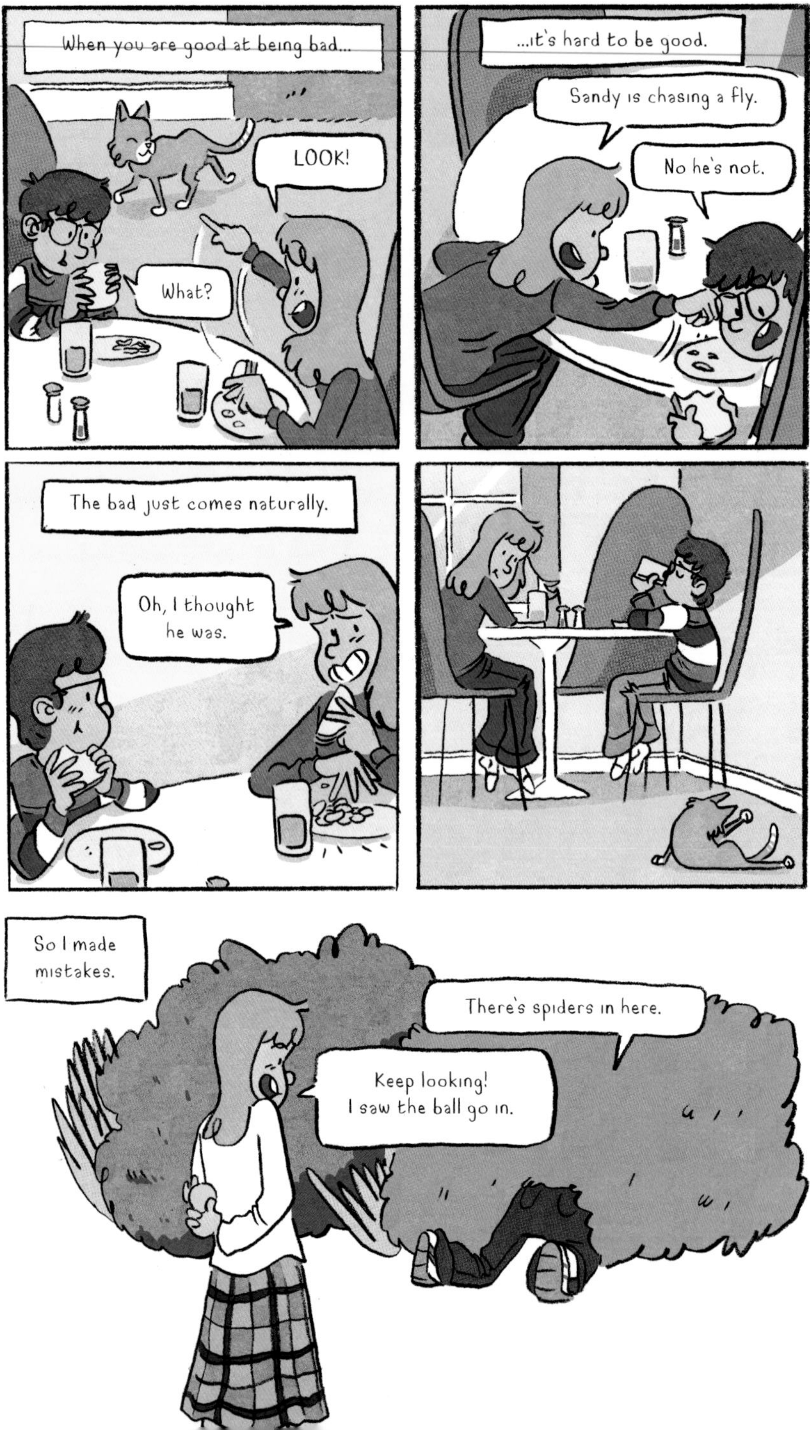
When you are good at being bad...
LOOK!
What?
...it's hard to be good.
Sandy is chasing a fly.
No he's not.
The bad just comes naturally.
Oh, I thought he was.
So I made mistakes.
There's spiders in here.
Keep looking! I saw the ball go in.

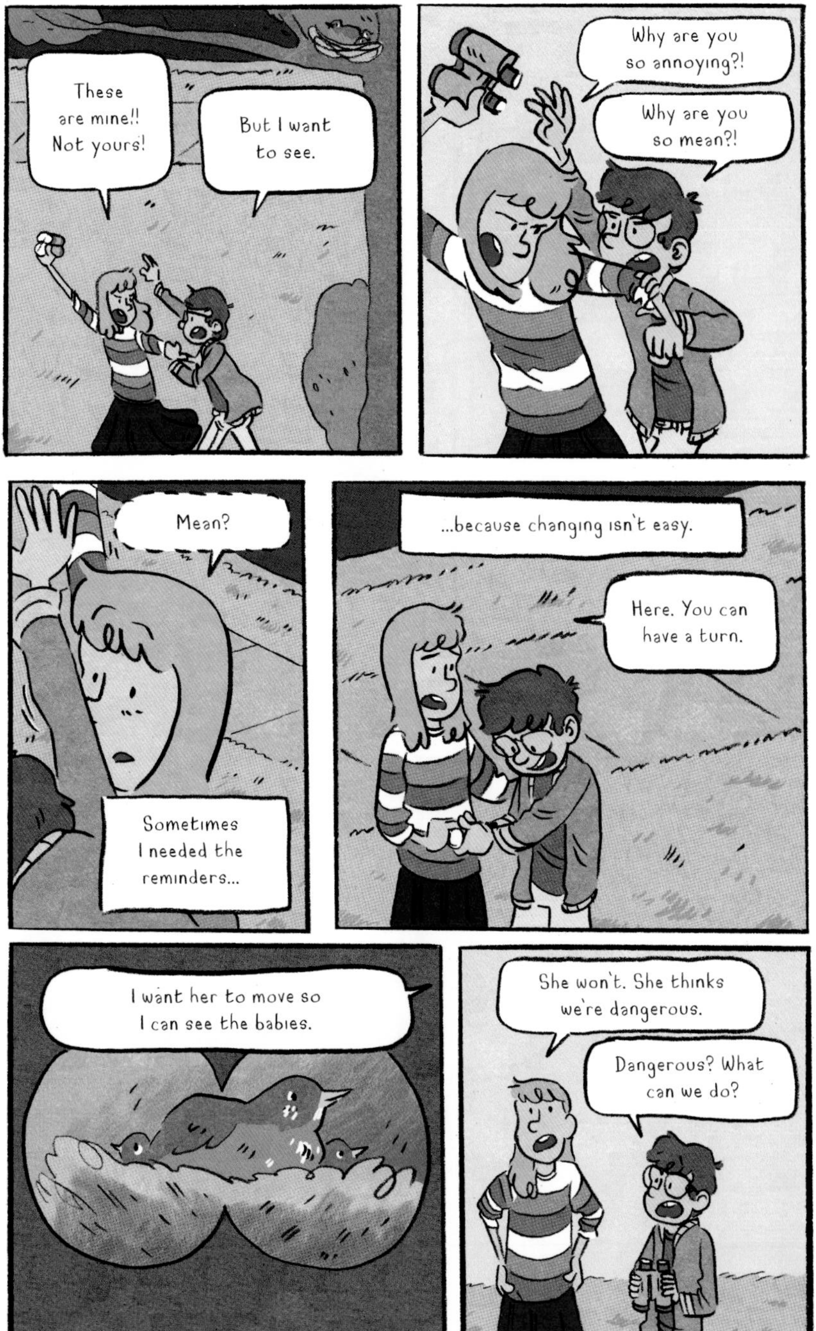

These are mine!! Not yours!
But I want to see.
Why are you so annoying?!
Why are you so mean?!
Mean?
Sometimes I needed the reminders...
...because changing isn't easy.
Here. You can have a turn.
I want her to move so I can see the babies.
She won't. She thinks we're dangerous.
Dangerous? What can we do?

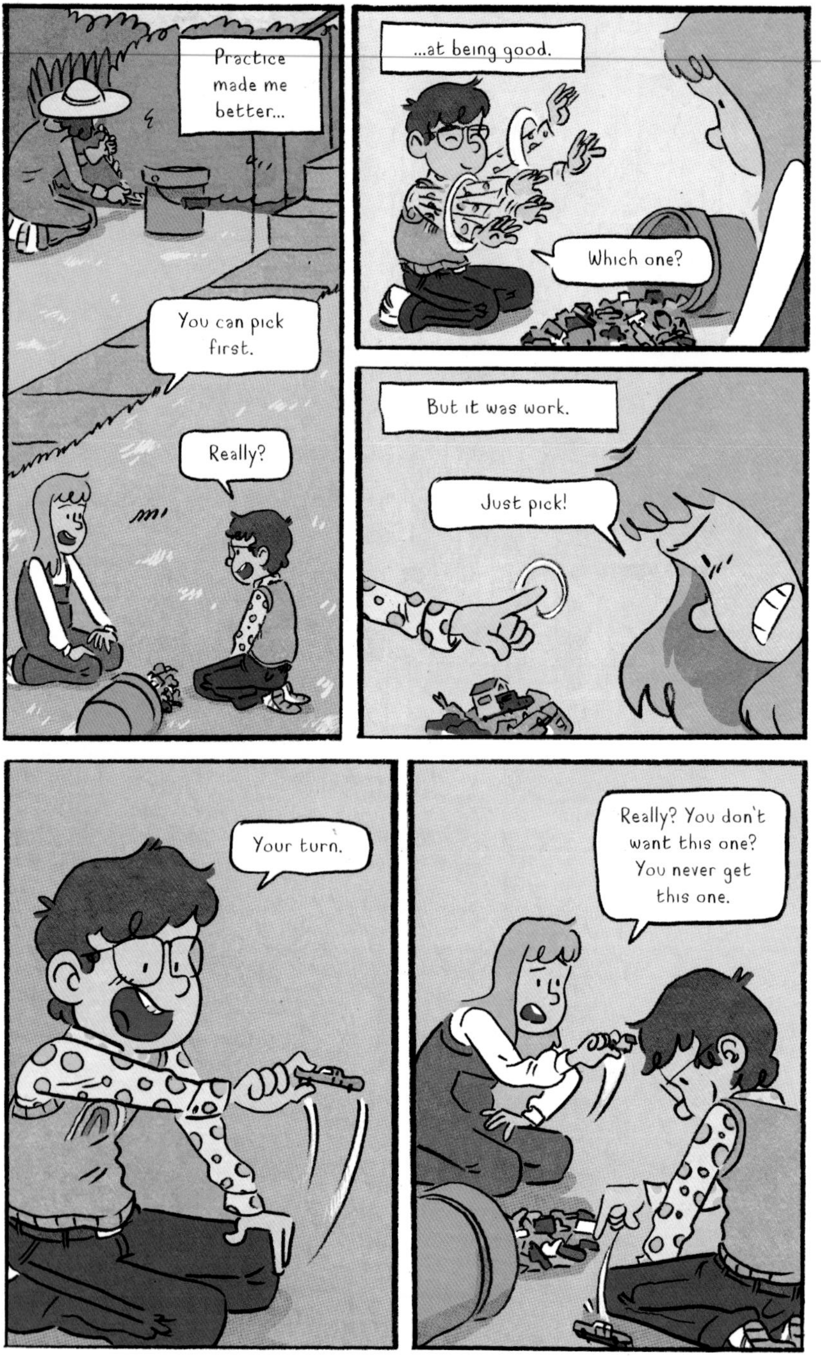
Practice made me better...
You can pick first.
Really?
...at being good.
Which one?
But it was work.
Just pick!
Your turn.
Really? You don't want this one? You never get this one.

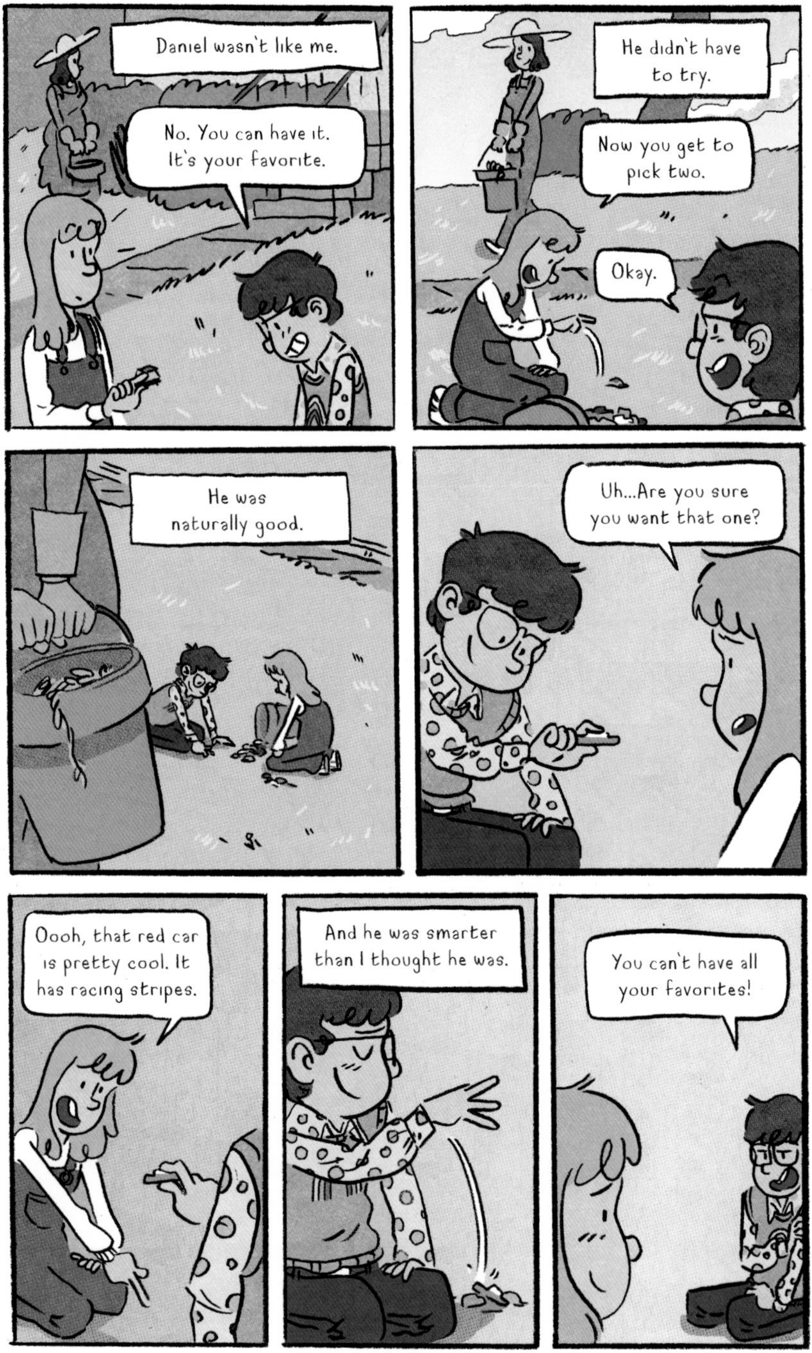
Daniel wasn't like me.
No. You can have it. It's your favorite.
He didn't have to try.
Now you get to pick two.
Okay.
He was naturally good.
Uh...Are you sure you want that one?
Oooh, that red car is pretty cool. It has racing stripes.
And he was smarter than I thought he was.
You can't have all your favorites!

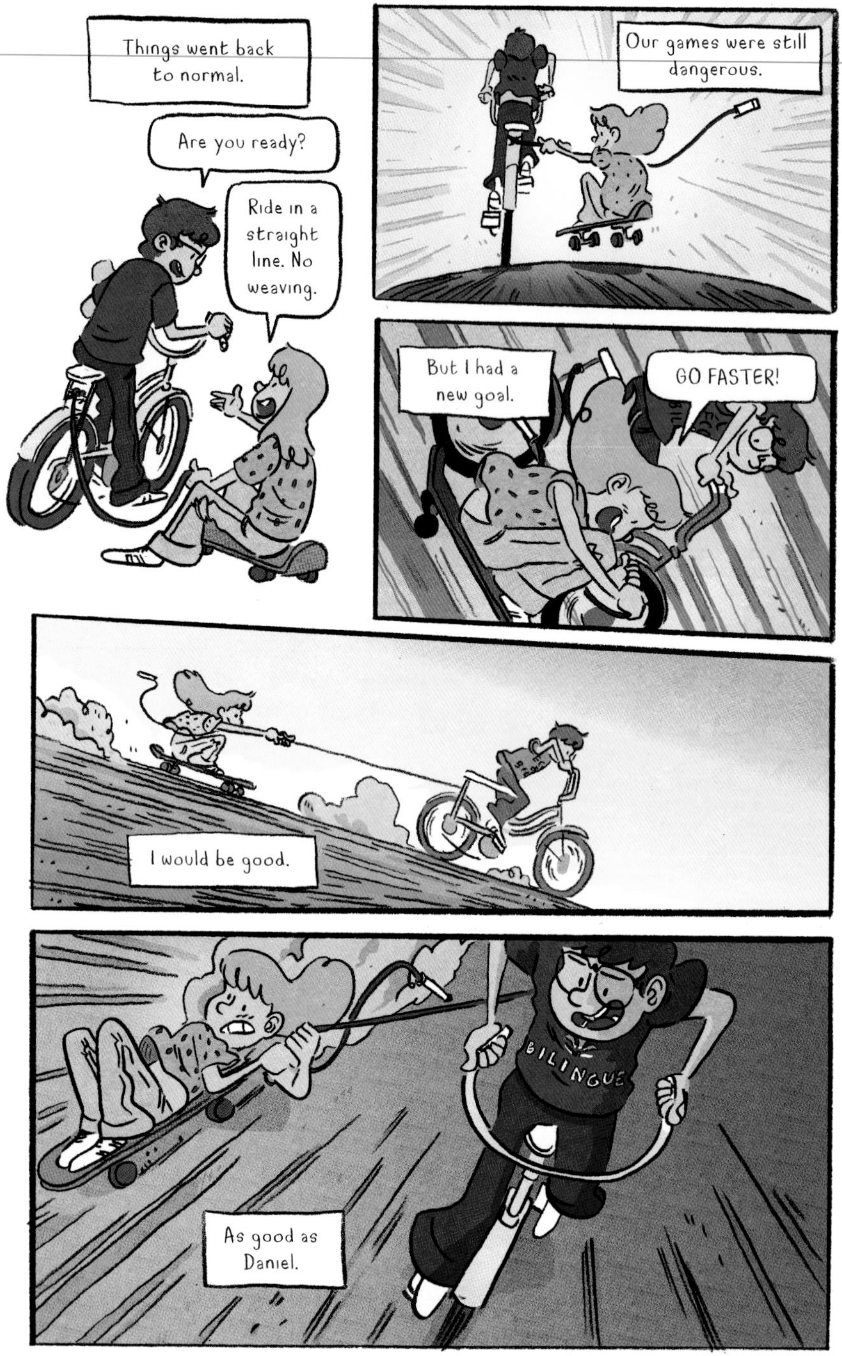
Things went back to normal.
Are you ready?
Ride in a straight line. No weaving.
Our games were still dangerous.
But I had a new goal.
GO FASTER!
I would be good.
BILINGUE
As good as Daniel.

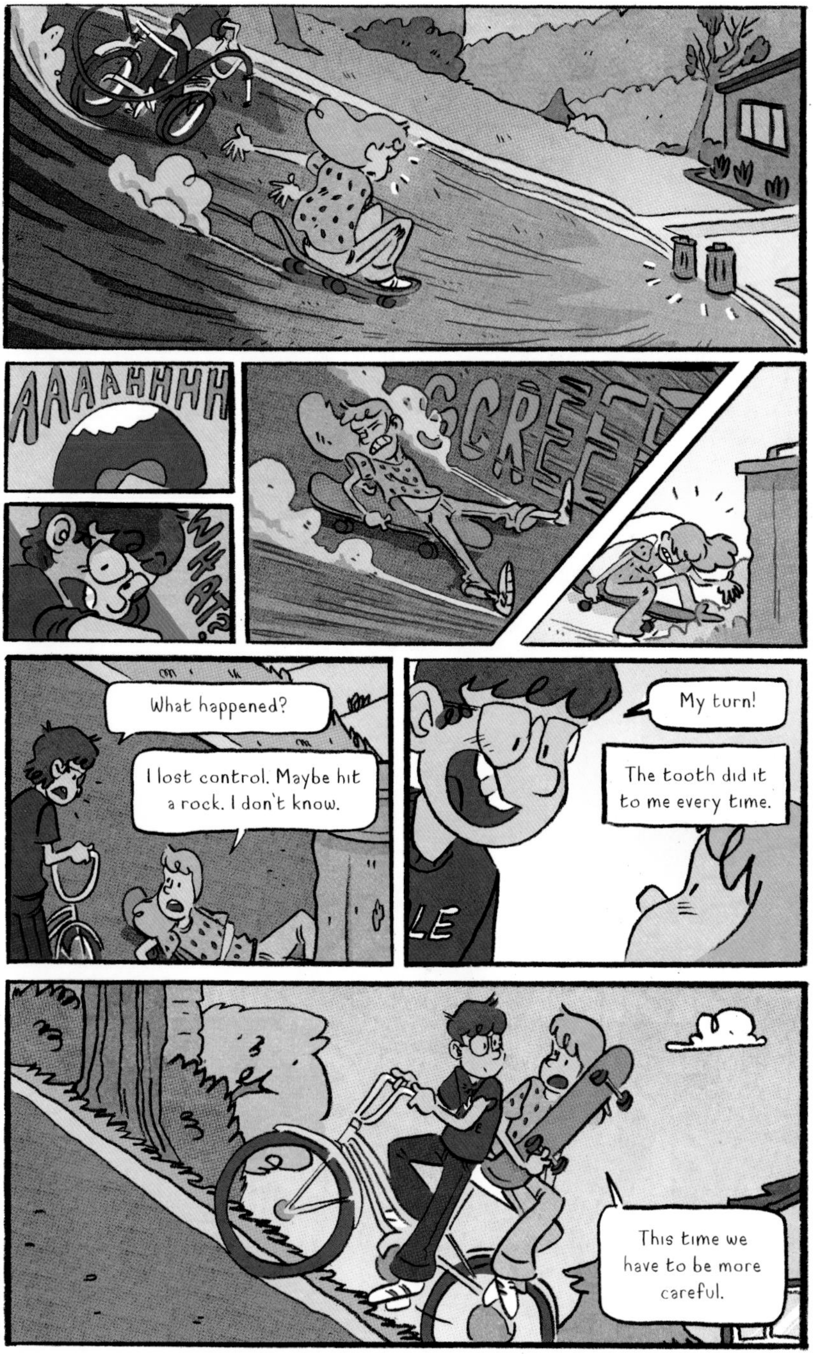
AAAAHHHH
WHAT?
SCREEE
What happened?
I lost control. Maybe hit a rock. I don't know.
My turn!
The tooth did it to me every time.
This time we have to be more careful.

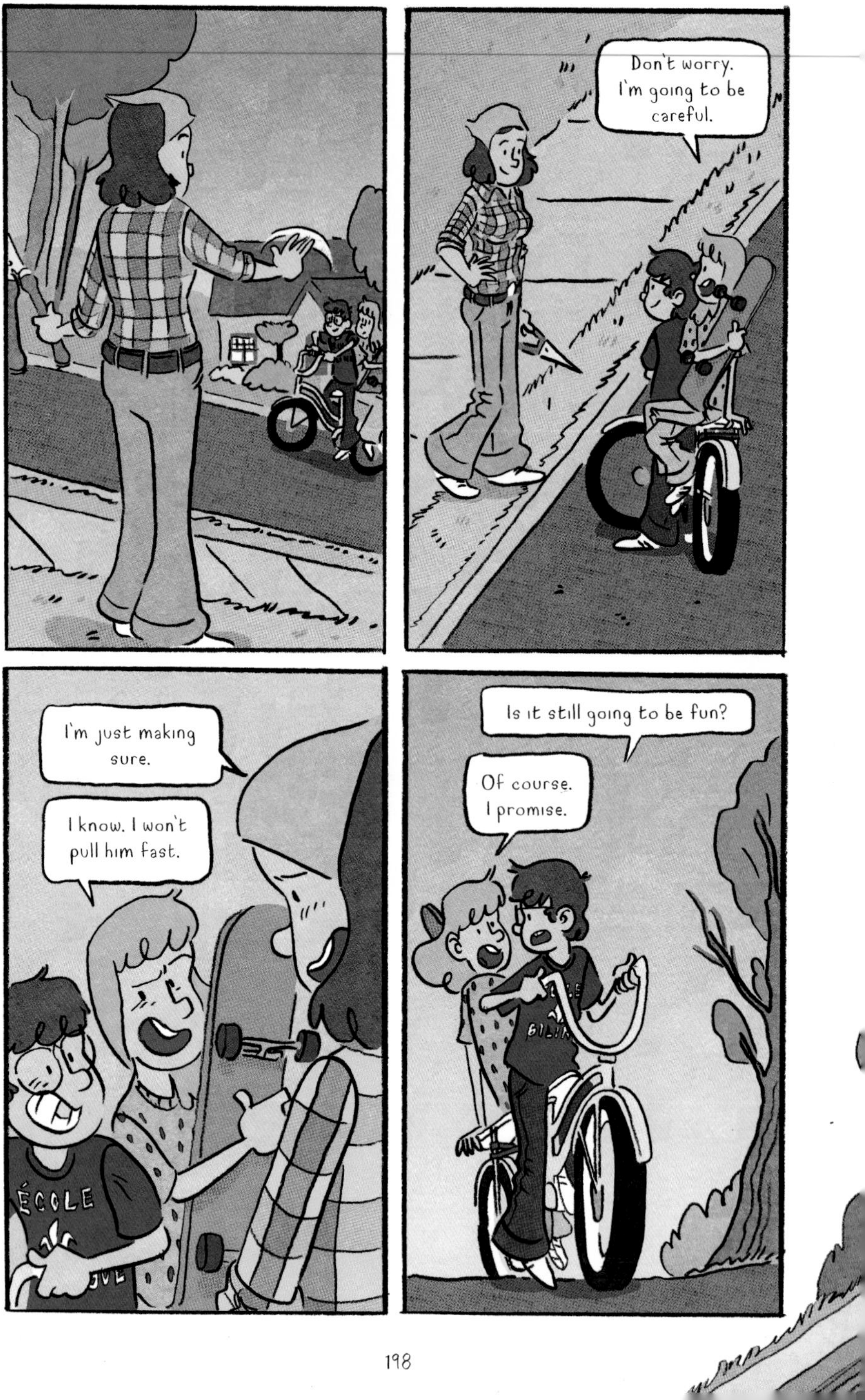
Don't worry.
I'm going to be careful.
I'm just making sure.
I know. I won't pull him fast.
ÉCOLE
Is it still going to be fun?
Of course. I promise.

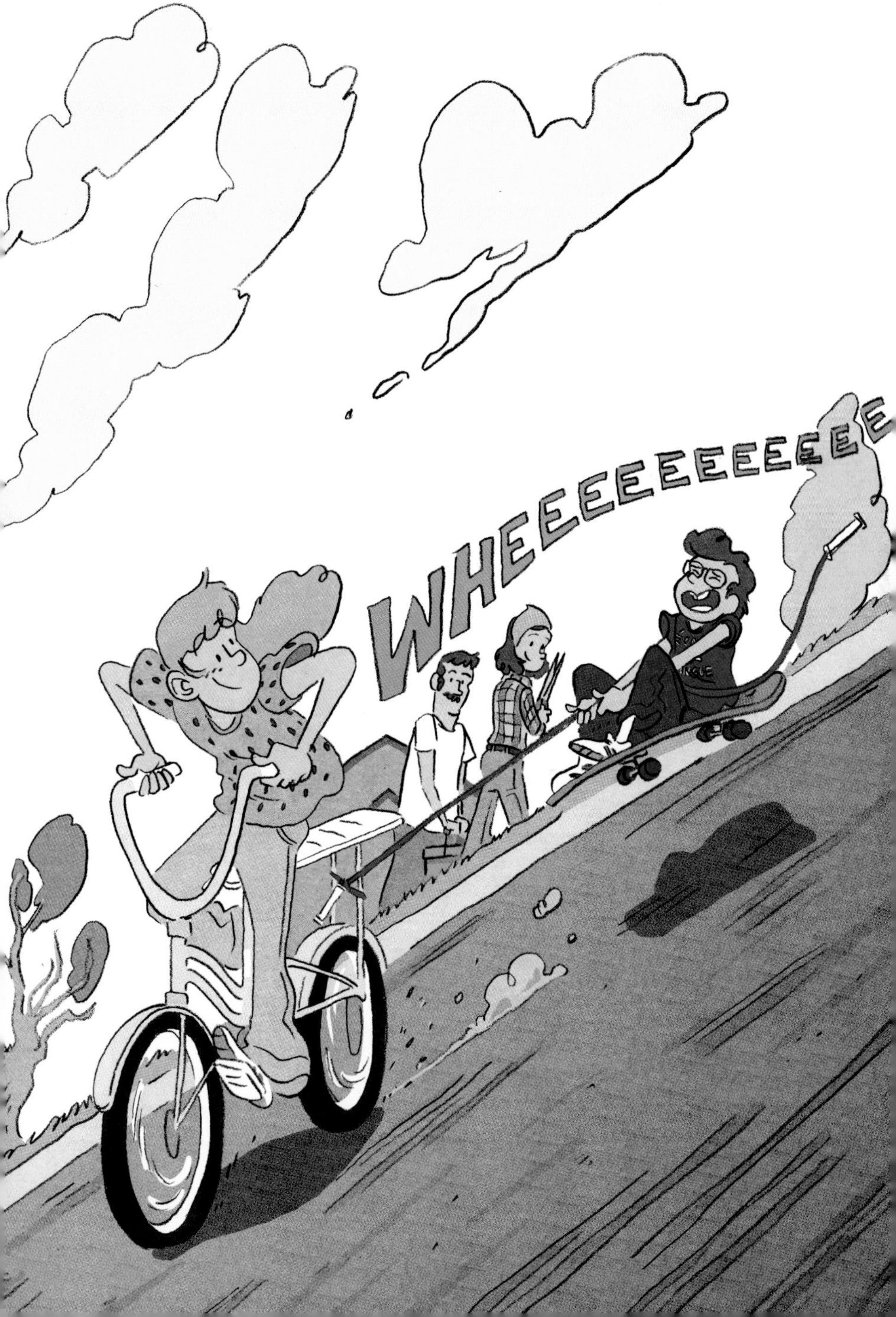
WHEEEEEEEEEEE

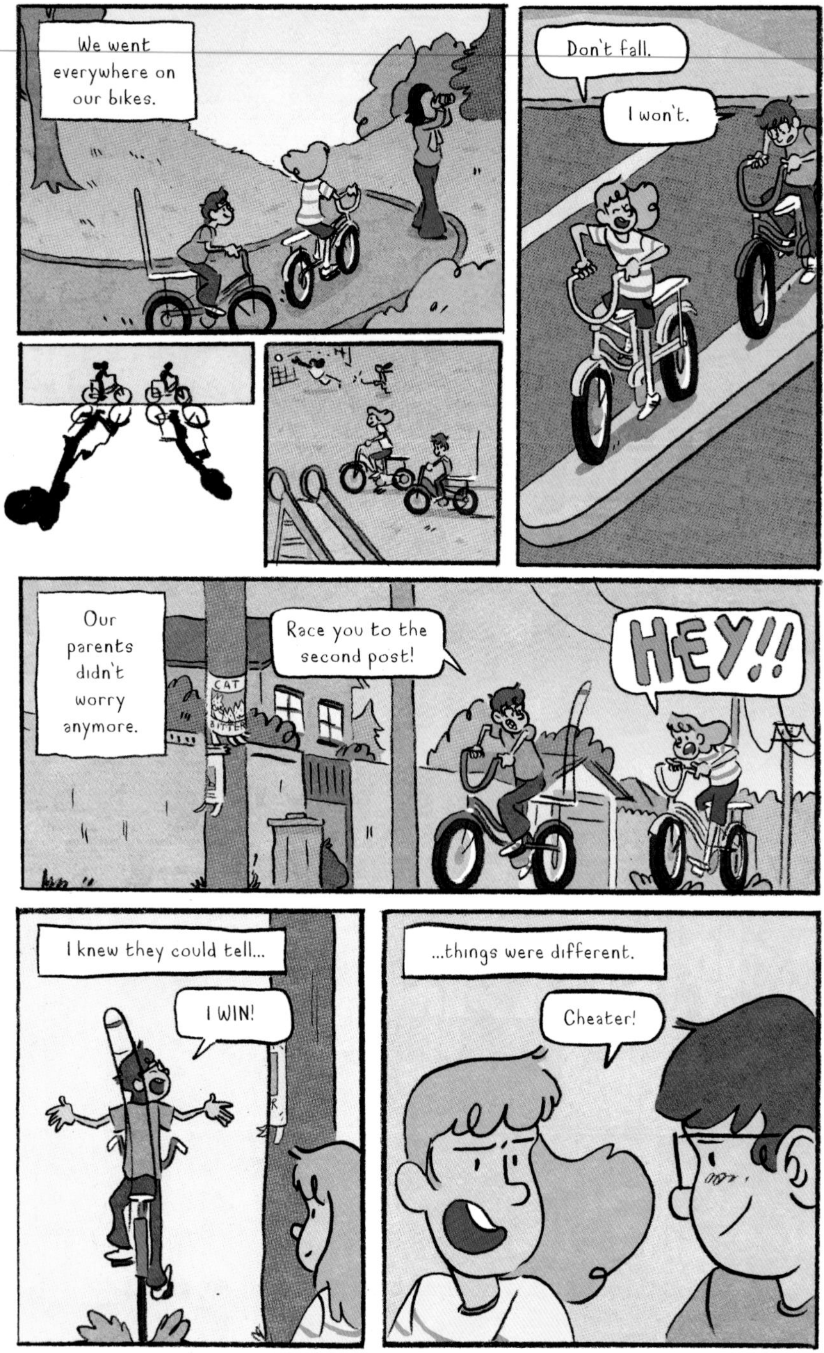
We went everywhere on our bikes.
Don't fall.
I won't.
Our parents didn't worry anymore.
CAT
BITTER
Race you to the second post!
HEY!!
I knew they could tell...
I WIN!
...things were different.
Cheater!

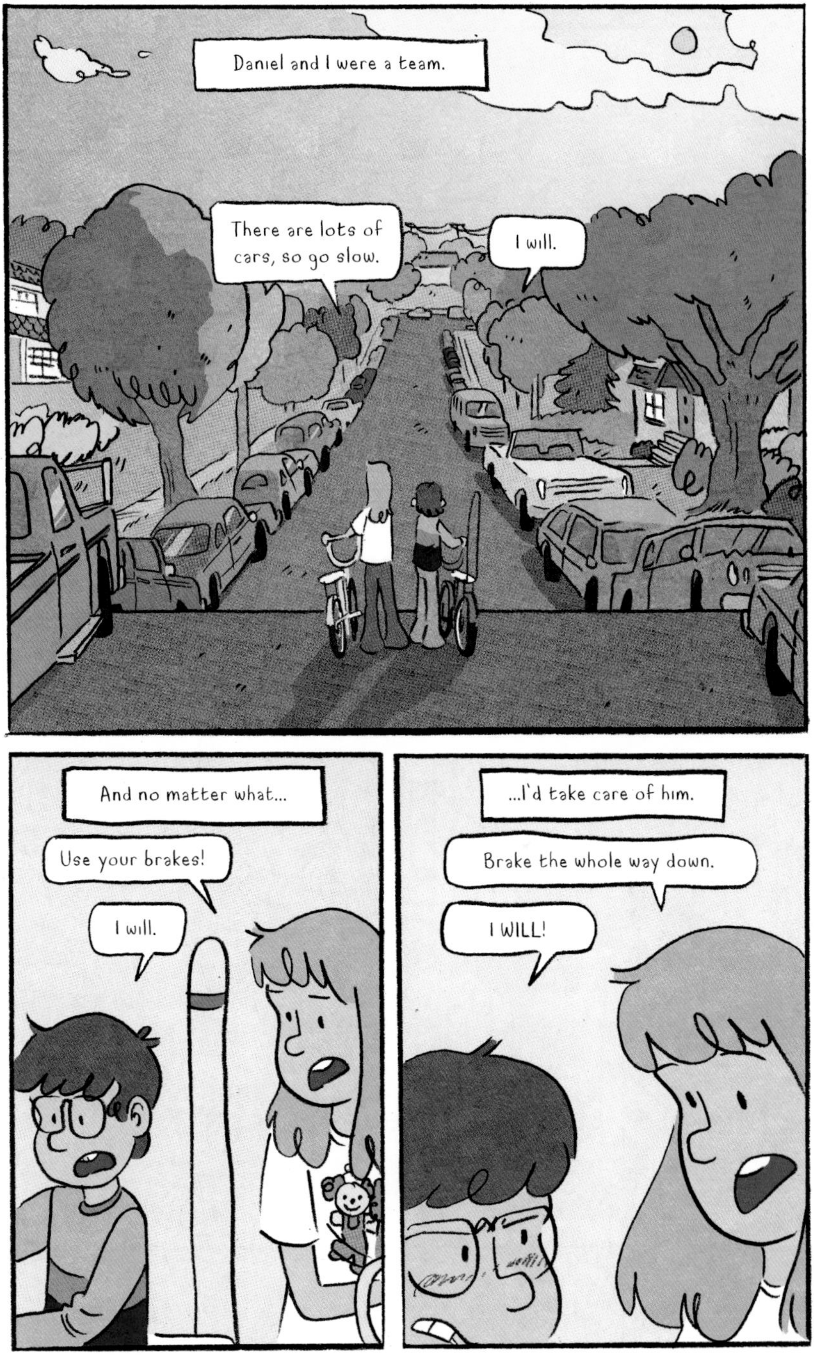
Daniel and I were a team.
There are lots of cars, so go slow.
I will.
And no matter what...
Use your brakes!
I will.
...I'd take care of him.
Brake the whole way down.
I WILL!

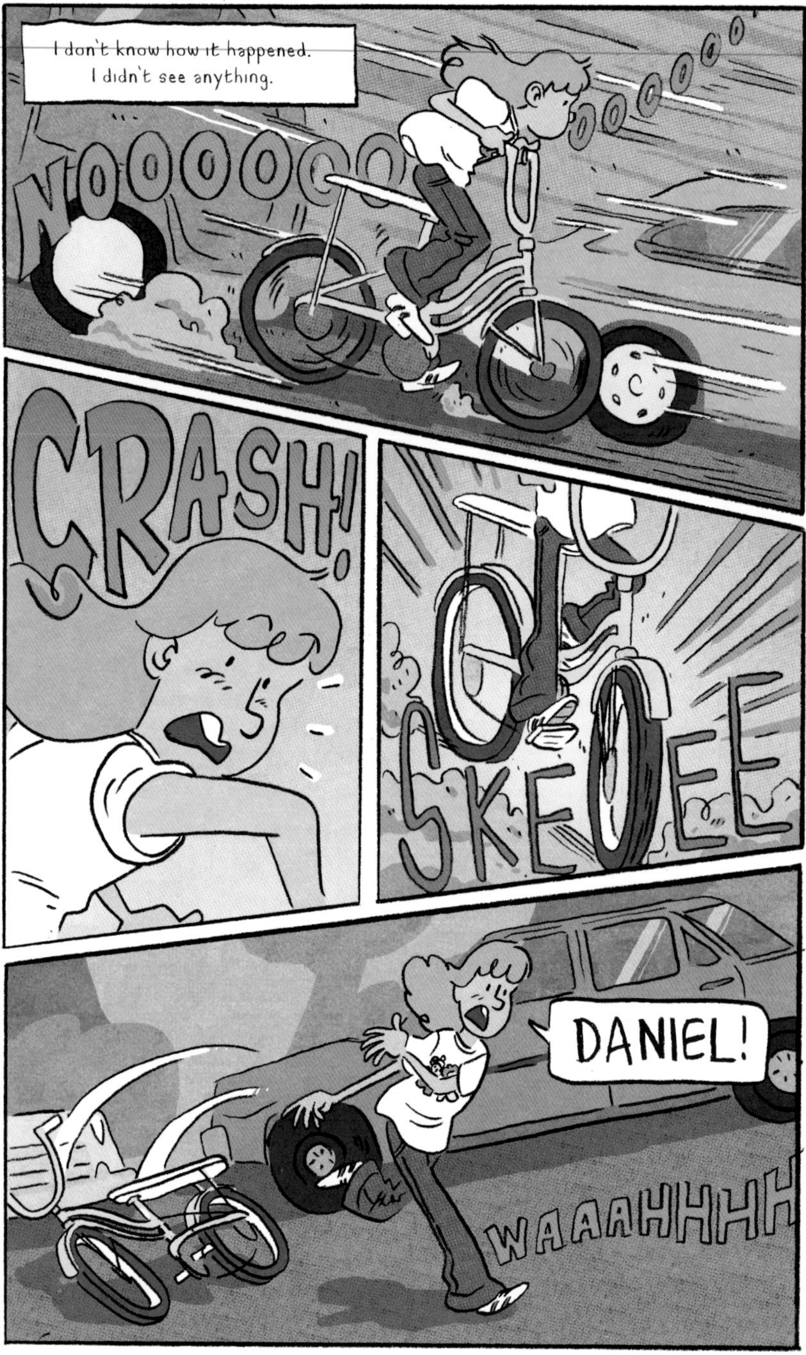
I don't know how it happened.
I didn't see anything.
NOOOOOOOOOOOOOO
CRASH!
SKEEEE
DANIEL!
WAAAHHHH

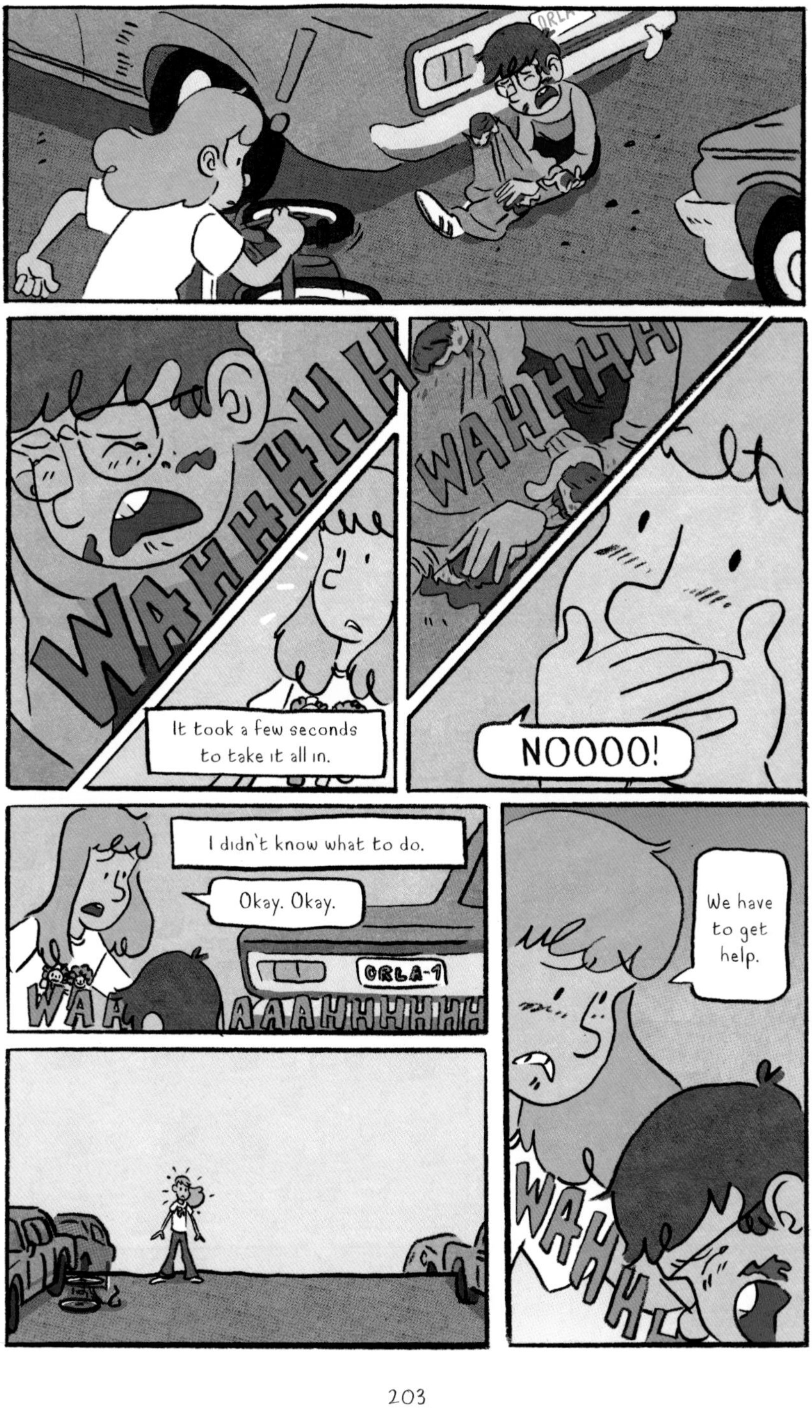
ORLA
WAHHHHH
It took a few seconds to take it all in.
WAHHHHH
NOOOO!
I didn't know what to do.
Okay. Okay.
ORLA-1
WAH
AAAHHHHHHH
We have to get help.
WAHHH

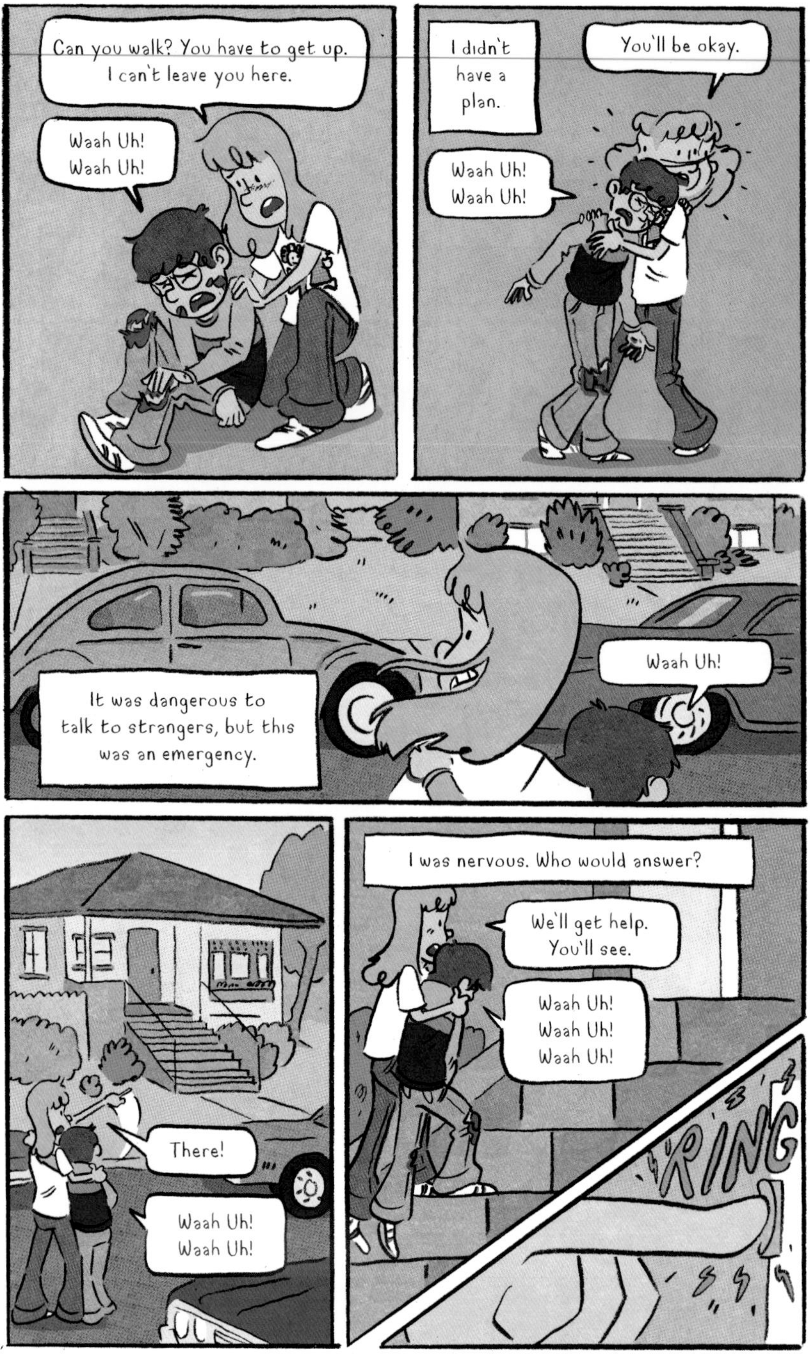
Can you walk? You have to get up. I can't leave you here.
Waah Uh! Waah Uh!
I didn't have a plan.
You'll be okay.
Waah Uh! Waah Uh!
It was dangerous to talk to strangers, but this was an emergency.
Waah Uh!
There!
Waah Uh! Waah Uh!
I was nervous. Who would answer?
We'll get help. You'll see.
Waah Uh! Waah Uh! Waah Uh!
RING

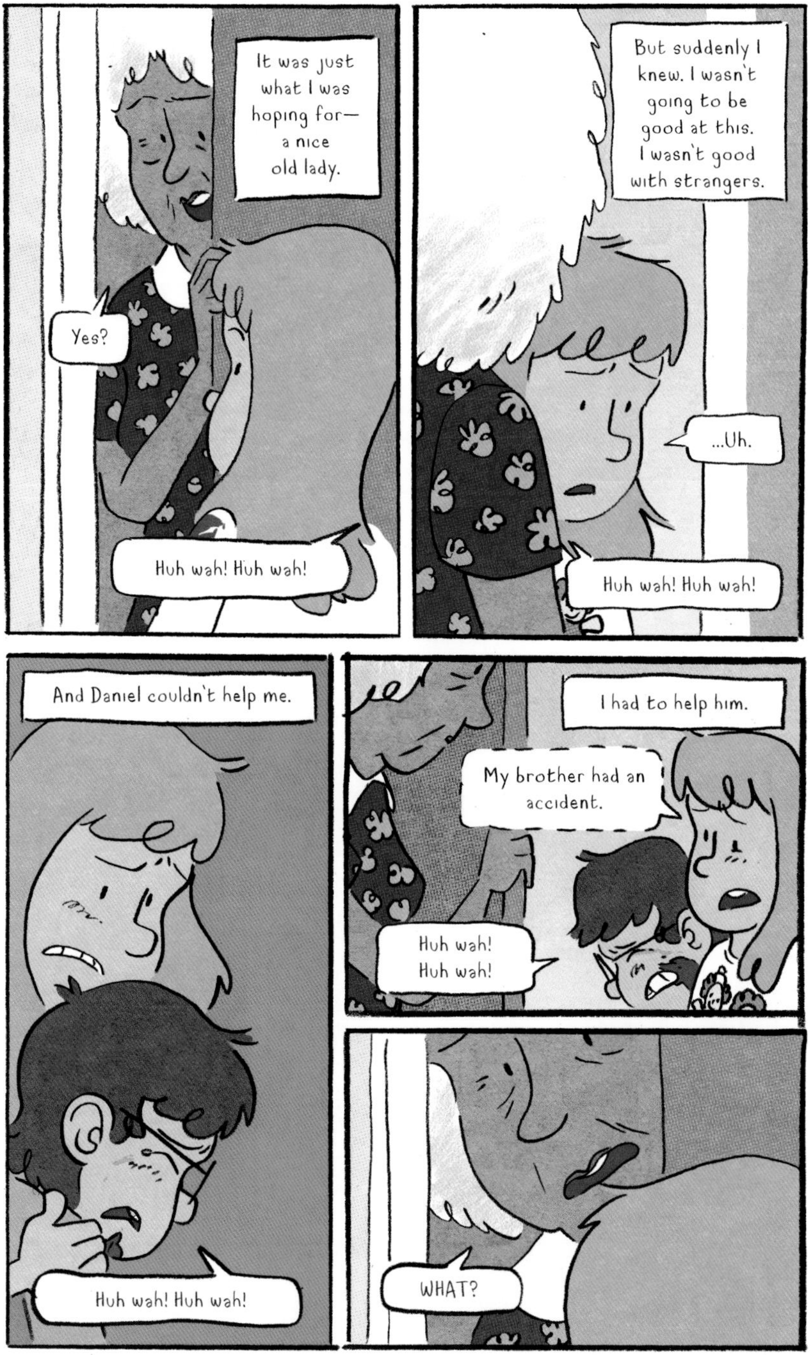
It was just what I was hoping for—a nice old lady.
Yes?
Huh wah! Huh wah!
But suddenly I knew. I wasn't going to be good at this. I wasn't good with strangers.
...Uh.
Huh wah! Huh wah!
And Daniel couldn't help me.
Huh wah! Huh wah!
I had to help him.
My brother had an accident.
Huh wah! Huh wah!
WHAT?

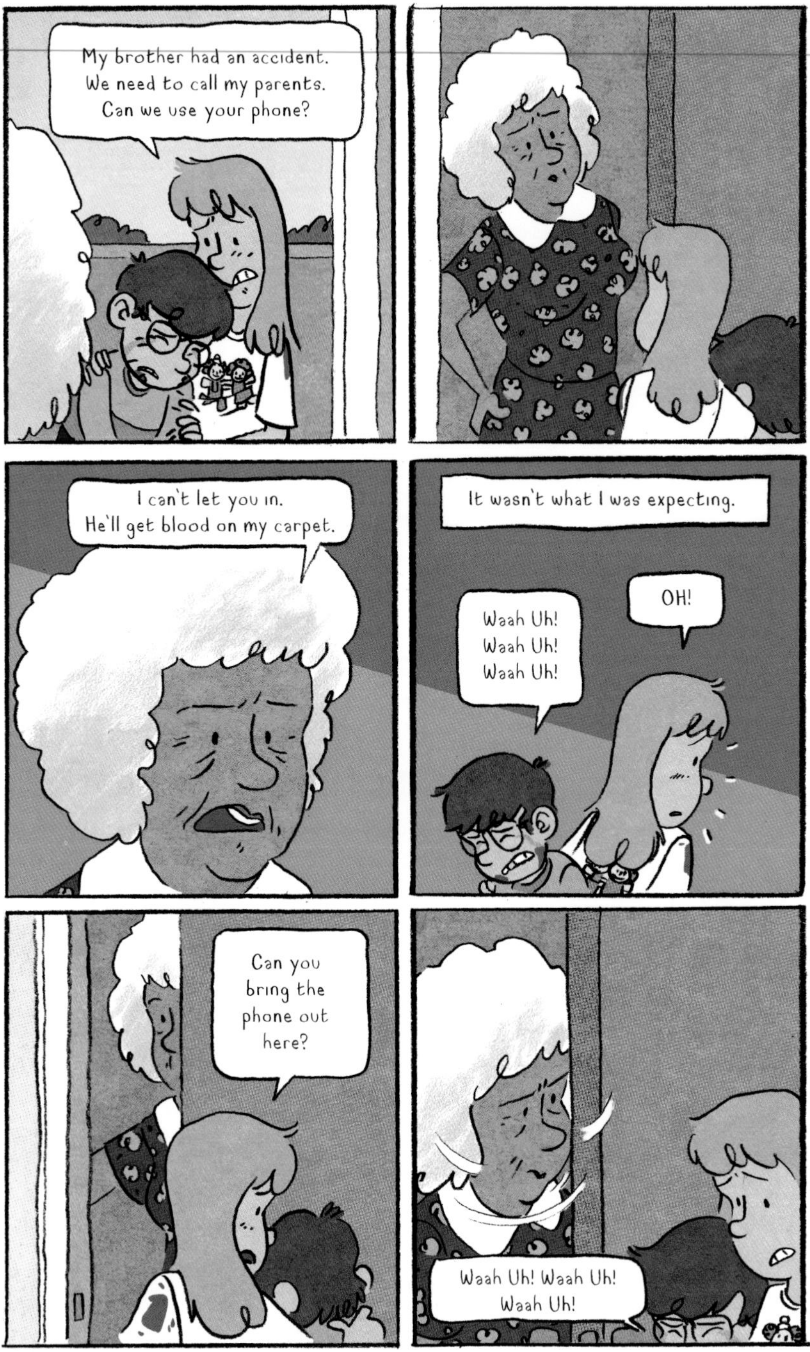
My brother had an accident.
We need to call my parents.
Can we use your phone?
I can't let you in.
He'll get blood on my carpet.
It wasn't what I was expecting.
Waah Uh!
Waah Uh!
Waah Uh!
OH!
Can you bring the phone out here?
Waah Uh! Waah Uh!
Waah Uh!

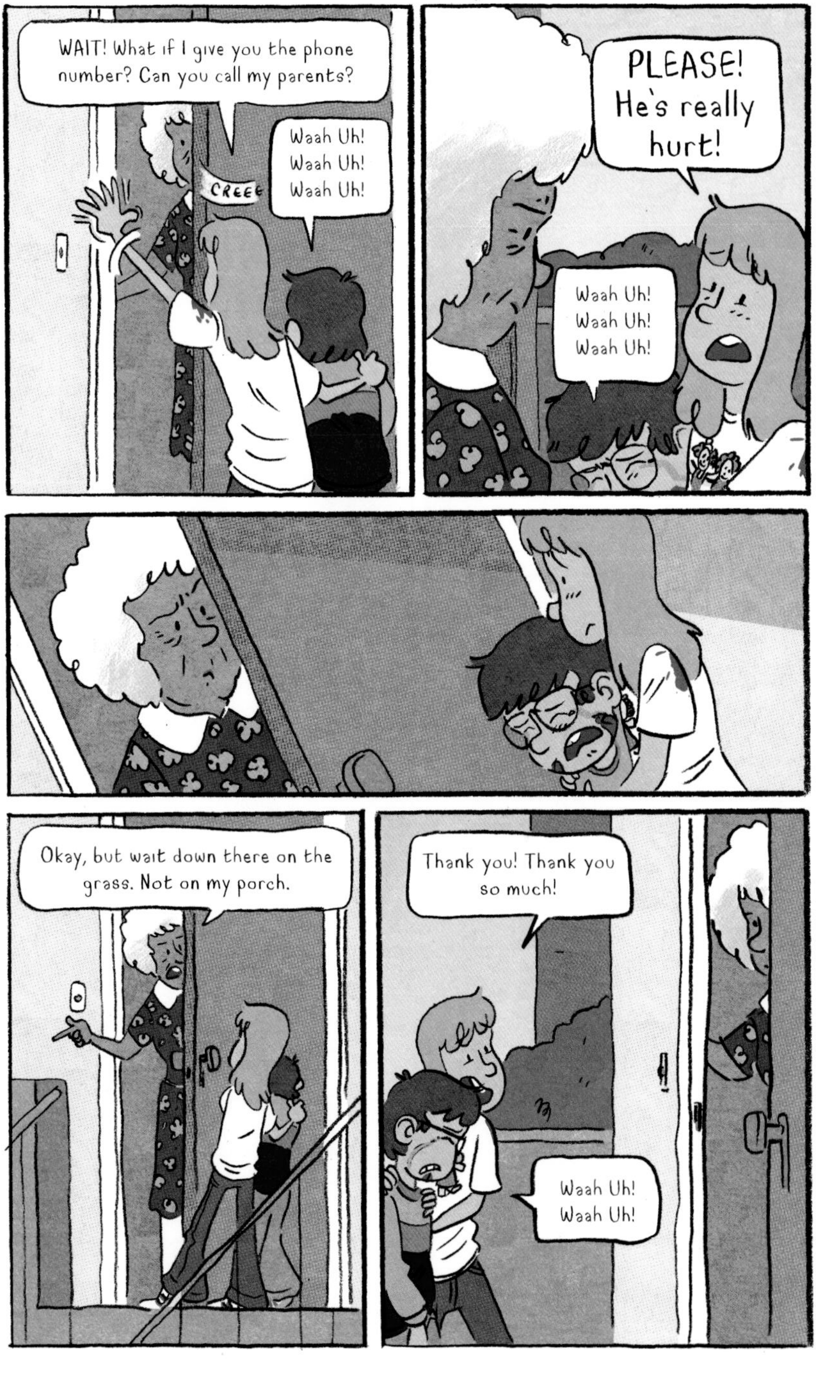
WAIT! What if I give you the phone number? Can you call my parents?
CREEE
Waah Uh! Waah Uh! Waah Uh!
PLEASE! He's really hurt!
Waah Uh! Waah Uh! Waah Uh!
Okay, but wait down there on the grass. Not on my porch.
Thank you! Thank you so much!
Waah Uh! Waah Uh!

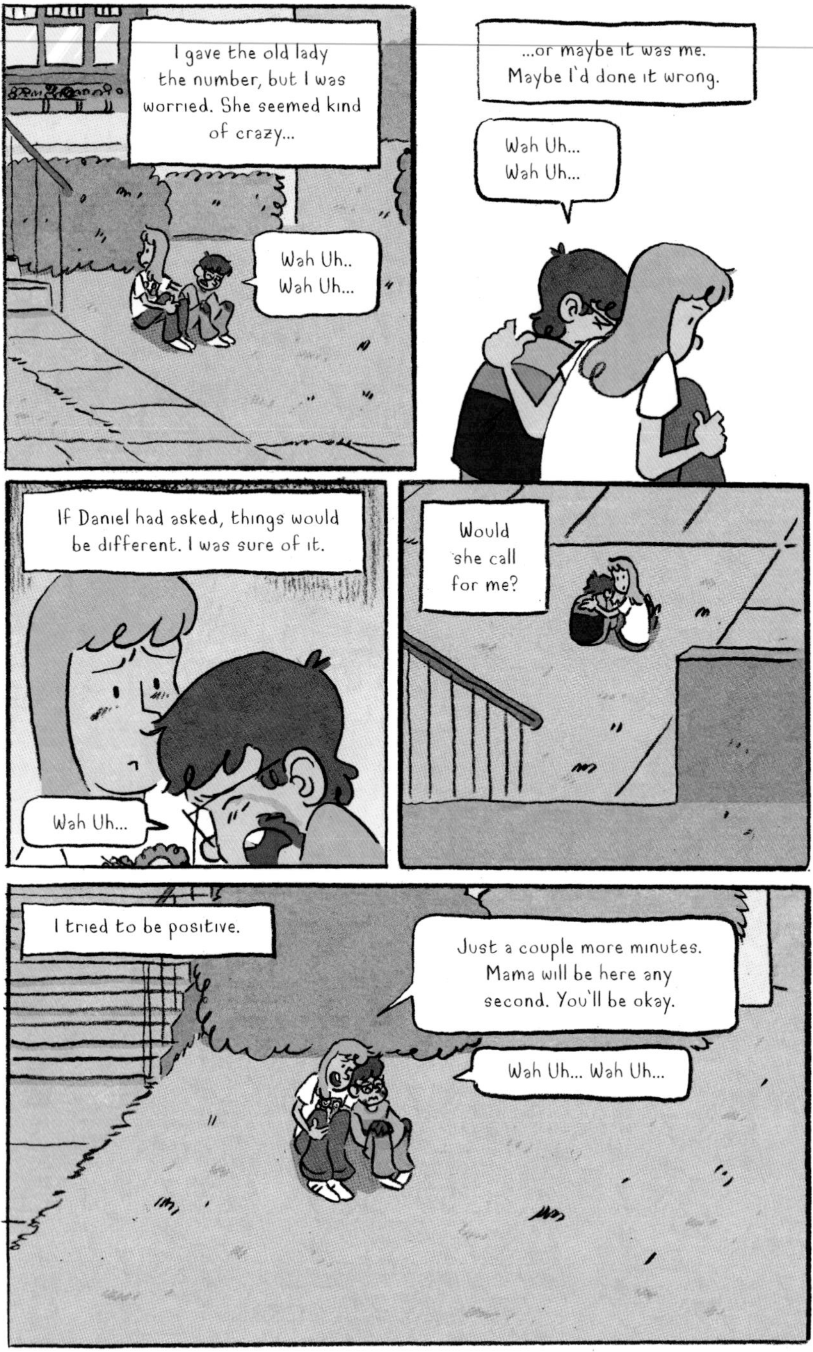
I gave the old lady the number, but I was worried. She seemed kind of crazy...
Wah Uh.. Wah Uh...
...or maybe it was me. Maybe I'd done it wrong.
Wah Uh... Wah Uh...
If Daniel had asked, things would be different. I was sure of it.
Wah Uh...
Would she call for me?
I tried to be positive.
Just a couple more minutes. Mama will be here any second. You'll be okay.
Wah Uh... Wah Uh...

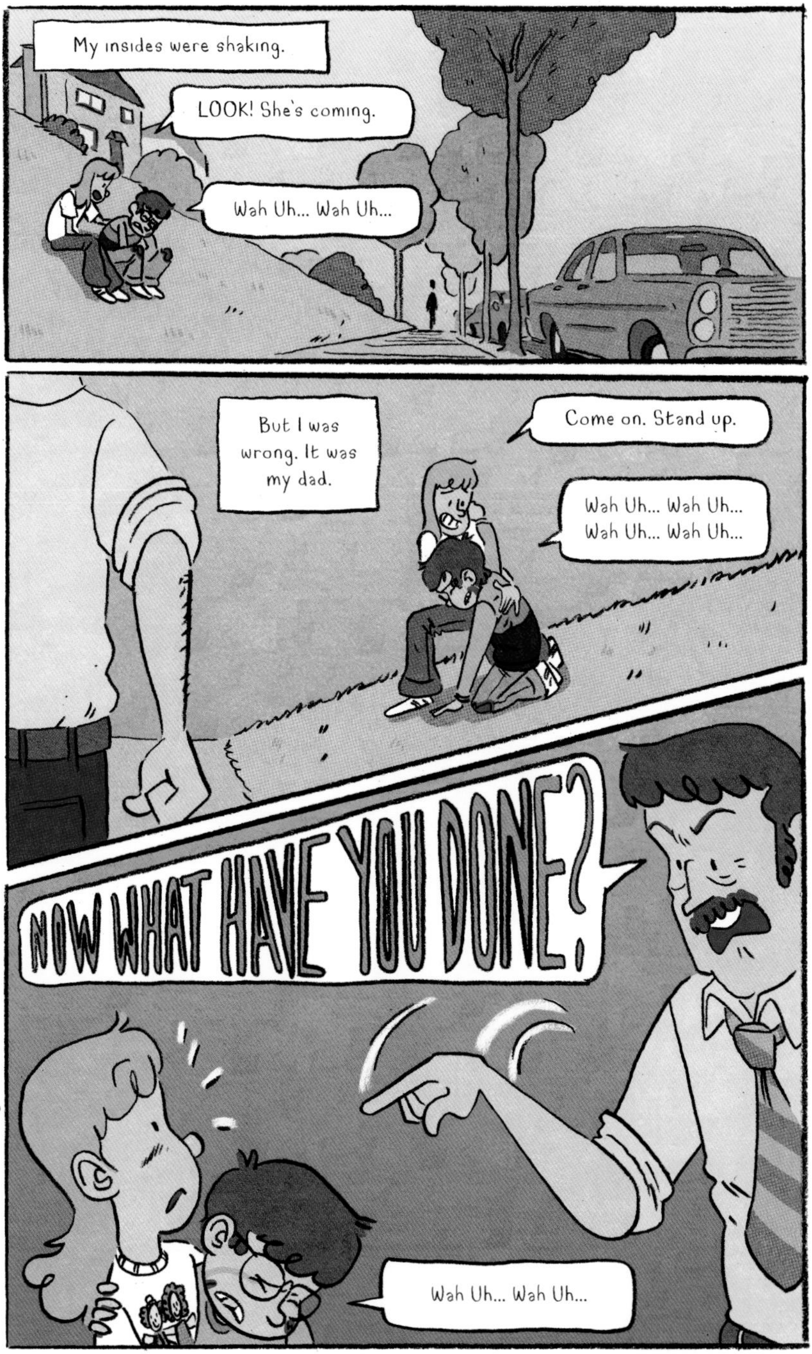
My insides were shaking.
LOOK! She's coming.
Wah Uh... Wah Uh...
But I was wrong. It was my dad.
Come on. Stand up.
Wah Uh... Wah Uh... Wah Uh... Wah Uh...
NOW WHAT HAVE YOU DONE?
Wah Uh... Wah Uh...

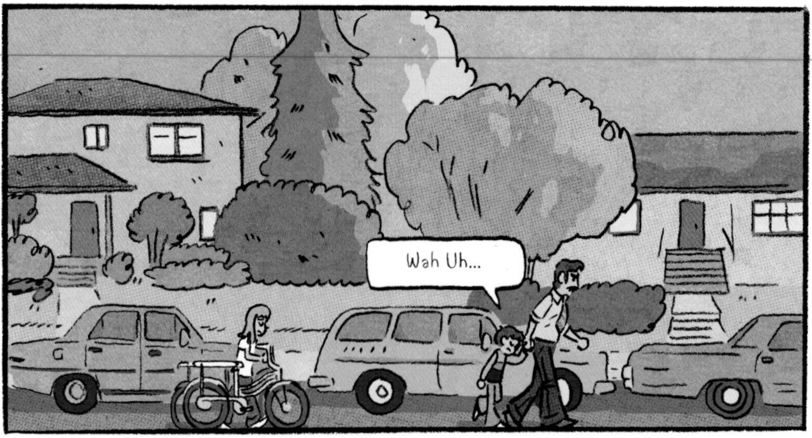
Wah Uh...

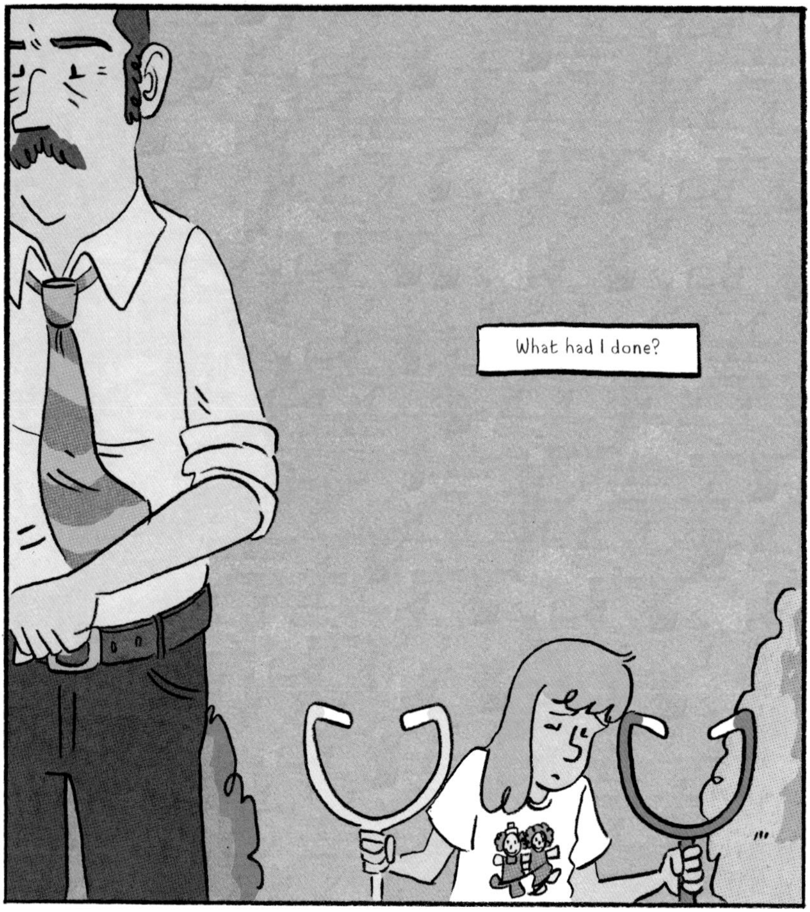
What had I done?

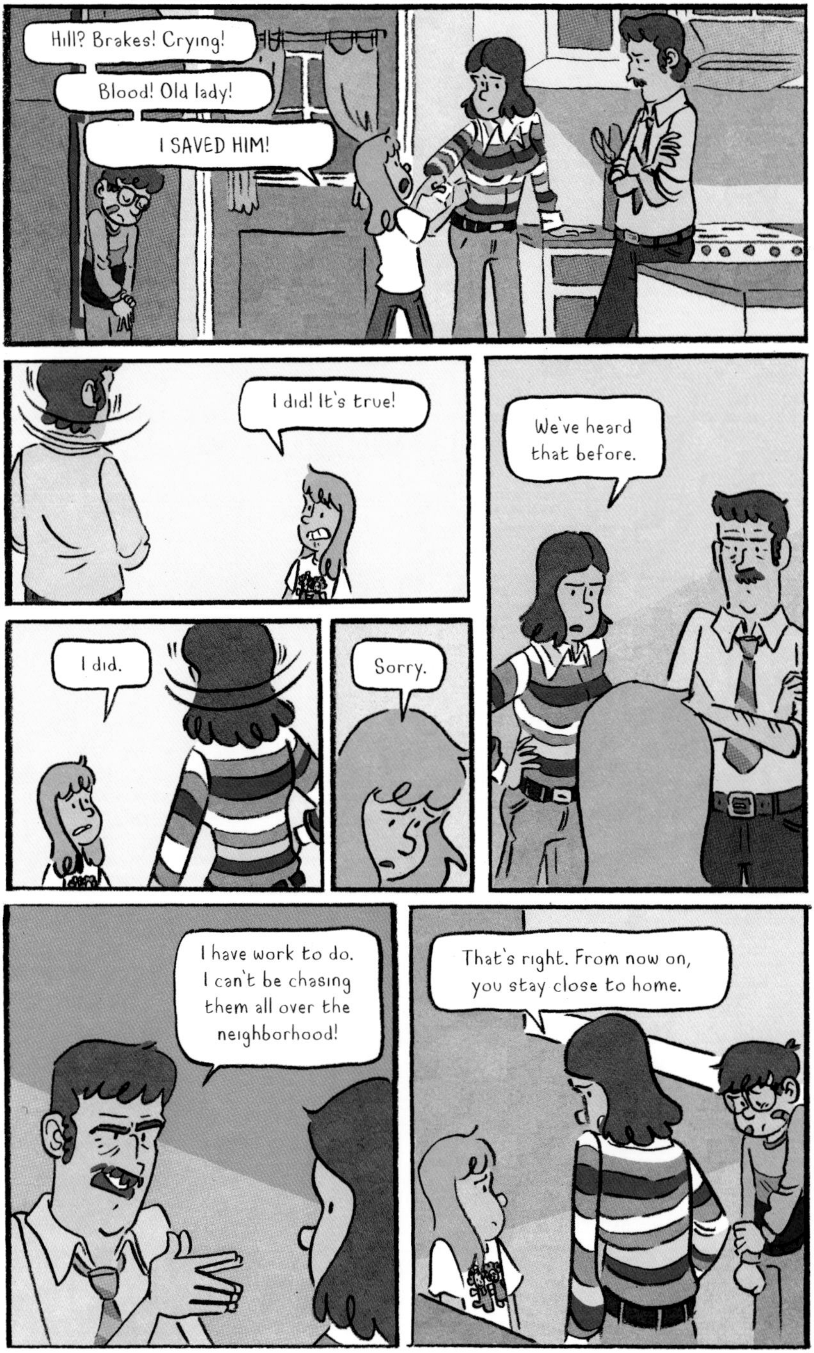
Hill? Brakes! Crying!
Blood! Old lady!
I SAVED HIM!
I did! It's true!
We've heard that before.
I did.
Sorry.
I have work to do. I can't be chasing them all over the neighborhood!
That's right. From now on, you stay close to home.

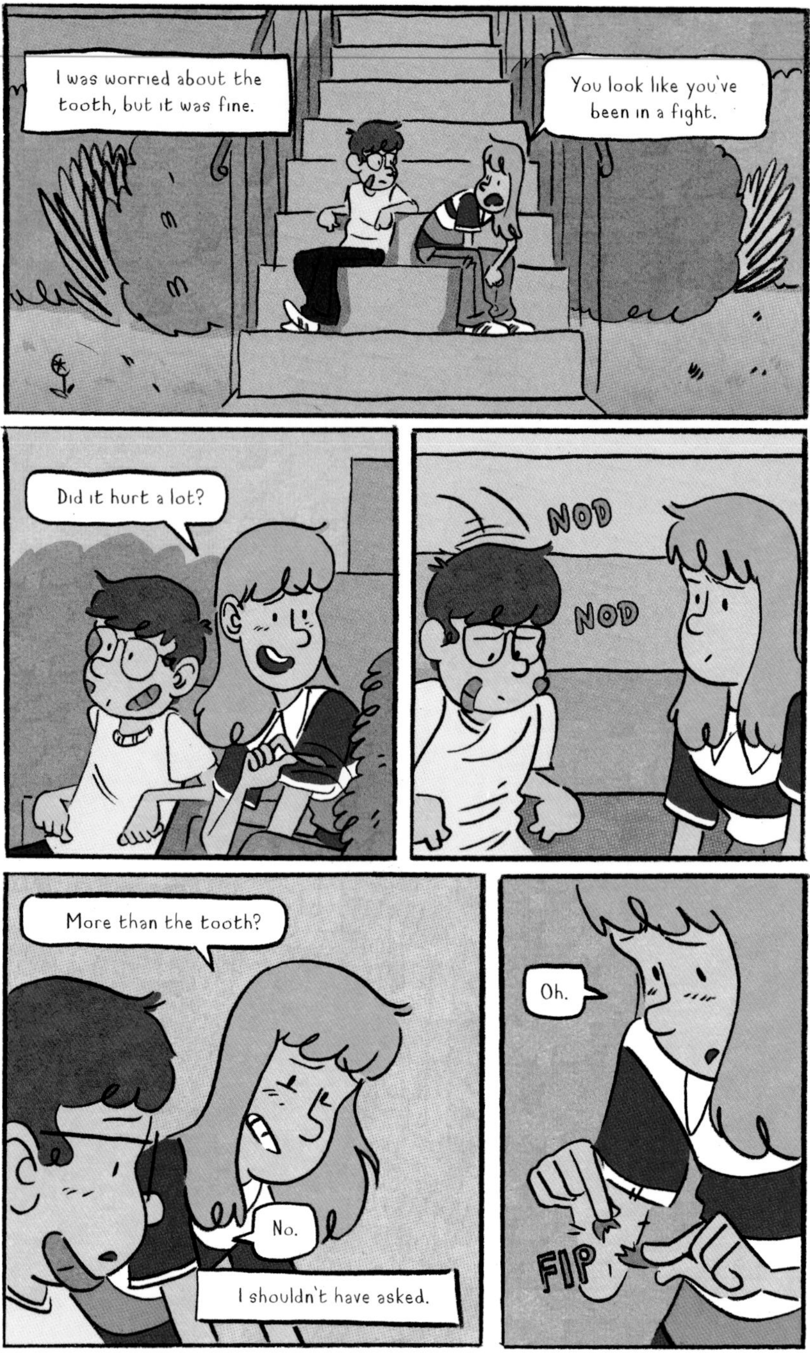
I was worried about the tooth, but it was fine.
You look like you've been in a fight.
Did it hurt a lot?
NOD
NOD
More than the tooth?
No.
I shouldn't have asked.
Oh.
FIP

10

The Biggest Power

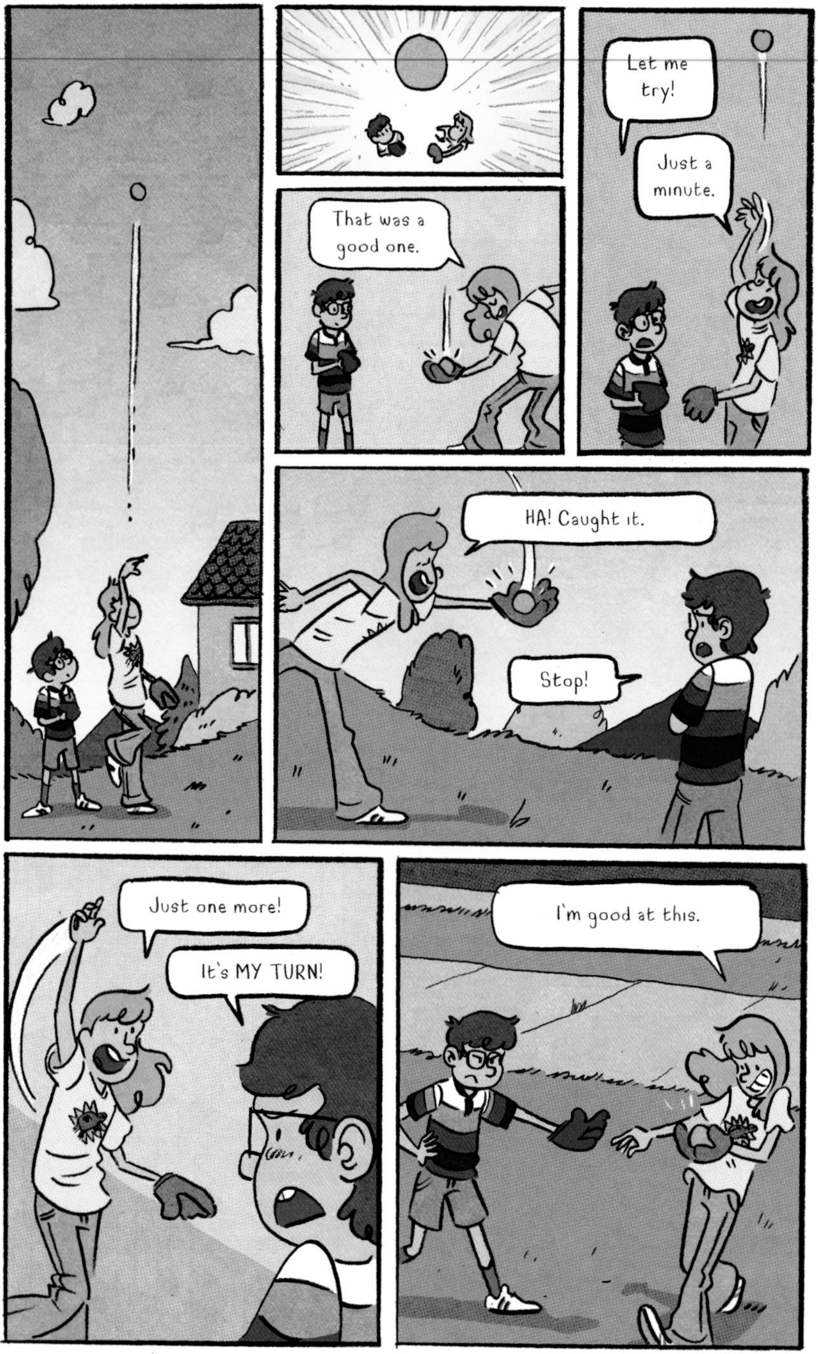

That was a good one.
Let me try!
Just a minute.
HA! Caught it.
Stop!
Just one more!
It's MY TURN!
I'm good at this.

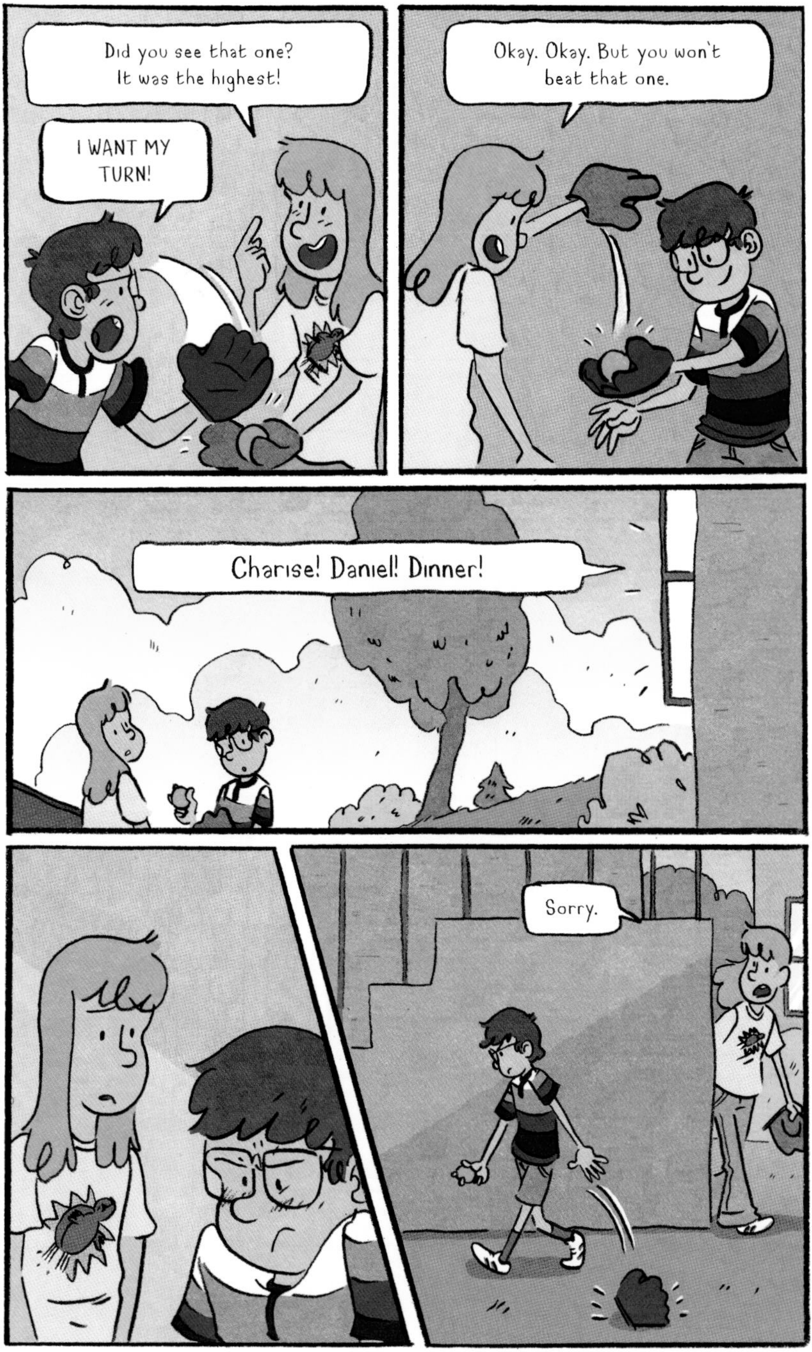
Did you see that one?
It was the highest!
I WANT MY TURN!
Okay. Okay. But you won't beat that one.
Charise! Daniel! Dinner!
Sorry.

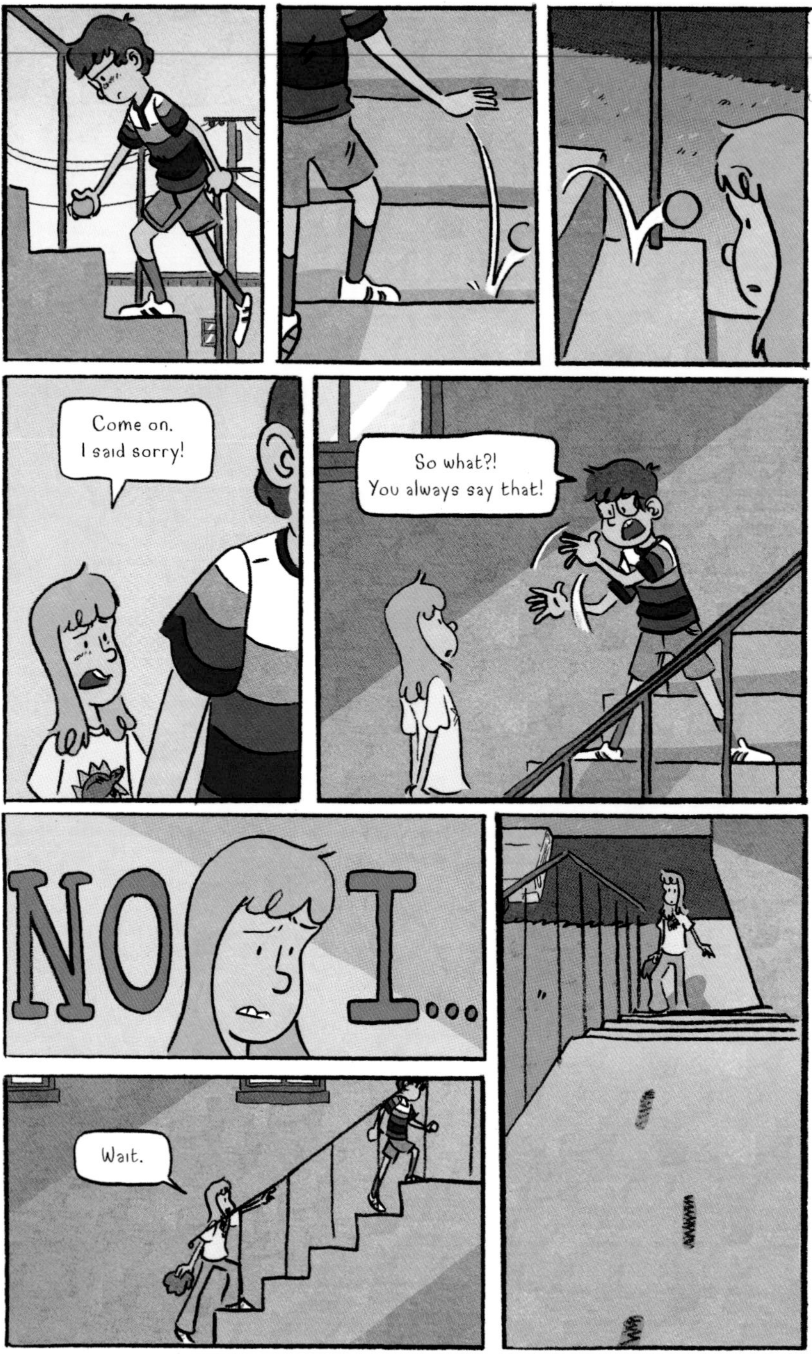
Come on.
I said sorry!
So what?!
You always say that!
NO I...
Wait.

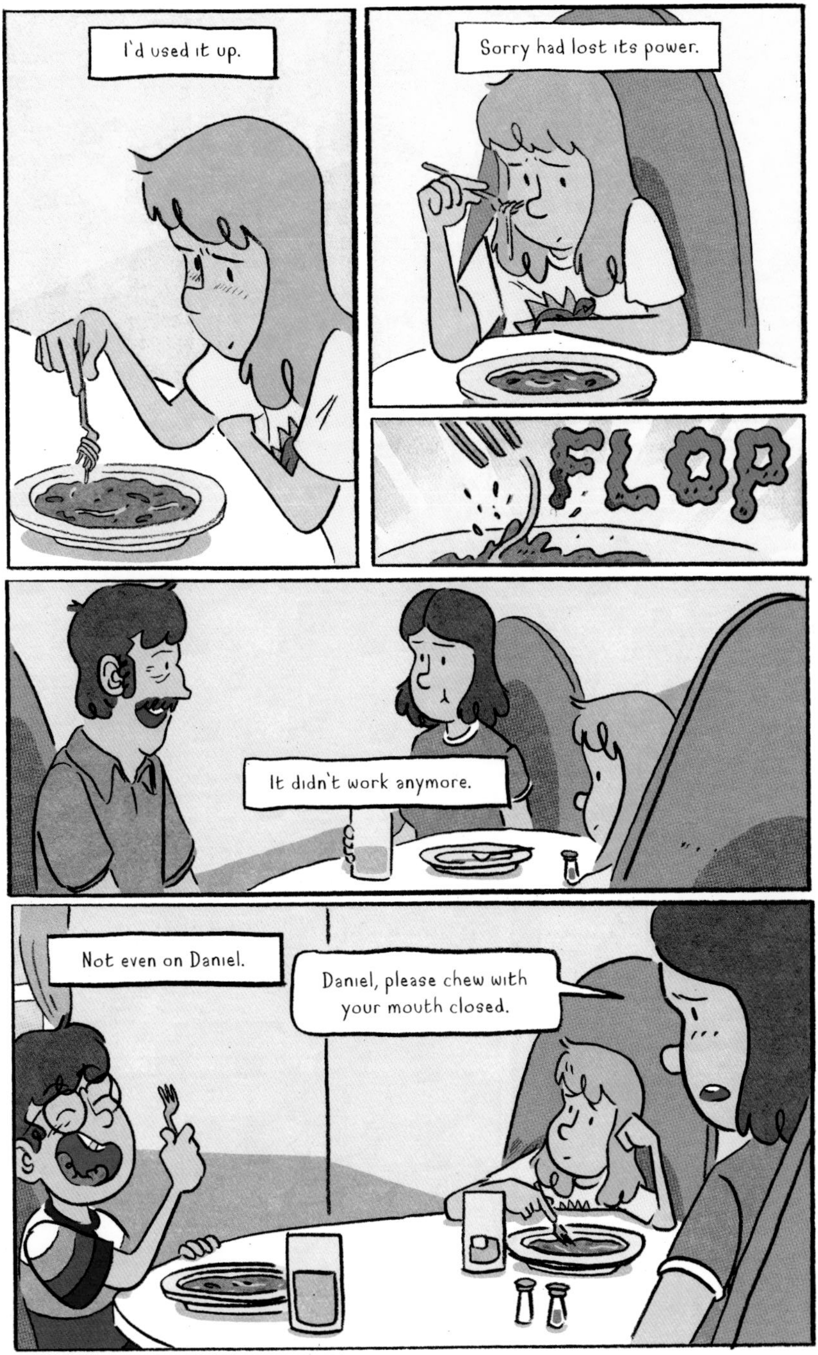
I'd used it up.
Sorry had lost its power.
FLOP
It didn't work anymore.
Not even on Daniel.
Daniel, please chew with your mouth closed.

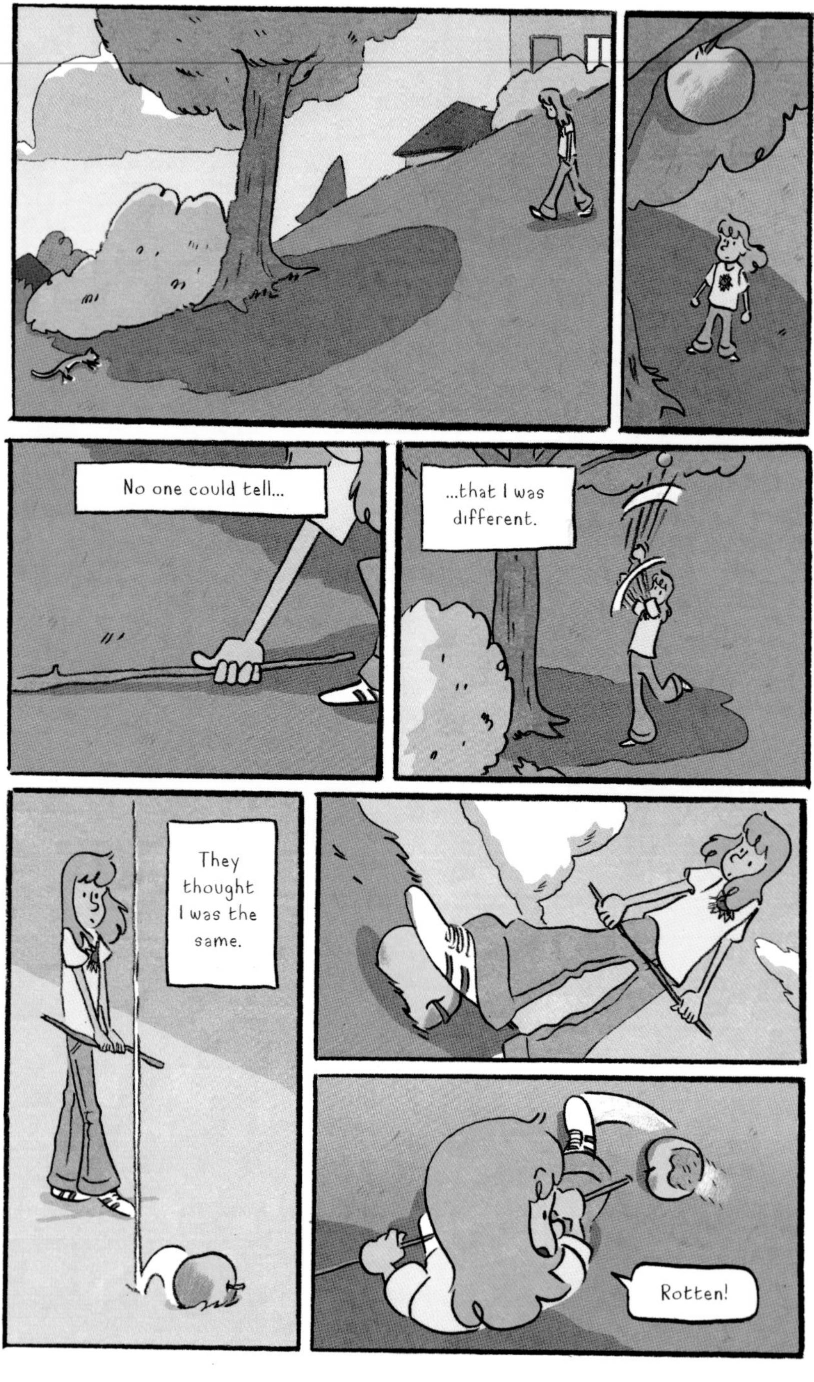
No one could tell...
...that I was different.
They thought I was the same.
Rotten!

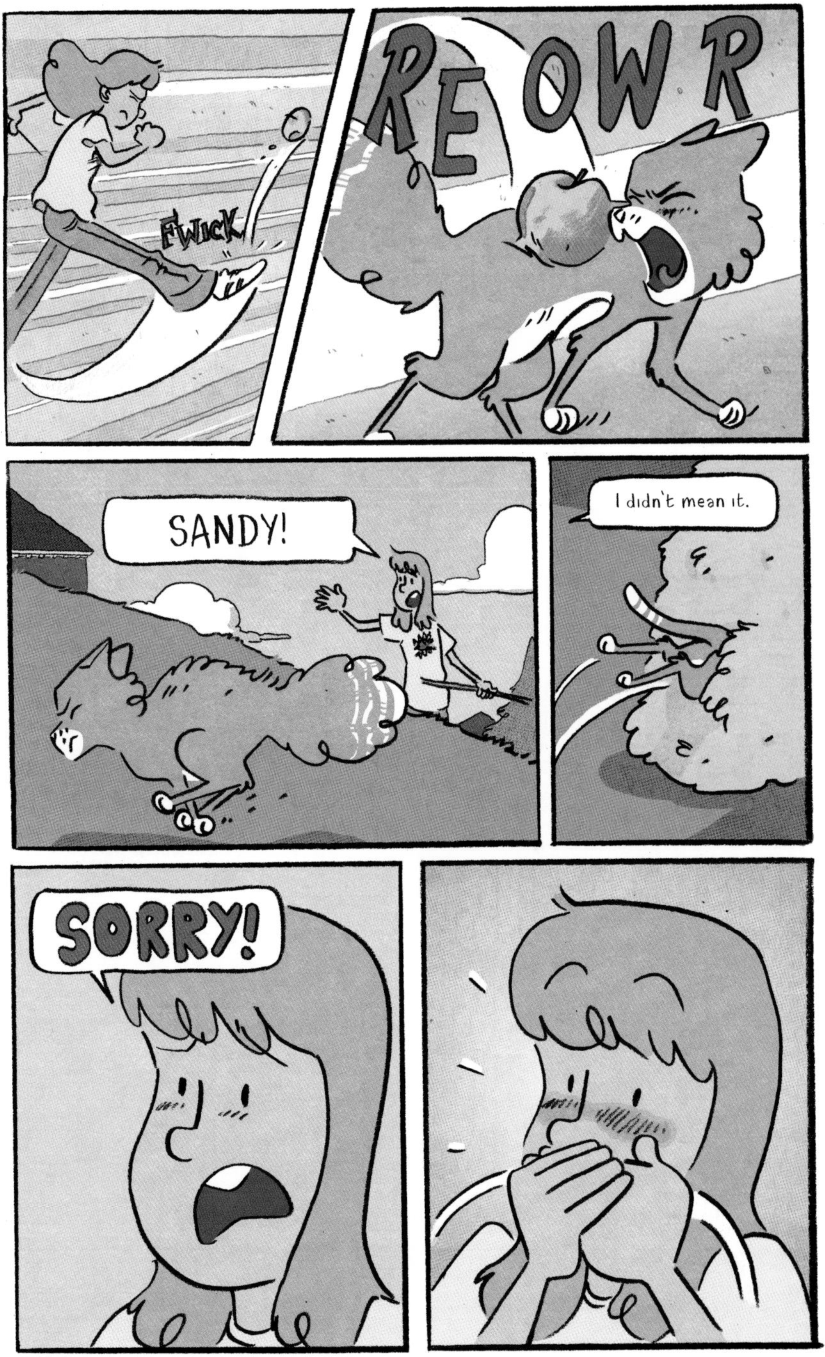
FWICK
REOWR
SANDY!
I didn't mean it.
SORRY!

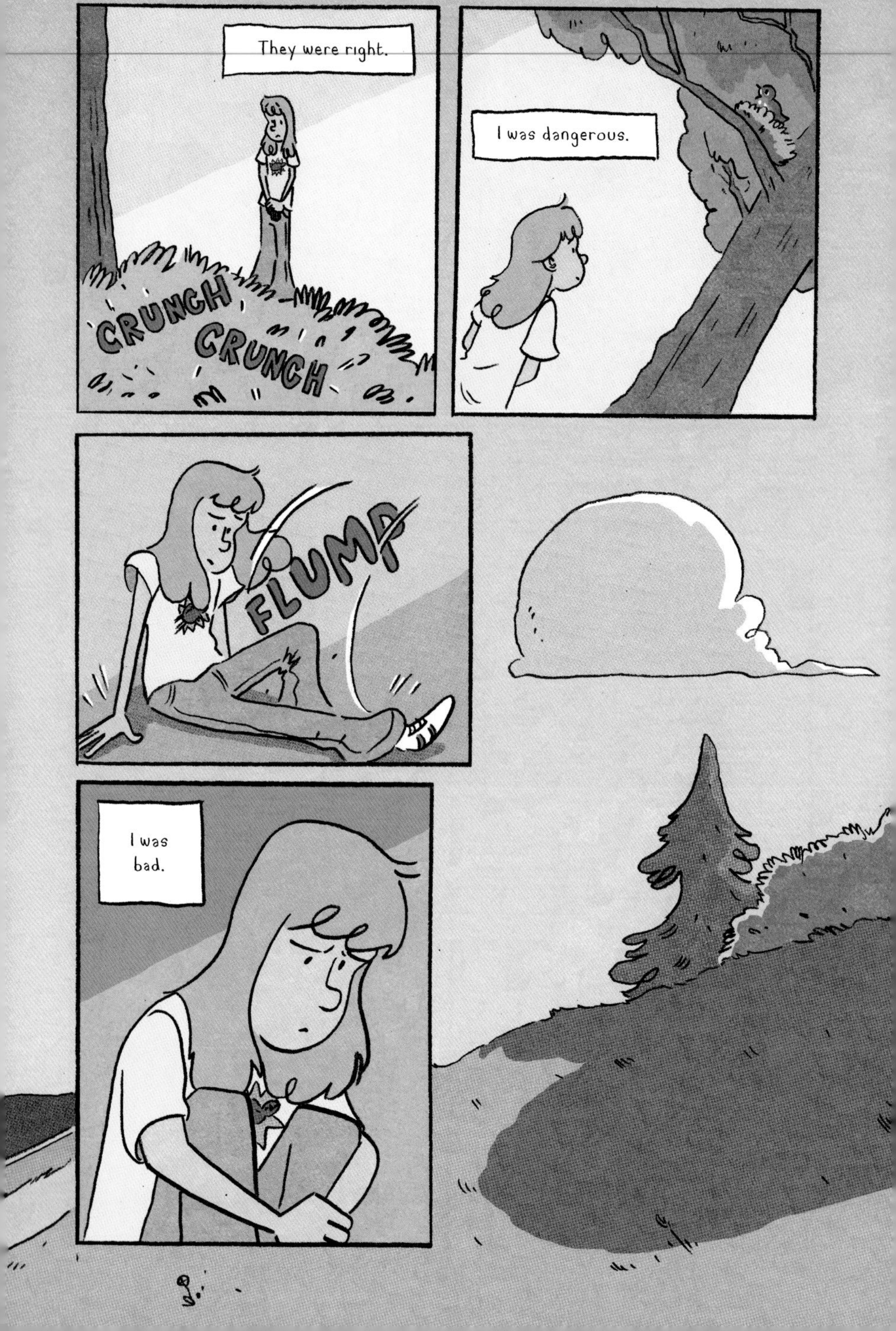
They were right.
CRUNCH
CRUNCH
I was dangerous.
FLUMP
I was bad.

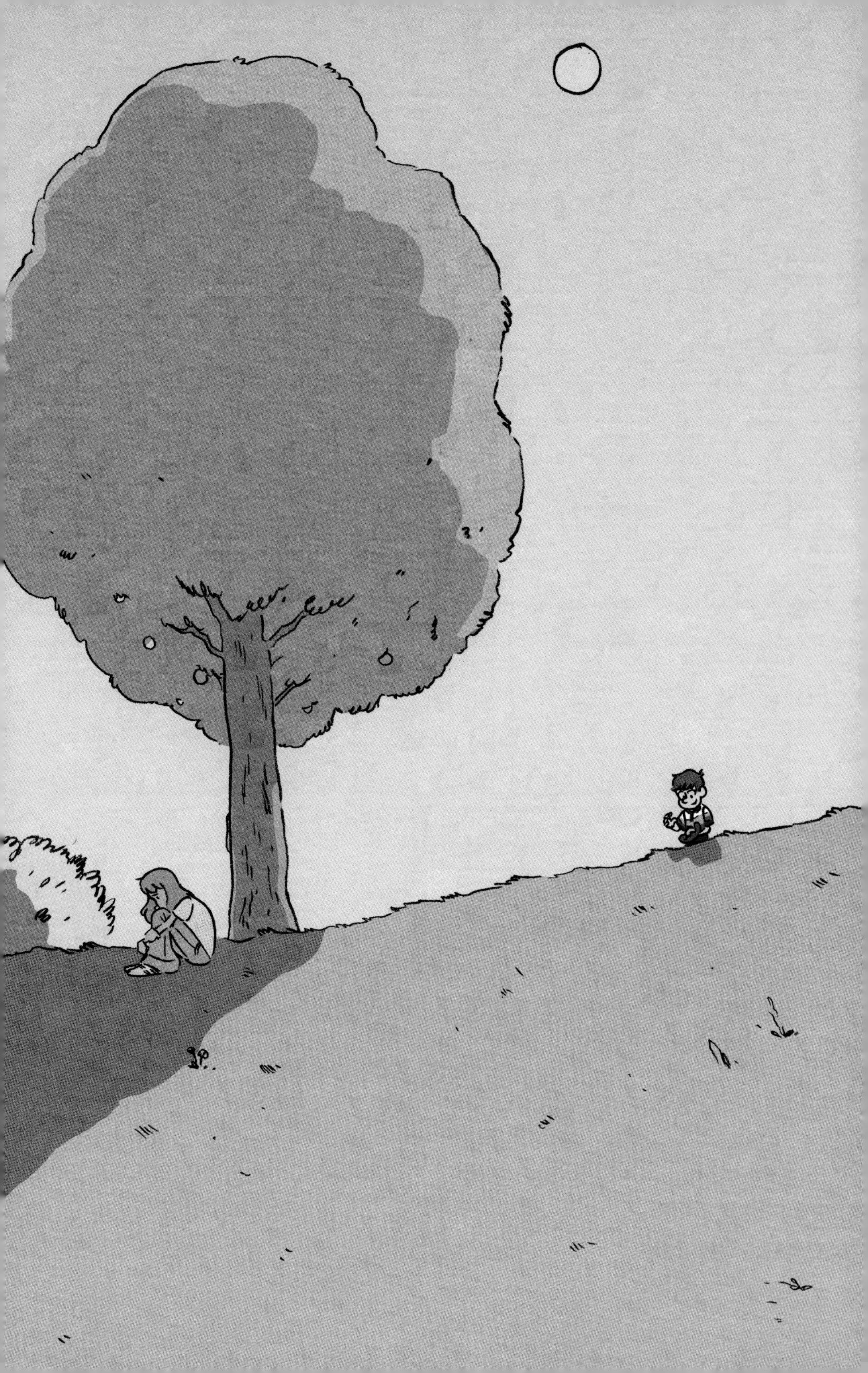

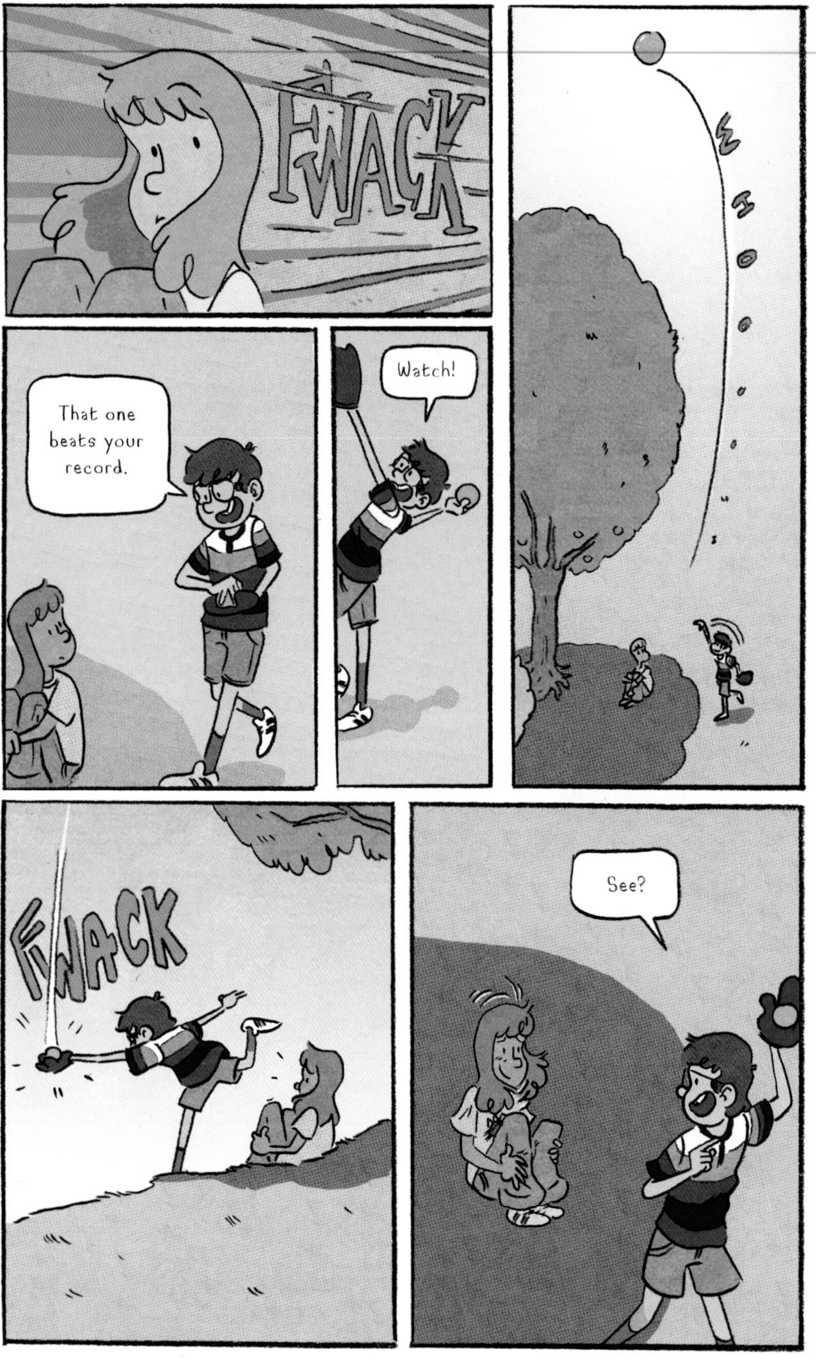

FWACK
WHOOOOOSH
That one beats your record.
Watch!
FWACK
See?

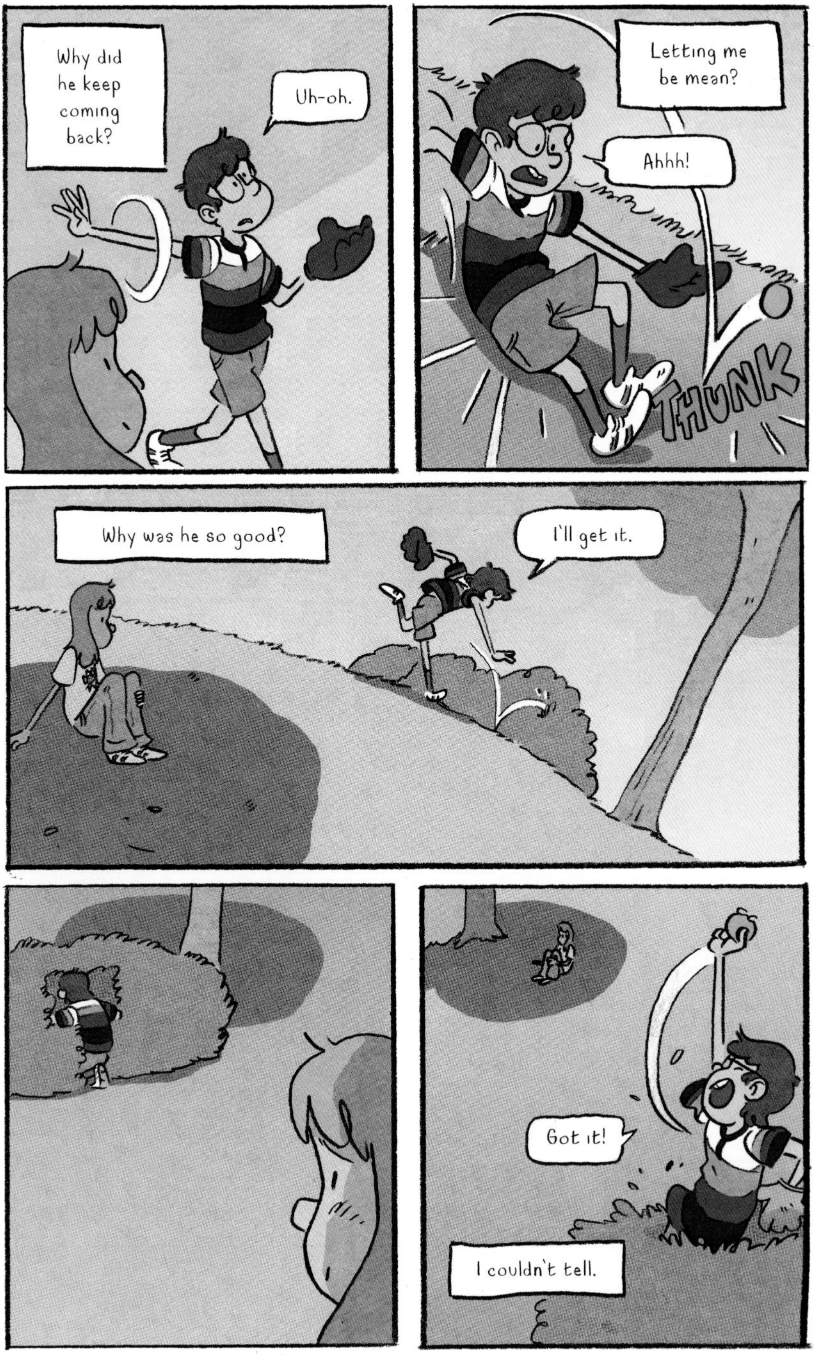
Why did he keep coming back?
Uh-oh.
Letting me be mean?
Ahhh!
THUNK
Why was he so good?
I'll get it.
Got it!
I couldn't tell.

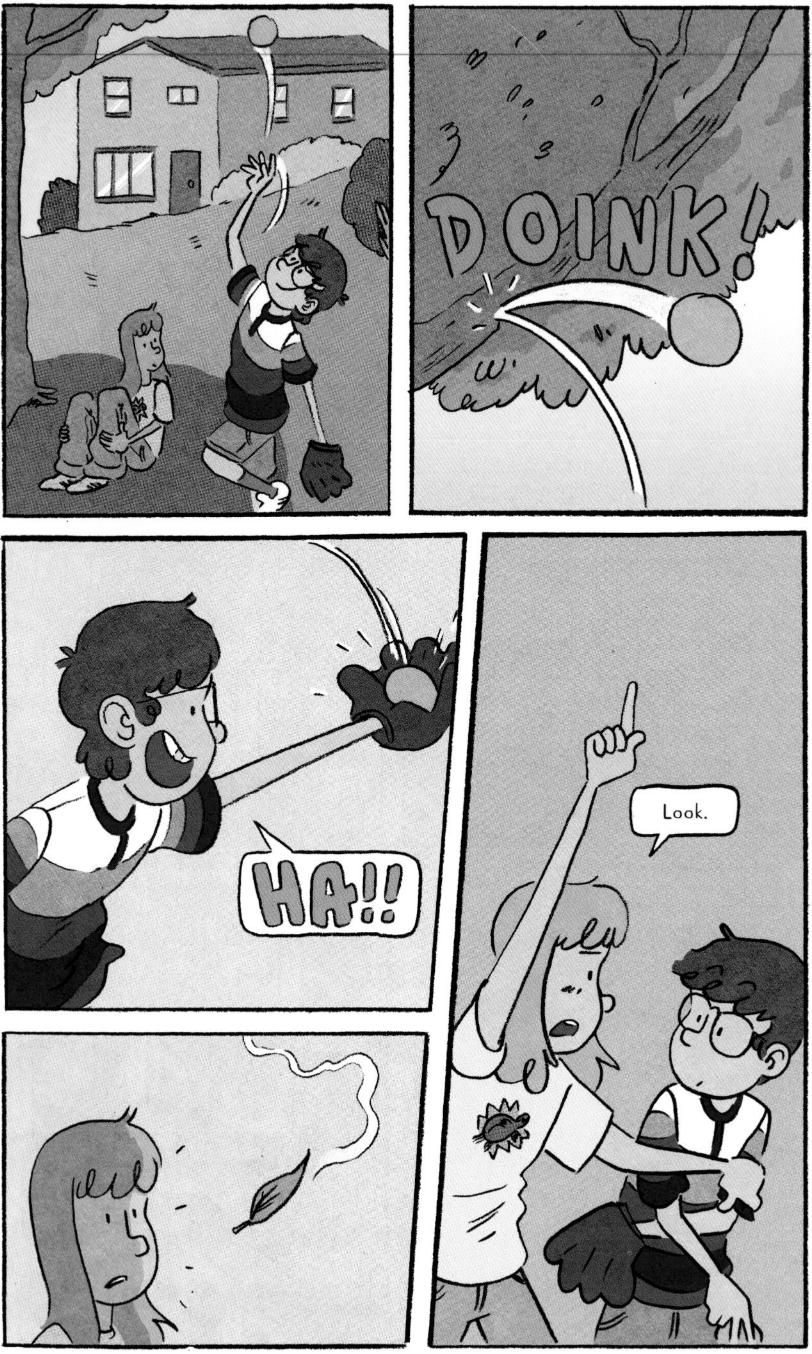
DOINK!
HA!!
Look.

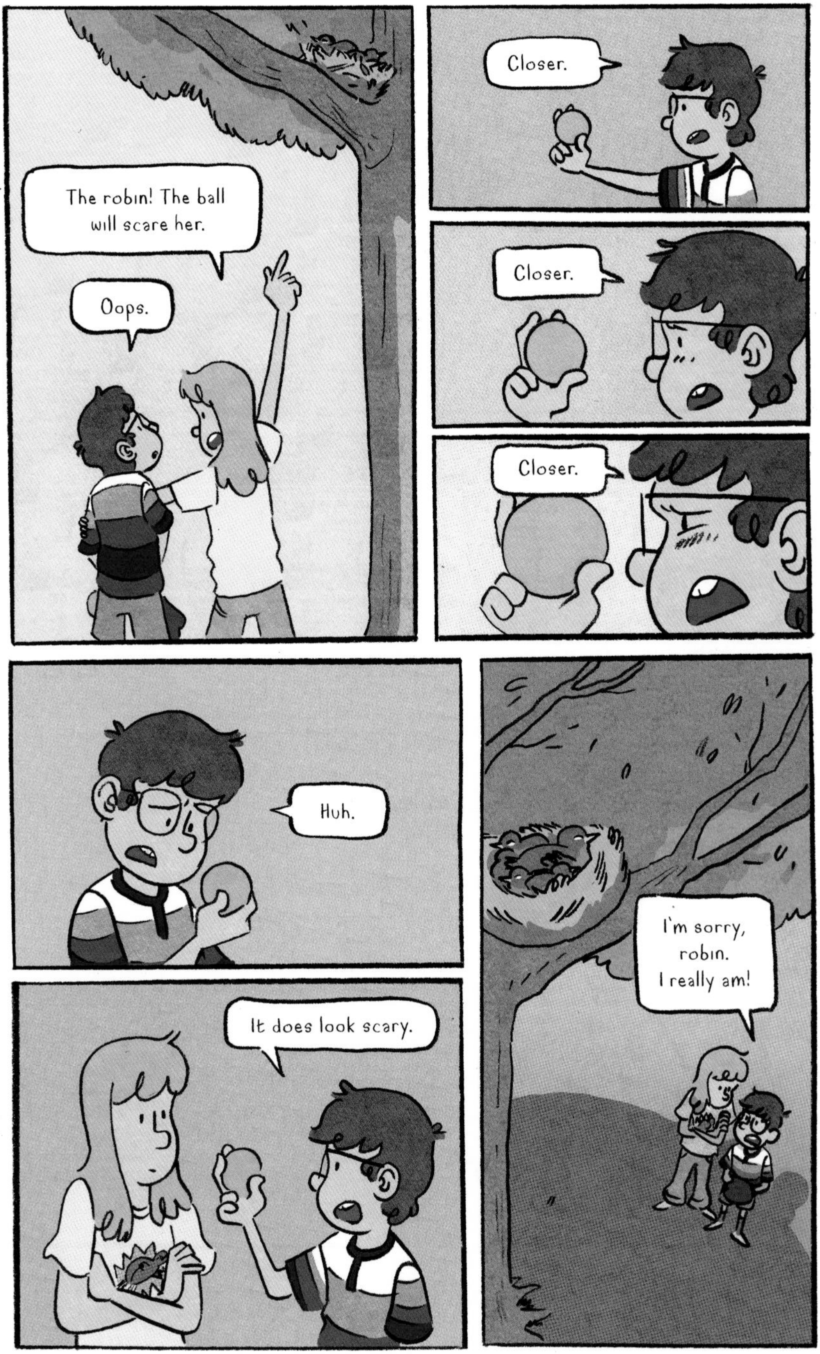
The robin! The ball will scare her.
Oops.
Closer.
Closer.
Closer.
Huh.
It does look scary.
I'm sorry, robin. I really am!

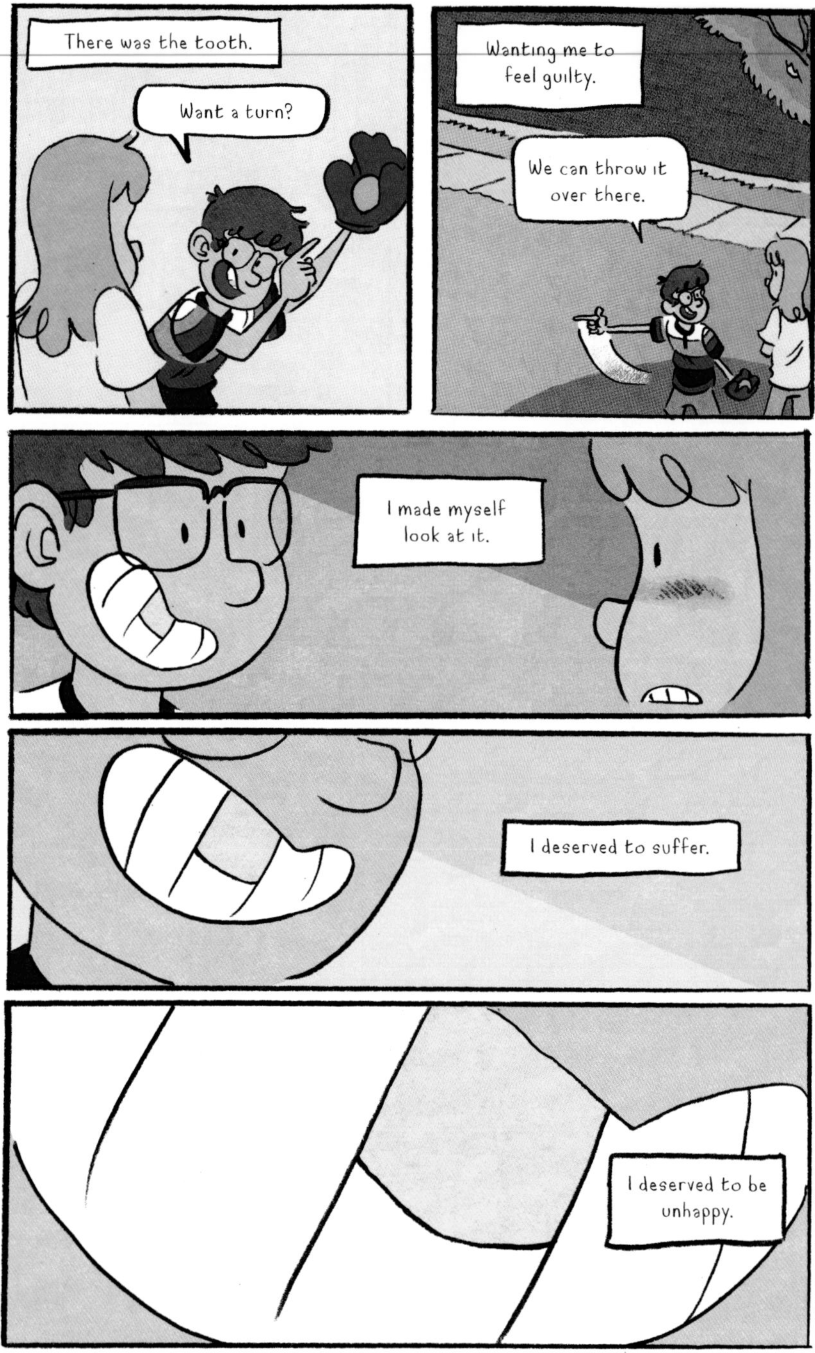
There was the tooth.
Want a turn?
Wanting me to feel guilty.
We can throw it over there.
I made myself look at it.
I deserved to suffer.
I deserved to be unhappy.

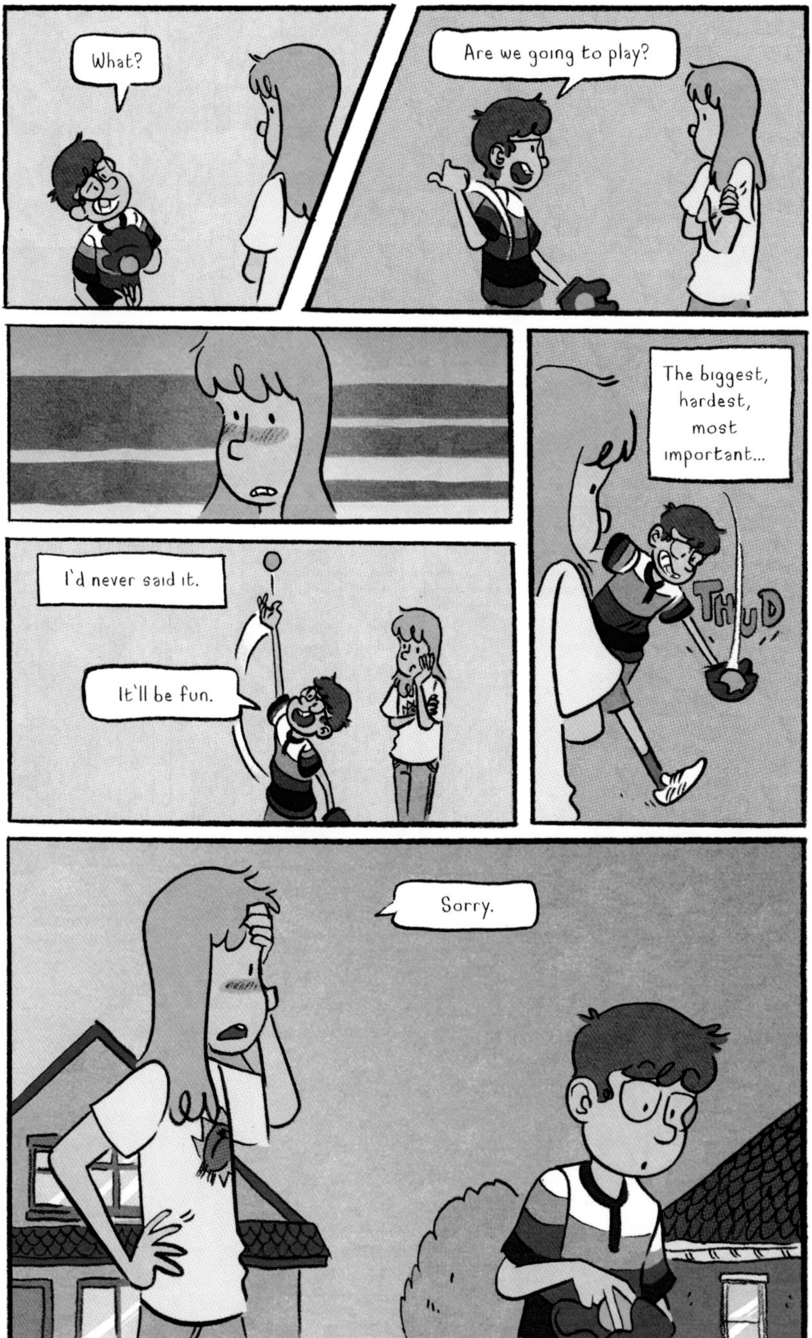

What?
Are we going to play?
The biggest, hardest, most important...
I'd never said it.
It'll be fun.
THUD
Sorry.

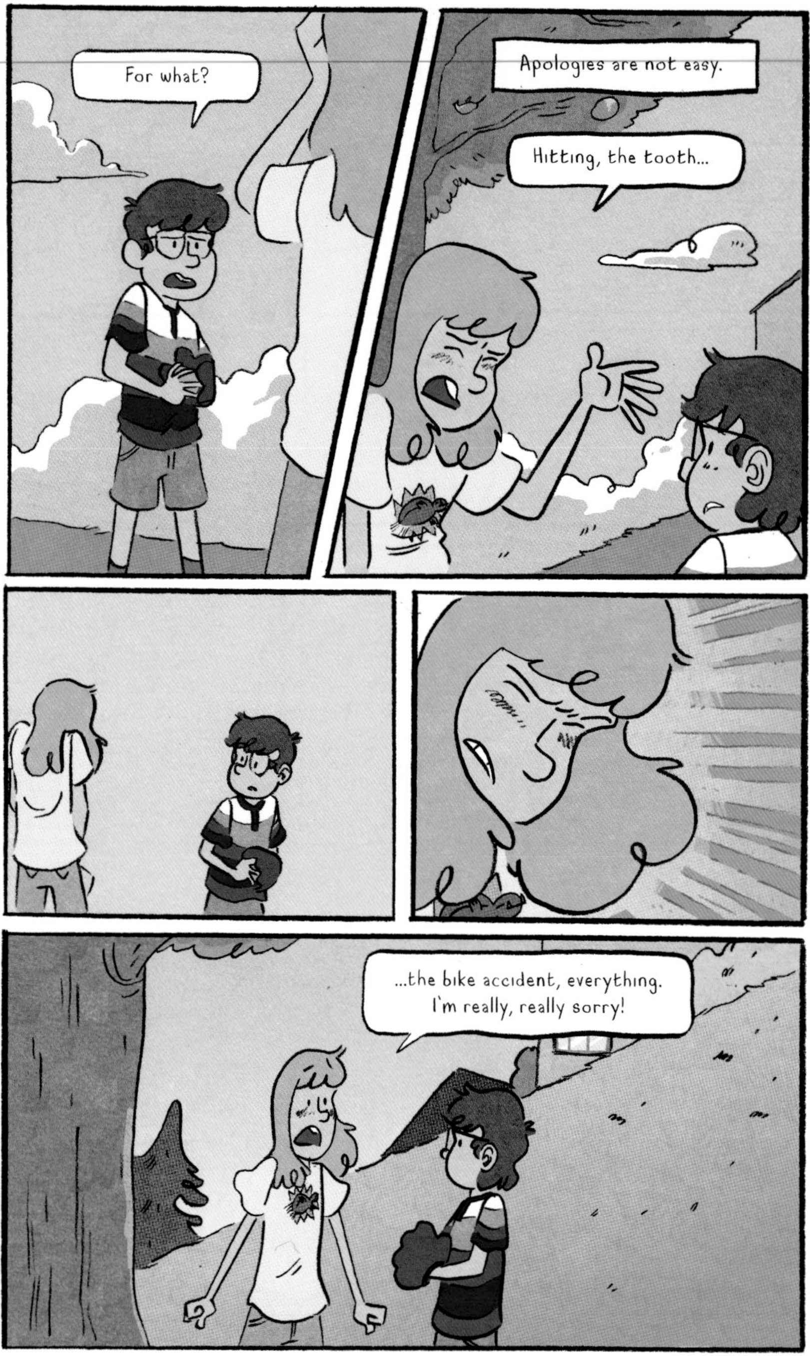
For what?
Apologies are not easy.
Hitting, the tooth...
...the bike accident, everything.
I'm really, really sorry!

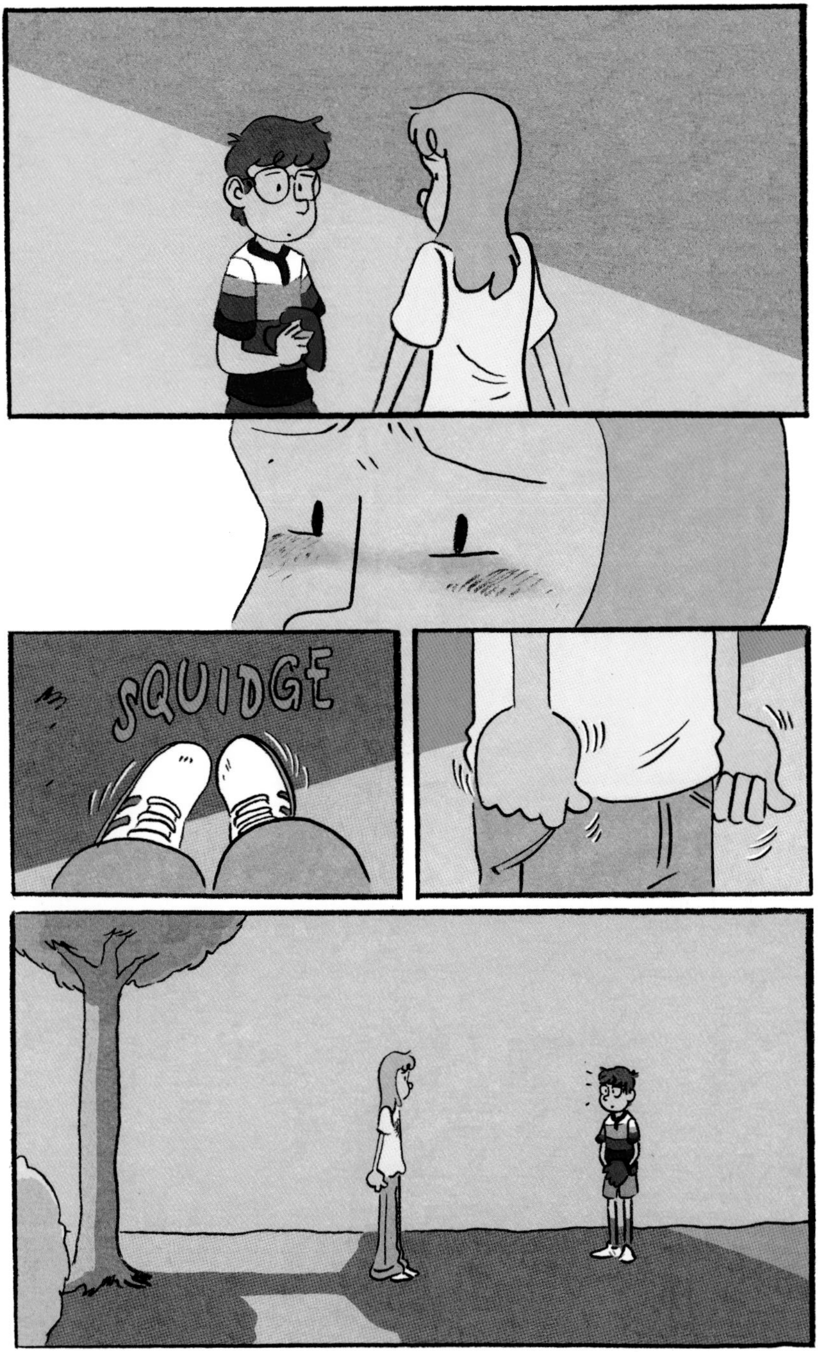
SQUIDGE

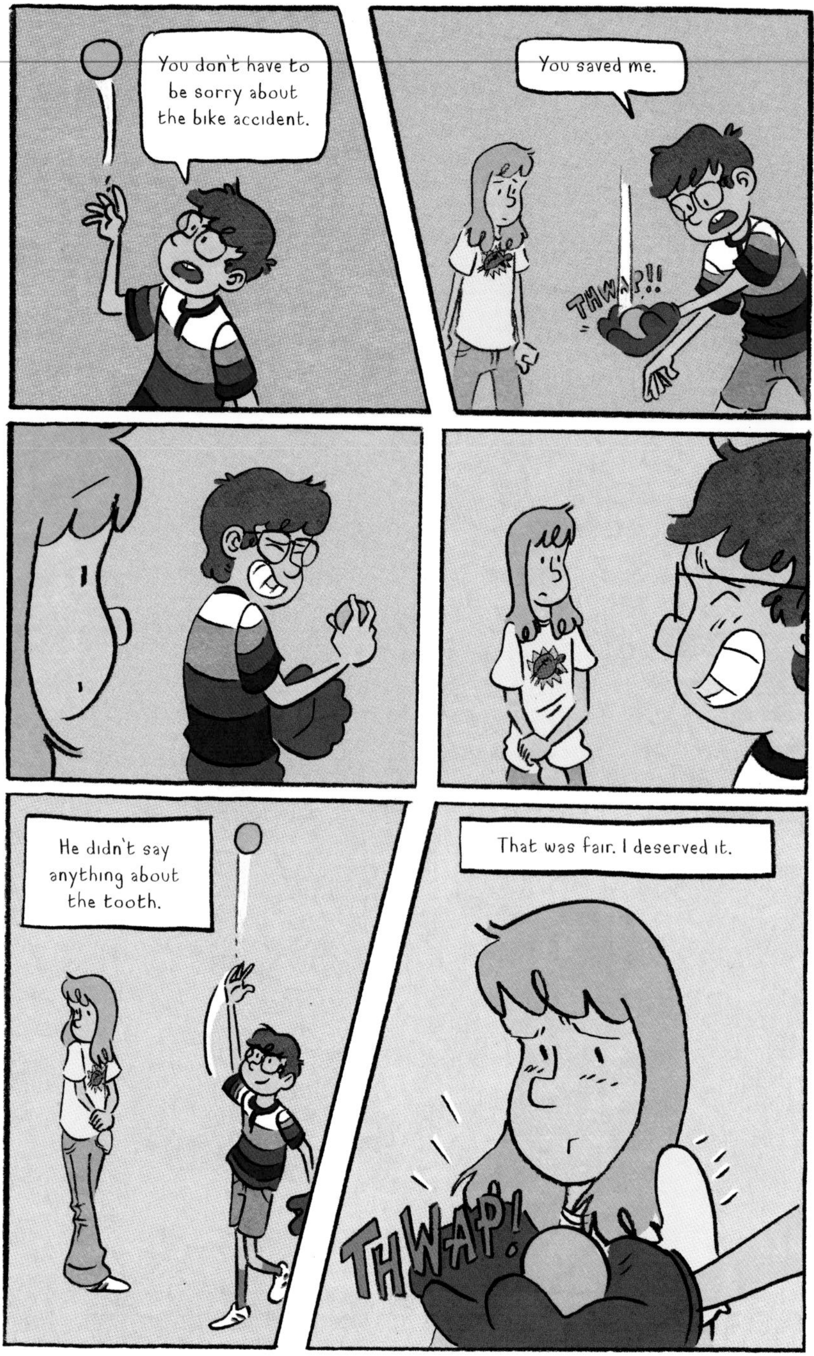
You don't have to be sorry about the bike accident.
You saved me.
THWAP!!
He didn't say anything about the tooth.
That was fair. I deserved it.
THWAP!

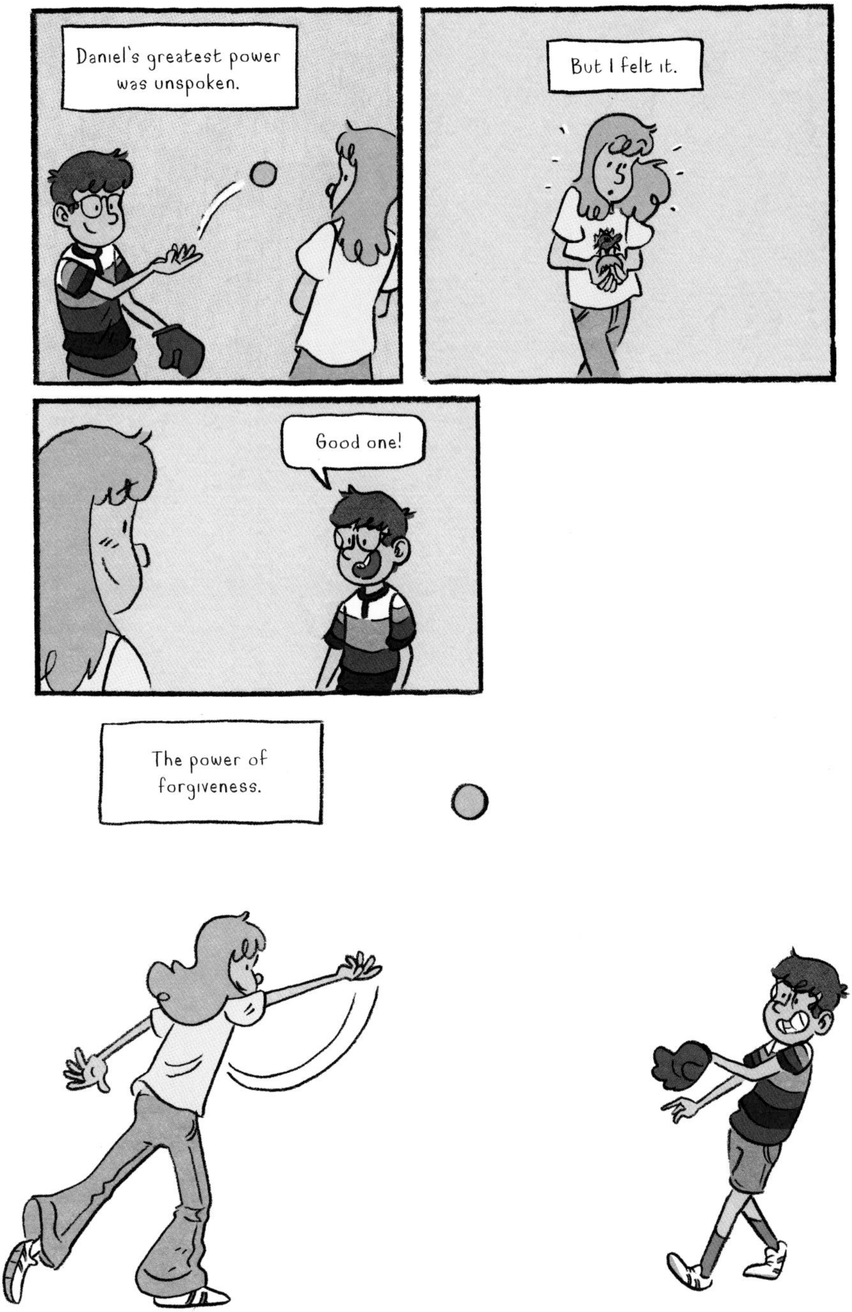
Daniel's greatest power was unspoken.
But I felt it.
Good one!
The power of forgiveness.

Years ago I took my brother's truck.
It still lives in my studio.
He doesn't know.

This book is dedicated to my brother, Daniel.
I wish I could go back in time.
To be more compassionate, patient, supportive,
understanding, and forgiving.
You are a silent teacher—the best kind.
Showing by example.
Thank you.
I love you.

I have to bestow a big parade of thank yous to Calista Brill,
Rachel Stark, and Alex Lu. Your work made this a better book.

And now look across the page—I'm waving a flag for Rory.
Thank you for your hours, your talent, and your vision.
You are awesome!

—Charise

To Charise Harper, thank you for sharing this beautiful story—
I still cannot believe how lucky I am to help tell it.

To everyone from First Second—Calista Brill, Alex Lu,
Kirk Benshoff, and Molly Johanson—as well as Rachel Stark and
Charlie Olsen, thank you for championing this book and
making me a better artist.

To the Haddonfield Friends School community,
thank you for your continued support of my art.

To my family, especially my nieces and nephews—
Cillian, Eleanor, Orla, and Onslow—a special thanks for inspiring me.

And to my wife, Emily. I don't have enough words
to thank you for always supporting me.

—Rory

:01

First Second

Published by First Second
First Second is an imprint of Roaring Brook Press,
a division of Holtzbrinck Publishing Holdings Limited Partnership
120 Broadway, New York, NY 10271
firstsecondbooks.com
mackids.com

Library of Congress Control Number: 2020919298

Our books may be purchased in bulk for promotional, educational, or business use.
Please contact your local bookseller or the Macmillan Corporate and Premium Sales Department
at (800) 221-7945 ext. 5442 or by email at MacmillanSpecialMarkets@macmillan.com.

FIRST
EDITION

First edition, 2021
Edited by Calista Brill, Alex Lu, and Rachel Stark
Cover and interior book design by Molly Johanson
Lettering assistance by Rory Lucey
Printed in China by 1010 Printing International Limited, North Point, Hong Kong

The book was penciled digitally in Procreate on an iPad, the final lines were drawn with a Staedtler
Mars Lumograph 6B pencil on Blick Hot Press watercolor paper and colored digitally in Photoshop.

ISBN 978-1-250-21905-3 (paperback)
10 9 8 7 6 5 4 3 2 1

ISBN 978-1-250-21906-0 (hardcover)
10 9 8 7 6 5 4 3 2 1

Don't miss your next favorite book from First Second! For the latest updates go
to firstsecondnewsletter.com and sign up for our enewsletter.